Timothy Asch and Ethnographic Film

Timothy Asch (1932–1994) was one of the best-known anthropologists of his generation and was among a small group of gifted ethnographic filmmakers who defined visual anthropology in the latter twentieth century. He worked with Margaret Mead, John Marshall and Napoleon Chagnon, lived and filmed on every continent except Antarctica, and won numerous international prizes. His work, which includes "The Ax Fight" and more than fifty additional films of Venezuela's Yanomamö Indians, and filming from Indonesia and Afghanistan, comprises the most widely used resource in the teaching of anthropology today. *Timothy Asch and Ethnographic Film* combines a biographical overview of Asch's life with critical perspectives, giving a definitive guide to his background, aims, ideas, methodologies and major projects. Beautifully illustrated with sixty photographs, and featuring articles from many of Asch's friends, colleagues and collaborators as well as an important interview with Asch himself, it is an ideal introduction to his work and to a range of key issues in ethnographic film.

Contributors: Douglas Harper, Nancy Lutkehaus, Peter Loizos, James J. Fox, Greg Acciaioli, Faye Ginsburg, Linda H. Connor, Patsy Asch, John P. Homiak, Wilton Martínez, Bill Nichols, Peter Biella, E. D. Lewis.

Edited by E. D. Lewis, Senior Lecturer in Anthropology at The University of Melbourne, Australia. He is author of *People of the Source* (1988), and co-producer with Timothy and Patsy Asch of the award-winning film *A Celebration of Origins* (1993).

Studies in Visual Culture
A series edited by Anthony Shelton

Volume 1
Shadow House: Interpretations of Northwest Coast Art
Jonathan Meuli

Volume 2
A Host of Devils: The History and Context of the Making of Makonde Spirit Sculpture
Zachary Kingdon

Volume 3
Timothy Asch and Ethnographic Film
Edited by E. D. Lewis

Frontispiece Timothy Asch, Canberra, Australia, 1980

Timothy Asch and Ethnographic Film

Edited by
E. D. Lewis

Routledge
Taylor & Francis Group
LONDON AND NEW YORK

First published 2004
by Routledge
11 New Fetter Lane, London EC4P 4EE

Simultaneously published in the USA and Canada
by Routledge
29 West 35th Street, New York, NY 10001

Routledge is an imprint of the Taylor & Francis Group

Typeset in Goudy by Bookcraft Ltd, Stroud, Gloucestershire
Printed and bound in Great Britain by The Cromwell Press, Trowbridge, Wiltshire

British Library Cataloguing in Publication Data
A catalogue record for this book is available from the British Library

Library of Congress Cataloging in Publication Data
A Catalog record for this book has been requested

ISBN 0-415-32774-1

Contents

List of illustrations   ix
List of contributors   xiii
Acknowledgments   xix
Preface   xxi

1   Introduction: Timothy Asch in America and Australia   1
    E. D. LEWIS

2   An ethnographic gaze: scenes in the anthropological life of   17
    Timothy Asch
    DOUGLAS HARPER

3   Man, a course of study: situating Tim Asch's pedagogy and   57
    ethnographic films
    NANCY C. LUTKEHAUS

4   At the beginning: Tim Asch in the early 1960s   75
    PETER LOIZOS

5   Efforts and events in a long collaboration: working with Tim   83
    Asch on ethnographic films on Roti in eastern Indonesia
    JAMES J. FOX

6   From event to ethnography: film-making and ethnographic   97
    research in Tana 'Ai, Flores, eastern Indonesia
    E. D. LEWIS

7   The consequences of conation: pedagogy and the inductive   123
    films of an ethical film-maker
    GREG ACCIAIOLI

8   Producing culture: shifting representations of social theory in   149
    the films of Tim Asch
    FAYE GINSBURG

 9 Subjects, images, voices: representations of gender in the films   163
    of Timothy Asch
    LINDA H. CONNOR AND PATSY ASCH

10 Timothy Asch, the rise of visual anthropology, and the Human   185
    Studies Film Archives
    JOHN P. HOMIAK

11 Tim Asch, otherness, and film reception   205
    WILTON MARTÍNEZ

12 What really happened: a reassessment of The Ax Fight   229
    BILL NICHOLS

13 The Ax Fight on CD-ROM   239
    PETER BIELLA

14 Person, event, and the location of the cinematic subject in   263
    Timothy Asch's films on Indonesia
    E. D. LEWIS

    Appendix: Writings and films of Timothy Asch   283
    Index   291

Illustrations

Photographs

Frontispiece   Timothy Asch, Canberra, Australia, 1980   iv
1.1   Tim Asch and magpie, Research School of Pacific and Asian Studies
        verandah, The Australian National University, 1980   5
1.2   Tim Asch and Tana 'Ai ritualists perform a sacrificial rite to "cool"
        the hut built for the anthropologists' use during the Tana 'Ai film
        project. Tana'Ai, 1980   9
1.3   Dealing with technical problems with recording equipment. Tana 'Ai,
        1980   11
1.4   Tim and Patsy Asch making camp, Tana 'Ai, 1980   12
1.5   Tim Asch unpacks the Arriflex camera in the "clean" tent.
        Watuwolon, 1980   12
2.1   North Country School, 1956   22
2.2   North Country School, 1956   22
2.3   North Country School, 1956   23
2.4   David Sapir by Asch, The Putney School, ca 1950   23
2.5   John Yang by Asch, The Putney School, 1950   24
2.6   Tim Asch by John Yang, California, south of San Francisco, 1951   24
2.7   Tim Asch by Minor White, California   26
2.8   Tim Asch by Minor White, California   26
2.9   Tim Asch by Minor White, California   27
2.10 Minor White by Asch, California   27
2.11 Minor White by Asch, California   28
2.12 Cape Breton   30
2.13 Cape Breton   30
2.14 Kanisaka's village, Japan   36
2.15 Japan   37
2.16 Man tapping his walking stick for his ancestors. Japan   37
2.17 Boy spinning top, Japan   38
2.18 Japan   38
2.19 Japan   39

2.20	Japan	39
2.21	Japan	40
2.22	Margaret Mead, 1957	40
2.23	Dodoth, Uganda, 1961	48
2.24	Dodoth, Uganda: courting dance	49
2.25	Thomas Beidelman, February, 1984	51
4.1	Tim Asch, Cambridge, Massachusetts, 1961	77
5.1	Tim Asch and Pak Foe Nalle in Rotinese ceremonial dress, 1977	88
5.2	Tim Asch filming a location shot on Roti, 1978	89
5.3	Timothy Asch filming Petrus Malesi on Roti, 1977	90
6.1	Tim Asch on the journey to Watuwolon, Tana 'Ai, July, 1980	103
6.2	Arrival at the house of Du'a Peni and Mo'an Koa, Watuwolon, July 1980	103
6.3	Asch and Klétus Ipir Wai Brama, the son of the late Source of the Domain, cut climbing notches in a tree trunk, Watuwolon, 1980	104
6.4	Asch filming a location shot of women dancing for the gren mahé ceremonies at the central ritual house of the Domain of Wai Brama, Watuwolon, 1980	105
6.5	Asch filming the dance of the clan headwomen at the central ritual house of the Domain of Wai Brama, Watuwolon, 1980	105
6.6	Patsy Asch and Tim Asch film the clan headwomen of the Domain of Wai Brama as they dance around a rice mortar at the central ritual house of the domain in preparation for the gren mahé rituals, Watuwolon, October, 1980	107
6.7	Asch loads film while Mo'an Koa Tapo looks on, Watuwolon, 1980	107
6.8	Tim and Patsy Asch filming Mo'an Déwa, Mo'an Sina, and Mo'an Koa discussing the exchange of a child between two clans, Munéwolon, 1980	108
6.9	Tim and Patsy Asch filming the discussion of an exchange of a child between two clans, Munéwolon, 1980	108
6.10	Tim Asch writes notes while Mo'an Sina and Mo'an Koa chant clan histories, Watuwolon, 1980	109
6.11	Asch watches the video of a burial with residents of Watuwolon, 1980	115
9.1	Tim Asch filming and Patsy Asch recording film sound with Asen Balikci, Afghanistan	167
9.2	Patsy Asch recording film sound, Afghanistan	167
9.3	Tim Asch with Asen Balikci filming in Afghanistan	168
9.4	Tim Asch and Linda Connor with Jero filming The Medium Is the Masseuse: A Balinese Massage	171
9.5	Tim Asch and Linda Connor filming a village cremation in Bali, 1978	173
9.6	Yanomamö	178

11.1 Tim Asch and Craig Johnson filming *Climbing the Peach Palm*, 1971   217
11.2 Tim Asch filming *New Tribes Mission*, 1971   217
13.1 A sample screen from *Yanomamö Interactive* with quadrants for
        different instructional purposes.   240
13.2 Contents of *Yanomamö Interactive*'s menus and options available
        through the menu buttons   241
13.3 Screen showing Chagnon's first comments on footage of the ax fight   243
13.4 Yanomamö genealogy, first level of detail, showing main protagonists
        in *The Ax Fight*   244
13.5 The extreme telephoto lens of Asch's movie camera and Chagnon's
        35 mm photograph   246
13.6 Selected still frames from *The Ax Fight*   257

Tables

6.1 Sample text of ritual language with full English translations and
        subtitles   110
14.1 Chronology of filming and post-production for Asch's Indonesia films   268

Contributors

Greg Acciaioli is Senior Lecturer in Anthropology at the University of Western Australia. He has conducted research in Indonesia since 1980 among both highland peoples of Central Sulawesi and the Bugis of South Sulawesi, covering such topics as migration, ethnic interaction, traditional healing, social change and development, and the resurgence of customary institutions under the auspices of Indonesian autonomy legislation. He has taught ethnographic film at both Columbia University and the University of Western Australia. Among his publications on ethnographic film is "Innocence Lost: Evaluating an Experimental Era in Ethnographic Film" in *TAJA* (*The Australian Journal of Anthropology*) 8 (2): 210–26 (1997). Recent publications on Indonesia include: "What's in a Name? Appropriating Idioms in the South Sulawesi Rice Intensification Program" in *Imagining Indonesia: Cultural Politics and Political Culture*, Jim Schiller and Barbara Martin-Schiller (eds.) (Athens OH: Ohio University Center for International Studies, 1997) and "Kinship and Debt: The Social Organization of Bugis Migration and Fish Marketing at Lake Lindu, Central Sulawesi", *Bijdragen tot de Taal-, Land- en Volkenkunde* 156 (3): 588–617 [2000]. He is editor (with Roger Tol and Kees van Dijk) of *Authority and Enterprise among the Peoples of South Sulawesi* (Leiden: KITLV Press, 2000). He would appreciate being contacted by any ethnographic film-maker who would like to collaborate on films about the resurgence of customary institutions in Indonesia or related topics.

Patsy Asch's first career was as a teacher who taught all ages, from three-year-olds to high school students, in Cambridge, Massachusetts, as well as students in the master's degree programs in Visual Anthropology and Film Production at the University of Southern California. In the late 1960s, she worked on the development of an anthropology course for ten-year-olds, Man: A Course of Study, under the intellectual guidance of Jerome Bruner. Between 1980 and 1999, she was employed as an ethnographic film-maker at the Research School of Pacific and Asian Studies at The Australian National University, where she collaborated on the production of ten films about Indonesia. Tim Asch was the

cinematographer on eight of them. Since Tim's death, she has studied media-
tion and counselling and now practises privately in Armidale, New South
Wales, Australia. Patsy Asch is co-author (with Linda Connor and Timothy
Asch) of *Jero Tapakan: Balinese Healer. An Ethnographic Film Monograph*
(Cambridge University Press, 1986, and Ethnographics Press, 1996) and is the
author of five articles about film and anthropology.

Peter Biella received his Ph.D. from Temple University in 1984 and, for the next
ten years, worked as an independent producer of ethnographic film and video
collaborations, with projects shot in Egypt, Costa Rica, El Salvador and the
United States. In 1991 he began an on-going series of publications about the
potential of interactive media for ethnography. Biella's collaboration with Gary
Seaman and Napoleon Chagnon resulted in *Yanomamö Interactive*, a CD-ROM
about Tim Asch's film, *The Ax Fight*, which is the subject of his chapter in this
volume. He maintains three large web sites, on Visual Anthropology, the US
Supreme Court's ruling about animal sacrifice in Santería, and the Japanese–
American Internment of the 1940s. Biella's forthcoming book and CD offer a
retroactive, epistemological reconsideration of his first fieldwork experiences
which were filmed in Tanzania in 1980. Biella directs a new program for digital
ethnographic video and multimedia production in the Anthropology Department at San Francisco State University.

Linda H. Connor teaches anthropology at the University of Newcastle, New
South Wales, Australia. Awarded a Ph.D. from the University of Sydney in
1982, she has carried out extensive field research in Bali over the last two
decades, and has written extensively on traditional healing and cultural trans-
formation in contemporary Bali. With Timothy and Patsy Asch, she is the
author of *Jero Tapakan: Balinese Healer. An Ethnographic Film Monograph*
(Cambridge University Press, 1986, and Ethnographics Press, 1996), as well as a
number of ethnographic films on Balinese healing and cremation ceremonies.
Her recent publications include *Staying Local in the Global Village: Bali in the
Twentieth Century* (co-edited with Raechelle Rubinstein, University of Hawai'i
Press, 1999); *Healing Powers and Modernity: Shamanism, Science and Traditional
Medicine in Asian Societies* (co-edited with Geoffrey Samuel, Westport,
Connecticut: Bergin and Garvey, 2000); and *Health Social Science: A Trans-
disciplinary and Complexity Perspective* (with Nick Higginbotham and Glenn
Albrecht, Oxford University Press, 2001).

Professor James J. Fox was educated at Harvard (A.B. '62) and Oxford (B.Litt.
'65, D.Phil. '68). He has taught at Harvard, Cornell, Duke, and Chicago in the
United States, and at various European Universities including Leiden, Bielefeld,
and the École des Hautes Études. He was appointed as Professorial Fellow in the

Research School of Pacific and Asian Studies at The Australian National University in 1975 and has since been appointed Professor of Anthropology. He is now the Director of the Research School of Pacific and Asian Studies. Professor Fox taught a course on ethnographic film with Tim Asch at Harvard and collaborated with Asch on two films, *The Water of Words* (1983) and *Spear and Sword* (1988), both dealing with life on the island of Roti in eastern Indonesia. He has also collaborated with Patsy Asch on two video documentaries, *In the Play of Life* (1992) and *Consulting Embah Wali* (2000), which explore the ideas and practices of a Javanese millenarian movement. He is author of *Harvest of the Palm: Ecological Change in Eastern Indonesia* and editor of numerous volumes, including *The Flow of Life: Essays on Eastern Indonesia*; *To Speak in Pairs: Essays on the Ritual Languages of Eastern Indonesia*; *Balanced Development: East Java in the New Order*; *Inside Austronesian Houses: Perspectives on Domestic Designs for Living*; *Origins, Ancestry and Alliance: Explorations in Austronesian Ethnography*; *The Poetic Power of Place: Comparative Perspectives on Austronesian Ideas of Locality*; *The Heritage Encyclopedia of Religion and Ritual in Indonesia*; and *Out of the Ashes: Destruction and Reconstruction of East Timor*.

Faye Ginsburg is Director of the Center for Media, Culture and History at New York University where she is also the David B. Kriser Professor of Anthropology. Her research interests include reproductive politics, social movements, and gender; the history of ethnographic film; and the development of indigenous media. Her books on media include *The Social Practice of Media* (edited with Lila Abu Lughod and Brian Larkin) and *Mediating Culture*, both forthcoming from the University of California Press. Among her awards are MacArthur and Guggenheim fellowships.

Doug Harper is Professor and Chair of Sociology at Duquesne University. He has held full-time appointments at the University of South Florida and SUNY, and visiting positions at Cornell University, the University of Amsterdam and the University of Bologna. His interests are in cultural sociology, and especially the use of visual methods in ethnography. His three books published by the University of Chicago Press are part of the growing visual sociology tradition. He is also founding editor of the journal *Visual Sociology*, and has edited or co-edited collections on visual sociology for academic presses in Holland and Italy. His articles and books have been translated into French, German and Italian. His current research, with Patrizia Faccioli, is a visual study of Italian culture, employing methods deriving from empiricism through semiotics to existential phenomenology.

John P. Homiak has been the Director of the Smithsonian's Human Studies Film Archives and the National Anthropological Archives since 1994. He is a cultural anthropologist who, for the past twenty years, has done research on the Rastafari Movement both in its Caribbean and global manifestations. He is presently working on two videos, one about Rastafari life in Jamaica entitled *Binghimon* and another on the African–Jamaican tradition of Kumina. He has done fieldwork in South Africa on the globalization of the Rastafari Movement there. Among his recent publications are "Movements of Jah People: From Soundscapes to Mediascape" in *Religion, Diaspora, and Cultural Identity* (John Pulis [ed.], Harwood Publications, 1999) and "The Body in the Archives", a review of the film *Bontoc Eulogy* by Marlon Fuentes, forthcoming in *Visual Anthropology Review*.

E. Douglas Lewis was educated at Rice University and received an A.M. in Anthropology from Brown University in 1975. He received his Ph.D. (1983) for a thesis written while he was a research scholar in the Institute of Advanced Studies, The Australian National University. Since 1977 he has lived and worked in Australia, Indonesia, and The Netherlands. He is Senior Lecturer in the Anthropology Program at the University of Melbourne. Lewis has carried out ethnographic research in Malaysia and on the islands of Flores and Timor in eastern Indonesia and is co-producer with Timothy and Patsy Asch of *A Celebration of Origins* (1993), a film about the ritual life of the Ata Tana 'Ai of east central Flores. His publications include *People of the Source: The Social and Ceremonial Order of Tana Wai Brama on Flores* (1988), a dictionary of the Sikkanese language of Flores co-authored with a Sikkanese collaborator (*Kamus Sara Sikka – Bahasa Indonesia* [1998]), and numerous papers on anthropological subjects.

Peter Loizos left Cambridge University in 1959 with a degree in English Literature and was a Knox Fellow at Harvard University, where he studied in the Department of Social Relations in 1959 and 1960. He went on to the Annenberg School of Communications at the University of Pennsylvania, where he took a Masters degree in Mass Media Communications. After working as a Film Project Manager for Smith Kline & French Laboratories in Philadelphia, he returned to the UK to join BBC TV Channel 2 as an assistant producer and film director, working with the science magazine *Horizon*. He joined the Department of Anthropology in the London School of Economics in 1966 where he completed his Ph.D. in Anthropology in 1974. He has carried out long-term fieldwork in Cyprus and has worked in northern Sudan. He is now Professor of Social Anthropology in the LSE. He is the author of *The Greek Gift: Politics in a Cypriot village* (Basil Blackwell, 1975), *The Heart Grown Bitter: A Chronicle of Cypriot War Refugees* (Cambridge University Press, 1981), and *Innovation in Ethnographic Film: From Innocence to Self-Consciousness 1955–1985* (Manchester University Press, 1993) and, with Evthymios Papataxiarchis, he edited *Contested Identities: Gender and Kinship in Modern Greece* (Princeton University Press, 1991).

Nancy Lutkehaus received her Ph.D. in Anthropology from Columbia University in 1984. She is an associate professor in the Department of Anthropology and the Program in Gender Studies at the University of Southern California. She is the Co-Director of the Center for Visual Anthropology at USC and a past editor of *Visual Anthropology Review*. Professor Lutkehaus is the author of *Zaria's Fire: Engendered Moments in Manam Ethnography* (Durham: Carolina Academic Press, 1995) and the co-editor of *Sepik Heritage: Tradition and Change in Papua New Guinea* (Durham: Carolina Academic Press, 1990), *Gendered Missions: Women and Men in Missionary Discourse and Practice* (Ann Arbor: University of Michigan Press, 1999) and *Gender Rituals: Female Initiation in Melanesia* (New York: Routledge, 1995). She is currently working on a book about Margaret Mead and the media.

Wilton Martínez is a Peruvian anthropologist, film-maker, and psychologist. His doctoral dissertation in Anthropology (University of Southern California, 1998) is concerned with the production, pedagogical use, and reception of ethnographic films. He currently lives in Baltimore, Maryland, and works as a lecturer and psychotherapist.

Bill Nichols is Professor of Cinema and Director of the Graduate Program in Cinema Studies at San Francisco State University. His *Representing Reality: Issues and Concepts in Documentary* (Indiana University Press, 1991) is a foundational text for the understanding of documentary and ethnographic film. He has also published a follow-up volume, *Blurred Boundaries: Questions of Meaning in Contemporary Culture* (Indiana University Press, 1994). *Introduction to Documentary* (Indiana University Press) appeared in 2001.

Acknowledgments

In 1995, Professor Jay Ruby prevailed upon me to take on the job of editing this book. I wish to thank both him for his early support and Professor Gary Seaman, who initiated the project that resulted in the present volume, for his assistance in the early stages of assembling the chapters. A number of individuals and institutions have materially assisted me in the course of assembling material, checking sources, seeking permissions, and verifying facts pertaining to Timothy Asch's life and work. They include Mr Peter Bunnell of The Art Museum, Princeton University, Ms Cynthia Close of Documentary Educational Resources, Inc., Dr Gregory A. Finnegan of the Tozzer Library, Harvard University, Mr Brian Morgan of The Putney School, Professor David Sapir, and Mr John Yang. The correspondence by email of Professor Douglas Harper helped keep me standing upright in the blizzard of paper in which the project was launched. And Greg Acciaioli read and made helpful comments on several parts of the text.

Mr Richard Sutcliffe of The University of Melbourne provided invaluable research assistance at a crucial juncture in the book's evolution and, more recently, Ms Claudia Damhuis, also of The University of Melbourne, recovered almost forgotten documents from my own files, thereby contributing to my own chapters in the book. In 1998, the Faculty of Arts, The University of Melbourne, provided a small but very helpful project grant for research assistance in the preparation of this book.

Earlier versions of Chapter 9 by Linda Connor and Patsy Asch and Chapter 11 by Wilton Martínez appeared in *Visual Anthropology Review: The Journal of the Society for Visual Anthropology*, volume 11, Number 1 (Spring 1995). They have been revised for publication here and are published with permission of the American Anthropological Association. Chapter 1 draws on material published previously under the title "Timothy Asch: 1932–1994. Anthropologist and Ethnographic Film-maker" in *Canberra Anthropology*, volume 18, numbers 1 and 2 (1995). That material is included here with the permission of the editors of *Canberra Anthropology*. Chapter 13 by Peter Biella is a revision of an article published in 1998 in *Visual Anthropology*, volume 11, pages 145–74 and is published here with permission.

For photographs used in this book, I would like to thank the following copyright holders. Figures 2.1–2.5, 2.10–2.25 and 9.6 are by Timothy Asch, courtesy of Patsy

Asch. Figure 2.6 is by John Yang, and reproduced with permission. Figures 2.7–2.9 are by Minor White, and reproduced courtesy of The Minor White Archive, Princeton University (© 2004 The Trustees of Princeton University). Figure 4.1 is by Peter Loizos and is reproduced with permission. Figures 5.1–5.3 are by James J. Fox, and are reproduced with permission. The photographer of Figures 9.1–9.3 is unknown; they are reproduced by courtesy of the Smithsonian Institution. Figure 9.4 is by Patsy Asch, and is reproduced with permission. Figure 9.5 is by Esta Handfield, and is reproduced with permission. Figures 11.1–11.2 are by Napoleon A. Chagnon, and are reproduced with permission from prints provided by Patsy Asch. The frontispiece, figures 1.1–1.5 and 6.1–6.11 are by E. D. Lewis (© 2004 E. D. Lewis).

Patsy Asch has been supporter, reader of this book in manuscript, confidante, springboard of ideas, and unending source of information, photographs, and assistance during this book's gestation. More than these, she has been a close colleague and friend for almost a quarter of a century. Thank you, Patsy.

E. Douglas Lewis

Preface

Science – indeed, all knowledge – accumulates and progresses through criticism and the sequential generation of new problems that arise from the solution of prior problems. One corpus of work, itself a solution to a problem or problems, generates new directions of inquiry and new problems to solve. The problem that preoccupied Timothy Asch throughout his career as an anthropologist and ethnographic film-maker and the fundamental problem he bequeathed to visual anthropologists was how best to represent culture visually through film. Those of us who worked closely with him on film projects – Patsy Asch, Elizabeth Marshall Thomas, Napoleon Chagnon, Asen Balikci, James Fox, Linda Connor, and myself – and others among his colleagues and students who participated with him in various facets of a complex life and career, learned this directly. Tim helped many of us solve problems arising from our individual research by refining the large problem with which he was always preoccupied and, in each instance, addressing it through his collaborations with us on our own work. For those of us who worked closely with Tim, the adventure of collaboration with a gifted film-maker generated, through the making of film, new lines of research. For others, the products of these collaborations pointed the way to new paths of ethnographic investigation and, in many cases, new paths of scholarship on film itself.

The essays in this volume have been written by a few of Tim's many collaborators, colleagues, and critics. This group may be taken as a small sample of those in the field of visual anthropology who have been directly influenced by Tim's work, and that includes just about everybody, not only professionals in visual anthropology, but all who have studied anthropology in a college or university.

Some of these essays tell the story of collaboration; some point to the ethnography which arose from collaborations with Tim; some address the new problems and lines of research suggested by Tim's work or those that have arisen from a critical examination of it; others take up Tim's devotion to the profession of teaching and his ceaseless search for better ways to use film in teaching students about the human world in which they live. All reflect on the new ways of seeing that each contributor, in his or her particular way, acquired through working with Tim or by close examination of his work.

From 16 to 20 March 1994, the Center for Visual Anthropology of the University of Southern California in Los Angeles hosted the Margaret Mead Ethnographic Film Festival and Timothy Asch Retrospective. Five of the chapters of this book grew out of papers by scholars who contributed to the special symposium on Tim's work that formed the core of the Festival in Los Angeles. The others were either first presented in November 1995 to a special session of the annual meeting of the American Anthropological Association in Washington DC, or were written for this volume.

Two days of the Mead Festival in Los Angeles were set aside for retrospective screenings of Tim Asch's films and colloquia in which Tim's collaborators, colleagues, and students spoke about various aspects of his work. The event was an encyclopaedic survey of the range of his achievements and even included a session of "Tim stories", of which everyone present seemed to have an inexhaustible supply. Although the disease that was to kill him eight months later was already taking its toll on his energy, Tim sat through almost all of the sessions, interjecting occasionally more or less audible remarks on the proceedings and, from appearances, thoroughly enjoying himself.

At the time of the Mead Festival I had known Tim for nineteen years and had been privileged to have collaborated with him on a project to film large-scale rituals in eastern Indonesia. So I gladly made the trip from The Netherlands, where I was then working, to Los Angeles to participate in that celebratory retrospective of his work. That week in March was the last time I saw him.

Following the Mead Festival, Professor Gary Seaman, Tim's friend and close associate in the Department of Anthropology at the University of Southern California, set about compiling and collating the papers presented in the symposium on Tim's work with the view toward publishing them as a *festschrift* for Tim. It is indeed unfortunate that that project could not be completed in what turned out to be the few months that Tim had left. Following Tim's death in October 1994, some of the papers presented during the Mead Festival were published in Volume 11, Number 1 of *Visual Anthropology Review* and Professor Seaman posted abstracts of the other papers on a USC World Wide Web site. Some of us believed that the papers could form the core of the first of what will surely be a number of critical examinations of Tim's films and philosophy of film-making. Then Professor Jay Ruby invited a number of speakers to address *The Legacy of Tim Asch* in a special session of the annual meetings of the American Anthropological Association in Washington DC, November 1995, a year after Tim's death. By then, Professor Seaman had decided that he would be unable to complete the editing of the volume of essays. Many of the contributors to the Mead Festival and others with an interest in Tim's work went to dinner after the American Anthropological Association session and, when the decision was taken to proceed with the publication of a collection of papers on Tim's work, I agreed to serve as editor of the volume and to take up the task of seeing the volume through press. Coordinating the work of twelve busy colleagues on three continents and bringing the project to a productive end required much more time than I had first envisaged, but the work is now complete. This book is the result of that collaborative effort.

The book can be divided somewhat unequally into three parts. The first consists of chapters which, in one way or another, recount episodes in Tim's professional life and includes excerpts from long recorded interviews with Tim conducted by Professor Douglas Harper in 1993 and in March 1994. The chapter by Peter Loizos recounts the beginnings of Asch's career in anthropology and film at Harvard University at the beginning of the 1960s, a place and time we now know to have been a pivotal and defining moment in the history of ethnographic film and visual anthropology. James J. Fox tells part of the tale of Tim's years in Canberra and their collaboration in making films on the island of Roti in Indonesia. Nancy Lutkehaus traces the origin of Asch's ideas about teaching anthropology to his participation in the MACOS Project of the mid-1960s. And Chapter 6 is a discussion of the Tana 'Ai Film project, its aims, the problems which arose in our attempt to document a large-scale ritual performance, and some of the solutions we devised for those problems.

The second part consists of explicative and critical treatments of Tim's work and professional activities. In this section, Greg Acciaioli analyzes the tension between Asch's desire to record the indigenous structures of the events he filmed and the restructurings that inevitably result from the process of film-making itself. Acciaioli argues cogently that this problem animated Asch's professional career and traces his development as a film-maker in terms of his experimentation with ways of illuminating both the lives of those he filmed and the essential problem of representation in anthropology. Faye Ginsburg sets out the progression of the ways in which Tim's films responded to developments in wider ranges of the social sciences and social theory during his career. Linda Connor and Patsy Asch address representations of gender in ethnographic film, with particular respect to Asch's work.

The last part focuses on problems that have come out of Tim's work, in one way or another, through the work of his colleagues. John Homiak reviews Tim's support for the establishment of the Human Studies Film Archives in the Smithsonian Institution in Washington, where a substantial portion of the footage that Tim shot in his career is now archived. Wilton Martínez examines the surprising results of studies done at the University of Southern California of the reception of ethnographic films among undergraduate students. Bill Nichols reflects on *The Ax Fight* in relation to the vexing problem of the relation of descriptive fact to interpretive frame and, in doing so, revises and expands remarks he made about Asch's film in 1981 in his influential book, *Ideology and Image*. Peter Biella reports on the fulfillment of a long-standing dream of Tim's: the development of a technique for combining still photographs, moving images, and text in a single hypertextual medium. The book closes with a survey of the eight films that Tim and Patsy made in Indonesia in collaboration with James Fox, Linda Connor, and myself and suggests that, as a corpus of work and despite being made with different anthropologists, these films may be the first corpus of ethnological films to come out of visual anthropology.

I shall here, at the outset, declare my colors with respect to the protagonist in this book. In the course of our collaborations, Tim and Patsy Asch came to be close and valued friends. In our work together, their aesthetic sensibilities, far more acute and more disciplined than mine, complemented my own scientific interests and propensities. In the field Tim saw, whereas my strengths lay in hearing and listening. It is well that our abilities were complements, for the ethnographic work we undertook demanded close attention both to those forms of action apprehended through vision and to those which required an understanding of spoken words to be understood. The work with Tim and Patsy has been the defining and directing episode in my professional career.

Our respect for Tim Asch as teacher, colleague, and friend, and for his work, will be plain to see in each of these chapters. But Tim told his students that his work should be seen not as an end, but as a beginning. It follows that it should be seen also as a challenge to new generations of visual anthropologists, as should the lives and works of all older generations. While this book is mainly a summary of selected aspects of Tim's work, it should invite criticism, and thus further progress in its field. I am sure Tim would have wanted it that way.

E. Douglas Lewis
Mount Toole-Be-Wong
Victoria
Australia
January 2001

Chapter 1

Introduction

Timothy Asch in America and Australia[1]

E. D. Lewis

From 1968 to his death in October 1994, Tim Asch produced more than fifty ethnographic films about the Yanomamö Indians of Venezuela, transhumant herders in Afghanistan, and the Balinese, the Rotinese, and Ata Tana 'Ai of eastern Indonesia. If one counts *Dodoth Morning*, which he shot in 1961, and footage he shot in Canada which was never made into films for release, he practised his art of ethnographic film-making on three continents and in Oceania. The films in distribution have had a profound influence on the science of anthropology and the way the discipline is taught in universities around the world.

Asch's career as an ethnographic film-maker began in the middle 1960s, just as portable synchronous sound technology for 16 mm production became available to film-makers.[2] Portable synchronous sound was a technology that would revolutionize the representation of ethnographic subjects on film, and Asch's exploration of the new technology's possibilities and his experiments with new techniques in ethnographic film-making helped create the field of visual anthropology and remake the discipline of cultural anthropology. In these explorations and experiments he was colleague, interlocutor and, sometimes, antagonist to a small number of film-makers, including Jean Rouch, John Marshall, Robert Gardner, whose work, it is now clear, defined visual anthropology in the second half of the twentieth century.

Asch was a university teacher and his main aim as an anthropologist was to make films for use in anthropological tuition. These films would illustrate general theoretical problems in the comparative understanding of mankind's cultures, and thereby not only improve the quality of university tuition in anthropology, but establish anthropology as the pre-eminent medium for communication between societies with quite different cultures and foster greater understanding by people everywhere of those whose ways are different from their own.

America, 1932–76

Tim Asch was born in Southampton, Long Island, New York in 1932. He was educated at the North Country School in Lake Placid, New York, and The Putney School in Vermont, from which he graduated in 1951. His classmates at Putney included the anthropologist David Sapir and the photographer John Yang. Together, they experimented with photography. The experience must have been profound: Asch himself went into photography and film-making, Yang became a photographer, and Sapir has increasingly focused on visual anthropology and still photography in his work.

In his late teens, Asch twice journeyed to California where, during the summers of 1950 and 1951, he studied with the photographers Minor White, Ansel Adams and Edward Weston. Asch has described his relationship with White as that between apprentice and master. He lived in White's household, going out each morning before dawn and again in the late afternoon to take photographs. Evenings were spent developing and printing the day's work. For Asch, this episode was a powerful encounter with an art form in the person of one of its masters. From White he learned aesthetics, techniques and discipline.[3] Patsy Asch has said that one of the things he learned from White and Weston was that his talent lay more in photographing people than landscapes (although his photographic subjects in his last years were largely drawn from nature). If White taught Asch his art, it was perhaps the photographic sequences of W. Eugene Smith that were the strongest influence on Asch's later mastery of documentary cinematography.

In the early 1950s, Asch's newly trained talent found its first expression on Cape Breton Island, Canada, where he lived for seven months in 1952. He returned to the community in 1960 to shoot his first film, and made visits in 1968 and shortly before his death in 1994. A special issue of the journal *Visual Sociology* under the editorship of Douglas Harper (1994) has been devoted to a selection of Asch's Cape Breton photographs.

After a year at Bard College, Asch was conscripted into the US Army in 1953 and served in Japan as a photographer for *Stars and Stripes* and the Japanese newspapers *Asahi Shinbun, Mainichi Shinbun,* and the *Nippon Times.* He lived for a time with a family in a rural Japanese village, his subject for an extensive (and as yet unpublished) photographic study. In 1955 he resumed his undergraduate studies at Columbia University. At Columbia he decided to study anthropology and became a teaching assistant to Margaret Mead, who encouraged his interest in ethnographic film.

From 1959 to 1962 he served as a film editor for John Marshall and Robert Gardner in the Peabody Museum of Harvard University, working mainly on Marshall's Ju/'hoansi (Bushman) films. In 1960 he met Peter Loizos, who documents Asch's relationships with Marshall and Gardner in Chapter 4 of this volume. In 1961 he traveled to Uganda, where he worked among the Dodoth as a still photographer and cinematographer for Elizabeth Marshall Thomas. In 1963 he completed the film *Dodoth Morning,* a short film about one morning in the life of a Dodoth family at harvest time.

From 1963 to 1965, Asch undertook a postgraduate course in African Studies at Boston University and studied with Thomas Beidelman at Harvard. After completing his M.A., from 1965 to 1967 he worked, under the leadership of Jerome Bruner, on *Man, A Course of Study* (MACOS), a film-based curriculum development project designed to bring the ideas of anthropology to primary school classrooms. Asch and his wife Patsy experimented with the Ju/'hoansi footage and the Netsilik Inuit films, which Asen Balikci developed for MACOS. This early work as an editor and on the development of film sequences for teaching contributed to Asch's growing belief in the pedagogical value of short films. In 1968 he and John Marshall founded Documentary Educational Research, a non-profit organization, to produce, distribute, and promote the use of ethnographic and documentary films, in part because no film distributor would agree to distribute all of the sequence films on which he had worked with the Marshalls. In 1971 DER incorporated as Documentary Educational Resources, Inc., which has grown into an international distributor of ethnographic films and promoter of research and development in visual anthropology.

From 1967 to 1976 Asch held teaching posts in Visual Anthropology at Brandeis University, New York University and Harvard University. Whilst juggling fractional appointments in three universities must have been difficult for a man with a young family, his professional situation was one in which there were few obligations of an administrative kind to his employers. He was thus relatively free to experiment with the development of undergraduate anthropology courses oriented toward film and to undertake fieldwork, which he did in 1968 and 1971 when he filmed the Yanomamö Indians in Venezuela in collaboration with Napoleon Chagnon. The years of the mid-1960s to the mid-1970s were thus the time in which Asch refined his thinking about, and his aims for, making films for research and teaching, and he found his first opportunity to put his thoughts about making films into practice in a collaboration with another anthropologist.[4] Loizos notes (Chapter 4) that by the early 1960s, Asch had set out for himself "a coherent and single-minded commitment to ethnographic documentary" and was already well along in "thinking through a programme of filming and classroom work surrounding film". We can see that in the 1960s Asch had clearly in mind how anthropological films should be made and what he wanted to do; as he himself wrote many years later about his work in Venezuela:

> When we first collaborated, Chagnon had a latent idea about the kind of film he wanted to make, whereas I knew exactly what kind of film I wanted to make.
>
> (Asch 1982: 16)

In 1968 Asch began his long and fruitful collaboration with Napoleon Chagnon, with whom he made field trips in 1968 and 1971 to the upper Orinoco valley of Venezuela to film the Yanomamö Indians. The collaboration resulted in at least forty-two films (see the Appendix, this volume: the number of Yanomamö films is difficult to determine exactly), including *The Feast* and *The Ax Fight*, which are ranked by many as among the best ethnographic films ever produced. The films of the Yanomamö series have received numerous awards and many have been staples in undergraduate university curricula in anthropology for over two decades. For a quarter of a century *The Ax Fight* has been a focus in anthropology and cinema studies of critical and theoretical thinking about the representation of culture through visual media. In this book, Nichols re-examines problems of representation addressed in *The Ax Fight*, Martínez reports research on the reception of the film among undergraduate university students, and Biella recounts an important experiment in transforming *The Ax Fight* into a "researchable film" through hypertext technology.

In 1975, with the sponsorship of the Smithsonian Institution of Washington DC, Asch collaborated with Patsy Asch and the anthropologist Asen Balikci in the production of research footage from which the film *Sons of Haji Omar* was produced. This project marked a major change in Asch's working methods: Patsy Asch collaborated in the fieldwork and production phases of the Afghanistan project and on the Indonesian projects that followed and was the editor of all of the Indonesia films. Patsy's intimate involvement with filming in the field and her editorial acuity were important factors in shaping Asch's last films, all of which reflect post-production dialogues between the Aschs on subjects ranging from how best to make use of particular footage to the basic aims of ethnographic film.

From 1969 through 1973, Asch taught in the Department of Anthropology, Brandeis University. After meeting James J. Fox in 1970 and moving to the Department of Anthropology at Harvard University as a lecturer in 1974, Asch and Fox taught a course on ethnographic film. Their common interest in film led to plans for a collaboration on a film project. Fox left Cambridge, Massachusetts to join the Research School of Pacific Studies (now the Research School of Pacific and Asian Studies in the Australian National University in 1975, but the two continued to plan a collaborative film project and in 1978 obtained a grant from the US National Science Foundation which provided partial funding for the work they had in mind.

In early 1976 Tim Asch left Cambridge, Massachusetts to join the Department of Anthropology in the Research School of Pacific Studies as a Senior Research Fellow. He lived and worked in Australia for six years until, in 1982, he took up his last position as Professor of Anthropology at the University of Southern California, where he became the first director of the Center for Visual Anthropology.

Australia, 1976–82

The six-and-a-half years the Aschs spent in Australia were extraordinarily productive. At The Australian National University, Asch was instrumental in bringing into reality what was then called the Human Ethology and Ethnographic Film Laboratory, a unit in the Department of Anthropology. The idea for HEEFL originated with Professor Derek Freeman, the head of the department at the time, who was interested in establishing a laboratory for the ethological study of human behavior and social interaction. HEEFL began with the human ethologists Adam Kendon and Peter Reynolds. With Asch's arrival, the mandate of the laboratory expanded to encompass ethnographic film-making.

During his six years in Canberra and after his departure for California, Asch collaborated with three Australian anthropologists in the production of research footage and ethnographic films on the eastern Indonesian islands of Roti, Bali, and Flores.

Figure 1.1 Tim Asch and magpie, Research School of Pacific and Asian Studies verandah, The Australian National University, 1980.

The Roti project

Asch's first collaboration at The ANU was with Professor James J. Fox (see Chapter 5). They planned to film large-scale rituals in five eastern Indonesian societies, the first filming to be of ritual contests during the ceremonial season on the island of Savu. As Fox had previously determined, Savunese ritual was spectacle in a way that contrasted with the more restrained oratorical performances which characterized ritual on the nearby island of Roti (Fox 1979). Given the combination of planned chorcography and spontaneous improvisation evident in Savunese rituals and the large scale of their performance, Fox and Asch were convinced that film was the best means to document the complex Savunese performances. In the end, delays in obtaining the permits required by the Indonesian government for research and filming prevented Asch and Fox from visiting Savu during the high ceremonial season on the island. So they shifted the site of their first work to Roti. The work on Roti resulted in two films: *The Water of Words* (1983) and *Spear and Sword* (1989). As it happened, a bureaucratic *snafu* in Jakarta resulted in the issue of two research permits, one for filming in the province of Nusa Tenggara Timur (which includes the islands of Roti, Savu and Flores) and one for Bali. This fortuitous confusion among Jakarta bureaucrats as to the whereabouts of Savu and Roti (see Chapter 5) opened the way for Asch's filming on Bali with Dr Linda Connor, the second of his Australian collaborators.

The Bali project

On their way to Roti in June 1977, Tim Asch and Jim Fox discovered that Margaret Mead was on the island of Bali attending a Pacific Science Association Conference. Mead planned to visit Bayung Gede, the village in which she had worked in the 1930s. She asked Asch, her former student, to record her visit to the village. On the way to Bayung Gede, Asch and Fox happened to meet Linda Connor, who was then in the middle of research for her Ph.D. in a village in central Bali. The following year, Fox, who was traveling from Europe, was to meet Asch, who was traveling from Australia, once again in Bali en route to Roti. As Asch told the story, Fox was delayed for several weeks and, worried about the state of his film stock, Asch decided to shoot a few rolls and send them back for processing and examination in Australia. But what to shoot? Asch went looking for Linda Connor, whom he had first met in Canberra before she began her fieldwork and, even though she was (again as Asch told it) in the last, frantic stages of her fieldwork, prevailed upon her to film something in which she was interested and which bore on her research topic. Asch rattled into Linda's village on a superannuated Honda, his camera positioned precariously on the back, gave Linda a brief but intensive lesson in recording synchronous sound and the two of them began filming. The result was the footage which became A *Balinese Trance Seance*. The collaboration with Linda Connor on Bali, which continued with a further season of filming in 1980 and for a number of years thereafter, produced five films. In this book, Linda Connor and Patsy Asch (Chapter 9) analyze their relationships to the Balinese and how they influenced the production of the Bali films, and Lewis (Chapter 14) locates thematically the Bali films in Asch's Indonesian corpus.

Working with Asch in Tana 'Ai: a personal memoir

I met Tim in the spring of 1975 in Cambridge, Massachusetts, where people were still talking about the wondrous festival of ethnographic films that he had screened during the second half of 1974 in conjunction with "Film as Ethnographic Experience", a course on ethnographic film which he and James Fox taught at Harvard. I still have the film list for the evening screenings (which regularly drew 250 to 300 students); it reads like a history of ethnographic and anthropologically oriented documentary cinema. When I arrived in Canberra in March 1977 to begin my Ph.D. research, Tim was one of the first people I met. He was then inhabiting – that is the only word – Room 7239, one of the larger rooms for research fellows in the Coombs Building, which housed the Research School of Pacific Studies.

The room was completely outfitted by Tim, which meant that no one could find a place to park oneself when visiting his lair. Cases and book shelves on wheels, equipment (mostly consisting of wires emerging from and disappearing into gadgets of uncertain provenance and less obvious function), dog-eared and spine-broken books (Tim could mangle a book in ways unimaginable by even the most fatalistic school librarian) and a fog of things (including a hammock) festooned the walls, ceiling, and every square centimeter of floor space. (This is the man who invented a mechanical baby-changer and installed it in a closet of one of his houses.) His first words to me were: "Great! Let's get some coffee. They have the best cookies in the world downstairs." "Downstairs" was the Coombs Building tea room, the "cookies" (I learned to say "biscuits" in Strine; Tim did not) were Arnott's, and the conversation was about film and research. We picked up just where we had left off in Cambridge, even though I never knew whether or not he remembered me.

My involvement in a collaboration with Tim can be traced to our correspondence which commenced not long after I began my Ph.D. fieldwork on Flores in September 1977. In those letters, we exchanged ideas about what we might film, should an opportunity arise to work together. Then, in the last month of my fieldwork in August 1979, the Source of the Domain of Tana Wai Brama, the ritual leader of the ceremonial domain on Flores where I conducted research, announced that the community would in the following year perform a complex of rites in celebration of the founding of the domain. Together these rites are called *gren mahé*, the "celebration of the *mahé*", the *mahé* being a clearing in a patch of forest where, so the mythic histories of the domain relate, the Domain of Wai Brama was founded.

After completing two years of fieldwork on Flores I returned to Canberra in September 1979. I discussed with Tim the possibility of filming the *gren mahé* the following year. Tim was, at the time, fully committed to filming on Roti and Bali but, as Jim Fox was unable to film in 1980, Tim quickly agreed to the idea. While not part of the original research protocol which Tim and Jim Fox had devised (see Chapter 14), the *gren*, as I described what I had heard of it, had all of the main features of the rituals which they wanted to film: it was large-scale, it was intimately linked both to the mythic origins of society and to contemporary social organization and it was of considerable importance for an anthropologist's program of ethnographic research. There were only two problems. First, I had never seen a *gren* and so could not say with certainty what it was. Second, the Ata Tana 'Ai plan many things but rarely do them on the dates they specify in advance, and so there was no way of guaranteeing that it would actually be performed in 1980. Nevertheless, Tim enthusiastically signed on. He, Patsy Asch, and I, accompanied by their teenage son Alex and an impressive mound of equipment, arrived on Flores in July 1980 to film the *gren*. The result of our collaboration has been one film in release, *A Celebration of Origins*, and two additional films which, to date, have not progressed beyond early post-production.

Tim Asch was an energetic and inspiring teacher, the best demonstration of the argument that creativity and originality in research contribute directly to effective teaching. Among the many things which he taught his colleagues in anthropology was the necessity of providing students (and professional colleagues) with written ethnography to accompany film. There are two ways to do this. In the first, one can make films on a subject already treated in a written ethnographic work. Thus, *The Water of Words* complements wonderfully James Fox's earlier book, *Harvest of the Palm* (1977), both the film and the book illustrating the ways in which lontar-palm tapping permeates all facets of Rotinese life. In the second, one can produce a written ethnographic account of the subject of a film. Of the two, Tim himself favored the second. *Jero Tapakan: Balinese Healer. An Ethnographic Film Monograph* (1986 and 1996), which Linda Connor, Patsy Asch and Tim wrote to accompany the first four of the series of Bali films, Tim described as just such an "ethnographic film monograph". The book contains a précis of the roles of healing and healers in Balinese social life, detailed shot-lists for the films and essays on the making of the films. The book is an unmatched exemplar of what Tim had in mind.

During the early phase of my work with Tim and before we commenced post-production of the Flores films, I often wondered about this apparent paradox in Tim's thinking: he was a consummate ethnographic film-maker who seemed obsessed with the importance of written ethnography. In the editing phase of our collaboration I discovered, through hours of discussion and argument with Tim, the solution of the paradox. Tim saw film as a sensually powerful and thus seductive medium. While it is unmatched as a technique for the iconic recording of human behavior, it is not a good medium for explaining itself, not, at least, without the film-maker stepping out of (or intrusively into) the film to offer explanations of what is going on. Tim deeply mistrusted the "Voice of God", especially when it manifests itself as voice-over narration. The danger Tim saw and one which has been confirmed in studies by his colleagues at the University of Southern California (see Martínez, this volume) is that, in using ethnographic film in teaching, people of one culture often react negatively, even with repugnance, when confronted with vividly moving images of the situationally appropriate but cross-culturally bizarre behavior in another. Since the inherent limitations of cinematic technique restrict the contextualization of images in film itself, the way to illuminate what is going on in film is to write ethnographically about the subject of the film, the actors in the film and the film-making process, and to ensure that the written materials are as easily available to students as the film itself. In this way, film becomes one part of a larger ethnographic enterprise and not an end in itself. Furthermore, only in this way can film contribute to anthropology's aim of bringing people together rather than driving them apart. The key to resolving the paradox was to realize that Tim Asch was first and foremost an anthropologist. For him film was always a tool, one which could be used well or poorly, in the service of anthropology.

Tim believed that the way to ensure that film served anthropology was for the film-maker to step into the background and to eschew the "authored" film. Early in his career, he realized that social life subsists in events, which themselves are composed of sequences of activities in which people do things for particular ends. These activities and the events they constitute can be filmed. Such films, because they are not directed and because the film-maker interposes himself into the activity as little as possible, can both be fashioned into edited films for audiences and can provide the anthropologist with an immensely rich source of ethnographic information.[5] Tim felt that this method was best employed when working with an anthropologist who is ethnographically expert in the community and society in which film is shot and who understands well the activities which become the subject of film (and who knows which questions to ask about them later on).

Collaboration in the production of an Asch film had several distinct facets. First, there was the collaboration with an anthropologist intimately acquainted with the community and people who would be the subjects of a film. Second, there was the collaboration between the film-maker and anthropologist with the people in the film themselves. In the first instance, the film-maker and anthropologist cooperate with the subjects about what to film, when to film, how to work together and over each of the myriad of small problems and opportunities which arise in filming.

Figure 1.2 Tim Asch and Tana 'Ai ritualists perform a sacrificial rite to "cool" the hut built for the anthropologists' use during the Tana 'Ai film project. Tana 'Ai, 1980.

Later the collaboration with subjects becomes more formal, when the film-maker and anthropologist return to the community to elicit further information about the filmed events using the technique Tim referred to as "informant feedback" (others have called it, more grandiloquently, "photo-elicitation"). Finally, there was the involvement, amounting in many cases to a further collaboration, of colleagues, friends, postgraduate students and undergraduate students as trial audiences in the final stages of post-production. In a sense, there was in Tim's work a fourth kind of collaboration, between him and his audiences. Tim listened to his audiences carefully; their comments, criticisms and enthusiasm for one film led to an ongoing interpretative re-evaluation of the past work which influenced the films that followed. This feature of Tim's work is perhaps most clearly seen in the relationship between *A Balinese Trance Seance*, which was shot in 1978, and *Jero on Jero*, shot in 1980. In addition to serving as an illustration of the feedback technique, *Jero on Jero* features Jero addressing on-screen questions put to her by Linda Connor – some of them questions raised by audiences of the earlier film.

Tim's method was to work as an anthropologist first and a film-maker second. To his collaborators he said, "Teach me about your people, so that we can film them." He said he preferred working with the "kids" – those still gingerly working their way through the basic problems of ethnography in their Ph.D. fieldwork – because the "grown-ups" were too busy making careers to be of much use and also because the kids were so much more excited about what they were doing. The kids (now all grown up, in part because of Tim's tutelage) included Linda Connor and myself, but he worked with grown-ups, too: Asen Balikci, James Fox, Napoleon Chagnon, to name a few. I cannot speak for the grown-ups, but as one of the kids I can say that all of us found working with him exhilarating. In my case, the work with him has turned out to be a defining moment of my career and much of my life since.

Tim's Indonesia projects carried his interest in filming events and activity sequences a further step. We set out on the Flores project with a number of aims in mind, one of which was to experiment with having some of the participants in the events we filmed explicate those events on film and for our audiences. To this end, we returned to Flores in 1982 with videotape transfers of all of the footage we had shot in 1980. In addition to showing people in the community some of the film we had shot, I worked through the footage more formally with a number of different informants, eliciting their comments and exegeses of the filmed events. The result of this experiment in "informant feedback" was an immense corpus of information on the *gren mahé*, which has enriched both the film we produced and the written ethnography on ritual in Tana Wai Brama. The success of this venture led us to invite Pius Ipir Wai Brama, a principal subject in A *Celebration of Origins*, to Canberra in 1984 where he assisted us in editing the film. In *Jero on Jero* and *Releasing the Spirits* we see the process of informant feedback in action. Thus, in his later work, Tim was actively engaging his films' subjects in the production of films for audiences, an approach to film-making which he further developed in Venezuela, where he taught video and film-making techniques to the Yanomami.

In making A *Celebration of Origins* we encountered not only the usual problems arising from editing undirected footage, but a number of others relating to the multiple themes we hoped to intertwine in the film. What we needed most was a way of gauging the effectiveness of the film as we proceeded with the editing. Tim's solution to this vexing problem was both simple and elegant: why not show the unfinished film to what we guessed would be the film's typical audience and then take account of their reactions in our editing? To this end, Tim employed a dual system projector which he had salvaged somewhere years before and then dragged across oceans and continents as his career led him from one place to another. With this mechanical monstrosity we could project the film with synchronized original sound at an early stage in post-production. With someone reading subtitles and voice-over narration, an audience could get a good idea of what the film was about. Using this technique, we screened A *Celebration of Origins* at various stages in its evolution for audiences of undergraduate students, graduate students, and colleagues in Los Angeles in 1986. I must confess that I harbor some less than fond memories of the dual system projector, but the results of Tim enlisting audiences directly into the film's making I found both generous and enlightening. We learned, for example, that audiences of students in the United States reacted with repugnance to close-ups of animals having their heads cut off in the *gren mahé* sacrifices. So Patsy Asch returned to the editing room and recut the sacrifice segments in such a way that neither reduced their centrality in the rituals nor caused audiences acute discomfort. We also identified problems with the complex three-tracked narrative structure of the film in time to solve them.

The nature of collaboration and the joint creation of ethnography became in

Figure 1.3 Dealing with technical problems with recording equipment. Tana 'Ai, 1980.

later years a subject for much thought and discussion between Tim and his colleagues. In particular, Tim was interested in the way that an ethnographic result, including films, was shaped by collaboration and the interplay of the collaborators' personalities. But there were other aspects of the problem about which Tim worried creatively. For example, when the time came to release a collaborative film, whose name ought to come first? Tim thought that all the names ought to come first, but given the linearity of words and film, this was impossible. I remember Tim playing at animated wheels, a kind of rotating mandala on which the collaborators' names would be inscribed in such a fashion that no one name could be seen as prior. It never really worked, but the intense and creative energy that went into solving the problem was entirely in character for Tim.

Tim's professional life was full of interesting problems. Working with him, one came to suspect that he loved each one of them. Many required the application of a formidable technical expertise (my favorite photograph from our first fieldwork together in Tana 'Ai is one of Tim working with a rat's nest of wires and, well, bits and pieces of junk, looking back over his shoulder and beaming at the camera). One such problem was what to do with all those used-up batteries that began littering the mountain in Tana'Ai on whose slope we worked.

Radios, tape recorders, torches (flashlights in American English), cameras, and the entire miscellany of equipment and gadgets we used in the fieldwork phase of the Tana'Ai film project all produce large numbers of batteries as refuse, batteries in all shapes and sizes, mostly alkaline, but who knows what exactly was inside those little tubes of metal? One of our aims in Tana'Ai was to make reliable transcriptions of the recorded speech which went with our films and of the interviews and "wild sound" which we took of people talking, chanting, arguing, and otherwise using words.

Figure 1.4 Tim and Patsy Asch making camp, Tana 'Ai, 1980. The Aschs and I set up our base camp at Watuwolon, in a fallow garden next to the house of one of the principal ritual specialists of the domain of Tana Wai Brama. The camera and other equipment were kept in a "clean" tent pitched on a bamboo platform. We stored film stock in insulated "eskies" (ice chests) coated with reflective material beneath the platform from which we hung burlap rice sacks to shade the film storage boxes.

Figure 1.5 Tim Asch unpacks the Arriflex camera in the "clean" tent. Watuwolon, 1980.

Transcriptions require the tedious playing and replaying of a tape recording, in our case using a small Sony TC 150 recorder (not the best recording apparatus but, in my opinion, because of its sturdy construction and unbeatable mechanical linkages, the best field transcription recorder ever made) which required four AA-size batteries. As the pile of "used-up" batteries from our work grew larger and as our carefully hoarded supply of alkaline batteries from Australia dwindled, Tim started thinking. When a battery goes weak and will no longer drive a torch (for it was our torches, in constant use, which seemed to generate the largest number of senile batteries), it still has power. But how to tap that power? Tim had an idea. It was simple: he went off with a couple of young kids and a machete into the nearest forest that had stands of bamboo, the universal constructor in Tana 'Ai used for everything from fences and floors to vessels for cooking rice. He took a D-cell into the bush with him and returned with bamboos whose inside diameters were just slightly larger than the D-cell. He then sawed off a number of the resulting tubes to just over the length of four D-cells and inserted batteries into them for a six-volt power source. He then cut four V-shaped notches, two opposite each other at each end of the tubes. He placed the coiled ends of wires at each end of the batteries and wound a string around the length of the tube and through the notches. With a tourniquet made from a small piece of nicely whittled bamboo, he wound the string until the coiled ends of the leads pressed firmly against the ends of the batteries, one at the positive pole and one at the negative pole. He soldered the leads into a jack compatible with the external power plug of our Sony TC 150 and, with this simple but to my mind impressively brilliant expedient, produced bamboo-encased power packs which, it proved, would drive the little Sony and many other gadgets for many hours. After the Aschs returned to Australia, I found that two or more of these simple devices could be rigged in parallel and so eight or twelve "dead" batteries provided power for many hours of tape recorder operation, especially if one also used the Tana 'Ai method for recharging batteries, which was to set them in the morning sun to warm up while the coffee was brewing. I used these gadgets for many years, most recently in 1993 when I returned to Tana 'Ai and found, at the bottom of a large wooden trunk I had filled with odds and ends from fifteen years of fieldwork, four of Tim's bamboo power packs, complete with leads and a selection of various kinds of plugs, still serviceable after all those years.

Tim's approach to rebuilding a Model A Ford in Canberra was the same: a clever application of technical imagination in the service of art. Of course, the thing also has to work well – at least for the five minutes you need it. Having myself spent a childhood making things with scavenged odds and ends, I loved this aspect of working with Tim: he did it even better than E.T. If he saw a problem, he solved it (if the problem was something broken or not working right, he'd fix it). He'd say, "Look, Doug, here's how we do it." At the time it always sounded as if he was employing memorized recipes and fix-it manuals, but he wasn't. He was making it up as he went along; it just looked as if the solution was old hat. Tim Asch was a *bricoleur*, wholly and joyously a Neolithic Man.

America, 1982–94

The last thirteen years of Asch's life were largely devoted to undergraduate teaching and developing the postgraduate program in Visual Anthropology in the Department of Anthropology at the University of Southern California. While he felt that he had found a sound method for making ethnographic films, he was enormously generous to those who had other ideas and was indefatigable in his support of his students when, as happened often, they found new insights and proposed new methods for making films in anthropology. As Patsy Asch has said, he believed in people more than in method and so would support whatever someone wanted to try. This is not to say that he was not critical, but he did not judge the work of others in terms of the films he thought they ought to be making. Instead, and especially with students, he tried to figure out what it was they wanted to do and then helped them find the best way to achieve their goals. The only exception to this side of Tim's character was when he suspected that a project would not accord full respect to the people being filmed. Having spent six months in the USC department, I know that students responded well to Tim's approach to teaching and to his generosity with time and ideas. Tim's students' films have won many awards (including an Academy Award nomination and an Independent Documentary Association award) and have been selected for screening at major festivals.

Following his six years in Australia, and shortly after arriving at the University of Southern California, Asch took over publication of the *Society for Visual Anthropology Newsletter*. Through his efforts and with the contributions of his students, Daniel Marks and Lucien Taylor, the *Newsletter* became *Visual Anthropology Review*, a leading journal for visual anthropology. In the 1980s Asch's films were increasingly used in university tuition in anthropology. In 1993 the Fifth Third World Film Forum (Freiburg, Germany) held a major retrospective of his work, and the program of the 1993 Margaret Mead Ethnographic Film and Video Festival (New York City) featured his films. Among the many awards his films received from such festivals as the Flaherty Festival, the Festival de Populi, the American Film Festival, and from organizations like the Royal Anthropological Institute and the International Scientific Film Association, his last film, *A Celebration of Origins*, won the Award of Excellence of the Society for Visual Anthropology (Washington DC, 1993). Tim was especially pleased at the news that *Celebration* received the Grand Prix of the Treizième Bilan du Film Ethnographique (Musée de l'Homme, Paris) in 1994.

This book describes and addresses critically some of Tim's achievements. His work is sufficiently important in anthropology that critical thought about his work will continue in the future. The advantages for anthropology of an expeditious examination of Tim's professional *oeuvre* include the prospect of a better understanding of the relationships of ethnography, cinematic technique, and the form of iconic recordings of culturally informed behavior. But I want to mention what I see as the central motif of his mature work: knowledge for the good. Increasingly, Tim was interested in the ethics of ethnographic film-making and anthropological research. This is a subject he wrote about, but it was also one he experimented with, most notably in his last major project: teaching the Yanomami to make their own videos.

In his professional life, Tim Asch was a man devoted to two things: anthropology and images of human beings captured in photographic emulsions. More than any other man, Tim created new ways of combining anthropology and images for the benefit of his students, his profession, and the whole of humanity. Tim was a Professor of Anthropology, and he professed his discipline in the fullest sense of the term to anyone who would listen. But the source of his gifts to us was not science, but the aesthetic sensibilities of the artist. His work, from the earliest photographs of Cape Breton's people to the last video frame shot in Venezuela and in every one of the millions of frames of 16 mm film which are his legacy to us, showed us not just the information to be discovered in human activities, but the fragile beauty which informs them.

While Tim Asch was a film-maker, he was an anthropologist first. I recall watching an early cut of our Tana 'Ai footage with Tim, Patsy and a professor from the USC film school, who objected to some of the poor lighting and graininess of the image in one particular sequence over which Tim, Patsy and I were congratulating ourselves. "How can you possibly use footage like that in a film?" he asked. Tim's response was that we had done the best that we could and that the image, while grainy, was there. It was great, said Tim, that we got this bit of action, which was important to my work. Tim Asch always subordinated the film and film-maker to the larger anthropological endeavor. In filming and editing he never let the profession of film-making get the upper hand or overtake his goals. He never chose spectacle over intelligibility, and in shooting and editing he never sacrificed the usefulness of his images for anthropological research for filmic effect. In short, he never let the expectations and boundaries of professional film-making get in the way of the subject and the work. He possessed in full the essential quality of the anthropologist: a willingness to learn and to do whatever is required, regardless of disciplinary borders, to get the job of ethnography done.

It has been said of the composer Howard Hanson, a compatriot of Tim's, that he was an artist, a teacher and an administrator and that he was equally gifted and effective in all of these fields. Working with Tim in the field, at the editing table and in the classroom, and watching him up close in one of the early years of the Center for Visual Anthropology at USC, I saw the same multi-skilled artist at work. I also saw the results. I still wonder how he did it. In the end, perhaps it was not so mysterious: Tim Asch may have been a *bricoleur*, but he was certainly a pro.

I am told that at the memorial service for Tim held in a courtyard of the University of Southern California, his family and friends passed around his thick and thickly framed eye glasses. Each person who chose to speak held them and so, for a moment, imagined the world as Tim saw it. For those of us who knew him but could not be there that day, and for millions of others around the world, now and into the future, there is his life's work of brilliantly perceived photographs and films through which we, too, can see the world as Tim Asch did.

Notes

1 Portions of this chapter first appeared in Lewis (1995). I would like to thank Greg Acciaioli for his thoughtful and, for me, illuminating assistance with that memoir and especially Patsy Asch, who knew Tim better than anyone and who generously shared her memory and knowledge of Tim's film-making.

2 The Marshalls used a synch sound system devised by Daniel Blitz, an engineer and friend of Laurence Marshall, in their fourth expedition to film the Ju/'hoansi in Africa in 1955. This was the first use of 16 mm synch sound in ethnographic film-making (Bishop 1993: 223).

3 Asch was not only White's apprentice, but also one of White's photographic subjects: two photographs of Asch, entitled "Tim Asch and Sandstone Sculpture" and "Tim Asch and Log", appear in White 1982.

4 He was also well acquainted with contemporary developments in what has come to be known as visual anthropology, including new films and debates about the place of film in the discipline; from 1971 through 1976 he served as audiovisuals editor responsible for film reviews in the *American Anthropologist*, the journal of the American Anthropological Association.

5 Alexander Moore has explored "activity sequences" in Tim Asch's Yanomami films (1995). See also Asch, Marshall and Spier (1973), which formulates a theory of events which can be seen at work in both the Yanomamö and later films.

References

Asch, Timothy (1982), "Collaboration in Ethnographic Film Making: A Personal View". *Canberra Anthropology* 5 (1): 8–36.

Asch, Timothy, John Marshall and Peter Spier (1973), "Ethnographic Film: Structure and Function". *Annual Review of Anthropology* 2: 179–87.

Bishop, John M. (1993), "Hot Footage/Cold Storage: The Marshall Ju/'hoan Bushman Archive". In Jay Ruby (ed.), *The Cinema of John Marshall*. Chur: Harwood Academic Publishers.

Connor, Linda, Patsy Asch and Timothy Asch (1986), *Jero Tapakan: Balinese Healer. An Ethnographic Film Monograph*. Cambridge: Cambridge University Press.

—— (1996), *Jero Tapakan: Balinese Healer. An Ethnographic Film Monograph*. Revised edition. Los Angeles: Ethnographics Press.

Fox, James J. (1979), "The Ceremonial System of Savu". In A. L. Becker and A. A. Yengoyan (eds.), *The Imagination of Reality: Essays in Southeast Asian Coherence Systems*. pp. 145–73. Norwood, NJ: Ablex.

Harper, Douglas (ed.) (1994), *Cape Breton 1952: The Photographic Vision of Timothy Asch. Visual Sociology* 9 (2). Kentucky: International Visual Sociology Association and Los Angeles: Ethnographics Press.

Lewis, E. D. (1995), "Timothy Asch, 1932–1994: Anthropologist and Ethnographic Film Maker". *Canberra Anthropology* 18 (1 & 2): 218–33.

Moore, Alexander (1995), "Understanding Event Analysis: Using the Films of Timothy Asch". *Visual Anthropology Review* 11 (1): 38–52.

White, Minor (1982), *Minor White: Photographs and Writings 1939–1968*. Millerton, NY: Aperture.

Chapter 2

An ethnographic gaze

Scenes in the anthropological life of Timothy Asch

Douglas Harper

I met Tim Asch in 1970 at a seminar in ethnographic film held at his house in Cambridge, Massachusetts. Although not enrolled in Brandeis University, where Tim was teaching, I became a regular participant in the seminar and Tim never really asked who I was or what I was doing there. We were cutting out-takes from the Yanomamö films into short films to learn about sequencing images. The discussions were exactly what I yearned for: talk about how images got their meanings, mixed in with a lot of love for the practice of picture-making. We learned by doing and were guided as much as anything by Tim's enthusiasm.

After a couple of months I screwed up my courage and brought in my photos. I had no idea that he had studied with Ansel Adams, Minor White and Edward Weston. My photographs were of tramps and railroad cars; some from the skid-row life in Boston. Tim flipped through them: "too dark, too light, too dark ..." I later discovered that he took them more seriously than his comments indicated.

I was seven months out of undergraduate school and had decided to apply for a Ph.D. program in anthropology. I asked Tim if he would write me a recommendation for the program at Brandeis, where he had an appointment. He said that, rather than that, I ought to leave with him (in three days) for Venezuela to do the sound for the next stage of the Yanomamö films. I have often thought back to that road not taken. When I told Tim that I couldn't accompany him to Venezuela, he replied that in any case I should drop the anthropology idea; I seemed more like a sociologist. In fact, he had already made arrangements for me to meet the sociology department at Brandeis and I ought to get moving lest I be late for appointments he had arranged. Tim helped me, like many people, to find who I was trying to be, and where I ought to go to do it.

Tim filmed in Venezuela with Napoleon Chagnon and then moved to Australia with his collaborator and wife, Patsy. Based in Australia, he and Patsy made several films in Indonesia and wrote extensively on ethnographic film and on their specific film projects. We did not meet for several years, although I followed his work through his films from Venezuela, Afghanistan, and Indonesia and his pervasive influence in visual social science. In the late 1980s I was invited to give a talk at the University of Southern California, where he directed the Visual Anthropology program. I stayed with Tim and Patsy and we spent several days making up for a decade and a half of lost time. We saw each other several times over the next years. Then, in the summer of 1992, Tim began treatment for lymphatic cancer. The next spring I was invited back to USC to learn about Tim's still photography. Like most people, I dated the beginning of Tim's visual work to his editing of Marshall's Ju/ 'hoansi films in the late 1950s. There was, however, a treasury of still photographic work which preceded his film career and for a while overlapped it. It was a separate vision: a belief in the potential of still photography to serve both art and science. The book *Cape Breton 1952: The Photographic Vision of Timothy Asch* developed from that first meeting with Tim in 1993.

Our first interviews took place over several days. We examined Tim's photographic work from the mid-1940s from The Putney School, which he had attended in his teens. There followed several rolls of street photography completed in New York, followed by a sudden leap in style and subject coinciding with Tim's two summers as a student of Ansel Adams, Minor White and Edward Weston.

We next examined the Cape Breton project, begun in 1952 and continued in 1960. Tim had been so excited by the project in the summer of 1952 that he stayed through the fall. He intended to begin studies at Columbia University but, having missed a semester, he was drafted into the Army. Tim next photographed in Japan for the US Army publication *Stars and Stripes*, and several Japanese newspapers. We dwelled upon images he made in a Japanese village where he stayed on extended leaves. We next examined several books of contact sheets made in 1961 in Africa as the photographer for the anthropologist Elizabeth Marshall Thomas and published in Thomas's book, *Warrior Herdsmen*.

In the next two decades, Tim concentrated mainly on film. During this time, however, he worked on social science curriculum development projects for elementary schools where he experimented, among other things, with making slide tapes. The most notable was a tape of Jonathan Kozol's classroom interactions. Before there were portable video cameras, Tim encouraged ethnographers to make slide tapes as an inexpensive and technologically simple way to convey a sense of a place, a process or social interaction. We examined his work in Trinidad in 1966 where he experimented by recording sounds and simultaneously taking slides very rapidly, and then refilming details from the slides to create even more images to place with the sounds. By using two projectors and a dissolve control, he could produce the feel of an encounter and even movement. These slide tape experiments were an important part of the transition from still photography to thinking about the moving image.

In his last years Tim returned to still photography in the form of 35 mm color prints, drugstore-developed and sequenced into his poems. In this work he had returned to the spirit of the work completed forty years before as a student of masters of the form.

During the summer and fall of 1993, Tim was treated for his advancing cancer. I returned to California in March 1994 for the Margaret Mead Ethnographic Film Festival and to complete our interviews. The interview tapes I did with Tim were distilled for *Cape Breton 1952* and for the present volume.

Though slowed by his illness, he and Patsy traveled back to Cape Breton in the summer of 1994 to resume work on the photographic and the 1960 film project. Members of the MacDonald family – father Dannie and mother Tina, and their children Michael, Stephen and Angus, with whom Tim had stayed in Cape Breton – had contacted Tim to encourage him and Patsy to complete the film begun on earlier visits.

Accounts of Tim's background, his work in California, and the Cape Breton project are told in the following interviews. I shall, in the following, add just a bit to the skeleton of this story. It is quite extraordinary that, of all of Tim's photographic projects, only the Cape Breton photographs have been published or even, for the most part, printed. A fuller publication of Tim's work is called for which would include his work from The Putney School, his art photography in California, the Cape Breton project, the Japanese village ethnography, a republication of the African work with Elizabeth Marshall Thomas, the high-school project with Jonathan Kozol, and his most recent photography and poetry. It is almost as if these projects were means to understandings which remained largely private. Once the projects were completed, he moved on. But perhaps Tim would not agree with this. Indeed, much of our discussion centered on his great disappointment that few of these projects had been published, or that they had been reproduced in a secondary role to text, as in the Marshall book.

We see, in the Cape Breton project, experiments in still photography that were eventually applied to anthropological filming: the use of sequences to portray socially purposeful actions. But Tim had not abandoned his orientation as an art photographer. Rather, he combined the sensitivities and orientations learned from leading art photographers with the shooting script technique developed by John Collier at Cornell University. Collier, it is to be remembered, learned the shooting script method from Roy Stryker, the director of the Farm Security Administration in the 1930s.

The interview sessions were transcribed by the staff of the Information Processing Center at the University of South Florida. I listened to all the tapes to correct the transcriptions. The original transcripts were several hundred pages long and largely unorganized, as our conversation moved freely from subject to subject.

The first step in the organization of this material was to sort by topic and to eliminate redundancies. I then put the roughly shaped pieces in chronological order and began editing in March 1994 to complete the interviews. Many friends and associates had traveled to the Margaret Mead Film Festival in Tim's honor, and we all competed for limited time to talk with him. Still, he and I were able to complete four more hours of recorded conversation, in which we discussed many of the photos we had selected for *Cape Breton 1952*. This method, often called "photo-elicitation", was a delightful way to remember experiences and to construct parts of a narrative. While I had done photo-elicitation with people I had studied as an anthropologist, I had never done it with an anthropologist. I then integrated much of the information from the second interviews into the text of our original discussions.

There are two basic methods of and attitudes toward editing transcripts. The folklorist seeks the most faithful recreation of the spoken text. This method does not pretend to attempt readability or logical transitions. The other method of transcription reproduces words of the conversation in order to develop a foundation for a constructed text. This has been my method in this project.

I have sorted topics and thus taken things out of the order in which they were discussed. In fact, I have mixed conversations between two interviews, one year apart, into the same text. In addition, I have edited the text to create a more reader-friendly grammar. At times I have added implied words which were left out of unfinished sentences. My goal has been, first and foremost, to tell Tim's story. But I have taken liberties with the spoken text to achieve what were clearly the intentions expressed in our conversations. In that I listened to the tapes at least twice and was a participant in the recording, I feel comfortable with my interpretations.

For those of us who knew Tim, reading these transcripts of conversation is an experience of *déjà vu*. We've known this voice of humility, insight, wisdom, and adventure. The transcripts allow us to return to a friend now departed. For those who did not know Tim, the transcripts show how an anthropologist operates in the field. Tim was a great anthropologist because he was connected to those with whom he lived. He took for granted that he would catch their fish, milk their cows, fight their battles. He was honored by the acceptance of the people with whom he lived.

Early years

TIMOTHY ASCH: I lived on 87th Street and York Avenue in an old brownstone. I got initiated into a street gang; there were very poor people across the street and relatively well-off people on our side of the street. My father was twenty years older than my mother. She adored him. When he died she fell apart; our family fell apart.

My dad ran Lennox Hill Clinic for thirty years. He had a lot of very poor patients and then he had a lot of very wealthy patients. The poor patients were artists like Misha Elman [1891–1967], who would practice their string quartets and whatnot before they went to the Town Hall to play. It was quite a nice household; artists gave him paintings instead of cash. He was one of the three founders of the New York psychoanalytic society, and the last person to be studied by Freud.

So when I was in trouble as a young kid, because my family life was falling apart, my mother sent me to one of my dad's friends, David Levy, who was a child psychiatrist. He said, "There's nothing wrong with him, just get him away from home as fast as you can." I must have been nine, ten, 1942. I had been kicked out of several schools because I was so disturbed and obstreperous. My mother said, "If you get kicked out of this school it's PS 91 for you." I thought that meant prison, actually. So by the time I was put on the bus I thought I was going to prison. Nobody went with me and I was too shy to ask questions about it.

So I was put on a bus; it changed at Albany; it went all through the night. I never went to sleep; I just looked out the window. In the morning I found myself in the midst of mountains in Lake Placid. We went between two very high peaks and two beautiful lakes called Twin Lakes, and then the bus stopped. Nowhere. There was six feet of snow on the ground. The bus driver said, "This is where you get off." I said, "Yeah, but what do I do?" He said, "Well, you just walk down that road and there's a school down there." I thought, "This is prison?" Now, I'd never seen mountains except in comic books. But there were mountains here, but the mountains were covered with snow and mist and clouds. You couldn't see the top which made you think they were all the higher. Anyway, I walked down the road and up comes a jeep; out of the jeep piles, I don't know, it was, like, twelve kids. It was like one of those circus cliaphone[1] things: people kept coming out. They were obviously late, and the leader of the jeep said, "You've got to do barn chores right away … we're going to be late for breakfast again, and Walter Clark [the director of the school] is really going to be angry at me so – race." I realized I had a problem. I'd never seen horses, I'd never been in the country, and I had a city suit on.

I just started joining in and helping. Then they all got in the jeep and left; they'd only done half their job. They fed the horses, cleaned a couple of stalls. I figured out how to work the manure bucket, which had to go all the way down to the end. The doors had to be opened; you had to pull special levers, you had to empty the thing and put it back again. I worked from about eight o'clock till noon and I said to myself, "If this is prison, I want to stay here; this is fantastic." So I cleaned out the remaining stalls and I watered a few horses that hadn't been watered. I did everything that I had to do. I walked to the school, and Walter Clark was furious. "Where have you been? We were about to call the police." But they never asked [what I had been doing], and nobody ever knew and I never said anything.

That was a great school.[2] My impression of New York City in those days was, for example, when I came back one early summer towards the end of the school year: in a bus with lots of other people packed in, there was this drip, drip, drip, on my nose … and some of it got in my mouth. It was very salty … I looked up and I was under this big fat woman's armpit. That was my impression of New York City. That's how badly I hated it.

I was at that school for about a year when someone sent me a Brownie camera. I had become very good with horses, and I photographed my horse with this little Brownie camera. The pictures came back from the drugstore and that was it. I knew that I would be a photographer. You know, lots of people don't know what they're going to do with their lives. I knew somehow I would be a photographer.

Later on, when I went to high school, I met David Sapir, the son of Edward Sapir, the great American linguist. He knew he was going to be an anthropologist.

Figure 2.1 North Country School, 1956. The 1956 photographs are among Asch's early experiments with capturing movement in his photography.

Figure 2.2 North Country School, 1956.

Figure 2.3 North Country School, 1956.

He had to, because his father was. So I started reading the things he was reading … and I knew I was going to be an anthropologist. So I knew two things already in high school, that I would be an anthropologist and that I would be a photographer. I just kept working at that.

When I was in high school I roomed with David. There was a sophomore named John Yang, a very sophisticated Chinese guy, who had already launched his career in photography. He was enamored of the nineteenth-century German salon photographers. He thought they were just fabulous; we all thought they were great. He had this book of their work; one day he had ripped up this book and thrown it away. This book was sacred. So

Figure 2.4 David Sapir by Asch, The Putney School, ca 1950.

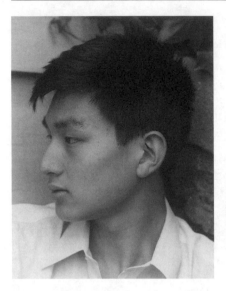

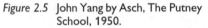

Figure 2.5 John Yang by Asch, The Putney School, 1950.

Figure 2.6 Tim Asch by John Yang, California, south of San Francisco, summer, 1951.

when he wasn't looking I took it out of the trash can and repaired it. But he found it again about a month later and he was furious that I'd found it … so he ripped it up again and destroyed it. We worked our way up from the soft-focus, German salon photographers to Alfred Stieglitz, Paul Strand, Edward Weston, Ansel Adams and Minor White. We thought Ansel was a bit shallow.

We were pretty savvy pretty quick. We had a six-week period where we had to do photographic projects. I was an extra at the Metropolitan Opera, so that was one of my projects. But I also did a project which meant that I walked the streets of New York City, sometimes from eight in the morning till ten at night. I made a little darkroom in the basement of my parents' house where you couldn't stand up; even a kid my size couldn't quite stand up: there wasn't enough room. But I developed these pictures and printed them.

We discovered that the Museum of Modern Art would give lending exhibits for fifty bucks. You'd get fifty of Edward Weston's pictures, fifty of Paul Strand's. We would get these twice a year and put them up in the dining room of this big high school – share them with everybody, talk about them. I would get up during lunch hour for ten minutes and everybody would be quiet. I'd say, "And we now have this exhibit from Ed Weston. He was born such and such … He's done this kind of work." And then Yang would do it. We had a darkroom that we kind of owned, and we worked incredibly hard trying to imitate these masters. We did terrible work.

We looked at each other at the end of our second year and said, "We don't know what we're doing."

My sister was a layout director for *Life* magazine and she had become close friends with [W. Eugene] Smith. Now Gene Smith was a master printer. Of course, he was one of the world's greatest photo-journalists. But he was in and out of mental institutions all the time; he was a pretty unstable person. My sister was so frightened that my mother would criticize her for introducing me to Gene Smith that she didn't. But I shouldn't have studied with Ansel Adams or Edward Weston or Minor White, I should have been working with Gene Smith. He kept slaves. He had people, young kids like me, who were slaves at his place, printing and working ... but they learned a lot.

So I didn't study with Gene Smith. I didn't even know who he was. But when his Spanish village story came out in *Life*, that changed my life.[3] I said, "This is it. I'm going to combine these two. I'll do the anthropology with the photography." I think *Life* was as impressed as I was with the quality of the images. They were exotic images of another society, but they were art. They had an artistic integrity and hold that were devastating.

California

TIMOTHY ASCH: I said to David Sapir, "What we ought to do is apprentice like they did in the old times." So I wrote seventeen letters, heartfelt letters. Twenty, twenty-five pages, handwritten ... Lisette Model, Berenice Abbott, Dorothea Lange, Alfred Stieglitz,[4] Edward Weston, Ansel Adams, Paul Strand ... just on and on and on.

DOUG HARPER: I think I found a response to one of those letters this morning. It's from Edward Weston, dated 1950, so you would have been eighteen.

TIM: Yeah.

DOUG: Can I get the letter and read the response?

TIM: Yeah.

DOUG: The letter, with a kind of scrawling handwriting: "Dear Mr Asch, I am disabled so far as writing goes ... so forgive the seemingly curt note. I gather from your letter that you are on the right track. Good luck. I'm not in a position to take on an apprentice. Have you considered the Photo League, New York? Or the California School of Fine Arts? My pyrosoda formula is the standard as given in the ..."

TIM: Eastman Kodak company and Ansco booklets.

DOUG: " ... except that I use one third the amount of carbonate and multiply my film speed by two or three in the field. As you can see I am giving out. Yours, Edward Weston."

TIM: I wrote letters to all these people and that's one of the nicer letters I got. Some people didn't answer. Other people said, "I'm sorry ... that I could never could take on an apprentice." Like, those medieval days of apprenticeships were dead. Ansel wrote me a postcard. That'll be over there somewhere, and it said, "Dear Mr Asch, I get so much correspondence and I'm so busy I just don't

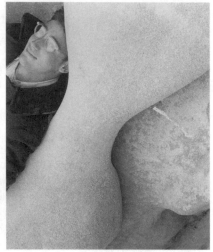

Figure 2.7 Tim Asch by Minor White, California.

Figure 2.8 Tim Asch by Minor White, California.

know whether I answered your letter or not." So I wrote him back a postcard saying, "No, you haven't." So he also mentioned the California School of Fine Arts, because he said he started the photographic program there, and it was going very well, and I should start there and see what I could do. Minor White was running it. I wrote them and they wrote back and said, "No, we don't take high school students; you have to be a college student or college graduate before we take you." So I wrote again – then I had something. I knew, "You're not going to shove me out all together, come on now." So I wrote and I wrote and finally this guy, Minor White, wrote back and said, "We give up; you can come."[5]

So I hitchhiked out west. I arrived in time to go to the first class and we were told by Bill Quandt, my first teacher, to go back and bring our portfolio with us after lunch. So I was sitting there waiting to show Bill Quandt my portfolio; I came back with the portfolio and there was this guy sweeping the floor and cleaning the windows, the janitor. He came over and sat next to me and said, "Let me see your pictures." I said, "Well, I'm a … you're a … I brought them back to show to my teacher." He said, "I'm not going to eat your pictures." So he looked at them and he said, "Good. Good. Want to apprentice with me this summer?" It turned out to be Minor White. So I did. He was living with Ansel Adams, in Ansel Adams's house, so I became one of Ansel's printers.[6]

Ansel had this huge railroad track 20 × 24 enlarger. He was a terrible person to work with because he was impatient, and he was a master craftsman, and it was boring. Eight-by-ten-inch negatives.

When I first went there I'd never met Ansel and I was looking around Ansel's drawers and I found this portfolio of Paul Strand's work in Mexico: the

Figure 2.9 Tim Asch by Minor White, California.

Figure 2.10 Minor White by Asch, California.

Mexico portfolio. I looked at that; I must have looked at it for five hours. Amazing pictures. It just changed my life. Then Ansel came in, like three o'clock in the morning, great big grizzly beard, put his head around the door and said, "Who are you?" I said, "I just flew up and I was so engrossed in these pictures." He thinks I'm a thief or something. But it worked out all right. I explained. He said, "Well, yes, you have good taste, that's beautiful work."

It was a difficult time in White's life because he decided very late to become a photographer. He worked kind of alone and earned a living teaching there. None of us had any money. I had saved fifty dollars as a riding counselor from the summer before – which would have translated into about a $275 today. That bought us groceries for about six, seven weeks. We lived down on Jackson Street, in the Chinese part of town. Minor had a jeep that he'd gotten, army surplus, for fifty dollars. That just barely got us around. He was very angry at what kind of a lazy teenager I was, and he wanted to discipline me to become an artist. So he'd say, "Get your eyes off the street and look around. You've got to be making things out of what you see visually here." He would kick me out of bed at 5.30 in the morning. I'd have to be sure all the 4 × 5 holders were loaded; all of the equipment was ready so that when we went out on expedition we wouldn't be missing something. Then I put it all in the jeep and got everything ready to go. We would get out just when the sun rose and we'd get the early light. Then we would come back and he would cook a little breakfast and I would develop the negatives. When I had time I would print the pictures from the negatives from the day before. Then we would go out and do the same thing with the evening light, anywhere from two to six.

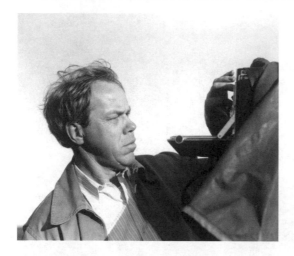

Figure 2.11 Minor White by Asch, California.

DOUG: Were you shooting, or Minor White?

TIM: We both photographed; we worked independently. I tried to stay close by. I had a lot of questions, a lot to learn. I knew nothing about the Zone System. For some reason, I don't know why, it only took me a few minutes to get onto what the Zone System was. I got some stimulus from working with him, but then often we might work for two or three hours without even being within earshot.

DOUG: This must have been a physical landscape that turned you on?

TIM: Well, again, I was interested in anthropology and people, without being able to articulate it. A lot of these people I wrote, most of them were photographing inanimate objects. Well, that's okay. That's a very contemplative, interesting thing to do, but it's not people. It's not anthropology. But, anyway, that's how I learned.

Then we ran out of money and we had to do jobs. I had to help him do some cruddy jobs, like photographing a little mobile. It was going to be put in some window in Abercrombie and Fitch in New York. He was very angry that I was spending so much time doing it. He said, "For jobs you just do it one, two, three. For your art you spend all month making a print if you have to. But learn how to be efficient …"

DOUG: I found two portraits of you in White's book, *Mirrors Messages Manifestations* (White 1982: 73 and 76). Can you tell us about those?

TIM: Well, when we were together we'd photograph each other. I have some photographs of him too.

Every day it was: come back at night, eat dinner, develop those negatives from the afternoon, print the ones from the morning and then, if there was time, make a decent print. But that could take you hours. I'd go to bed at three; he'd get me up at 5 or 5.30. I'm a teenager; I want twelve hours sleep. But I knew I was learning something; it was hard. I had a steel grip on a piece of the jeep so I wouldn't fall out because I was always dozing off. When I was working I wasn't sleeping, but as soon as I got in the jeep … zzzzzz. It was terrible. Then after six weeks of this, Minor didn't get up one morning. I said, "What's the matter?" He said, "Well, I'm sick. You go out and shoot." So I went out and shot in the morning. I did all the routine. I came back. I cooked breakfast. I developed film. Night came. Next morning, he wasn't going to get up. "I'm still sick." – "Well, I'm not going out." – "Just go out, just leave me alone." So when I came back I said, "Look, I've made up my mind, either you get up or I go get a doctor." – "No, there's nothing wrong, just leave me alone." So that night I said, "Well, that's it. It's getting late now and I'm not going to be able to get a doctor. This is ridiculous, nobody stays in bed this long." He said, "You don't understand. You were nothing. I was trying to train you and now it's just worn me out."

He spent three days in bed, trying to teach me how to be an artist, trying to teach me how to be efficient. I had an exhibit at the end of that year. Bill Quandt, who was my teacher at the school, looked at the work. I was very proud of it. He looked at the work and he said, "There is nothing original in any of this. You've just been imitating these people. I don't see anything of you here. I don't see any future for you."

I bought it. You know, I'm so stupid and gullible. When he said that, I looked at the work on the wall in an entirely different way. He was right.

Then I went down to see Edward [Weston]. We used to walk the beaches a lot and I found a cormorant which was very pleasant and friendly, pet-like, which would help me eat my sandwiches and whatnot. I took a beautiful photograph of this cormorant flying off of the rocks. Edward said, "Now there – now, Tim, that's something. It's something moving. God, man, you can stop imitating art."

I went out there and worked hard as an artist, and I realized that I couldn't make a living. I could do the work but I could never make a living at it. It wouldn't be worth it anyway because I didn't have anything original, it would seem, to contribute. If I had anything original to say photographically, it would be filming people and nobody was filming people there. So, I could have banged my head against a stone wall year after year after year out there, and I never would have broken away. I felt that Weston and Minor White and Ansel Adams were driven; that they had a purpose in life and that really interested me.

Cape Breton

TIM: I went to Bard College and they didn't have any anthropology to speak of, so I decided to go to Columbia. My sister introduced me to John Morris, the picture editor for *Black Star*, and he suggested I see John Collier. So I went to see John Collier; he said, "Okay, you go to Cape Breton Island."

DOUG: John Collier had been an FSA[7] photographer in the 1930s, if I remember correctly.

TIM: Right. His father had been the Indian Commissioner for twenty years and John had spent a lot of time growing up on the Navajo reservation. He'd done a book called *The Awakening Valley*. That also impressed me tremendously. I thought, "Now there's an example of something I'd like to do."

DOUG: So Collier was a guy who kind of fit between things also. He was a

Figure 2.12 Cape Breton.

Figure 2.13 Cape Breton.

photographer but he didn't have graduate degrees in Anthropology, did he?

TIM: No, but he worked in an anthropology department. Alexander Leyton and other people at Cornell understood his talent and how his talent could help their research.

They did an interesting study, one of those rare things which should be done much more often but usually never works – to collaborate across disciplines. Because of Alexander Leyton as a leader, the psychology, sociology, and anthropology departments wrote a grant to study the effects of the life-changes that were taking place at a place called

Digby County, on the western end of Nova Scotia. On that whole part of Nova Scotia and Cape Breton, you had people living on the perimeter of the land in little fishing villages. The person who had the most prestige was the person who'd catch the most number of cod in a day, a week, a month, a year, and/or the person who could fiddle best on the Friday night dances. Life was fairly simple, and then the war came and we had to send meat to our troops overseas, so back in the United States and Canada we had to eat a lot more fish. You couldn't compete, catching one fish at a time, with the draggers dragging the sea. There was a two-mile offshore limit, but they just dragged right inside and got all the spawning grounds and everything. So the bottom of the market dropped out for these small-time fishermen; there was an over-supply of fish at the same time they fished out the fishing grounds.

Industry had to be drummed up, so in the larger towns in the center of Nova Scotia you had workers migrating from the perimeter by the sea to work in the factories. But, interestingly, a lot of them would not move all the way in to work. They couldn't stand the noise and the dislocation of the city. They lived somewhere in between, and they had chickens and so forth, and they could get to the center every day, where they had to work, fairly easily. A lot of them lived like that. The mental health problems were interesting.

I went to see Collier up at Cornell and I saw all of his photographs; it was just the kind of thing I wanted to do. I was a little upset that he wasn't an academic because somehow I knew that I would have to be an academic to do this work. It was sad that there was that distinction. But he was a wonderful person. He said, "We don't have any sort of a control group of what this used to be like, but in Cape Breton they still live this way, so why don't you go to Cape Breton Island?" So again my summer was planned out for me; this was probably November.

I had a room-mate who restored old cars and I asked him what kind of a car I should get to do this fieldwork that summer. He said, "Oh, get an old Model A Ford." They were twenty-five, fifty bucks. So he got me one for fifty dollars; it was in good shape. I drove off in May, up to Cape Breton Island. I met the Colliers and their group in Nova Scotia, and then I went on. I lived in a swordfishing village, and a coal-mining town, and in Mabou Mines with the McDonald family, which is where Patsy and I made the film several years later.

DOUG: What kind of themes were you trying to explore when you were shooting?

TIM: That was a problem for me. I wasn't problem-oriented and I didn't have themes – I wasn't good at focusing on a story, on developing a narrative. I was good at exploring and doing fieldwork, but it was my first experience at constructing a narration.

I was going to come back late August and I stayed, I think, until November, till it was really cold. So I really had to stretch my money out, which meant that my lunch was one can of sardines, because they were twelve cents a can. And sometimes that's what I would have for dinner. So I really had to stretch it. I ate out of grocery stores while I was on the road. In Mabou Mines the

McDonalds fed me. I worked, like on the swordfishing boat, and so I was fed. So my expenses were primarily that I had to pay for gas.

DOUG: Do you remember working with the shooting script Collier prepared for you? Did you actually look at that and work with that?

TIM: Yes, I did. Not everywhere; it wasn't appropriate on the swordfishing boat, or the coal mining. But, yes, when I was living with the McDonalds I did.

DOUG: The notion of shooting script, I believe, traces back to Stryker, who was friends with Robert and Helen Lynd during the time they wrote the Middletown books.[8] Stryker's conversations with the Lynds focused on what they called "visual ethnography". You've got Stryker saying things like, "I don't give a damn for the spectacular; I want these photos to mean something twenty years from now. I want them to show how people did the little things of life, not the big things. Let the photo-journalist take care of that."

TIM: But that script also would have derived right out of Alexander Leyton's project for rural documentation. I got into my Model A Ford, left Long Island and got to Cape Breton. I felt so free and so exhilarated. I had heard about this village several years before, on a Putney School trip. I approached it from a direction where I'd never approached that part of the coast before. I stopped a little kid that I saw in the field, to ask directions, and his Scot brogue was so thick that I could barely understand it. I felt that I was in an exotic place, and it was. I was on my own and I was discovering things. So I got to the end of the road at Mabou Mines; that's where the end of the road was. There was this great old house and there was this woman; she came out with a couple of milk pails in her hand. I stopped the car and went up to her. I turned off the motor and she looked at me kind of half-frightened, half-annoyed and she said, "What do you want?" I said, "Well, I was looking for a place to live and to photograph that was really beautiful. And this is such a beautiful place." "Well, we don't want any strangers here." I said, "Well, I was hoping maybe I could work for my keep and live outside in a sleeping bag." "We don't want any strangers here and what could you do anyway? You're obviously a city person; what do you know about working on a farm?" I looked at her milk pails and I said, "Well, I can milk a cow." She said, "You can milk a cow, my foot." And I said, "I can!" She said, "All right, come on down to the barn." So I went to the barn; there were three cows. She milked her two while I was still trying to milk mine. If you haven't milked a cow for a long while, you know, your hands lose their strength.

I knew how to milk cows. But my hands were so weak that I was almost crying for the strength I needed to do that work. So she finished her two cows and I heard her say, as I was milking, "Poor cow."

So she went back up to the house, and then I finished and I went back up to the house. She said, "Well, I'll tell you, you can wait till the others come back from mission." This was a family of sixteen people and they were all, fifteen of them, at mission except for her. Once a year they have this big church mission where they go for a whole week. They come back at night but they spend all the day there. It's a big thing. So they finally came back. The man of the house,

Dannie, was always looking for a companion. Although I was very young, I was just barely old enough to be his companion.

We went on real drinking binges, which he wouldn't have been able to do as well without me. We went to the race tracks several times, and I did a lot of haying and lumbering, lobster fishing, so I was integrated into that family that baked seven loaves of bread a day just to feed themselves. Old Grandma had to have one of the kids, one of the thirteen- or fourteen-year old kids, sleep with her to keep her warm at night. That was always a chore that nobody wanted. So that's how I found that family.

I came back late, in November. I wrote Columbia and I asked them if I could extend my summer. They said, "You can do that; we'll let you take this semester off if you're so productively employed at the moment, but you have to remember you'll be eligible for the draft." So twelve days before I was to go back to school, having paid my tuition, I was drafted. When I came back from Cape Breton, just before I was drafted, I worked like a fiend and I storyboarded the Cape Breton experience. I had tons of sheets of this stuff. I was trying to work with it. Then I got drafted, and I was gone for two years. There was nothing I could do with the photos. John Collier was very upset that I didn't follow through with something that they could use. The photos would have been part of the Digby county project but it just didn't work. Being drafted, what could I do? So when I came back, this was really behind me; this was two years later. I just threw myself into my studies.

I started photographing people when I went to Cape Breton and realized that it wasn't so much an issue; it wasn't so much an art, but a question of documentation.

[During the next years I finished Columbia and] went to the Peabody Museum at Harvard to make those Bushman films with John Marshall and Bob Gardner. After six or eight months, they said, "You haven't made a film." So they were nice enough, although I was doing slave work – they were both nice enough to say, "Hey, you'd better make a film. You're not going to learn anything [doing our editing]." So John Marshall staked me to some film and I went back to Cape Breton in 1960. Patsy and I went together and we just loved it. I'd written to the McDonalds. I still have letters there. I had sent them some of the photos.

The film was called *One Day of Many*. It was a day in the life of these people. I didn't have any portable tape recorders. Except Bob Gardner had the first wet-battery-operated recorder, so I took that and I made some tapes that we'll use in the finished film, of Dannie telling stories and some singing. Wild stories. We didn't really think of a good narrative structure. All we could come up with was "Well, let's just do a day in the life of these people." So it had a lot of the miscellaneous activities. We did farming. We didn't do any logging. We did some haying because that was happening. We did some farming and there was a little bit of fishing. We decided to just focus on one child. So it was a day through the eyes of a child. So we came back to Harvard with that footage and

I didn't do anything with it for a while because I wasn't really an editor then, and it's hard editing. But then one day John and I had an argument and I went in the basement of my house where I'd set up a little editing studio and I edited the film that afternoon, basically in a fit of anger. It really got me going. It made me an editor overnight. It was a pretty good job.

Now, I refined it. I showed it to John and he thought it was great. So did Bob Gardner. They loved it.

[We shot] about half an hour and the film is about twenty minutes. I finished editing it but it didn't seem to have much purpose or life, except as home movies, so I took it back and showed it to them and they loved it.

It's a beautiful film just the way it is; it really turns out. But now the question is how to finish it. They want it; they feel they need it. So that's enough. I think it's beautiful and I'd like to finish it but I don't know how. But because they have asked me to finish it it's enough for me to make the effort to go up [and do it].

There were sixteen in the family, some of whom have died. The mother's dead, and the grandmother's dead, but there are all these kids, some of whom were three at the time. One of 'em was just born when we were there. So that kid would be thirty-three years old. They were enticed by the government to move out to the town so they could get an education and become carpenters and plumbers and electricians. That way they could make a contribution to the development of the country instead of being locked away in these self-sufficient farms where they weren't a contribution to anybody, and they were pretty poor. They wanted the money so they were eager to go along with it, but they lost a way of life that they now feel was really very valuable. And they're not sure what they've lost, and they feel that our film can help them understand what they lost.

So the film isn't finished. We would go up and interview them and we would show them the film; we would show them the still pictures. Patsy and I will have to do this together.

Japan

TIM: I came back late from Cape Breton. Twelve days before I was to go back to school, having paid my tuition, I was drafted, in 1952. I went to see my draft board representative and she said, "You can fight it if you want but I've got three boys in Korea right now, and as far as I'm concerned you're going to Korea." I kind of gave up. I'd never had a job really, I mean a paying job. I was ready for a paying job. I wasn't ready to go back to school. I'd had this great experience in Cape Breton. It was very meaningful to me. Going back to Columbia, taking a lot of academic courses, didn't appeal to me. So I just gave up. So I went to Japan and I had the best two years of my life.

First of all, basic training was an absolute gas: until it came to bayonet practice and you really had to kill people. If you weren't out there killing somebody with your bayonet you were kicked in the ass and your face was rubbed in the

... well, it was survival; if you couldn't do it, man, you'd be dead. I'd go out in the truck in the morning and I'd learn how to fire all these new weapons ... but I'd be the first in line. But there were hundreds of people out there. They didn't care who fired first because they were going to have to be there all day; they just milled around and whatnot. So I was always first on line; then I went back in the KP truck. When the KP truck got back to the kitchen patrol duty I just walked through the kitchen and out the other end to the library. I spent the entire day in the library with earphones on listening to music and reading. I would get back to the barracks just as the other guys were marching in or something. I got away with that the whole time I was there. I had a fieldwork specialty of a field linesman; I had to teach communications and so forth. My friends were being shot off of telephone poles because we had made that great leap from South Korea to Enchon and then we were consolidating the whole country, and there were pockets of guerrillas that were just waiting to shoot at field linesmen. I didn't like that idea so much so I had several jobs in Tokyo.

If Cape Breton was my first culture away from home, Japan was my first exotic culture. It took eight hours to take what should have been a half-hour trip from Yokohama to Camp Drake outside of Tokyo. The train just crept along. I guess there were lots of other supply trains and things. It was so beautiful. There's a lot of poverty, what we would call poverty, but there was something beautiful about it. These people wrote in art. Their Kanji characters were, to me, works of art.

I had a fantastic time; I did fieldwork on leaves in a couple of villages. On Friday afternoon, whenever I could, I would take off and I would explore. I'd take the trains. The Japanese didn't see many foreigners; all the foreigners were behind barbed-wire fences at army posts; there was no fraternization. You were thought of as bad or weird if you spent any time in the countryside or visiting. You might visit a few temples or something but otherwise it was a "no-no". I did a lot of this. For instance, to give you an example, I learned to sail on Lake Bewako. After a few weeks of sailing, there was a terrible storm. I was the last boat out, except for one other boat that had three guys in it – Japanese – and they were terrified. They knew they were going to drown. They had been slammed up against some fishing weirs – big nets with poles – and they were trapped. So they called out, "Help us, help us, help us." I sailed back and forth; I was with one other person. He was pretty heavy, so when the wind was pushing the boat over he could actually get out of the boat and stand on the keel and keep the boat from going over. I could sail in any direction because I had that extra weight. So I made a plan and I rehearsed it several times with the guys who thought they were going to die. I finally threw them a rope; we managed to drag their boat away from the weirs. It was a lot of work; it was exhausting but it was pretty thrilling. I was on an assignment and so I came back once a month to Odsu, on Lake Bewau, to get paid. So the captain comes out to see me and says, "Asch, what the fuck do you think you're doing? Who are these idiots that come by every day? They're asking for you and they bow

Figure 2.14 Kanisaka's village, Japan.

and they're an annoyance." I said, "What are you talking about?" They were two of these guys who I saved. They wanted to give me a gift; they were thrown off the post.

If you were an American in those days, and you were in civilian clothes or Army clothes and you did what I did, which was to take my grammar book, that I was now on page thirty-eight of, and sit next to some elderly respectable gentleman on the subway and quietly go over your grammar, and after two or three minutes of quiet, silent contact, ask him some questions you have about the grammar, boy, you were gone. He would take you home; he would feed you, he would introduce you to his family. He had to know what this American was; there were none around. They had to be dissected. How could they have won the war? Who are these people? They hated us. But they treated you as a human being, as an individual. But still they hated you. There were members of the family you could see were despising you, but they tolerated you. When they realized that you were actually pretty nice they changed.

I never slept in a hotel. Ever. Before the sun set I was sidling up to somebody and I was taken home. I was fed. I found the village I wanted to stay in by asking school teachers, because they knew the most about the environment and the area. They said there was a beautiful village, so I went to this place. The Buddhist priest in any temple has to let you in for the night. An aspect of being Buddhist is that they have to take care of wayfaring strangers, and I knew that, so that's another way that I used to get a free meal and a place to sleep. Then I said, in the morning, yes, this is the most beautiful place in the world;

Figure 2.15 Japan.

Figure 2.16 Man tapping his walking stick for his ancestors. Japan.

Figure 2.17 Boy spinning top. Japan.

Figure 2.18 Japan.

I want to live here. I asked, "Is there a family I could stay with?" He said, "You wash the dishes." And about a half an hour later there was a cackle of people yelling and screaming at each other, three groups. I said, "Oh god, it's so crude of me – it's so typically American of me to ask to stay with a family – I shouldn't have done that." But, no, they were arguing to see which would get me. The guy who got me was named Kanisaka. He had, as a kid, had a friend come back from the Japanese–Russian 1905 war who said, "Kanisaka, it's a great world out there you really ought to go." He put a little bundle of things together, the way he always did when he went out in the field to work, and he never came back. He wanted to become a ship's captain, and he finally did, after years and years of helping build the American railroad and so on and so forth. He'd kept sending money back to the village. His house was the first house to have a tile roof; his child was the first to get an education outside the village. His son went to the only university in Japan at the time, the University of Tokyo, graduated with a BS and then got a master's degree in calligraphy. At that point he came back to the village and so Kanisaka came back from the world to the village. They were there two months together and then the son was drafted and went to Manchuria and was killed in three months. I was the replacement. So my master's degree is in his *tokonoma*[9] and my bachelor's degree is in his *tokonoma*, and I became part of that family.

Figure 2.19 Japan.

I saved all my leave for six weeks at a time, so I had three six-week leaves. The first time I went to the village they gave me a place to live; then they gave me the first bath. Because, you know, they had a village tub and people got into it one at a time. So I was the first one, because I was the guest. I'd been in Japanese baths before where you go in naked, but I wasn't comfortable. You see, right after the war, when I was in Japan, people bathed together nude. It was a pretty traumatic experience for me to begin with but it was kind of nice. Then Mrs MacArthur got on the radio and said that if the

Figure 2.20 Japan.

Figure 2.21 Japan.

Figure 2.22 Margaret Mead, 1957.

Japanese wanted to become respected members of a world society they would stop practicing a number of rather uncivilized behaviors such as bathing together in the nude. The next day, in all the big pools in Japan, there was a big fence across the middle. You could go underneath the fence if you wanted to but there was a fence dividing the pool into male and female. It was after this that I was in the village, and I didn't see how I was going to get out to the tub easily without being seen by everybody, so I declined. I pretended I didn't know any Japanese at all. That night everybody in the village came around to the family where I was living and they talked about me. They said, "It's true, it's true what they say about these Americans; they're filthy. Disgusting. He walked over the mountains. He's all sweaty. It's been a day and a half and he hasn't had a bath." So the next night, of course, I had to take my bath. I went out; nobody was watching and I had my towel around me. I took my towel off and I looked around and everybody seemed to be watching. Oh god, it was awful. So I got into the tub and I sat there, and I started to boil like a lobster. When I came out I almost passed out trying to dry myself. That night the whole village came around again and they said, "It's true what they say about the Americans, so disgusting, white and peaked and hair like a monkey … oh, it's disgusting." So it took me a while to become accepted in the village, but eventually I was.

Kanisaka was a fisherman so he fished at night and came in when the sun rose. So … we fished and then we'd sleep. I did the work that a son should do. I did farming. I did a lot of walking when I could to take photographs. The food was awful, it went right through me. They were very poor; they grew rice but they had to sell it.

DOUG: We were also talking about these photographs from Japan.

TIM: I guess it's that whimsical element that caught my attention. This bundle, this little animate bundle here, that's washing these clothes was just too funny, humorous, lovely, for words (Figure 2.15). Anthropologically speaking, there is another dimension. The mother is right here and she's washing clothes. So this kid is just learning how to wash clothes, doing what her mother does, at a very early age. So this, to me, was a piece of art, or at least, I was practicing my work as an artist. As an anthropologist we need the mother, and then we need some way of connecting the two. Then we need a study of how this child, with its siblings, is socialized in this Japanese family, within this village. I mean, we work our way outward from the photograph. So this is the micro-element which happens to be an attempt at a piece of art, by somebody who's attempting to be an artist.

But to go beyond means to settle down in this community for a year. I could use this family perhaps as an illustration of the kinds of things that I wanted to talk about, such as the process of socialization that takes place between men and women, and mothers and boys. It's a tremendous contrast.

Whereas she's very subservient and compliant, and works with her mother and the kid, the boy the same age is beating up on his mother and telling her where to get off, and isn't taking any kind of disciplinary anything from her.

DOUG: You'd made the decision to frame tightly, her filling up the frame pretty much. You framed it in a way that was anthropologically responsible, if you will, and yet you've made a photo that we dwell on. I see these little things in it, like, for example, the sandal, which looks like it's hand-made. It's cold out; she has a big heavy jacket on, but she has no socks on.

TIM: True. Her nose is dripping.

DOUG: Let's talk about the other one from Japan (Figure 2.16).

TIM: Again, by now I know a lot about Buddhism and Shintoism, and the difference between the two and the different roles they play in Japanese society. It's winter, in the afternoon, and I was watching people come down from the temple. I asked him about this; he's tapping this marker here which is a marker for one of his ancestors.

DOUG: The photo is beautiful, in terms of shape and shadow and light and form. I didn't even see the stick.

TIM: Yeah, these little elements.

DOUG: There's a level of meaning here: deference to ancestors and the daily experience of acknowledging one's ancestors.

TIM: But I saw it exactly the way you did to start with, in terms of shape and form, as an artist, and then I took it and then I wanted to find out more about the meaning of the event.

Anthropology

TIM: When I got through with Cape Breton, Japan and the Army I had more of a purpose going back to school. Having left Bard I went back to Columbia more purposefully, took anthropology in a serious way and did a thesis on community studies; at which point my famous teacher, Morton Fried, said, "Tim, you can't do a thesis in community studies; it's death." I didn't say to him, I said to myself, "Wait a minute, I have been working all my life, and have gone into anthropology to make a living for the rest of my life, because I want to go to various communities around the world, study these communities and film them carefully and do the best community studies I can, and that's not a future?" Fried says, "Well, Tim, first of all you have to have a problem. It's not the community. You have to have a problem to focus on and when you focus on this problem the community is only a background. Nobody does community studies any longer; they've been done. We have enough studies of communities; we don't need any more. We know what communities are all about. Now we're interested in problems in human development." This is like 1955, '56. He says, "You can do a thesis in community studies if you want to. I'm just telling you it's a waste of time. Your time. My time. I don't even have to read it."

I spoke to Margaret Mead and she said, "I'm the first one that ever did a community study. Yeah, I have to agree with Morton Fried; he's right, but if you want to do a community study … I mean, Tim, you're so naïve." I wanted to use Laurence Wylie's book, *Village in the Vaucluse*, as a model. "Tim," said Margaret, "that is a contribution to the cause of higher education; that's not really a community study." I recognized it as a great piece of work, as an artistic piece of work, and as a community study. Later other people did too, but then they were very critical of it. Later, he got recognition; he got a full chair at Harvard on the strength of that book. A full chair at Harvard ... that's your ultimate prize, so to speak. So I did the best I could with that thesis and he rejected it; I had to re-write it. I didn't use *Village in the Vaucluse* but I used [Conrad] Arensberg's book, *The Irish Countryman*. I used four or five others, and it wasn't good enough. It wasn't scholarly enough. It wasn't well enough done. It wasn't whatever. It was "old hat" theory and everything. I graduated and everything, but the thesis wasn't accepted; it wasn't a requirement to graduate. I started working in September, and the next spring it really rattled me that I hadn't finished this thing. It was incomplete, I guess, as a thesis; it had to be completed within a certain amount of time. So I worked on it in the spring. I re-wrote it, did some more reading. I was very dejected – I knew it wouldn't pass but I sent it in anyway. Fried wrote me back and he said, "Tim, I had no idea that you could do such good work. This is wonderful. I loved your thesis. I think it's great. I'm giving you an A and everything's fine – your thesis is accepted and I'm very pleased." Boy, I'll tell you, it just was such a lift. Here was the romantic and the artist, behind the times.

Visual anthropology

TIM: I had taken my introductory anthropology course with Morton Fried. He hated film and visual things, but he showed a couple of films in the course. When I saw them, once again I said "That's it!" I knew I would become an ethnographic film-maker. I felt anthropology was a really exciting subject and I felt I would just make it that much more exciting for students by making good films that would relate to the subject. So, again, I was absolutely convinced of what I was going to do.

Bob Gardner had asked Margaret Mead if there was somebody that they could find to help edit John Marshall's Bushman films. Mead said, "Oh well, Tim Asch, he'd be interested." She was my advisor. I met her my sophomore year; it was kind of a strange meeting. I'd heard about her and I wanted to do photographic work. Morton Fried and the others wouldn't support it; they said I'd flunk out if I spent any time on it, and so I went to see Mead. Mead sat me down and she said, "Okay, are you married?" – "Yeah." – "Children? How much money have you got?" She got all her statistics organized that she wanted and then she said, "Okay, now here's what you're going to do: this summer you're going to work for me on these twenty-nine thousand negatives I have of Bali which haven't been worked on too much. And then you're going to do this and then you're gonna do that. Then next semester you're going to take these four courses and the semester after that you're going to take these four courses and then you're going to go to graduate school and you're gonna … ." She had my whole life planned out. It frightened me to death. So I walked out of her office and I didn't come back for about a year and a half.

In the mid-forties she had come back from the field and talked in a comparative sense about work that she'd done in Iatmul and Bali: about childhood rivalry and rejection and problems of childhood, sibling rivalry and so forth. If she'd just given her paper, people would have believed her, no problem. But she showed some film and when they saw an example of rejection people said, "How do we know the mother wasn't stung by a bee or something?" There was a huge bruha about it; they booed her out. So she didn't dare say a word about visual media in anthropology for a long while. It was a hard time for me, growing up with that, because I saw the value of it but it was definitely something that Connie Arensberg and Morton Fried, my advisors, were not going to accept.

DOUG: So what you wanted to be, a visual anthropologist, wasn't something that you could be?

TIM: I couldn't. No. Oh, absolutely not. I'd be laughed at. It was at that point that Gardner called and Mead said that I should be the person that they should get. It turned out the reason they wanted me was they needed a flunky; they didn't want an editor who would take a film away from them. They needed somebody who would do a lot of dirty work and learn. So I went up there and I learned. Patsy had gone to Radcliff and said that Cambridge was a wonderful place to live, so we should leave New York and go to Cambridge. We fixed up a nice rented house and didn't pay any rent; we rented it out to roomers. I worked at the Peabody Museum and Patsy taught at an elementary school. It was a great life, but it lasted about three years and then I decided I'd better go back to school.

Bob and John had fallen out, and I was left to handle a lot of the material. Bob went to New Guinea and I ran the base back at Harvard. John went to Yale. I looked at all John's material; there were half a million feet of film. I saw that there were sequences there. Margaret Mead had taught me something about sequences in her book, *Balinese Character*, and in her field methods course, which I had taken and been a TA [teaching assistant] for. I was very impressed with the idea of sequences of photographs, which tell you a story that single photographs don't. John's father [Laurence K. Marshall] had told him when he filmed to film everything and to film in detail. So John had sequences of behavior, like arguments or altercations, or processes, in great detail. Yet the name of the game in making film is to make a big narrative structure in an hour that tells you a lot. *The Hunters* does that – the great narrative thing – but it's also a little bit of a sequence in that it's about hunting.

But then how to make the next film? John had his heart set on making a film about the problems that a girl has when she's betrothed to be married before she's born. She grows up knowing she's going to have to marry that guy over there who she thinks is disgusting and ugly or whatever, or just making that adjustment, because she's not going to sleep with him until puberty and that's late; it could be fifteen, sixteen for these kids. But she'll be married when she's eight, and they'll be living together for maybe eight years before they sleep together. It's a different cultural thing. It fascinated him. He was also in love ,with this girl. So he had something like three or four hours of film that he'd been working on for a long while that I helped him splice. My god, it had thousands of splices; we had spliced it day-in and day-out for days. Then finally, the night before he was supposed to go back to Yale, we saw it. He wouldn't talk about it because he was there in film, living every minute. But he couldn't talk to me.

The upshot for him was that I obviously didn't understand a thing that was going on, and that the film was, therefore, a failure. He walked away from it, and said, "Re-constitute it." We didn't even have a record. It should have been a fascinating film, but Gardner said, "Take every piece of work print, every cut, and put it back in the original sequence."

Africa

TIM: I guess it was 1961, John's sister Elizabeth [Marshall] was going to write her second book, called *Warrior Herdsmen*[10] ... and they asked if I would come along. So I left John's project and went with Elizabeth to Africa. And that was a fantastic experience. I was about thirty, had one child; the second was born when I was in the field. Patsy was teaching and taking care of the kids. I was there for a little over three months, I guess.

DOUG: This would be the third time that you took a still camera to the field, after Cape Breton and Japan. How did you approach the subject photographically?

TIM: Again, the same thing, by just living with these people. Getting to know them as well as I could. I'd learn as much of the language as I could and then think about the same community study structure: you know, subsistence; every activity that came along. The new twist was ritual and ritual sacrifice. Age groups and age sets of men getting together sacrificing cows, talking about political things. Another new twist was raiding from the Turkana, down the great East African Rift Valley escarpment, and the constant problems and fears and whatnot that that engendered. But these were cattle people; their lives revolved around cattle. So that was a new subject.

DOUG: How was it that you went along on this trip?

TIM: They thought my still photographic work was great and they needed still photographs for the book.

Elizabeth brought lifelong care-taking friends that the family had known, two people, a man and his wife, from Sweden. They had always taken care of the two young Marshall kids. They were good Swedish-Boy-Scout-type people. I don't know how old but they seemed quite old, but hardy and strong. They kind of ran the camp. Then Elizabeth and her husband Steve worked together. They were there before I was. Steve came back to work and then I went over. So there were just four of us.

DOUG: Elizabeth had been with her brother in the early 1950s, shooting the first Bushman footage?

TIM: Yes. The whole family had gone; she was going back. In fact, it was her father who found this particular place, these pastoral people, and it was her father who found where they all went to study the Bushmen. Elizabeth and I worked somewhat independently. She would interview people and get life histories. That was going to be her way to develop strategy for a narrative of the book. I was with her some of the time, but I also went a lot of places alone and watched and asked questions and filmed activities. It was very interesting, very nice. I've never worked like this before; they spent a lot of time organizing this expedition. They had beautiful tents and things. So we had a compound, a fenced-in compound, like everybody else, only everybody else had cattle inside their fenced-in compound. At night it was standard procedure that you would sit down before dinner, which was being cooked for you by somebody else, and have a drink. And then we would have our little shot of whiskey, or whatever, and discuss the day. Elizabeth and I would compare notes: what we'd done, what we'd learned, who we'd met, what we had begun to understand about the culture. The two of us worked together piecing things together, which was a very nice way to work. Elizabeth was very perceptive.

I began to learn the language. That was interesting because when I first arrived in Nairobi I had to take buses and whatnot to get to Katali, and when I got to Katali I was picked up by, I think, a cook or somebody and this Swedish guy. I just learned as much of the language as I could from the driver. I learned about seventy-five words on the way …

DOUG: On the way? On the first day?

TIM: On the first day. On the way there. Then I woke up in the morning before anybody else, and jumped over the fence and climbed a hill nearby. I could look down and see these rings of pastoral compounds, and I could hear people waking up and it was another exotic, romantic trip really. I mean, everybody must feel this way in such a strange new place, but for me, god, I was so enthusiastic! So I ran down to this first compound – people had been told that somebody like me was coming but they didn't expect me to come out of the blue before anybody else had gotten up. They invited me into this compound and they were yelling and screaming at me. I was talking a few words of their language and trying to communicate with them.

DOUG: First day you were there?

TIM: First day I was there, using my seventy-five words. They couldn't believe it. I'd come out of outer space and I already seemed to know something of their language. But my enthusiasm began to wane. You know, it was a very strenuous meeting, that first meeting. First of all there were so many flies. I had never seen so many flies in my life. There was this one woman that was full of life. She was a great woman, and she had flies all over her eyes, and she had a little child with pussy eyes. This was a congenital thing that happens to most people and it cures itself. Sometimes when you're thirteen or fourteen or fifteen you kind of lose this pus and everything, but when a child is born a couple of drops of medicine just kills that disease and you don't have to think about it again. Anyway, there she was with this kid with eyes black with flies and that was kind of wearing. And then they gave me something to eat. This cow starts urinating and this guy jumps over the fence quickly with a gourd to catch the urine, that he then cleans out a gourd with it. Now the urine is acid, right? And the gourd's full of milk which is base. The only way to clean out the gourd is to use acid to clean the base. But then they offer you milk. And when he's through, he puts the gourd down and washes his hands and he gets them all clean in the urine. Then he shakes his hands off, and then he comes over and he scoops up some grain and he gives it to you. So you kind of dig around in the middle, hoping to get something that hasn't been urinated on. If they eat it, if they can do it, why can't you?

By the way, in many cultures, if you can't eat a people's food you're considered a witch. And this was a culture full of witches. If you couldn't eat their food, forget it, man, you were a witch. So anyway I ate some of this food but I finally just wore out. And I went back up; everybody was up. They were having breakfast. I just went into my tent and sat down and read more of Isak Dinesen's *Out of Africa*.

I really fell in; I loved it. After a couple of days – millions of flies everywhere – it was terrible – after a couple of days I didn't notice a fly; I just got used to it.

DOUG: So how did you plan your shooting script for what you were doing with your still cameras?

TIM: I had to find things. Again, some people would develop a structure and go out and get it. I was just always open. Anything that happened I filmed in detail. I did shoot sequences. Yeah. And that came directly from Margaret Mead's Field Methods course: sequences of still photographs translated right into John Marshall's sequences of film events; filming events for what they were.

I photographed the rituals, which were so unique and interesting and exotic. Age grades and age sets would go to a particular ritual grove for a particular reason, and they would have a meeting there and sacrifice cows and everybody would eat these cows. That was always good. You learned a lot about the anatomy of an ox, what was good meat and what wasn't good meat. It was fascinating. There was a lot of singing. And there was a lot of very stern and sober ritual going on.

DOUG: Did you feel you were making visual records of things that you had less than a perfect knowledge of?

TIM: Yeah. That certainly is true. Because Elizabeth really didn't know the language, so she had a good interpreter. She wasn't there that long. But she had a good interpreter. And we both used him and learned a lot. But even he didn't know the meaning, when you get into ritual. People don't talk or explain their rituals very easily, before, during or even after. So there were a lot of things that I filmed that I didn't understand. I realized that my heart was as much in still photography as anything. But because I was working for Bob

Figure 2.23 Dodoth, Uganda, 1961.

Gardner, who they didn't particularly like, and John Marshall, and we had done all these films, so she thought, "He's really a film-maker and I'm going to have to work hard to get him to do still photographs." So it was written in the contract that I couldn't make a film. But then I said, "I'm not coming if I can't make a film." So she said, "Okay, it's written in the contract that you can't make a film, but, of course, you can make a film, but when it seems okay to do it." So, again, I didn't have any money. I was earning $4,000 a year and I had kids and expenses and we just didn't have much money. So I think the Peabody Museum or somebody gave me an hour's worth of film or three-quarters of an hour's worth of film. So I had, again, the same camera I used in Cape Breton and a little bit of film. I made a film at the end, this time in color. So I went to do still photography and I did a very conscientious, good job.

But then at the end, we had to pull the camp down and leave quickly. So I made a film in the morning, just a little bit before sunrise and again before ten o'clock. It's a terrific film. It's one of my best films. It's called *Dodoth Morning*.[11] Again, it's a "day in the life". It's about twenty minutes and it shows quite a few activities, and an argument. It's a much better film than the Cape Breton film. And I finished it. But again, I didn't finish it for quite a while. And again, we didn't have a tape recorder. But David MacDougall gave me sound from the tribe next door that speak quite the same language. I dubbed his sound onto this film. It worked perfectly terrible.

DOUG: I'm curious as to how you photographed for three months in Africa. How did you try to build a visual ethnography with still photography there?

TIM: I was mainly interested in getting photographs for a book. Elizabeth wrote a best-seller first, *The Harmless People*, so I figured this could be a best-seller, so it was a job. I conscientiously wanted to get the best pictures possible. I didn't have my own agenda in doing an ethnography. I probably should have. I wasn't in a position to. I didn't have enough knowledge about the subject either. It wasn't till I went to Boston University's African Studies to get a master's degree that I decided to pull that ethnography together.

DOUG: What about these photos for the *Warrior Herdsmen*?

TIM: I made good prints and I wanted to work with the layout and reproduction. I expected a book like the ones you and I go and see, those thousands of books that always intimidated us. I expected to get nice reproductions and whatnot. All I got was this shitty reproduction: photos in a middle section of the book. Then it came out in paperback and it didn't even have the pictures in it. I said to Elizabeth, "Elizabeth, everything you said about our collaboration and how important it was and now it's in paperback (of course, the pictures would be printed badly

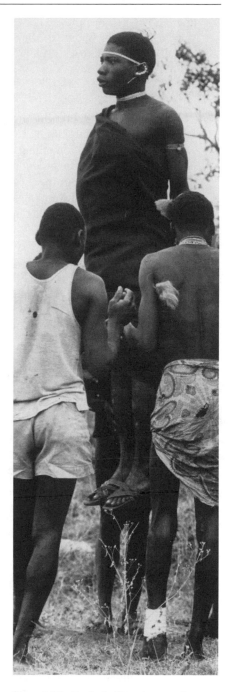

Figure 2.24 Dodoth, Uganda: courting dance.

anyway, but …) but they're not even there." I don't know what she did, but she did something about it. They brought a paperback edition out that she actually managed to get the pictures back in.

Back in the States

TIM: I had finished with John's Bushman project to a point where it was obvious I had to go on to do something else. So I decided to go back to school so I'd be in a better position to do something constructive. I was ready to get more of an education. I went to African Studies. I guess that was two years, 1964 or '65,[12] and it was wonderful. But that degree in African Studies was more in politics than in anthropology; I wanted anthropology. Then I decided that it wasn't taking me anywhere; it was just too dull and dry; it wasn't doing the trick. I thought what I will do is go to the National Film Board of Canada. I made that decision without even telling Patsy. I was going to go the next week, and I would carry cups of water and coffee and sweep the floor until I could get a job, and then I would bring Patsy and the family up to Montreal. I didn't tell Patsy, but I told David Sapir, a photographer on the board there: remember the guy that I did photography with in high school with John Yang? Sapir said, "Oh, well, wait a minute, that's fine but don't do it yet. There's a new guy named Tom Beidelman in East Africa, which is your subject, so go see him." So I went to see this guy … I went to his office and … he seemed like an inter-esting … sort of character. After a long while I decided I'd had enough and I went to leave, but he put himself against the door knob and he went on talking. So he said, "Let's go have a beer." So I said, "Okay." Anything to get out of here. So we went to have a beer; I had thirteen beers with him – I never drank so much beer in my life. Patsy had expected me home for dinner and I didn't come home until 10.30. He was just non-stop talking and actually, when we started having beer, he turned out to be a really fascinating guy. A tremendous human being.

So when I came home at 10.30 looking for dinner, Patsy was pretty annoyed. She cooked us dinner and … whispered in my ear as we were going out, "You don't ever have to bring him back here again." It turned out that we all became very, very close friends. … Tom's a great person. He was by far the best teacher I ever had. He was one of the best teachers anybody had ever had who'd worked with him.

He was at Harvard; very enthusiastic. I just sort of dropped out of BU for a while and transferred to Harvard and took tutorials with this guy. He put the intellectual ideas and concepts of anthropology into a context that meant something to me. I was totally devoted to some of the ideas that he was inter-ested in, like most of E. E. Evans-Pritchard's ideas about social anthropology. I started reading Max Gluckman and the case study method; that fitted right in with sequences. You do a core case study in detail and generalize from that. Now I had something that wasn't dead and something that was meaningful.

Figure 2.25 Thomas Beidelman, February, 1984.

I worked and I read; I had a terrible time the first week. He said, "Okay, you'll take this tutorial with me, now you'll read a book, sometimes two books a week and write two papers." It took me weeks to read a book. It was the beginning of the semester and they had a speed-reading course, so I quickly took it, but it was all semester and I wasn't going to learn how to speed-read for a year at this rate.

The guy who taught the speed-reading course gave such a tremendous overview about what it was really all about, and I was so desperate to learn, that I picked up the structure of what he was trying to teach. Actually, the whole bit about a machine that went over words faster and faster, and taught you how to read faster, had nothing to do with learning how to speed-read. Learning how to speed-read is taking a book and attacking it for the two or three ideas that are in it. So I picked that up and I took the first book, *Witchcraft, Oracles and Magic Among the Azande*, which must be seven hundred pages, and I figured out that the way I usually read, it would take me four weeks to read the book. I usually had to take copious notes because I read kind of slowly. Well, I attacked this book for ideas in the book. I read it in three hours; I couldn't believe it. I read a book that would take me maybe three or four weeks in three hours and I seemed to know more about what was in that book than I'd ever understood from any book I'd ever read. I didn't have to take notes because it was all in my head. What was at the beginning of the book was still in my head at the end of the book. I took a lot of notes; I wrote my paper right then and there. So in four hours I'd done the whole assignment. It was liberating. Just because one guy was a great teacher, was so enthusiastic and was able to transmit that, I was able to get the skills I needed ...

Holy mackerel, this was amazing. Then I had an hour left, or two hours left, still, before dinner. So I said, "Okay, I'm going to read the book again and see what I've missed. I'll just look for things that I might have missed." I didn't get anything more out of attacking the book again. I knew that book. I hadn't taken notes but I'd penciled a lot of things so I could go back to that book any time and get most of the basic ideas out of it that I needed. So that was very liberating. So I then became an anthropologist, at that moment. That's what set me up professionally for ever after.

In the meantime I had helped John make quite a few films. You had the mother, who was doing more scientific anthropology, making films with Frank, while John was developing sequences. The plan was that, when he was through developing sequences, then to make a larger film. If you haven't got a larger film now, you know how to make, for god's sake, these little sequences, which are valuable for teaching; I knew they were. It turned out that I was right because about a year later I started working with Jerry Bruner, the social-psychologist at Harvard, who with Elliot Morrison and others developed *Man, A Course of Study*. We used some of those films for their national social studies curriculum. The films were short; they were open-ended; they weren't didactic; they didn't tell you what to look for and how to interpret what you see. They were sequences that could be manipulated a dozen different ways by good teachers. It was a good pedagogical technique to develop these sequences and to shoot them. I also worked with Carlton Gajdusek and Richard Sorenson at the National Institute of Health and their big shtick was to make a research film. They were very compulsive about it. You went out in the field and you made a research film by bringing back everything you shot and putting it in the order in which it was shot and annotating it as well as possible and freezing it for ever. Then you'd have this document of disappearing cultures.

So I combined those two ideas into one idea: a technique whereby you go out with an anthropologist, if you don't know the language yourself, who knows the language and the culture. I refined that further by realizing that you can't go out with grown-up anthropologists – they don't have the time to get the information you need – so you work with a graduate student who's doing the Ph.D. They have a problem; you film the core case study of their problem, and you will get translations, transcription and analysis of everything you need to make a rich film, which would also be a rich anthropological document. You come back and make a research film before you cut it up. All the sequences and everything you've shot in the field, in the order in which it was shot, with as much information as you can bring to bear on it. Then you edit films if you want to for teaching, short films that I like to use for teaching, or you edit more television-type films, or theatrical film, like *Dead Birds*, and TV films like *The Bushman Woman*. So one method sort of fulfills all obligations to the rest.

Later photography

TIM: It wasn't until 1980, when I stopped working for a while at The Australian National University and I started writing poetry, that I found a medium where I could provide a narrative. They worked because they were short; it was shorter than a short story. But they have to be short. I can't handle something beyond a certain size. So poems were great because they were one or two pages, and I could fiddle with them and push them around. I always knew where I was and I always had a structure to work with. So I really got some confidence then, as an artist. Then I started having a lot of confidence in my own photography.

I had gone back to Australia to visit and I went to the Australian National Gallery where they had an exhibit of photographers, mainly French photographers. I looked at Jacques-Henri Lartigue and Cartier-Bresson again and I said, "Tim, this is what you want to do. You're interested in the exact moment. You're interested in that wonderful moment that Bresson and Lartigue get and you hate the darkroom, and it's all so goddamn tedious and slow, so go out now and use the existing technology, the drugstore, and use color (which you hate but use it anyway) because that's what you have to use to use the technology, and you'll get immediate results." I went out right after that exhibit and I started taking pictures and I gave them to the drugstore. Horrors! I'd been taught by Minor White and Weston to mix my own chemicals; I had a scale and chemicals I didn't even buy from Kodak; I bought them from a chemistry lab and I mixed them all myself. Now I was sacrilegiously giving it to the grocery store. But I was only interested in the image. Then I started to grow. God, I was old by that time. We're talking 1982 so I was fifty years old when I finally got confidence in myself as an artist. Which is what I desperately tried to do when I went out west.

It's all in the print; with black and white still photography, it's in the print. Normally you wait six months to accumulate enough pictures to go to the darkroom to develop and print them. Then you never really could do a good job of printing because it takes six months of printing every day to be able to make a museum print (one or two) in one day. If you drop that, if you stop doing that and do something else for a month or two, you're right back where you started from. Six months of hard labor. That's why this new digitized stuff is so liberating, because you can do so much more, without the chemicals.

You're only going to get that image, and learn how to get it, and become an artist, by doing it and then getting immediate feedback, and going out and doing it again. As a dilettante and a professor, and doing other things, I can still do that now. I can go out and work hard all weekend and, admittedly, I should be doing it for a year at a time constantly, but anyway, I could get a lot done on a weekend. Monday night I can get the pictures; I can look at them and think about them in the morning when I get up, and crop them; and then I can go up to the color printer and have them printed. I am developing that way as an artist. But it didn't work till I was fifty years old.

DOUG: Why did still photography get dropped out of your anthropology?

TIM: My still photography?

DOUG: Well, yours and anthropology's?

TIM: Visual anthropology is ninety-five percent video and film.

DOUG: What happened? Why did still photography get dropped out of the mainstream?

TIM: Well, there are thousands of schools that teach anthropology courses in this country and I would say it's only recently, and not even to any great extent, that there's any credence or value given to still photographic work. I told you about the difficulties I had in going through school, and I had Margaret Mead to work with. I was just told that I'd never get through school if I persisted in having an interest in still photography. Basically you go to school and there is so much to read. It's amazing what you have to read to learn something about the field. So you learn everything you know about anthropology by what you've read, then you go out to the field and what you eventually learn is based on how well you've been able to observe visually and to analyze what you have observed. So why haven't we made better use of visual media to help us? As soon as you've done that, all of those observations go into written notes. You come back, and the test of how good an anthropologist you are is, how good you are at analyzing your data: that's what being an anthropologist is, writing a Ph.D. that analyzes your data. How well can you do that?

DOUG: You've come to the place where you began, which was the single image.

TIM: Right.

DOUG: But you've said that value is artistic.

TIM: Yeah.

DOUG: Where does the anthropology come in?

TIM: It's the single image, not in relation to rocks and scenery, but in relation to human beings.

DOUG: For example, we were looking yesterday at the photo of the two girls walking down the street in India. Where's the anthropology of that image?

TIM: I don't see it. For me, the anthropology is in an analysis of how culture works: an illustration of a given aspect of culture. Those two women walking down the street is an illustration of two women walking down the street in India. But without being put into a sequence it doesn't tell us much about the culture. It's like a painting on the wall. It's a work of art. It's quite beautiful. But what does it tell us? I wouldn't care whether that Indian woman was totally impressionistic or not. I'm looking at that as an artist.

DOUG: So that picture's about color and shape and form?

TIM: Yeah. It's exotic. It's quite different from anything from my own culture.

DOUG: Maybe that's a start of an anthropological statement. It's two girls, maybe it's about their friendship; it's about the fact that girls walk alone in the streets; it's about the clothes they wear, their body language and the material culture that they would encounter as they walk down the street: buildings and the sidewalks, what the spaces are like. Even though it is a beautiful image, in terms of its formal properties, it still is full of information which is the beginning of anthropological knowledge.

TIM: But then we need a sequence, and in addition we need some analysis. Actually there have been lots of very sensitive people, like Ruth Benedict, who wrote poetry but wanted to be a scientist. So there's a lot of that in a lot of us. We want to be the scientist but we also want to be the poet. Well, fine, they don't often work together, but you can work on them separately. So being in Los Angeles and working hard, I loved going off and escaping on the weekends. I've done this a lot. I've only done one or two of these poems but I have a lot that I'm trying to do. On the weekend, if Patsy is in Australia, I'll just go off by myself and walk a beach or something. There was the early training with Weston and Adams. It's a wonderful inspiration for doing this.

As with lots of people, there are moments in one's life where one is going down a road, and there are several directions one can go. Sometimes there's some real blockage there and you can't go where you want to go. When I got through with Columbia I wasn't inspired to go on to graduate school, so I reverted back to photography and decided to become a photo-journalist.

Unfortunately, just at the time that *Life* magazine was soon to go out of business, *Look* magazine was going out of business. It soon seemed to me that it dissipated. But those people didn't despair and die because the magazine folded; they went on working. So I decided to be a photo-journalist. It's only that Bob Gardner had talked to Margaret Mead and wanted me to go to the Peabody Museum, so I didn't make that decision. I was hauled out of the photo-journalism, that I really wanted to get into, and I went to Harvard and worked on these films because it seemed, wow, it's anthropology and it's a chance to learn something new. Certainly I should know something about films and movies since I'm interested in visual media. So I went on to that. But then that road ended and it was a question of what to do next. Well, it seemed obvious with that kind of training that one would have to go back to school, so I went back to school. There are times when one has to stop and make a decision about where to go next. It wasn't a direct line; it was kind of halting, but always there was that very strong interest in still photography because Minor White, in particular, instilled a kind of discipline in me at a young age; and once having that discipline, it influenced my whole life. But it also kept me tied down to and interested in still images, which I never let go of.

Notes

1 A calliope.
2 North Country School in Lake Placid, New York. Many North Country students went on to high school at The Putney School in Vermont.
3 Minor White's papers, which include correspondence with Asch, are held by The Art Museum at Princeton University. Peter Bunnell of The Art Museum writes that the article by Smith to which Asch refers appeared in the 9 April 1951 edition of *Life*. He adds: "[the article] was clearly important to Tim, for in a letter to Minor White of 5 May 1951, he talks about the essay. This letter Tim wrote in response to a

letter from Minor telling him he would take him on again as an apprentice for the summer of 1951 (we do not have a copy of that letter)" (Peter Bunnell, personal communication with E. D. Lewis).

4 Peter Bunnell notes that Stieglitz died in 1946 (personal communication with E. D. Lewis).

5 Peter Bunnell has written (personal communication with E. D. Lewis) that Asch studied with Minor White during the summer of 1950 while Asch was still a student at The Putney School, and again during the summer of 1951, the summer after Asch graduated from Putney. Bunnell adds that The Art Museum at Princeton holds no letter from Asch to White requesting permission to study with White. The correspondence between Asch and White held at Princeton begins in the fall of 1950, after Asch's first summer in California. Bunnell notes further: "I can find no record that Tim enrolled officially in any course at the California School of Fine Arts – he appears on no class list. So the arrangement, surely set up by Minor who did teach summer school with Quandt, must have been informal."

6 Bunnell writes that in 1950 Minor White was renting Ansel Adams' home. "Adams lived much of the time with his family in Yosemite. However, Adams' darkroom was in the basement of the house and Tim would have had experience there with Adams when he was in San Francisco to make prints and process film etc. In 1951 Minor White left the Adams' house and moved to a loft at 135 Jackson Street and it was there that Tim stayed during the second summer" (personal communication with E. D. Lewis).

7 Farm Security Administration of the US government.

8 Robert Lynd and Helen Lynd, *Middletown: A Study in Contemporary American Culture* (1929) and *Middletown in Transition: A Study in Cultural Conflicts* (1937). Roy E. Stryker was professor of economics at Columbia University and led a historical section in the Department of Agriculture which documented the plight of farmers in the 1930s during the Great Depression.

9 A *tokonoma* is a niche, alcove, or recess opening from the living room of a Japanese house in which religious icons and objects of significance to the family are kept.

10 Elizabeth Marshall Thomas, *Warrior Herdsmen* (1965).

11 *Dodoth Morning*, 1963, distributed by Documentary Educational Resources Inc., Watertown, Massachusetts. The film was reviewed in *American Anthropologist*, volume 81 (1), March, 1979.

12 Asch was enrolled in the African Studies Program, Boston University, from 1963 to 1965.

References

Harper, Douglas (ed.) (1994), *Cape Breton 1952: The Photographic Vision of Timothy Asch. Visual Sociology* 9 (2). Kentucky: International Visual Sociology Association and Los Angeles: Ethnographics Press.

White, Minor (1982), *Mirrors Messages Manifestations: Minor White, Photographs and Writings 1939–1968.* Millerton, New York: Aperture, Inc.

Chapter 3

Man, a course of study

Situating Tim Asch's pedagogy and ethnographic films

Nancy C. Lutkehaus

Although Tim Asch was probably best known – and will be most remembered – for his many ethnographic films, a major portion of his adult career was spent teaching and writing and talking about teaching, especially championing the use of ethnographic film in the teaching of anthropology. In addition to writing several articles that dealt specifically with pedagogy and film, Asch promoted and collaborated on the production of study guides to accompany filmic material. He taught an uncountable number of undergraduate and graduate students at Brandeis, Harvard, New York University, The Australian National University, and the University of Southern California and gave numerous lectures and workshops at universities in America, Europe, Australia and Asia. He was also instrumental in the establishment of the Center for Visual Anthropology's Master's Degree program in Visual Anthropology (MAVA) at the University of Southern California, where he urged students to write study guides to accompany their visual projects and the written portion of their degree requirements. Finally, for more than a decade, in collaboration with myself and others, Asch conducted workshops at the annual meetings of the American Anthropological Association for college and university professors on the use of ethnographic film in teaching anthropology.

During the 1960s and 1970s Asch was involved in the creation of the National Anthropological Film Center at the Smithsonian Institution, which is dedicated to the preservation of ethnographic research film footage and its documentation. Asch conceived of the NAFC as an archive for use by teachers across the country. He remembered Margaret Mead as having scoffed at his idea that eventually teachers across the nation could call an 800 number at the Smithsonian from their public libraries and, through a special phone/video carrel system, scan unedited research footage and place an order for the segments appropriate for their own pedagogical purposes (Asch 1991: 13). Of course, with the development of personal computers, CD-ROM technology and the internet, we are on the verge of being able to do this today.

Why film?

In a description of a course he taught at Brandeis University, Asch noted:

Today's students have been brought up in a markedly different world from that in which classical pedagogical techniques were developed. Their exposure to television and the movies, radio, phonographs, and photographs, the instant communication of today's world, has led them to expect more from their education and has created a need for new teaching and learning strategies.

(Asch 1974: 385)

This statement seems to imply that Asch believed that students required a more intellectually and emotionally stimulating learning environment than they were experiencing and that this in turn required new strategies for teaching anthropology, strategies that involved the use of sound and visual images. He always stressed that film was to be used in conjunction with, not in lieu of, written materials. "With the combination of film and written materials," he wrote, "students have a better chance than mere book-learners of arriving at an accurate understanding of the cultural forms and social relations of an unfamiliar society" (Asch 1974: 394).

But why was film necessarily the answer? Was film simply a more dramatic or sensorially stimulating means of engaging students' attention? Or was there something more specific about the filmic experience that enhances the ability or desire of students to learn anthropology?

According to Asch, film was an ideal medium for conveying to students a sense of "what it means to be a professional anthropologist" (Asch 1974: 386) and how an anthropologist works in the field. Film could represent in the classroom the raw data of concrete examples of behavior that an ethnographer encountered in the field, in "the total social environment in which the behavior occurs" (Asch 1974: 386). Having observed behavior *in situ*, students could then apply their knowledge of theories and models of society to an understanding of that behavior; order – and meaning – could be made out of chaos. Pedagogically, "the theory becomes tied to reality in the student's mind as its value is demonstrated" (ibid.). This model may sound familiar; it is, of course, the very structure of *The Ax Fight* (1975), one of Asch's best-known films.

Film could allow students to re-experience the experience of the anthropologist in the field. For example, in *The Ax Fight*, Asch's voice-over expression of amazement and confusion at what is going on before him (and us, the audience) as he records with his camera mirrors our own confusion: what is going on here? Then, in the second sequence of the film, we are made privy to the information the anthropologist gradually acquired that allowed him to interpret and understand what we have just experienced. Order now emerges from the previous chaos.

Implicit in the concept that film allows students to re-experience the experience of the anthropologist in the field is the assumption of the indexical quality of the cinematic sign, that the filmic image, like a photograph, enjoys an existential bond between itself and that to which it refers. This quality is what film theorist Bill Nichols refers to as the "sense of the magician's 'voila!'" (Nichols 1981: 240) in documentary and ethnographic films. The excitement and awe that documentary film produces in the viewer is based on the sense of replication: what you see is what was there, at a particular time and place. It may have occurred some place we will never actually visit ourselves and it may be amazing to us, but it occurred nonetheless – and we now have the chance to figure out what it all means.

From a pedagogical perspective it does not actually matter that the ax fight took place in 1971 and that the Yanomamö have changed considerably since then, if what we want to convey to students is the "you are there" and "you figure it out, too" experience of the ax fight. As a case study, an event such as the ax fight can live on and on, as the anthropological principles that underlie understanding that specific event remain the same. From this perspective, a teacher might be less interested in having students understand Yanomamö culture and society *per se* than in having them understand the significance of kinship and alliance as sociological principles or the methods anthropologists use in the field to unravel complex behavior.

The post-modern turn in ethnography and the social sciences and the questioning of what constitutes "truth" and the so-called "crisis in ethnographic representation" have led many of us not only to denounce the validity of ethnographers' written representations of societies – for example, are the Yanomamö really the fierce people, as Chagnon contends, or are they the gentle people that Lizot presents? – but also to question the veracity of visual images as objective representations of reality. My intention is not to repeat the criticisms that have been made against the biases inherent in ethnographic representations. Asch's own understanding of this problem developed over time (see, for example, Asch n.d.). Changes in social theory also led Asch to change the way he made ethnographic films (see Ginsburg, this volume; Lutkehaus and Cool 1999; Marks 1995; Ruby 1995). I am interested instead in understanding the historical context in which Asch's initial belief in the power of visual images and their transparent ability to convey experience arose. I want to return to an earlier, more innocent – and, in retrospect, perhaps more hopeful – moment in the past in order to gain insight into how the belief in the value and significance of film for the teaching of anthropology developed in Asch's thinking.

Intellectual mentors and models

Asch frequently acknowledged the important influence of his association with Margaret Mead at Columbia University and his experience working with John Marshall editing Marshall's huge corpus of Ju/'hoansi footage (Asch 1991). He credited Mead's insistence (and, indirectly, that of Gregory Bateson) on the value of sequences of photographs as a research method as having laid the foundation for his recognition of the significance of the filmic sequence, both as an aid to research and to the teaching of anthropology.[1] Even earlier influences were his own experiences at the North Country School and The Putney School, institutions noted for their adherence to the progressive education movement promoted by John Dewey.[2] Dewey believed that children learned best through direct experience, through being allowed to cultivate their natural curiosity, and through taking responsibility for their own learning (Dow 1991: 13).

But Asch also cited his association with Harvard psychologist Jerome Bruner as having convinced him of "the power of film, particularly of short sequence films, in teaching social science" (Asch and Asch 1986: 352). During the mid-1960s both Tim and Patsy Asch participated in the development of an elementary school curriculum called *Man, A Course of Study* (MACOS), which was funded in part by the National Science Foundation. The curriculum, developed under Bruner's guidance, used the subject matter of anthropology as its core and engaged the participation of several anthropologists of that era, including Robert Adams, Asen Balikci, Irven DeVore, Richard Lee, Lorna Marshall, Elsa Miranda, and Douglas Oliver, as well as ethnographic film-maker John Marshall and the fledgling anthropologist/film-maker Timothy Asch. In the discussion of MACOS that follows, I rely heavily on Dr Peter Dow's history of the project (1991).[3]

With the exception of Peter Loizos's brief mention of the Netsilik Eskimo films that anthropologist Asen Balikci produced for it (Loizos 1993: 30–31), visual anthropologists have not paid critical attention to the development of the MACOS project. I suggest that in the underlying pedagogical principles developed for MACOS we find a major source of Asch's theory of the pedagogical value of film in teaching anthropology and his early philosophy of ethnographic film. Specifically, these include:

1   the psychological and cognitive reasons for the use of filmic images in teaching anthropology;
2   the production and use of sequence films;
3   the concentration on studying two or three cultures in depth;
4   the importance of contrast as a principle of learning and the role film can play in facilitating the perception of contrast among different societies and different behaviors;
5   the attempt to show students what an anthropologist actually does in the field.

The MACOS project not only sheds light on Tim Asch's early career, but also illuminates a significant moment in the history of anthropology and its role in American culture. The central – and most innovative – element in that project was the production and use of ethnographic film. I suggest, moreover, that ethnographic film – and the MACOS project – deserve greater recognition for the role they played in the history of American anthropology than anthropologists have given them thus far.[4]

The Sputnik era: a role for visual images in the teaching of science

On 4 October 1957 the Soviets launched Sputnik 1, a 184-pound satellite, into Earth orbit. This feat sent the United States into a tail-spin, as it convinced many Americans that the USSR had achieved scientific superiority over the US. Almost all Americans educated after the launch of Sputnik are the products of the aftermath of this event. It led to sweeping reforms in the American educational system (something that Congress had not done since 1917), inaugurated by the National Defense Education Act that President Eisenhower signed into law in 1958 and the decision of the relatively new National Science Foundation (itself a post-World War Two creation) to become involved in curriculum development. With funding from NSF, Jerrold Zacharias, a physicist at the Massachusetts Institute of Technology, initiated a reform in physics education. There were two major innovations in the new curriculum proposed by Zacharias's Physical Science Study Committee (PSSC). First, short-circuiting the usual role of education specialists, Zacharias proposed having research scientists work directly with high-school teachers to develop the curriculum. Second, the development of the new curriculum involved a collaboration between research scholars and media specialists. An abandoned movie theater was converted into a film studio, a film director was hired away from CBS, and ninety films, each about twenty minutes long and accompanied by texts, problem books, question and answer cards, and other teaching apparatus were produced in order to bring the world of contemporary physics to the high-school classroom (Dow 1991: 22).

The success of Zacharias's new physics curriculum led him to convene a symposium at Woods Hole in 1959 of thirty-four research scientists and psychologists concerned with the psychology of learning and thought to brainstorm further applications of research science to the development of elementary- and secondary-school science curricula. The participants in this symposium included two cinematographers.[5] Jerome Bruner, one of the developmental psychologists who attended the Woods Hole symposium, published the recommendations of the ten-day working symposium in a small book, *The Process of Education* (1960).

Among the topics discussed at the symposium were aids to teaching, their relationship to intuitive and analytic thinking, and their stimulation of the motivation to learn. Commenting on the use of films in the new PSSC physics curriculum, Bruner noted three characteristics of a successful science film:

1   By directing attention to the important questions and problems, a film should "help assure that all the great mass of fact and concept and theory and application that constitute any field of knowledge will fall into a coherent pattern in which the more important aspects will be clearly differentiated from the trivial." Although this is difficult to achieve with the printed word, "on film it can be accomplished at times with a gesture" (1960: 87).

2   Each film should "show a real scientist in action, presenting him not as a disembodied intellect but as a normal, active, occasionally fallible human being, dealing rigorously and respectfully with real problems and deriving not only satisfaction but at times excitement from the intellectual pursuit in which he is engaged" (ibid.). The purpose of this emphasis was to "elucidate the nature of scientists and of the scientific life …" (ibid.).

3   A film should be "scrupulously honest." The experiments seen on the screen should be carefully performed and accurately reported.

While extolling the virtues of the use of film in teaching science, the final words in the book issued a note of caution. Critical of "the film or television show as gimmick, the television system without substance or style in its programs, the pictographically vivid portrayal of the trivial" (1960: 91), Bruner wrote that the challenge educators faced was "to integrate the technique of the film maker ... with the technique and wisdom of the skilful teacher" (Bruner 1960: 92).

Initially surprised, as well as intellectually ignited, by the public response to the Woods Hole symposium's findings, in 1964 Bruner decided to embark on his own development of a science curriculum by applying insights from his research into the psychology of learning. Bruner may be best remembered among instructional specialists for his conviction that one can teach a version of anything to anyone if the material is appropriate to the student's age and level of development. A key element in his theory of instruction was the importance of images (Dow 1991: 48). Children, Bruner thought, should be immersed in concrete materials that are rich in imagery and possess the power to stir emotions and stimulate thought. More-over, wherever possible, these should be the same materials that scholars use. Psychologically, the transition from raw data to formal thought involved the creation of images in a child's mind; thus many of the early steps in the introduction of formalism, Bruner argued, should be handled through the use of visual materials, including films.

Film was the best medium to establish communication between scholar and students, and it could make the academic specialist more human by showing him "in his shirtsleeves" (Dow 1991: 48). Thus:

> ... students should be introduced to the romance of academic disciplines by watching specialists at work on the screen – archaeologists digging up ancient artifacts, anthropologists studying preliterate peoples, historians uncovering ancient records, etc.
>
> (ibid.)

From Endicott House to ESI: the birth of the MACOS Project

During the Kennedy administration, Jerrold Zacharias, the intellectual force behind the creation of the new physics curriculum and the Woods Hole sympo-sium, chaired the education panel of the President's Science Advisory Committee. Critical of what he considered to be "fuzzy-headed thinking" among social studies teachers, he convened a group of scholars to clarify the aims and pedagogical methods of the field (Dow 1991: 54). At the Endicott House Confer-ence Zacharias organized in June 1962, the predominance of history in the elementary school curriculum was challenged by social scientists, who suggested that children needed to be exposed to the scientific approach to the study of human behavior. This meant the inclusion of social science in the curriculum at all levels (Dow 1991: 43). The sociologist Robert Feldmesser argued that, from their earliest years, children should be introduced to the methodology and conceptual structure of the various social sciences so that

> they could develop a critical and questioning attitude about the social world
> equivalent to the attitude of mind that characterizes students of the natural
> sciences.
>
> (ibid.)

Bruner argued that in order to deal with the problem of data overload, which over
time would overwhelm students with the richness of the historical record, they
needed to be taught general principles and how to think abstractly about concrete
events and details (Bruner 1966: 76):

> It is the behavioral sciences and their generality with respect to variations in
> the human condition that must be central to our presentation of man, not the
> particularizations of history.
>
> (Dow 1991: 77)

An additional reason to shift away from teaching history toward the social or
behavioral sciences was "the need for studying the possible rather than the
achieved" (Bruner 1966: 36), a necessary step if we were to teach children how to
adapt to a changing world. Adaptation was the key concept here.

In these statements we see a 1950s' discourse about the need for more and better
science teaching applied to social studies and the humanities. It was in the Endicott
House Conference that the seeds of the MACOS project were sown. A group of
social scientists continued to meet in Cambridge after the conference. Under the
tutelage of Zacharias's non-profit organization, Educational Services Incorporated
(ESI), they began to formulate ESI's Social Studies Program. The anthropologists
who participated in the group at this point included Douglas Oliver, Sherwood
Washburn, Michael Coe, and Robert Adams (Dow 1991: 55).

The central pedagogical principle of their proposed curriculum was that students
should be encouraged to take responsibility for their own learning. The curriculum
exercises were designed to "activate the student, turn him into his own social scientist, his own historian, his own evaluator of what is wisdom and what is folly in
man's conduct of his affairs" (Dow 1991: 58). In other words, students should be
taught how to think, not just to memorize facts.

The content of the course was to be "man, his nature and evolution as a
species." Whereas Oliver had suggested a carefully structured six-year evolutionary scheme that began with the study of primates and hunter-gatherers and
culminated with Greek civilization, Bruner favored a topical and comparative
approach organized around the questions "What is human about human beings?",
"How did they get that way?" and "How can they be made more so?" (Bruner 1966:
74; Dow 1991: 72). He and his cohorts identified five great humanizing forces:
tool-making, language, prolonged childhood, and the urge to explain the world
(Bruner 1966: 75). The problem, Bruner said, was to rescue the phenomena of

social life from familiarity. The techniques they proposed to aid teachers in this task included the use of contrast, hypothesis-making (i.e. the stimulation of informed guessing), active participation, and the stimulation of self-consciousness about the tools of thought (e.g. categorization, causal explanation, language, etc.).

Bruner's aim was to construct a new model for social studies education that would change the existing pattern in both form and content. To that end, he encouraged the use of a diversity of instructional media, including film, games, graphics, sound recordings, "hands-on" materials, and a variety of print, including fiction and poetry (Dow 1991: 73).

In 1963, the Ford Foundation gave ESI a million dollars to begin implementing the Social Studies group's curriculum proposals. This was the inception of Man, A Course of Study. At the American Anthropological Association meetings that year, Douglas Oliver, director of ESI's Elementary Social Studies Program, contacted Asen Balikci, who had recently completed his Ph.D. at Columbia University, and offered him the opportunity to lead an expedition to film the Netsilik Eskimo at Pelly Bay, among whom Balikci had done research. This was the beginning of the famous Netsilik Eskimo series of nine ethnographic films (Balikci 1989; Loizos 1993: 30–31). During the next three years Balikci and his cameramen shot over 180,000 feet of Netsilik footage (Balikci 1989; Dow 1991). When Oliver resigned as director in 1964, Jerome Bruner, formerly in charge of the project's Instructional Research Group, agreed to become the new head of ESI's Elementary School Program.

During the summer of 1965, a pilot program was ready to be tested at the Underwood School in Newton, Massachusetts. Both Tim and Patsy Asch were involved with the project at Underwood that summer (Lutkehaus 1994). One of Tim's innovations, his idea for an "environment chamber", a life-size filmic simulation of the environment of the Kalahari desert, is not only an example of Asch's wide-ranging creativity, but also of his early experimentation with multimedia and interactivity in teaching.[6] By rear-projecting scenes from the Kalahari on a huge translucent screen and accompanying these images with a tape recording of desert sounds,

> Tim took children on a trip through the Kalahari seasons of the year and exposed them to the cycle of a Bushman day. The students could imagine themselves side by side with the people they were studying, hearing the soft Bushman language, absorbing the sounds of the Kalahari environment, and listening to a Bushman musician playing mournful sounds on his hunting bow. Fashioned from inexpensive tracing paper and cardboard tubing and using a single carousel projector coupled to a tape recorder, the environment chamber was designed to be easily replicated by a resourceful teacher in an ordinary classroom.
>
> (Dow 1991: 98)

The environment chamber was Asch's version of what later became the IMAX screen and technology.

The psychological reasons for the use of film in teaching anthropology

The pilot test at the Underwood School demonstrated that most children found the ethnographic films engaging. Dow reports that

> [w]hether or not the deeper lessons were learned, unnarrated films about baboons, Eskimos, and Bushmen had the power to capture the attention of 10 year olds and to stimulate their desire to learn. ... Following Underwood, MACOS became a film-based course.
>
> (Dow 1991: 95)

But films were important to the project for reasons other than their ability to capture students' attention and imagination:

> Like laboratory studies in the natural sciences, ethnographic films allowed students to subject behavior to repeated observation and analysis. Instead of telling students how people in other cultures behave and why, the films permitted children to figure things out for themselves through direct observation.
>
> (ibid.)

Film enabled a giant leap forward in the project innovators' effort to get students to take responsibility for their own learning.

The project's experimentation with educational media confirmed the inadequacy of the conventional textbook and its failure to incorporate much of what the curriculum reformers had learned about children's learning. Unlike a textbook, film and other new forms of instructional media helped to promote the idea that there could be more than one right answer or one way of explaining a body of data. Finally, the MACOS innovators realized that films that showed the new curriculum actually being used by teachers and students in the classroom could be as powerful a medium for teaching teachers to teach as it was for teaching children. They hoped to create an archive of films for teacher-training as rich as the course films themselves, but lack of funding prevented this goal from being reached.[7]

The production and use of sequence films

The MACOS curriculum was unique in its use of unnarrated ethnographic films that depicted short sequences of behavior for students to analyze and compare with other such material. Although excited about the use of film in the curriculum, Bruner had always had reservations about the passiveness of most film viewing. He wanted to explore how film could be used to get students to ask questions. He suggested that the Netsilik material be cut into short "film loops" (loops of film four minutes in length). Each loop should pose a question such as "Why did the Eskimos gather moss, and what did they use it for?" This could then be followed by further material that illustrated how moss was used. Bruner called these films "Marienbad teasers" after *Last Year at Marienbad* (1961), the enigmatic French film popular at the time.

But Quentin Brown, who was working with Balikci on editing the Netsilik footage, found that the "Marienbad" approach did not work out well in practice because there was no simple answer to how anything was used in the culture. In the end, Bruner's loops were abandoned. But the experiment led Brown to try to put together longer films, without narration, that could stimulate the viewer to raise questions. In 1963 he edited a half-hour silent film, *Fishing at the Stone Weir*.

Brown and Balikci were surprised, and delighted, to discover that the response of adults to viewing *Fishing at the Stone Weir* was positive: "Hey, this is how you get the viewer involved. Don't tell him anything. Let him try and figure it out for himself." This reinforced Brown and Balikci's decision to construct films from unnarrated sequences of complete activities. The sequences, which lasted from five to ten minutes, were designed to provide enough information to allow the viewer to follow a complex event involving several participants from beginning to end (Dow 1991: 64). When Brown added sound from wild recordings to his second film, *Jigging for Lake Trout*, it was even more successful than the first. From then on sound became an important element of the sequence films (Balikci 1989).

Tim Asch's predisposition toward the use of sequence films acquired from his association with Mead and Marshall must have been further reinforced by the decision of the MACOS designers to incorporate the unnarrated sequence film as a central pedagogical tool in their curriculum. The scientific rationale for the use of sequences as representations of naturally occurring human behavior (Moore 1995) was underscored by Bruner's conviction of their pedagogical value in stimulating students' curiosity and thinking.

Concentration on studying two or three cultures in depth

Everyone at ESI agreed that the only way to get any idea across to children was to pursue a subject in depth:

> If you want children to commit their minds to a subject, you must give them time to immerse themselves in the data so that they become emotionally engaged in the material at hand.
>
> (Dow 1991: 260)

Following this principle, the MACOS curriculum exposed children to a small number of well-documented animal studies, followed by a detailed look at the seasonal migration cycle of a subsistence society. In addition to the Netsilik material, MACOS included ethnographic film and data on the Ju/'hoansi provided by the Marshalls as well as material on East African baboons recorded by Irven DeVore in Kenya.[8] The sequence films were the primary means for providing students with detailed information about these few cultures or animal societies from which comparisons could be made. Bruner's ultimate aim was for children to learn a few basic abstractions, such as life cycle, adaptation, ecological balance, innate and learned behavior, technology, social organization, child-rearing, and belief systems that were to be "derived from an immersion in the details of the human and animal case studies" (Dow 1991: 113). He was especially concerned that children understand the concept of reciprocity, the glue that held society together: "Social organization," he said, "is marked by reciprocity and exchange – cooperation is compensated by protection, service by fee, and so on. There is always giving and getting" (ibid.: 83). For Asch, too, alliance and reciprocity – especially as exemplified by Mauss's theory of the gift and gift exchange – was an important concept that he used the Yanomamö and Ju/'hoansi films to exemplify. He also structured his university courses around a focus on two or three societies, usually the Ju/'hoansi, the Yanomamö, and the Balinese.

The role of film in the perception of contrast

Closely related to the concept of concentrating on two or three societies was the idea of the importance of contrast. According to Zacharias, "without contrast you cannot see" (Dow 1991: 181). For Bruner, too, contrast was a fundamental aspect of learning to generalize, as well as to understand the concepts of continuity within change. Thus, contrast was built into the heart of the MACOS curriculum: humans versus animals, humans versus the higher primates, humans versus prehistoric man, humans versus primitive man, and the human adult versus the child. The notion of the life cycle – one of the abstract concepts the curriculum aimed to teach children – was to be taught through the comparison of information from animal and cultural materials that dealt with growing up, socialization, status and role, transitions between life-cycle stages, and the comparisons between the life cycles of humans and other animals. MACOS had two parts: a "Man and Animals" unit that examined humans as a species, and a "Primitive Cultures" unit that looked at what it meant to be human by comparing the Netsilik, the Ju/'hoansi (later withdrawn from the course), and ourselves (Dow 1991: 113). Films, with their ability to manipulate time, were ideal for depicting the life cycle of salmon and herring gulls in contrast to Netsilik and Ju/'hoansi material on the stages in the life of hunter-gatherers.

For Asch, the use of contrast ideally took the form of first showing students a sequence film depicting a single event or social relationship, such as Marshall's film *Debe's Tantrum*, in which five-year-old Debe throws a tantrum when his mother tries to leave him at home as she goes off to gather food for the family. Students were then asked to study an American family at a time when the mother was performing a specific job while also having to take care of her children. Comparisons could then be made between the two different cultures. By first viewing the Ju/'hoansi film, students also had an opportunity to generate research questions for their own fieldwork based on their observation and analysis of the filmed event.

The attempt to show students what an anthropologist actually does in the field

Thus, the role of film in the MACOS course was to present students with actual ethnographic data from which they could formulate questions and derive hypotheses based on their own observations. Of course, without narration an important source of information – what the Eskimo themselves thought or said – was absent. Like the fledgling anthropologist who has not yet mastered a local language, the process of hypothesis-making was both simplified and focused on the students' own logical thought processes. Ultimately, as in Tim Asch's university anthropology courses, students were asked to compare their observations and newly acquired knowledge with their own culture. The aim was for students to recognize the continuities and similarities between them (Balikci 1989).

The most successful types of films the MACOS project produced were those that showed students interacting with scientists, discussing questions about the scientists' research. We can consider this a variation of the film that shows the scientists at work, which was one of the pedagogical aims of the Woods Hole scientists, to make scientists appear as real human beings, as sympathetic individuals doing interesting things that students might aspire to do themselves in the future.

Debate in Congress over MACOS

From 1967 on, the MACOS curriculum began to be used in classrooms across the country from Boston to California and internationally in such far-flung places as Canberra, Australia. One of the most challenging aspects of the new curriculum was getting teachers to feel comfortable using it. In addition to funding from the Ford Foundation, ESI had received funds from the National Science Foundation to aid the development of the MACOS curriculum. Bruner and his associates also received funds from NSF to set up programs across the country to train elementary school teachers in the use of the new curriculum. By 1971, however, a backlash began when conservative parents in Florida, Maryland, and Arizona challenged MACOS as inappropriate for the instruction of elementary school children. Quoting excerpts from the teachers' manuals and student booklets, critics such as Reverend Glenn of Citizens for Moral Education argued that the curriculum "advocated sex education, evolution, a 'hippie-yippie philosophy', pornography, gun control, and communism" (Dow 1991: 179). These critics were incensed that taxpayers' dollars had been spent to support the development and dissemination of the curriculum.

By April 1975, the issue of MACOS had reached the House of Representatives. When authorization of the NSF budget, which included $110,000 for "information workshops" for MACOS, was discussed in the House Committee on Science and Technology, Congressman John B. Conlan, who represented a conservative district in Phoenix, Arizona, spoke out against the MACOS curriculum. MACOS, he said, is designed to mold children's social attitudes and beliefs along lines that are almost always at variance with the beliefs and moral values of their parents and local communities. … Recurring themes … include communal living, elimination of the weak and elderly in society, sexual permissiveness and promiscuity, violence, and primitive behavior.

(Dow 1991: 200)

In Conlan's eyes, the MACOS curriculum promoted "a dangerous plan for the federally-backed takeover of American education" (Dow 1991: 211). He introduced an amendment to the authorization bill that required Congress to review all NSF curriculum projects prior to implementation. Although some congressmen defended the curriculum and Margaret Mead had previously testified in its defense (Dow 1991: 204–207), as the House debate on the authorization bill progressed it became apparent that the central political issue had shifted from the content of MACOS to the question of freedom of choice within the educational community. Was it appropriate for Congress to pass judgment on any program funded by taxpayers' dollars before it was released for public consumption, or were local school districts to be allowed to choose between a variety of available course materials, including government-sponsored programs (Dow 1991: 213)?

When the vote finally came, Conlan's amendment was defeated by the slim margin of 215 to 196 (Dow 1991: 214). But the story of MACOS did not have a happy ending with the defeat of the Conlan amendment. The Senate also debated the pros and cons of the MACOS curriculum. One of the witnesses brought in to testify against the program was Dr Onalee McGraw, the same person who had started the debate in Arizona against MACOS that led Conlan to raise the issue in Congress. She questioned the propriety of the NSF's role in assisting the Educational Development Corporation (EDC, formerly ESI) with the publication of the MACOS course materials, saying that the curriculum's subsidies and association with the NSF gave it an unfair advantage in the public market place of educational materials. This criticism and other objections to the curriculum led to three separate federal investigations of NSF's involvement with curriculum reform (Dow 1991: 217) and MACOS suffered from the negative press the curriculum had received nationwide. NBC, for example, advertised a news commentary on the program with the headline "Horror Flicks. Is Your Ten-year-old Watching 'X-rated' Films at School?" (Dow 1991: 220). The result of the controversy was the premature decline of the MACOS curriculum and NSF's termination of several of its science and social science curriculum projects. Moreover, as Dow notes, Congressman Conlan spoke for a new political constituency that was "intolerant of academia, suspicious of federal reform initiatives, and fiercely protective of the autonomy of the local school district" (Dow 1991: 210). Twenty years later, these words have a far too familiar ring.

The fate of the MACOS project provides us with a cautionary tale, one that reminds us that the best intentions of well-meaning scholars and scientists to improve education do not evolve in a social vacuum. The schoolroom is not just a laboratory for training the mind, but a place where the moral outlook of the next generation is formed. Although the innovators of MACOS articulated the values that they felt the curriculum should instill in students, they misjudged the social climate of American society at large and the impact of the political and social upheavals of the era of the Vietnam war. In retrospect, we may wonder at their naïve faith in the reception of their innovative theory of instruction. In this tale, however, we also see evidence of a similar naïveté towards the power of images, a concept that has taken us much longer to perceive and understand.

Conclusion: the paradoxical power of images

MACOS must certainly stand as the most ambitious and carefully designed elementary school program that has ever focused so centrally on anthropological material. The use of unnarrated ethnographic film served as the core of the MACOS curriculum. It also made the project unique. Although other curricular reforms may have experimented with the incorporation of film, it is doubtful that any were as extensive as MACOS, either in terms of the central pedagogical value ascribed to film or in terms of the amount of film shot and produced.

Thus, at one level, the story of the MACOS curriculum illuminates a moment in American history in which anthropology as a subject matter and social science played a national role, provoking political controversies about what to teach children about their common humanity, and how to teach it. We can see in the creation of the MACOS curriculum the development of a place and rationale for the significance of ethnographic film, not only as a research and archival tool, as Mead, Bateson, and others before them had proposed, but also as a pedagogical tool in teaching anthropology.

One of the major contributions of the Sputnik era reforms in education such as MACOS was the extensive experimentation with a variety of instructional media, including film, still photographs, physical materials, and games, rather than a single text. The developers of MACOS jokingly referred to their innovations as "the new technology of the knowledge industry ..." (Dow 1991: 258). Little did they know how prescient they were. We can see MACOS as a precursor to the experiments with multimedia formats in the teaching of anthropology that many of us are experimenting with today.[9]

At another level, the development of the MACOS project also illuminates the historical context and intellectual milieu in which many of Tim Asch's pedagogical principles and theoretical precepts about ethnographic film were developed or strengthened: his conviction of the importance of film as both a research and a pedagogical tool and his vision of how to make ethnographic films.

As early as 1973, however, two years after *The Ax Fight* was filmed and two years before it was released, Thomas Hearne and Paul DeVore reported evidence that the images of the Yanomamö produced a range of responses in students that were quite different from those expected by Asch and Chagnon, the film-maker and anthropologist (Hearne and DeVore 1973). Some years later, Asch encouraged

Wilton Martínez and me to undertake a study of the reception of ethnographic films among students at the University of Southern California. The results of this study (Martínez 1990, 1992 and Martínez, this volume) confirmed and expanded the earlier observations of Hearne and DeVore. We have learned that in teaching with ethnographic film it is necessary to take into careful account the protean nature of images and their cinematic "excess" (Nichols 1981: 141). The paradoxical power of visual images in a documentary or ethnographic film is the multiple meanings they can convey through the excess information they communicate to viewers, and how much viewers' own experiences influence how they read a film. If our understanding of film reception has become more sophisticated today, this does not necessarily mean that the way in which we are using film in teaching anthropology has necessarily changed as well. This, of course, is a message with which Tim Asch was constantly concerned, and one that he continually refined and shared with others throughout his academic career.

Acknowledgments

An earlier version of this paper was presented at the Annual Meetings of the American Anthropological Association in Washington DC in 1995. I would like to thank Dr Peter Dow and Dr Jerome Bruner for their willingness to discuss the history and philosophy of the MACOS project with me. I would also like to thank Patsy Asch for her editorial assistance and comments on earlier drafts of this article.

Notes

1 Mead had told students to take not just single photographs, but "sequences of photographs, a whole roll or maybe two rolls about one event" (Asch 1991). Although I do not discuss this latter influence in any detail at present, recent articles by Dianne Hagaman (n.d.), Ira Jacknis (1988), and Andrew Lakoff (1996) contribute greatly to the analysis of Mead and Bateson's (Bateson and Mead 1942) use of film and photography in their Balinese research.
2 Patsy Asch kindly pointed out these influences to me.
3 A participant in, as well as chronicler of, the project, I had the chance to talk with Dr Peter Dow about MACOS and Asch's participation in it in 1994. Both Patsy and Tim Asch also provided information about MACOS, as did Dr Jerome Bruner in an interview I conducted with him in 1996.
4 The failure to recognize their role reflects both positive and negative developments in our society that reflect: the changing status of anthropology as a science and as an academic discipline, the controversy over multiculturalism in the American curriculum, and the internal debates and divisions within anthropology itself.
5 Mr John Flory of Eastman Kodak and Dr Don Williams of the University of Kansas City (Bruner 1960: vi).
6 To study the application of the MACOS program, Tim videotaped most of the summer school classes at Underwood using an early prototype of a portable video system.
7 At least two such films were made, however. They include A Time for Learning (1973) and What Makes Man Human (1973). Both films were produced and distributed by Educational Development Center, Inc., Cambridge, Massachusetts. Shot in a classroom in a Boston area school, they show teachers and students in action using the MACOS curriculum materials. In addition, Tim made an innovative slide tape, teaching MACOS. Patsy Asch has commented that "Tim believed his slide tapes were more innovative and pedagogically stimulating than his films" (Patsy Asch, personal communication with E. D. Lewis).
8 The Ju/'hoansi unit, which was developed by Patsy Asch, was later withdrawn from the course.
9 For example, some of Tim Asch's colleagues have taken his Yanomamö film, The Ax Fight, and created an interactive CD-ROM version for classroom use (Biella, et al. 1997 and Biella, this volume).

References

Asch, Timothy (1974), "Using Film in Teaching Anthropology: One Pedagogical Approach". In Paul Hockings (ed.), *Principles of Visual Anthropology*. The Hague: Mouton Press, pp. 385–420.

—— (1991), "Sequence Filming and the Representation of Culture". Unpublished manuscript (version dated 2 February 1991).

n.d. "Bias in Ethnographic Reporting: A Personal Example from the Yanomamö Ethnography". Unpublished manuscript.

Asch, Timothy and Patsy Asch (1986), "Images that Represent Ideas: The Use of Films on the !Kung to Teach Anthropology". In Megan Biesele with Robert Gordon and Richard Lee (eds.), *The Past and Future of !Kung Ethnography: Critical Reflections and Symbolic Perspectives*. Essays in Honour of Lorna Marshall. Hamburg: Helmut Kuske Verlag, pp. 327–58.

Balikci, Asen (1989), "Anthropology, Film and the Arctic Peoples: The First Forman Lecture". *Anthropology Today*, (2): 4–10. April 1989.

Bateson, Gregory and Margaret Mead (1942), *Balinese Character: A Photographic Analysis*. New York: New York Academy of Sciences.

Biella, Peter, Napoleon A. Chagnon and Gary Seaman (1997), *Yanomamö Interactive: The Ax Fight*. Fort Worth, Texas: Harcourt, Brace and Co.

Bruner, Jerome S. (1960), *The Process of Education*. Cambridge: Harvard University Press.

—— (1966), *Toward a Theory of Instruction*. Cambridge: Harvard University Press.

Dow, Peter B. (1991), *Schoolhouse Politics: Lessons from the Sputnik Era*. Cambridge: Harvard University Press.

Hagaman, Dianne DiPaola (n.d.), "Connecting Cultures: Balinese Character and the Computer". Unpublished manuscript.

Hearne, Thomas and Paul DeVore (1973), "The Yanomamö on Film and Paper". Paper presented at the Anthropological Film Conference, Smithsonian Institution. Washington DC May 1973.

Jacknis, Ira (1988), "Margaret Mead and Gregory Bateson in Bali: Their Use of Photography and Film". *Cultural Anthropology* 3 (2): 160–77.

Lakoff, Andrew (1996), "Freezing Time: Margaret Mead's Diagnostic Photography". *Visual Anthropology Review* 12 (1): 1–18.

Loizos, Peter (1993), *Innovation in Ethnographic Film: From Innocence to Self-Consciousness 1955–1985*. Manchester: Manchester University Press.

Lutkehaus, Nancy (1994), "Image as Teacher: Timothy Asch and the Use of Film in Teaching Anthropology". Paper presented at the University of Southern California Symposium in honor of Timothy Asch. Department of Anthropology, University of Southern California. Unpublished manuscript.

Lutkehaus, Nancy and Jennifer Cool (1999), "Paradigms Lost and Found: The 'Crisis of Representation' and Visual Anthropology". In Jane Gaines and Michael Renov (eds.), *Collecting Visible Evidence*. Minneapolis: University of Minnesota Press, pp. 192–222.

Marks, Dan (1995), "Ethnography and Ethnographic Film: From Flaherty to Asch and After". *American Anthropologist* 97 (2): 339–47.

Martínez, Wilton (1990), The Ethnographic Film Spectator and the Crisis of Representation in Visual Anthropology. Master's Thesis. Los Angeles: University of Southern California.

—— (1992), "Who Constructs Anthropological Knowledge? Toward a Theory of

Ethnographic Film Spectatorship". In Peter Ian Crawford and David Turton (eds.), *Film As Ethnography*. Manchester: Manchester University Press, pp. 131–64.

Moore, Alexander (1995), "Understanding Event Analysis Using the Films of Tim Asch". *Visual Anthropology Review* 11 (1): 38–53.

Nichols, Bill (1981), *Ideology and the Image: Social Representation in the Cinema and Other Media*. Bloomington: Indiana University Press.

Ruby, Jay (1995), "Out of Sync: The Cinema of Tim Asch". *Visual Anthropology Review* 11 (1): 19–35.

At the beginning

Tim Asch in the early 1960s

Peter Loizos

Early in 1960, Tim Asch took a risky initiative when he decided to befriend Peter Loizos, then a student at Harvard University. Tim was working then at the Film Study Centre, at the Peabody Museum, Harvard, logging the Ju/'hoansi footage shot by John Marshall, and getting to know it. Later he was to become involved in editing some of it with Marshall. Robert Gardner was then Director of the Center, having helped Marshall complete *The Hunters*, and himself preparing for a major project in Melanesia. Tim labored in a cutting room next to Gardner's office.

I was the interloper – restlessly treading the mills of graduate studies in Harvard's Social Relations Department. The anthropology components were sometimes taught at the Peabody, and there my eye had been tugged by the word "Film", which pointed down to a subterranean domain where Gardner reigned, tall, languid, a Demon King in the guise of a gentle Bostonian. Film was such a relief from statistics, Parson's theory, and McClelland on the Achievement Motive. Gardner tried to shoo me away and then, when I wouldn't go, tested my resolve by making me read through Spottiswoode's exhaustive film textbook – chemistry and all. Then as a reward for persistence, he offered me Kracauer's second film book in proofs. That was really exciting. Realism – that was what film was best at, Kracauer argued. There was a lot to be thought about in his approach. Finally, Gardner offered me the use of a clockwork Bell & Howell, the handheld combat camera used in the Second World War, and a couple of hundred-foot rolls of outdated color stock, with the thought that it was time to try something practical after all this reading. "You can only learn so much from books," he said, a remark which should be inscribed over the entrance to every film school, if not to every university.

It was soon after this that Tim raised his eyes from his Bushman (Ju/'hoansi) chores, and with a mixture of curiosity and diffidence, introduced himself. He had seen me coming in and out of the basement, and wondered what I was doing. I had seen him, and had been having similar thoughts. As soon as he realized that I was being allowed to shoot some film, and that I hadn't the least idea of how to do it, his manner became wistful, not untinged with envy, as if Gardner were a father who had favored one of his children unfairly over another, but that this unfairness was an inevitable part of life. He characteristically dealt with whatever dissonance he experienced at my good fortune by generously inviting me home to supper to meet

Patsy, his wife. As we left the Peabody, with its overtone, for him, of a daily grind and a rather frustrating one, his manner changed and he became voluble, enthusiastic. This was to be the first of many evenings with the Aschs, in which I came to appreciate their energies and dreams about using film in teaching and anthropology, and we exchanged views on everything which came to mind, which was a great deal.

Tim had already done a great deal. He had studied still photography with Minor White, Edward Weston and Ansel Adams and served in the US Army, where he worked as a photo-journalist for *Stars and Stripes*. Part of this had been in Japan, and he showed me some of his pictures from there and told me how he had been able to wander in the Japanese countryside, spending time in villages. That sounded almost the most romantic and fascinating thing I could imagine. He had a picture of a tiny Japanese girl, a huge sun-hat tied under her chin with a bow, somewhere between two and three years old, studiously scrubbing at a garment by some water. "And do you know," Tim said, to convey to me what the picture meant to him, "that little girl will spend *all day* rubbing at that dress, just because she has been *told* to. It's *unbelievably* different. In America, we … we have *no idea* … what it means to bring up children like that … ." He told me to read John Embree's book, *Suye Mura*, when I said how interesting a Japanese village sounded. I obediently went off to read the Embree book, and found it as good as Tim had said.

Tim had taken his enthusiasm for such explorations to Columbia University, about which he was enthusiastic. He had wanted to do a "community study" (like *Suye Mura*) but had been told that this was no longer considered an acceptable project. "You have to be interested in theory, now. They don't want ethnography for its own sake. And I don't want to do that kind of anthropology … ." His idea was to do a descriptive ethnographic study in which photographs and cine films would be an indispensable component. It was notable, perhaps, that his ambitions were not in the arts, towards images for the sake of images – a social aesthetic he might have taken in from Adams and Weston – but towards documentation, a service to the idea of social science.

The year 1960 was a good one to have met in, because it marked the start of a period of intense creativity in realist documentary, some of which spilled over into ethnographic filming. Robert Gardner was preparing himself for the expedition which would allow him to make a major ethnographic film, *Dead Birds* (1963). John Marshall was also in and out of the Peabody, intense, introverted, and becoming involved in the editing of Bushmen "sequence" films, such as *A Group of Women* (1961) and *A Joking Relationship* (1962). Much later he was to film for Frederick Wiseman the painful revelations of *Titicut Follies* (1967), a study of a Massachusetts asylum. Tim was also to work with Marshall in various ways on these films, and to found with him Documentary Educational Resources, a center for the distribution of documentary films for education. Tim, then, was serving what proved to be an instructive apprenticeship with John Marshall. I was totally undecided about my future but knew it had to be film. Tim and I had a lot to say to each other about common interests. We were, whether we understood it or not just then, at the beginning of life-long love affairs with film, with anthropology, and with the relations between them.

Tim already knew that he wanted to work in anthropological film, while I was drawn more strongly to fiction and the kinds of films which were shown on the "art house" circuit. But it did not greatly matter, because at that point all films, any films, were exciting to us, and we could learn from seeing them and discussing them, and exchanging reactions to films. There was a cinema called The Brattle in Cambridge, where I recall seeing a documentary made by Lindsay Anderson about the Aldermaston March,[1] the symbolic start of the British Campaign for Nuclear Disarmament. Memory suggests I saw it with the Aschs. At the Peabody, Gardner let us watch Rouquier's *Farrebique*, a well-wrought study of the seasons on a French farm, and Godard's *Breathless*, which was the most radical departure from Hollywood we could imagine. But the film which caught all our imaginations was Richard Leacock's *Primary*, which Tim, Gardner and I saw in the Peabody basement because Gardner had got it in.

Figure 4.1 Tim Asch, Cambridge, Massachusetts, 1961.

The impact of *Primary* on us then can hardly be overstated. There is an early shot inside a campaign car, traveling up a snowy road somewhere in Wisconsin, about which several things were quite extraordinary. First, you knew the camera and sound were inside the car at the time, because you could hear the people in the car talking, and the track was so dirty you knew it could not have been studio-recorded, and second, as the windscreen wiper worked, you could hear it too, and in some way I cannot now explain, this was the most immediate, the most *real* event I had ever seen in a film. This sequence, and much of the film, had a freshness and impact which made everything else we had been seeing in documentary suddenly look old-fashioned, and that included a film as recently made as *The Hunters* (1957). *Primary* seemed to leave Hollywood for dead, as a world of candy-floss. But whereas I could only be amazed by it, Tim and Bob knew who had made it, and what else was going on.

Tim knew a man in New York called Mitch Bogdanovich who had been working on the technicalities of the synch sound problem for Leacock and the Maysles brothers. He also knew about that totemic object without which synch sound was practically unthinkable, the Nagra tape recorder. He knew that it cost some thousands of dollars and that the designer was a man called Kudelski. And he knew a lot more about the explosion of observational documentary which was taking place in New York and elsewhere.

Tim had a strong practical side. He made things with his hands and was ready to learn to take a camera to pieces, and knew about registration systems, which was why an Arriflex had a better film image than a Bell & Howell or a Bolex. His practicality was, I now see, that of a man preparing himself for a major production. But at the time this was hidden, and it was simply a difference between him and me. With an education in classics and literature which seemed designed to make me as ignorant as possible of anything which had resulted from the industrial revolution, I could only wish then that Tim could have implanted some of his knowledge, skill and confidence about machines into me. Being generous, he would have done so.

By now I had shot my first roll of the film Gardner had given me and was unhappy with the results. There were a few acceptable images but too many indecisive, pointless camera movements. I could not see how to move forward. Tim suggested I check the Bell & Howell out one weekend and that we shoot something together. We took one or two 100-foot rolls of black-and-white film (much cheaper than color, then) and drove with Patsy Asch and a baby called Caya to a fair somewhere in New Hampshire. Tim showed me that if you took a light reading off the back of your hand in open sunlight, and looked at the range of subjects in sun and shade, you could work around that reading for the rest of the day. He explained about "the grey scale". As I had been taking a separate exposure for every shot, and wasting a lot of time and mental energy doing so, this trick of the trade was helpful.

We took a long time in the little fair, shooting kids on swings and carousels, and a game with a mallet, a ball, and a bell where, if you hit the target hard enough, the ball sped up a column and made the bell ring. At the end of a long afternoon's shooting (amusing to think how we spun out our meagre supply of stock) we were elated. We had to wait days to see the material developed and printed, but when we did, it was nearly all useable, thanks to Tim's skill with the light meter. We realized that there were now real possibilities for editing the material together to give an evocation of all the things going on in that little fair at the same time. We edited and re-edited the material, learning a great deal as we went about duration, editing time. If you saw a man hit the target with the mallet, how long did you need to cut away to a kid on a swing, in order to come back in time to see the ball hit the bell? We tried that a lot of different ways. There was nothing very theoretical involved – simply the need to make something simple "work" in conventional film-editing terms.

Later on, as I laboured on a different mini-project by myself, Tim, indentured to the Bushman material, would look over my shoulder and say, "That cut won't work" – and to my chagrin, he would turn out to be right. Why had he always seen it long before I did? His view, looking back now to his own feelings then, is that he was as uncertain about what he was doing as I was. It did not come through to me that way.

Gardner now sent me across Boston on his Lambretta to collect cowrie shells from an arcane stockist for his Baliem Valley Expedition. He gave me one or two other minor chores too, so I started hoping that he would need me in some menial capacity on the expedition itself, and I know that Tim also ached to go. It would have been a painful test of our friendship if one of us had been picked, but neither of us was. Later, after Gardner had gone, Tim had the major responsibility of looking at rushes for him, to make sure there were no serious camera problems. I dropped in one day and saw some material with him – vicarious participation being better than none at all. Tim was not happy. He couldn't see what sort of film Gardner was aiming for. There were masses and masses of material, of ritual, of warfare, of people gardening, and much more, but Tim insisted that there was something fundamental that was missing. "There's no interaction," was the way he summed it up. He reckoned that whatever Gardner was filming, it lacked the flow of social communication, the give-and-take of everyday life. It had the virtue of being a sound realist position, although I doubt if we put it into such a clear-cut conceptual box. I felt defensive of Gardner, but hadn't the least idea either. "And he isn't shooting synch sound," Tim added. We had both seen that the future was synch sound, and we were puzzled as to why Gardner, who apparently had shared our enthusiasm for its possibilities, was not using it. Later, in his contribution to *Boston Marathon*, he would do so. That film, which Gardner worked on with a team of other film-makers, was an effective observational documentary using synch sound, and giving the impression of condensed real-time coverage of an ongoing event. Gardner must have been sufficiently taken with *Primary* to want to try his hand at film-making in this vein.

There was nothing to keep me in Boston and, with Gardner's help, I moved first to a master's programme in the second year of Philadelphia's Annenberg School of Communications, where Sol Worth appeared from time to time to tell us that he could not teach us how to make films, and we had just better get on by ourselves. Perhaps that was good advice, but at the time it felt cold and dismissive. Worth was, I believe, dealing with health problems. I stayed on in the city for two more years to work as an in-house documentary producer for Smith Kline & French, a blue-chip pharmaceutical company, visiting Tim and Gardner several times in the next few years. By 1965 Tim had made a trip to the East African Dodoth (a pastoral people like the Maasai) formally employed as a still photographer by Elizabeth Marshall Thomas, which allowed him to do some creative work, and he showed me some excellent stills. But what he was much more excited about was cine footage he had shot. It had all been done in his last day there, and without the approval of his employer who, as is usually the case with employers, had seemed to have wanted all his energies available for her project. In any case, Tim had now shot some serious footage. He regretted that it had been shot mute and not synch, but he showed it to me in a black and white one-light work print, and it was visually accomplished. In my own life, I was getting further and further away from shooting a synch sound ethnographic film. Tim had also been working with John Marshall on Bushman material, and was excited by the idea of building up short "sequence films" in which a single event was the core for a short film. The idea was to get away from the style of film-making embodied in *The Hunters*, and to work with much more naturalistic, spontaneous, unmediated material, whether of ritual performance, production, or the quiet periods of rest and play which punctuated the hot afternoons of Bushman life.

With hindsight, a quality which informs this whole essay, I now appreciate that in the early 1960s Tim was setting out a coherent and single-minded commitment to ethnographic documentary. In daily conversation with Patsy, John Marshall, and other collaborators, he was thinking through a program of filming and class-room work surrounding film which carried him forward for the rest of his life. It is possible to see that his early photographic training might have encouraged him to follow Robert Gardner's direction, and make films which were image- and symbol-led, and which explore the societies in which they are made with a sense of awe and a hunger for resonant humanistic themes.[2] Tim had the eye and he had the sensitivity, and Gardner would probably have encouraged him, had he wanted to go in such a direction. Tim's warmth and interest in other peoples' lifeways would have carried him forward to work in what Bill Nichols has termed the "Family of Man" approach. But, it seems, he did not.

There were strategic decisions which he had to make. In the summer of 1966 he was thinking hard about returning to graduate school to undertake a Ph.D. in Anthropology. At this point, Jerome Bruner offered him a good salary to work on *Man, A Course of Study*, the MACOS project, which was to combine ethnographic film innovatively with classroom instruction as an experiment in national primary school curriculum development. Tim was torn between the wish to become a fully qualified anthropologist and the desire to accept a good salary, better than new Ph.D.s were getting, for work on an exciting project. He had never had a proper job with a good salary, and his family was growing. He reasoned further that as a professional anthropologist he would only study one or two cultures in depth during a professional lifetime whereas, if he became a specialist film-maker who collaborated with a series of individual anthropologists, he would become satisfyingly involved with a number of cultures. So that decision proved decisive. If we compare Tim's approach with Gardner's we see an interesting contrast: Gardner has in his professional life collaborated several times with a seasoned professional anthropologist, such as Franz Staal, over a series of films in India (*Altars of Fire* and others). He has also had less fully collaborative involvements with younger people, in which he has remained intellectually sovereign, retaining overall responsibility for the finished films. And he has undoubtedly played an influential role in a number of other films where film-makers rather than anthropologists were in the driving seat.

Tim worked with anthropologists who could and did take intellectual responsibility for knowledge-in-depth of the chosen society (Chagnon, Balikci, Fox, Connor, Lewis). That is not to play down his creative contributions to the films which resulted, but to stress that he took a clear position on the division of competence and, indeed, on the kinds of films he wanted to lend his name and labors to. He rarely mentioned Gardner's films over the many years we met and discussed new works without stressing the distance between his goals and Gardner's. "Bob sees himself as an *artist* … " Tim would say, suggesting that Gardner was thereby freed from disciplines and responsibilities which he, Tim, had willingly taken up, burdensome though they sometimes might be.

One might ask at this point whether Tim's collaboration with John Marshall influenced him more strongly than his contacts with Bob Gardner. In my view, once *The Hunters*, with its echoes of Flahertian heroes struggling with the difficulties of a supposedly hostile environment, had ceased to satisfy Marshall, he was set firmly on a realistic course as a film-maker. That seems a rather thin phrase to convey a life spent in such intense involvement with the San people and their fortunes. Marshall showed early on an extraordinary capacity for intense involvement with the people with whom he had grown up and whom he had filmed so sensitively. Tim's creative life certainly showed a similar, if not quite so exclusive, capacity for sustained involvement. And the commitment to realist accounts and properly contextualized events never wavered. But Tim also struck out in a different direction from John Marshall: his commitment to the educational, indeed, scholarly side of ethnographic film-making developed throughout his working life, in close collaboration with Patsy Asch, and that desire to make film work for an educational anthropology is, perhaps, his most distinctive personal legacy.

The changing political environment of the 1960s and 1970s shifted film-makers away from a detached observation to a consideration of the fate of their subjects. Tim's concerns became less single-mindedly with filming itself, and his interest in the ethically responsible use of film developed in tandem with collaborative film-making. He was to do his first major creative work among the Yanomamö Indians in Venezuela, and later there were to be collaborative projects in Afghanistan and Indonesia. The Afghanistan project sharpened his concern with the ethical use of film, when he suddenly found that material he had shot for one purpose had been transmitted in quite a different way by the BBC to make a program about the Afghan civil war. Tim was shocked to discover how film-makers could lose rights to original material, which could be traded between paymasters in ways which diluted or destroyed the original implicit or explicit filming contracts, and he started a campaign to alert anthropologists and film-makers to the issues in which they were too often, quite literally, innocents abroad. His essay on contracts (Asch 1982) should be required reading for any documentary film course.

On a more personal note, after our first intense months of contact, there was a secure if argumentative friendship in place and we planned to make a film together one day. I was to do some serious anthropology and Tim was to be the film-maker. I had got so much pleasure and stimulation from Tim and Patsy, and learned so much that, although I seemed to be heading off in another direction, it did not seem right or reasonable that we would not eventually collaborate. That agreement must have been initially made in 1960 and reconfirmed at intervals during 1961–63. After several zigzags, I finished an anthropology doctorate and then felt ready to think about making a film. It must have been 1970 or 1971. I had shot hardly any film in the decade since we met, but had produced or directed a dozen assorted films. I wrote to Tim, with whom I had lost touch, proposing he think about making a film in Cyprus with me. A letter came back making it clear that Tim had moved a long way since we had met. He had done his first major Yanomamö expedition, and was now on his way back for more. He was clearly very involved in his own work, and not at all the dejected assistant editor I had first met. He was now able to give me a useful piece of advice, consistent with all his considered views on filming and anthropology. "You don't need a cameraman," he wrote. "You know how a film ought to be made, so shoot it yourself!"

At the time this letter came to me as an unpleasant surprise. I had been mentally relying on Tim to shoot for me, and thus overcome my insecurities about machines. A collaborative film was now revealed as anachronistic. But the more I thought about his letter, the more his advice seemed right. It would clearly be highly disruptive to introduce a film crew into a Cypriot village. So the letter decided the matter for me. A film resulted, in due course: not synch sound, but at least shot by me. And for that move out of dependence I was indebted to Tim. Small wonder he became an inspired teacher of film-makers.

This short essay has tried to evoke Tim at the start of a long, productive and single-minded career in ethnographic film and education. Tim inspired all sorts of people in his life, through his personal warmth, the seriousness of his purposes as an educator, and his energetic enthusiasm for exploring his own culture and other peoples'. He certainly gave me a great deal of stimulation, and challenging benchmark standards to argue with, and he has done that for many others.

This essay has inevitably been a personal evocation but perhaps, to anthropologists and film-makers who have sympathy for the concrete and the specific, it may be judged none the worse for that. If I have imparted a sense of Tim Asch as an intense, restless young man at the start of the lifelong engagements which sustained him, and which he sustained, its purpose is achieved.

Notes

1 *March to Aldermaston* (1959).
2 At one point during my Peabody sojourn, Gardner and I contemplated making a fiction film together. My outline was essentially naïve realist, a De Sica- and Fellini-inspired story of a boy who runs away from home and lives rough, turning from a normal middle-class child into a waif. Gardner took this and added all kinds of dark, powerful imagery with psychoanalytic resonances which I thought sat uneasily with my boy-on-the-run realism. We agreed that Boston's garbage dump would be an important location, but the project foundered on the refusal of our imaginations to meld.

Reference

Asch, Tim (1982), "Collaboration in Ethnographic Film Making: A Personal View". *Canberra Anthropology* 5 (1): 8–36. [Reprinted in J. R. Rollwagen (ed.), *Anthropological Filmmaking*. Chur, Switzerland: Harwood Academic Publishers, 1988: 1–29.]

Chapter 5

Efforts and events in a long collaboration

Working with Tim Asch on ethnographic films on Roti in eastern Indonesia

James J. Fox

Introductory comment

Collaboration can be a complex affair. My collaboration with Tim Asch covered a period of well over ten years. Our work together had its assortment of ups and downs, successes and set-backs, but it did lead eventually to the production of two films, *The Water of Words* (Asch *et al.* 1983) and *Spear and Sword* (Asch *et al.* 1988), about life on the island of Roti. Much more footage exists from our two film trips together and there is the hope of yet more films to come. Let me explain how our collaboration came about and how it developed over the years.

Cambridge, Massachusetts

I first met Tim in Cambridge, Massachusetts in 1970. I was teaching in the Department of Anthropology at Harvard and Tim was teaching at Brandeis. At first, we had merely a passing acquaintance – the occasional meeting, a brief chat, a gradual getting to know one another. At the time, Tim was deeply involved in his work on the Yanomamö and I was anxious to see as much of that extraordinary material as I could. The Yanomamö were a great lure and revelation. As film review editor for the *American Anthropologist*, Tim would also occasionally ask me to do a brief review of some film, which he would then arrange for me to view, usually at the Documentary Educational Resources (DER) studio. In time we began to consider the possibilities of collaboration.

My first collaboration with Tim was to teach an ethnographic film course with him at Harvard in the fall semester of 1974. This was a remarkable course for several reasons. It was the first general course at Harvard on ethnographic film and had an unusual format. It was definitely an anthropology course, but it was taught as part of the General Education curriculum and it had attached to it an evening film series entitled "Film as Ethnographic Experience". The evening series was open to all Harvard students.

Our course had an official enrolment of nearly eighty students which made it a good-sized class, but the evening films drew upwards of 250 to 300 students. These films were shown on Thursday evenings in one of the largest lecture halls in the

University, Lecture Hall B in the Science Center and, for most sessions, the auditorium was entirely filled. In the course, we tried to present ethnographic film as a serious subject of study and insisted that students must view the films we were discussing more than once. The evening film series allowed us this second showing and also gave us the opportunity to show other films in relation to the principal films in the course. It was therefore a necessary part of the course but offered a way of attracting a wider audience to ethnographic films.

The film series began with several sessions of "classic" films – Nanook of the North, The Wedding of Paolo, Grass, Jaguar, The Hunters and Dead Birds. We also showed a number of Tim's films on the Yanomamö such as A Father Washes His Children and The Feast, films that reflected different aspects of Yanomamö life. We also showed other films to present contrasts – Les Maîtres Fous and The Old Amish Order; various films on the Navajo, including one made by the Navajo themselves; films on American life – Happy Mother's Day, Three Domestics – and some of the Granada series, such as The Last of the Cuivas.

A film that particularly interested me was Eric Crystal's Ma'Bugi: Trance of the Toraja, which focused on spirit possession among the Toraja of South Sulawesi. It was a film made on the thinnest of shoe-string budgets and from the viewpoint of a professional film-maker could perhaps be criticized for evident shortcomings. Nevertheless, I felt it was remarkable for its use of sound and its reliance on a "native voice" in its narrative of a ritual (for my review of Ma'Bugi, see Fox 1976). It was a film that influenced the making of The Water of Words. Throughout the course, Tim was hard at work on The Ax Fight. His work gave the class the opportunity to see how work on particular footage develops and indeed to contribute to its development in their discussions. We were able by the end of our film series to show something very close to the final production version of The Ax Fight.

It was during this course that Tim and I began to discuss the possibilities of future collaboration. The idea was to produce a series of films about eastern Indonesia. It was also during this time that I was offered the position of Professorial Fellow at the Research School of Pacific Studies in The Australian National University. I decided to accept the offer and left Cambridge during the summer of 1975.

Canberra, Australia

Tim and I kept in close correspondence after I had moved to Canberra. At the time, Professor Derek Freeman, who was Head of the Anthropology Department in the Research School of Pacific Studies, was particularly interested in developing a laboratory for the ethological study of social interaction. Although my interests and Tim's were more ethnographically oriented, our concerns had enough in common to form the basis of what was originally called "The Human Ethology and Ethnographic Film Laboratory", which became an adjunct unit of the Department of Anthropology. Tim was hired as a Senior Research Fellow and joined the Department in 1976. Adam Kendon, who was already a Senior Fellow in the Department, was also attached to the Film Laboratory and did his research through it.

In late 1977, Derek Freeman proposed a further initiative to obtain funding from within the Institute of Advanced Study. To do this he gave the Human Ethology and Ethnographic Film Laboratory (HEEFL) a new name, "The Laboratory for the Iconic Recording of Human Behaviour", which he felt might better attract funding in a competition dominated by requests from the natural scientists in The ANU's Institute of Advanced Studies. The work of the Laboratory was, initially, to be divided into two research groups: one consisting of Tim and myself would work on ritual performance, and another consisting of visitors (Dr Stephen Levinson and Dr Penelope Brown and others who were about to arrive in Canberra to take part in a two-year working group headed by Dr John Haviland) would work on the recording of language in cultural context. In the end, Derek's efforts were successful in obtaining funding for a technical officer and a small operating budget to add to the funds already allocated to the Laboratory from the Anthropology Department budget.

To begin our work on ritual performance, our initial plans were to film the succession of ritual contests that are held at intervals during a three-month period of the ceremonial year on the island of Savu. These are large-scale rituals and require comprehensive recording to be studied properly. Just before I left the US, I had presented a paper at the University of Michigan on the ceremonial system of Savu (Fox 1979). In it, I tried to contrast the spectacularly intensive ritual encounters of the Savunese that are carried out without oration with the verbal performances that constitute ritual on the island of Roti. Tim and I felt that film was the appropriate – indeed, perhaps, the only – means to document and to analyze the combination of choreography and spontaneity that characterize the rituals of Savu.

After I had moved to Canberra, Tim and I continued our planning for the study of ritual performance. We would begin on Savu and from there move to other islands to make a series of films on different styles of ritual in eastern Indonesia. We formulated this project as "The Comparative Eastern Indonesia Project" and we initially designated five cultures as the focus of our efforts: (1) Savu, (2) Roti, (3) Flores (Sikka/Tana 'Ai), (4) Bali, and (5) Bugis or Buton.[1] To do this work, we applied to the US National Science Foundation through Documentary Educational Resources's base in Cambridge. We were successful in obtaining this NSF grant – not at the level we ambitiously hoped for, but with enough funding to begin our project.[2]

By the end of 1976, Tim and Patsy had moved to Canberra; we had an NSF grant and we had applied for permission from the Indonesian Institute of Sciences (Lembaga Ilmu Pengetahuan Indonesia: LIPI) to do research and filming in eastern Indonesia. We hoped to be on Savu by February or, at the latest, March of 1977, in time for the high ceremonial season.

It was at this point, however, that our carefully made plans began to come unstuck. The Indonesian invasion of East Timor in 1975 cast a shadow over all research in the Timor region. The island of Savu happened to be administratively part of Kabupaten Kupang of West Timor. Formal permission from LIPI to carry out film research was delayed and continued to be delayed beyond any hope of reaching Savu for the high ceremonial season in 1977. I contributed a further complication to our situation by accepting the offer of a year's Fellowship at The Netherlands Institute of Advanced Study which required that I arrive in The Netherlands by early September.

In the end, LIPI research permission was granted but since we had missed the ceremonial season on Savu, we decided to direct our first efforts to filming ritual on Roti (also administratively within Kabupaten Kupang, in which we were granted permission to film).

From Bali to Roti

I left for Bali on 17 June 1977 (for a short holiday with my family before going on to eastern Indonesia) and Tim followed with all the equipment and film stock on 24 June. However, on his arrival all the equipment and film stock were immediately impounded since we had not yet been to Jakarta to obtain our official letters from LIPI. We tried to negotiate the release of the equipment, but – quite correctly – were unable to do so without proper documentation from LIPI. Tim therefore went on to Jakarta on 28 June and I followed two days later. Our collaboration had begun.

The paperwork in Jakarta went slowly but smoothly. It resulted in one marvelous mistake. Acting on the recommendation from LIPI, the Ministry of Internal Affairs (Departemen Dalam Negeri) issues the official letters for research and notifies provincial governments of the research that has been approved by Jakarta. In our case, a young staff officer, who had no idea where the islands of Savu and Roti were located, issued us permission to do filming on Bali. When I showed him on a map where Savu and Roti were actually located, he issued a second set of documents giving us permission to do research in the Province of Nusa Tenggara Timur. This fortunate bureaucratic confusion enabled us, from the very start of our filming project, to work in two provinces of Indonesia and opened the way for all of Tim's eventual filming on Bali.

This permission also allowed us to do some immediate, completely unexpected, filming on Bali. When we returned to Bali, we met Margaret Mead, who was attending the Pacific Science Association Conference which was being held at the Hotel Bali Beach in Sanur. She intended to return to her old village, Bayung Gede, with her former research assistant Made Kaler, and she asked us to record the event. We agreed, especially since Tim had once been Margaret Mead's student and we had formal approval to film on Bali. The filming and recording in Bayung Gede turned out to be the first time that Tim and I actually worked together in the field and my diary notes of that date give some idea of how well we managed:

> July 23, 1977: Drove in jeep and car to Lake View, a restaurant overlooking Lake Batur in Kintamani, where we picked up Linda Connor.[3] There we transferred the equipment to the jeep and Tim, Made, and I went on ahead to Bayung Gede to announce M's arrival and to set up to film it. Arrived and had

to overcome initial reluctance since we had not notified the *camat* [District Officer]. Gave instructions both to the driver of the jeep and to the village officials about what to do for the film. Balinese take to theatrical direction and everyone cooperated. Chaos with filming and taking sound. Tape recorder got stuck and Tim exposed an entire roll of film [without sound]. Eventually we got a few good shots with some good sound, especially of M and Made making offerings at the temple ...

Our main problem was that Tim had set up a radio-operated rig attached to the Arriflex that was supposed to turn on the Nagra that I was carrying whenever he began to film. (Tim's idea, which I thought was brilliant, was to establish an automatic means of synchronizing the sound I would be recording to the film that he was taking.) Unfortunately the rig short-circuited almost immediately and I could not manually override the remote control system and was therefore unable to do any recording. The problem, which could have jeopardized the entire day's shooting, was one which we were able to overcome. It took us only ten minutes or so to discard the rig and readjust our equipment. Despite the confusion, within a short time, we were able to coordinate our efforts and to get back to filming and recording.

Our first efforts produced some interesting "historical" footage, which I did have the chance to see later in Canberra, but not all of the footage had good accompanying sound. Tim sent all of the film to Margaret Mead and I can only assume that it is sitting somewhere in some archive.[4] It might still be useful to do something with this footage when there are some of us, like Linda Connor and myself, around who can remember where the filming was done and what happened in the course of our brief excursion to Bayung Gede.

Ufa Len, Termanu

If it was on Bali that we began our first filming together, it was on Roti that we had to face the challenge of a full and extended collaboration. One of our difficulties was in allocating time to our main work together. To reach Roti took us over five weeks. Tim arrived on Bali with all our equipment on 24 June and we finally managed to reach Roti on 2 August, arriving in the settlement of Ufa Len in the domain of Termanu in the late evening of that day.

This travel time included not just the time in Jakarta, Den Pasar, and Kupang that was required to arrange our documents; it also included several days in Solo in central Java where we had been invited to attend the *Bedyo Ketawang* at the Kraton of the Susuhunan with a view to possible filming in the future. This royal dance performance commemorates, with extraordinary refinement and elegance, the encounter between the Susuhunan's ancestor and the Queen of the South Sea, which forms a charter for the Mataram dynasty. Attendance is restricted to the court circle and a few privileged guests who are allowed to view the dance from behind a glass enclosure. Tim and I were given permission to attend through

Figure 5.1 Tim Asch and Pak Foe Nalle in Rotinese ceremonial dress, 1977.

the good offices of the Bupati of the Kraton, K.R.T. Hardjonagoro, who was also the Director of the Museum Radyapustaka.

Because this was to be the first in a series of filming trips, we were concerned to announce our intentions, to look for other possibilities for future filming and make every effort to facilitate matters for our next trips. The time we spent was, we felt, an investment in future filming in Indonesia but it left very little time for actual filming on Roti.

From the perspective of film, Roti appeared to offer nothing but disappointment. Tim's first remark on getting off the plane at midday at the airport of Penfui at Kupang on Timor was on the quality of light – sharp, direct, unshadowed, and overwhelming. Roti, which was then accessible by small plane from Kupang, was even worse. Compared to the lush greens of Bali or Java, Roti was stark and bare. Worse still, there was nothing that resembled the ceremonies of the Kraton of Solo or the temple pageantry of Bali. Indeed, as I had warned Tim, the Rotinese are, for the most part, notable non-ritualists. In the same paper in which I described the exuberance of Savunese ceremonial contest, I characterized the Rotinese as a population enamoured with speaking. Rotinese are content mainly to talk their way through ceremonies. Language is everything; performance counts for little. The challenge we faced was therefore to make a film about ritual where ritual is primarily verbal performance, not visual performance.

Tim was also hardly prepared to deal with the verbal onslaughts of the Rotinese. The fact that he was only beginning to speak Indonesian only increased Rotinese teasing. I was continually called upon to translate and interpret. Initially, I did this as faithfully as I could but I soon realized that Tim's answers failed to reach their mark. We therefore took another tack. In reply to some sharp repartee, I would have Tim say something in English and would then follow with an answer that purported to be Tim's reply, but was as sharply pointed as I could make it. I remained, however, to all appearances the innocent translator. Tim's reputation increased as his verbal barbs stuck and, in the course of our stay, the time spent on these encounters escalated together with the palm-gin drinking that must accompany such verbal duelling. Most of these encounters were orchestrated by Pak Mias Kiuk, who is one of the characters in *The Water of Words* and with whom we stayed in Ufa Len.

Pak Mias was an irrepressible character – an archetypical Rotinese – with great wit, cunning intelligence, and a lively sense of mischief. My wife and I first took up residence in one of Pak Mias' houses when we arrived in Termanu in 1965; when I returned to Roti in 1973, I again spent much of my time with him. It was for this reason that Tim and I went directly to Ufa Len when we arrived on Roti. During our stay, Tim and I may have constituted camera and sound crew but, true to form, Pak Mias assumed the role of director of our Rotinese filming. Diary notes from the day of our arrival in Ufa Len identify Pak Mias' role in our filming and foreshadow the film, *The Water of Words*, that we eventually made.

> August 2, 1977. Explained the idea of the film to Pak Mias who immediately grasped the concept and began setting out what we must film – beginning with lontar tapping. Next the link to Dou Danga (*ledi tua lai dua* ["tapping the tree twice a day"]), link from Tio Holu//Dusa Lai to *manaseko meti-ala* ["those who scoop-net in the tide"]. This must be a film produced by Rotinese. Interestingly, Pak Mias who has never seen a movie was the first to realize what we had come to do.

Figure 5.2 Tim Asch filming a location shot on Roti, 1978. The footage became the opening scene of *The Water of Words*.

Figure 5.3   Timothy Asch filming Petrus Malesi on Roti, 1977. Asch and Malesi are sitting on the *tetus* (mortuary monument) built in honor of Stephanus Adulanu of clan Meno. This photograph was used as a still in the closing titles of *The Water of Words*.

These mixed-language notes are key signposts to sequences in *The Water of Words*, which Pak Mias narrates along with the chanter, Petrus Malesi, who was a member of clan Dou Danga, the clan whose ancestor is credited with devising the proper techniques of lontar-palm tapping and of the cooking of its juice. The reference to women who "scoop-net in the tide", a sequence of which is shown in the film, alludes to the ritual association of the lontar palm with the sea. A germ of an idea for a film about Roti was evidently there from the beginning, though it took some time to take its full shape.

Whatever ideas we were beginning to develop, they had to be put to one side, as we plunged into filming within days of our arrival. As it happened, a ritual event was about to occur which we both felt was worth filming. Diverted from Savu, we had arrived on Roti and had to seize whatever opportunities were presented for the filming of ritual. Unlike Savu, Roti has no ceremonial season whose rituals follow a lunar cycle. The rituals that occur are those of the life cycle and depend on developments within individual communities. The ritual event that was about to occur was the payment of bridewealth by a member of clan Nggofa-Laik for his bride from clan Meno. Nggofa-Laik is the paired clan of Pak Mias' clan, Ingu-Beuk, and Pak Mias was to act as one of the representatives for the groom.

Since the bride's branch of clan Meno resided in the settlement of Taka Daen, most of the residents of Ufa Len and the neighbouring hamlet of Sosa Dale would therefore go as a group to Taka Daen to represent the groom. The night before the ceremony, the chief spokesmen on both sides, Ayub Adulanu from Meno who was village head of Ono Tali, and Frans Biredoko who was the village head of Nggodi Meda, which included both Ufa Len and Sosa Dale, met at a small feast given by the groom's family and worked out among themselves (without necessarily informing others) a mutual strategy for the next day's proceedings. I attended the feast but was only able to learn the general outline of the amounts of bridewealth and counter-gifts agreed upon, based on Pak Mias' estimates.

Filming on the day, 6 August 1977, went smoothly, even though it was our first effort together on Roti. The bridewealth payment ceremony was a circumscribed event and certainly showed the way Rotinese talk themselves through ceremonies. Eventually, the day's footage became the film *Spear and Sword*. The film itself follows closely what we recorded and we had only to fill in the gaps that occurred when the camera was not running but the tape recorder remained on. The film conveys the seriousness of such ritual negotiations as well as their humor. It also makes evident the ordinary reality behind high-sounding "verbal frames" such as "Spear and Sword" (Rotinese: *Te-Tafa*). Embodied in the film is a view of Rotinese ritual performance that I have described at some length, particularly in relation to funeral rituals (Fox 1988). Rotinese rituals consist of – or at least are ordered by – a succession of marvelous-sounding verbal frames. These frames have great metaphoric value. They cannot, however, be taken literally. A ritual proceeds by working through these verbal frames, each of which marks a stage or a component of the ritual. Interest for the Rotinese lies not in the frames themselves, which are well known, but in how they are "interpreted" or "implemented" in the performance. For those frames that refer to objects of exchange, local interest centers on what will be offered, as "Sword and Spear" for example, and whether the offered objects will be accepted, rejected, or form the basis – as usually happens – for further negotiation.

In the case of the ritual we filmed, basic agreement had been reached the night before between the spokesmen on both sides, although the spokesman for the bride's side had not informed all the other members of his side on what he had agreed. Clearly, the participants were enlivened by the presence of the camera and tape recorder but negotiations retained their usual character. By the time drinking began, the self-consciousness of the performance diminished.

As Tim always insisted, *Spear and Sword* needs a proper study guide to explain the background to and intricacies of the event and of the dialogue. Some understanding of the verbal frames that guide the participants is needed and more information would certainly help to explain the interactions toward the end of the film when the chanter, Petrus Malesi, is called upon to provide a chant that can be interpreted as an ancestral charter for the practice of bridewealth payments. As it stands, *Spear and Sword* has proved reasonably popular among students in that it conveys a sense of Rotinese repartee and humor.

If all filming were as easy as our first effort, one could imagine endless collaboration between ethnographer and film-maker. Unfortunately, nothing went as effortlessly as that first day. There were a number of niggling problems with the equipment that required Tim's constant attention; there were also the frustrations for Tim which arose from not being able to communicate well. But what impressed the Rotinese were Tim's energy and activity which, because he could not explain what he was doing, could only be observed. Within a few days, Tim was given the nickname *Sangu Ana*, "Mini-Typhoon", and jokes about the "typhoon" blowing in and out were added to the repertoire of teasing. Our main problem, however, was that no new "event" offered itself for filming.

Tim, in my view, was a brilliant "event film-maker". *The Feast*, *The Ax Fight*, Jero Tapakan's séance in *A Balinese Trance Seance*, the *gren mahé* ritual in *A Celebration of Origins*, as well as (in a minor key) *Spear and Sword* are all event films presented and analyzed to reveal cultural significance within a circumscribed form. Had we filmed on Savu, as we originally intended, I am certain that we would have encountered ritual events of high drama but, on Roti, such events are not so much muted as merged in a continuing round of talk. Court cases, for example, of which there are many on Roti, have their dramatic moments, but such cases rarely seem to end; rather, they go through phases as parties to a dispute regroup and realign themselves for their next encounter. We filmed one such dispute which, as a case, remained unresolved and, as an incident, was unrelated to anything else that we filmed.

For the rest of our first trip, we therefore set about filming sequences that would accumulate toward a film about life on Roti. For Tim, this was to be a film that would be the visual accompaniment to my book *Harvest of the Palm* (Fox 1977), which describes the economic significance of a particular way of life organized around the use of the lontar palm. For this, we filmed the techniques of palm tapping and juice cooking.

For my part, I wanted a film that would document the mythic significance of everyday life as recounted in ritual language recitations. For this we filmed a number of ritual language recitations, particularly by the poet Petrus Malesi.

For Pak Mias, reliance on the lontar palm was a part of Rotinese self-presentation. Pak Mias, seated in his house, talking directly to the camera about lontar tapping, provided sufficient exaggeration and overstatement to give a good sense of how the Rotinese think of themselves. Earlier that same day, we had tried to film Pak Mias in one of his fields speaking to his son Os, but the strong, intermittent winds that sweep Roti in July made good sound recording difficult.

We were more successful in getting good footage of women fishing in stone weirs along the shore and watering their dry season gardens. But by this time, we were nearing the end of our supply of film. We left Ufa Len on 16 August with plans to film the Independence Day ceremonies on 17 August in the domain of Keka. In Keka, we finished our work and the last of our film.

On leaving Roti

We left Roti with fragments for possible films but nothing that seemed sufficient to justify our efforts. All of the elements that went into the making of *The Water of Words* were already there but they were not apparent to us at the time. Rather than feeling satisfaction, we felt that we had to look to further filming to make something of what we had done. It was at this point that Tim and I parted.

Tim's task was to get the film and equipment back to Australia; my task, on my way to The Netherlands, was to retrace our steps through the bureaucracy to ensure that we could continue our filming the following year. In Kupang, I managed to obtain a letter of support from El Tari, the Governor of the Province, himself a Savunese, who wanted us to continue our filming and, in particular, to do filming on Savu. In Jakarta, I submitted a formal report on our activities to LIPI along with the Governor's letter and reapplied for visas for the coming year. Again, our request was for visas to film on Savu in March 1978.

Unfortunately, the same inexplicable and frustrating bureaucratic delays occurred again to prevent us from filming on Savu. When our research visas were finally issued, Tim went immediately to Bali to begin filming there. I joined him later in August 1978 and we went on to continue our filming on Roti. Again on our arrival, we were captured by an event – the death of an old woman of clan Biredoko, whose mortuary ceremonies involving almost all branches of this powerful clan had to be extended to await the arrival of her son from Jakarta. Filming this event took many days and a good deal of our supply of film. Most of this footage remains to be worked on and offers prospects for another film, perhaps to be called A Death in a Clan, in our series of films on Roti.

On our two trips to Roti, apart from the ritual events we focused on, Tim shot footage of a variety of common everyday activities – activities around the household, a local dispute, a church service – from which other films can be made. A particular challenge would be to make a film about "speaking" – which is, for Rotinese, their proudest preoccupation. Such a film might include all of the different kinds of verbal performances we filmed.

Back to the future: the goal of an electronic study guide

In one particular area of our collaboration, I have been woefully delinquent. From the beginning of our work together, Tim always insisted that the films he made should be accompanied by a proper study guide to be used by students interested in understanding the film and the society that it is about. I have, however, never written the appropriate study guides to either of the films we made together – always with the lame excuse that we had more films to complete and that what was needed would be a single study guide to the entire opus. My book, Harvest of the Palm, was supposed to serve as a kind of introduction to Rotinese life and livelihood.

The Water of Words, in particular, needs a study guide because it is a dense film that operates on various levels. At its simplest level, it provides exact documentation of the traditional techniques of palm tapping both for male and female palms. At another level, it presents life on Roti as Pak Mias wished to present it and would like outsiders to imagine life on Roti. The film, however, intentionally provides contrapuntal views of Rotinese life that contrast with Pak Mias' narrative. At yet another level, The Water of Words is a ritual film narrated by a Rotinese poet. From its opening scenes to its concluding shots, the film follows a ritual format. It is a film about "origins" and its opening scenes are of "places" of origin in Termanu. The film ends at a ritual site, Meno Tutus, the mortuary platform of the Head of the Earth in Termanu.

The poetic narrative of *The Water of Words* contains excerpts from and allusions to the most important of Rotinese ritual chants. These chants embody what are believed to be the foundations of Rotinese culture. Little of this structure, however, can be appreciated without the exegesis that a study guide could offer. The film thus remains unexplicated and, as yet, half-done. Until recently, *The Water of Words* stood as a foundation without an edifice or, adopting a Rotinese metaphor, a trunk without a tree.

With some strong prodding from Chris Gregory, who developed his introductory course on Anthropology at The ANU around key ethnographic films, I began to prepare what was supposed to become an electronic study guide. As a first step in this direction, the video of the film was digitized in MPEG and Quicktime and was made available internally on the web for use by students within The ANU. It has subsequently been made available on the World Wide Web and can be viewed at http://www.anu.edu.au/anthrop/WOW-home.html. This site consists of (1) the film itself, (2) the full film script, (3) a sequence index which divides the film into its various sequences, (4) a video index which allows a viewer to go to any segment of the film, (5) a photo gallery with special images from the film, and (6) poem pages which feature each of the separate poems that make up the film.

At a very simple level, one can select any sequence for immediate viewing and, for that sequence, one can refer to the script or to any of the poems that form a large part of the script. This is, however, only the first step in the development of this study guide. As a first step, the system has been designed, as far as is feasible, to be further expanded and possibly upgraded as new developments in technology become available.

In this system, *The Water of Words* is divided into various sequences that are equivalent to the chapters of a book. Each chapter could be used to focus on a different realm of Rotinese life: ritual topography, origin narratives, social relationships, political structures, all aspects of livelihood, and even an ethnography of speaking. One intention is to transfer to the same format a selection of approximately 300 slides (taken over a period from 1965 to 1993). These slides could also serve as icons to illustrate aspects of the different chapters. The tapes of ritual chants, gathered over a similar time-period, together with texts and translations, could also be added to provide oral as well as visual dimensions to a potential electronic encyclopedia of Rotinese culture. Indeed, a great deal of the footage that we have so far not used in making a specific film could be similarly added for study purposes. The advantage of this system is that it is entirely modular. Like a tree, it can branch in many different ways. As it grows, its trunk can remain firmly based in our film, *The Water of Words*. As a model of development, this structure would approximate a favored botanic metaphor of the Rotinese themselves.

In his work, Tim always stressed the importance of the stimulus that comes from using film in teaching. Tim used the responses of the students in our ethnographic film course at Harvard to guide him in shaping *The Ax Fight*. The more accessible *The Water of Words* and *Spear and Sword* become for introductory teaching, the more it may be possible to respond to students' ever-changing perceptions, reactions and queries by adding new dimensions to a developing study guide.

It is also worth noting that there is an Indonesian language version of *The Water of Words*, entitled *Air Kata-Kata* (Asch *et al.* 1984), with an excellent translation of the script and accompanying voice-over by Raharjo Suwandi, a graduate of anthropology at The ANU. The video version of this film has been used in Indonesian language courses taught at The ANU and it is also, I am told, used in teaching anthropology in Indonesia.

Tim's return to the US in 1982 did not end his collaboration with the Anthropology Department at The Australian National University. Patsy Asch provided the critical link to keep this collaboration going, dividing her time between the University of Southern California and The ANU. Her involvement was central – indeed, absolutely indispensable – to the making of both *The Water of Words* and *Spear and Sword* and has been equally essential in the making of the films about Bali and Flores. She, too, has now visited Roti and has taken high-band video of the final mortuary ceremonies in honour of Pak Mias. This has only added to the material from Roti on which there is so much work still to be done.

Therefore, instead of dwelling on the past, I would prefer to look to the future and to the possibility of more work, especially now with the development of new technologies for visual anthropology.

Notes

1 We referred to this last possibility initially as an "Islamic sailing population of Southern Sulawesi" and contemplated filming either a group of Bugis or "Butonese".

2 Asch's and Fox's NSF grant was entitled "The Ceremonies of Savu: the development of a methodology for the analysis of large-scale ritual performances via the use of film and video-tape".

3 Linda Connor was at that time a research student at the University of Sydney and was carrying out her fieldwork on Bali.

4 Tim sent the film to Margaret Mead accompanied by a long four-page letter, dated 19 January 1978, with apologies and explanations about the quality of the working print and the sound.

References

Fox, James J. (1976), "Review of E. Crystal, *Ma'Bugi: Trance of the Toraja*". *American Anthropologist* 78 (3): 723–4.

—— (1977), *Harvest of the Palm: Ecological Change in Eastern Indonesia*. Cambridge, Massachusetts: Harvard University Press.

—— (1979), "The Ceremonial System of Savu". In A. Becker and A. A. Yengoyan (eds.), *The Imagination of Reality: Essays on Southeast Asian Coherence Systems*. Norwood, New Jersey: Ablex Publishing Corporation, pp. 145–73.

—— (1988), "Chicken Bones and Buffalo Sinews: Verbal Frames and the Organization of Rotinese Mortuary Performances". In D. A. Moyer and H. J. M. Claessen, *Time Past, Time Present and Time Future: Essays in Honour of P. E. de Josselin de Jong*. Verhandelingen van het Koninklijk Instituut voor Taal-, Land- en Volkenkunde No. 131. Dordrecht: Foris Publications.

Films

Asch, Timothy, Patsy Asch and James J. Fox, (1983), *The Water of Words: A Cultural Ecology of an Eastern Indonesian Island*. 16 mm color. 30 minutes. Watertown, Mass: Documentary Educational Resources.

—— (1984), *Air Kata-Kata: Sebuah Film tentang Lingkungan Hidup dan Budaya Satu Pulau di Nusa Tenggara Timur*. [Indonesian Version of *The Water of Words*] 16 mm color. 30 minutes. Watertown, Mass: Documentary Educational Resources.

—— (1988), *Spear and Sword: A Payment of Bridewealth*. 16 mm color. 25 minutes. Watertown, Mass: Documentary Educational Resources.

Chapter 6

From event to ethnography

Film-making and ethnographic research in Tana 'Ai, Flores, eastern Indonesia

E. D. Lewis

The heuristic film, or, on not working to a script

> Unlike feature film-makers, ethnographic film-makers record events as they
> happen – no scripts, no actors, no sets, no retakes. ... The film must also
> capture the essence of the people, their passions, their fears, their motivations.
>
> (Asch 1992: 196)

The Tana 'Ai film project, which Tim Asch, Patsy Asch, and I began in 1980, had
three main objectives. The first was to make a recording of a major ritual which
would be of use in my research on the religion of the Ata Tana 'Ai of Flores in
eastern Indonesia. The second was to test and refine techniques by which film and
video are used with informants to elicit data for the ethnographic description and
analysis of the life of a community. The third aim was the production of films on the
ritual life of the Ata Tana 'Ai for university teaching and public screening. Among
other things, we filmed three rituals which were central to my research in Tana 'Ai:
the *gren mahé*, a large-scale and rarely performed complex of rites in which all
members of the community participated; the exchange of a woman between two
clans; and a second-stage mortuary rite. We planned to produce a film about each
of these rituals, the first of which, *A Celebration of Origins*, treats the *gren mahé* and
is now in distribution. Drawing upon our work in Tana 'Ai, I will here address three
topics pertaining to the method and theory of using film and video in anthropological research and the construction of a cinematic account of an event of paramount
importance in a Tana 'Ai community.

Before beginning work with the Aschs in 1980 I had carried out two years of
research on the island of Flores, some seventeen months of that time in Tana Wai
Brama, the largest of the seven ceremonial domains into which the Tana 'Ai region
is divided. Shortly before his death on 14 August 1979, the Tana Pu'an ("Source of
the Domain"), the ritual leader of Tana Wai Brama, announced that the community would undertake a performance of *gren mahé* following the next rice harvest in
June 1980. *Gren mahé* ("the celebration of the *mahé*") is the rarely performed
culminal rites of the ceremonial system of Tana Wai Brama. Whereas most ritual is
a means for communication with spirits or the ancestors of houses and clans, in *gren*

mahé the whole community gathers to invoke and address its deity. The people of Tana Wai Brama told me that the *gren* should be performed about once in every seven years, but in 1980 it had been almost twenty years since the last *gren*. Because *gren mahé* is the only ceremonial event in which all of the people of the community participate, it is of particular significance for understanding the organization of the society of the Ata Tana 'Ai and, when I left Tana 'Ai to return to Canberra in late August 1979, I was very keen to return to Flores to continue fieldwork the next year when the *gren* was to be performed.

Tim Asch thought that the *gren mahé*, as a large-scale ritual in eastern Indonesia, would be worthwhile as a subject of filming and together we embarked upon the Tana 'Ai ritual project. The Aschs and I set out for Flores with the primary, but only generally formulated, intention of filming the *gren mahé* in Tana Wai Brama. We had very few concrete plans and certainly no script to which we intended to work. As in all exploratory ethnography, we intended to follow events as they unfolded and, insofar as those events were controlled by their participants, to allow those participants to direct our work. While we located ourselves in what, on ethnographic grounds, we knew to be the social and ceremonial center of the domain, we sought in no way to influence the occurrence or direction of the events which we filmed. Tim and Patsy maintained cameras, tape recorders, and other equipment for filming at the ready at all times and we were thus able to begin filming on only a moment's notice. Given that we knew very little of the event we hoped to film before it occurred, this was the only reasonable way to proceed.

In a discussion of "opportunistic sampling" (which they contrast with "programmed sampling", "filming according to a predetermined plan"), Sorenson and Jablonko (1975: 153) exhort ethnographic film-makers to

> Seize opportunities. When something interesting happens, pick up the camera and shoot. Opportunistic filming, a freewheeling yet indispensable approach to visual documentation of naturally occurring phenomena, takes advantage of events as they develop in unfamiliar settings.
>
> (ibid.: 152)

The term "opportunistic filming" might seem to describe the method we employed in making the Tana 'Ai films and, indeed, Tim Asch on occasion used this term in reference to the methods which he employed in his cinematography. I believe the term "opportunistic filming" is inaccurate to the extent that it masks the complexity and subtlety of the process which Tim Asch and other film-makers have employed in recording particular events and the dynamics of collaboration with an anthropologist. To begin with, the term opportunistic has connotations of unplanned, and thus random, activity and overtones of exploitation. In regard to the Tana 'Ai films, the Bali films produced by the Aschs in collaboration with Dr Linda Connor, and the Roti films produced with James Fox, a better term would be "heuristic filming". Heuristic means "serving to find out or discover" (OED) and, in American usage,

providing aid or direction in the solution of a problem but otherwise unjusti-
fied or incapable of justification; of or relating to exploratory problem-solving
techniques that utilize self-educating techniques (as the evaluation of feedback) to improve performance.

(Webster's)

The *gren mahé* footage was shot as part of a larger project which has aimed to study
ritual as an element in the life of the Ata Tana 'Ai related to other aspects of Tana
'Ai life and in relation to other societies of eastern Indonesia. Much research had
already been done on these subjects and we went to Tana 'Ai in 1980 equipped
with what I had learned of ritual there during my first fieldwork. The project was
thus located in a larger problem situation, itself defined by the study of ritual as a
preoccupation of long-standing in anthropology and the emerging ethnology of
eastern Indonesian social and ceremonial systems.

There were two main problems which animated the Tana 'Ai film project. The
first was the ethnographic and ethnological problem of social organization in Tana
Wai Brama and its relation to the domain's ceremonial system and the religion of
its people. Insofar as religion involves ritual practice and practice requires actors,
film is an excellent medium for recording data pertaining to this general field of
anthropological study. Second was a cinematic problem which bears on questions
of method in the recording of anthropological data: how best to film a large-scale,
lengthy, and complex event involving many more people and simultaneous activities than can be accommodated within the frame of the camera as recording device.

Filming the *gren mahé* thus cannot be described as opportunistic in the sense that
the term has been used in the literature on ethnographic film because it was motivated by scientific problems and justified by the likelihood that it would enable us
to solve those problems. But there is a more compelling justification for describing
the Aschs work in Tana 'Ai as heuristic film-making.[1]

Once made, the film served not only as a source of data of use in solving the problems which generated it, but also led directly to new and interesting problems and
further questions about the function of ritual in the community of Tana Wai
Brama. It served as a means for finding out, for discovering, more about Tana 'Ai
than was known before. The film provided, in short, a powerful heuristic for further
ethnographic research, but it was only one part of a larger and longer trajectory of
discovery.

One finds in the first few paragraphs of many introductory textbooks on anthropology the profession that anthropology is the study of culture (or of society or of
human behavior or of the orderliness of human social life). The truth is that these
are high order constructs – theories, in other words. The immediate subject of
anthropological investigation is events, and the data from which the ethnographer
works are facts about events in which people do things, sometimes alone, but more
often together and interactively. These facts are recorded in one way or another (if
only in memory). Events and texts of events are thus the data which anthropologists as ethnographers study directly, not culture or society, and for which they

attempt to provide an account in ethnography. In the writing of ethnography, culture or (depending upon the anthropologist's intellectual propensities) society unfolds as a theory of these recorded data. Events evolve in time, in which they are rooted and of which they are an expression. Perhaps better than any other medium, film captures the temporality of events and it is this which makes film attractive to anthropologists as a medium for recording data.

Communication, verbal and of other kinds, is an important element of the social events which ethnographers record. When an anthropologist records behavior, much of what is recorded is communication and almost all of it has communicative value. In the case of records of verbal communication, what is produced as a record is a text of the event, written down, tape recorded, or filmed. Such records are texts because they are extracted from the situation – the context – of which they are an integral part. In a sense, the production of such textual records can be viewed as a part of the event which defines the situation; in any case, the recording of an event cannot satisfactorily be viewed as apart from or outside of the event itself.

A good illustration of this point is the fight sequence at the end of the *gren mahé*:[2] through the camera we see the fight or, at least, a selected part of it. But, for a fleeting moment, we also see Patsy Asch enter the frame from the right, wearing earphones, pointing a microphone at some of the fighters, and motioning urgently to Tim Asch, the cinematographer, to move forward and closer to the action. If Patsy had been edited out of the final montage, all we would see would be that part of the fight which Tim selected for filming. But another observer, one taking a broader perspective, would have seen and remarked upon (or recorded) another event as an integrated and seamless whole: an event which consisted of some men fighting, some men attending closely to the fight with lassos of vine ready to capture and restrain too violent fighters, scores of on-lookers, men chanting as they circle the nearby *mahé* altar, and three film-makers recording part of the event cinematically. The point is, of course, a simple one that has been made frequently in anthropology: the participant-observer is an observer because he records the event as it evolves; he is a participant because he cannot help but be so. His presence and activity are constituent elements of the event. Furthermore, since it is impossible for consociate human beings not to communicate (even silence or refusal to communicate communicates something about a person's construction of the situation), the participant-observers, in the case at hand the film-makers, are ineluctably active participants in the event rather than merely passive ones. Like it or not, they contribute to some extent both to the definition of the event and to its evolution. As Crawford (1992: 78), citing Breitrose, has put it, they are the fly in the soup rather than the fly on the wall.

It is precisely because of the interposition of the investigator that events such as the fighting at the end of the *gren mahé* raise questions of general scientific and ethnographic interest. The fighting we see in the film of the *gren mahé* seems at first chaotic, a breakdown of the order of ceremonial events which the previous footage of the ritual has adduced. But is it chaotic, unplanned, and random behavior? Information from two sources, one internal to the film and the other external to it, leads to the suspicion that it may not be. First, we see in the film that only some people are fighting and that all of the fighters are young men. Thus, not all of the defining elements and persons in the event are in chaos. Other people, most of them women and older men, are not fighting at all, but are doing other things. These other things include watching the fight, but there is more. We see a man smoking a cigarette calmly take an infant from Pius's arms as Pius (a young chanter and one of the film's narrators), excited by the fight, prepares to charge into the mêlée. The lassos have to have been made and imply preparation for an expected or intended occurrence. A man brandishing a bicycle chain has planned for the fight by bringing the chain, from which we can infer a degree of intentionality on the part of at least one of the fighters. Toward the end of the sequence we see Sina and Koa, two of the community's leaders who organized the *gren*, calmly consulting in the midst of the milling throng of fighters and spectators while other men dance and chant around the *mahé* altar. The fact that we can discern these distinctively different kinds of behavior within the larger situation in which the fight is only one element means that, while the fight may appear chaotic, it is embedded in a larger order. It is thus part of the definition of that order. Furthermore, because of the social distinctions apparent (it is only the young men who are fighting), a sociological analysis of the event is possible. Contrary to our initial impression, we may conclude that the scene is not one of chaos at all, but is exactly what, on closer examination, it can be seen to be: a fight engaged in by a minority of the people present and controlled by watchers at the center of an ongoing and evolving event which, at the more inclusive level of analysis, manifests a specifiable order. We can further conclude, on the internal evidence of the film alone, that the fight is part of the order of the event under study.

The second, external source of information about the fight is itself from two sources and offers perhaps even more compelling support for the thesis that the fight is more than an example of chaotic behavior and random occurrences. First, long before the *gren mahé* took place, I was told by people in the community that fighting was likely to happen in the *gren*; indeed, some of my informants seemed to look forward to a fight with pleasurable anticipation. I was told stories of fights in previous *gren mahé* and Pius, in his comments on the film, refers to those fights and implies that fighting is part of the plan of the *gren mahé*. He even offers his own theory of why fighting must occur in the *gren mahé* when he remarks:

> Usually, fighting happens because people are drunk. In the past it was according to tradition that men must fight. When we begin to go around the *mahé*, there must be a little fighting. But in the old days, it was not just a little fighting. Men would fight until some were stabbed and some died. It is said that men must fight so that their work will yield fruit.[3]

As he views himself in the film being led out of the *mahé* grove and away from the fight by a group of women, he remarks mirthfully:

Because my wives were there – the two of them – along with my mother and sister, they bound my arms. ... They were too strong for me; they were so many.[4]

Second, it is known from other ethnographic reports that fighting, combat, and other forms of competition are common in the ritual complexes of other eastern Indonesian societies, notably on the islands of Timor, Savu, and Sumba. The fighting that occurred in the *gren mahé* thus bears affinities of context to other societies in the region. Again we have evidence for the significance of the fight as an expected and planned element of the ritual complex within which it occurs. We are thus confronted by an interesting problem: why does fighting occur in the *gren mahé*? The film, as heuristic, both confirms that this is a legitimate and interesting problem and provides a source of data for addressing that problem.

However, heuristic film-making of this sort is not without its difficulties. When to turn the camera on and when to turn it off were always problems for us in Tana 'Ai (when does an event "begin" and when does it "end"?) Having not recognized that something is happening, should we begin filming once an event has already begun and even though we missed the beginning? How should we budget a limited supply of film for events we were not certain would occur and, when they did, how long they would last? Working in such a way, it was inevitable that we made what were, in retrospect, mistakes. But the most interesting problems we encountered were those which arose in post-production, when we began transforming the iconic recordings of events in the film record into ethnography.

The textualization of the cinematic record

... as anthropologists we most fruitfully admit films in evidence when we can relate them most effectively to sources outside the film itself. Many films have been preceded by ethnography, or give rise to additional ethnography as a by-product of the filming process, so films do not need to be thought of as 'stand-alone' texts.

(Loizos 1992: 50)

Film-making, as any other means of creating texts of events, involves both abstraction and reduction, an abstraction from the contexts within which events occur and evolve, and a reduction, both in time and in content (or "resolution"). The redescription of the content of events recorded on film and the re-establishment of the context of those events are the most difficult problems to be overcome in ethnographic film-making. They are solved, well or poorly as the case may be, in post-production, in analysis and editing of footage and in the creation of montage. With respect to the Tana 'Ai project, it may be useful to survey some of these problems by recounting the way we worked through our material and how we constructed our films.

Figure 6.1 Tim Asch on the journey to Watuwolon, Tana 'Ai, July, 1980.

Figure 6.2 Arrival at the house of Du'a Peni and Mo'an Koa, Watuwolon, with equipment, July 1980.

Sound recordings and subtitles

A general aim of the Tana 'Ai project was to provide film from which could be drawn ethnographic data on Tana 'Ai ritual. Much of what is important for the ethnography of Tana 'Ai is to be found in what people say to one another and how they say it. Thus, we approached sound recordings – of conversations and espe- cially, the chanting in ritual language which is a core feature of all Tana 'Ai ritual performance – with the same care we devoted to recording action on film. Indeed, there were occasions when we filmed because of what people were saying rather than because of other things they may have been doing.[5] Our usual method was to leave the tape recorder turning continuously when filming, even though the camera might be going on and off. For the purposes of my research, it was important to have complete recordings of ritual chanting and conversations, especially those which occurred between ritual specialists as they planned, organized, and negoti- ated the rituals. In addition to synchronous film sound (i.e. sound recorded contin- uously while we were filming), we made many hours of supplementary recordings of talk which we did not film.

Sound recordings are of little use unless they are transcribed and, as required, translated. To this end, we engaged a local Ata Tana 'Ai (a daughter of Mo'an Rapa Ipir Wai Brama, the late Source of the Domain), who transcribed sound recordings while we were in the field in 1980. After we returned to Canberra, I corrected these transcriptions as required and entered them onto a computer using a word-processing system. The work of translation, the analysis of these transcriptions, and linking them, first to the events in which they occurred, and second to the 16 mm footage, both illuminated the events we recorded and gener- ated many puzzles which could only be resolved through further fieldwork. These transcriptions have been of very great value for the writing of ethnographic accounts of Tana 'Ai. They also

Figure 6.3 Asch and Klétus Ipir Wai Brama, the son of the late Source of the Domain, cut climbing notches in a tree trunk. Watuwolon, 1980.

Figure 6.4 Asch filming a location shot of women dancing for the *gren mahé* ceremonies at the central ritual house of the Domain of Wai Brama. Watuwolon, 1980.

Figure 6.5 Asch filming the dance of the clan headwomen at the central ritual house of the Domain of Wai Brama. Watuwolon, 1980.

provided the basis for the creation of subtitles for the films we are producing, and it is this aspect of the work on which I would like to focus here.

Subtitling, as I have discovered in working with the Aschs, is an art and one that is subject to a number of technical constraints. First, one can include only a limited number of characters in a subtitle (in our films this number is 32) and the viewer of a film must be given sufficient time both to read and absorb a title and to absorb the visual image which it accompanies. Second, a minimum time must be allowed between each subtitle, even though the moving image is continuous. Here a number of difficulties arise. First, people often speak quickly and, in speaking, they overlap with one another. These facts often make it impossible to reduce all that is said in a given verbal exchange to translated subtitles, even when the translation is reduced to its simplest grammatical form and one which employs the fewest possible words. In much of our recorded material, there is more than one line of discourse, i.e. people may be talking about several things at once, not all of which can be accommodated in subtitles. In the most difficult instances, several people may be talking at once about different things, all of which pertain directly to the event being filmed. It is impossible to track all of these simultaneous utterances in translated subtitles.[6]

Subtitling the ritual speech of the Ata Tana 'Ai presents acute problems in this regard. Tana 'Ai ritual language is a genre of speech with a highly constrained grammatical order. Ritual speech can almost always be transcribed as couplets, with (usually) no more than four words per line, each of which pairs semantically with a word in the same position in the subsequent string (*ina nian tana wawa, ama lero wulan réta*, "mother earth and land below, father sun and moon above", is an example). Given its formulaic character and the usual pattern of eight words to a couplet, one could be forgiven for thinking that creating equally brief translations and, from them, succinct but complete subtitles would be a simple matter. But in this genre of speech, information is packed densely and most of the grammatical markers which occur in ordinary speech are either eliminated or greatly elided. One consequence of the form of ritual language is that utterances may lack subjects or verbs or predicates. Frequently in ritual language, actors or agents are not specified. In order for translated subtitles of couplets to make sense, grammatically more complete sentences in which subjects, actions, and objects are restored must be devised. This requirement, which leads to the expansion of the representation in English of the original utterance, can make continuous subtitling of the original speech all but impossible. Furthermore, the analysis of such speech as text requires a considerable knowledge of the language, the mythology, and the culture and social organization (the context) within which the speech occurs in Tana'Ai. Moreover, men usually speak ritual language very quickly and, as a result, the informational content of the speech itself in a given time is extraordinarily great, a feature of ritual language which is abetted by the grammatical elision of the form.[7] Thus, contrary to expectation, meaningful translations of a single couplet of ritual speech into English usually require a text considerably longer than eight words. These texts are exceedingly difficult to reduce to sensible subtitles. The same

Figure 6.6 Patsy Asch and Tim Asch film the clan headwomen of the Domain of Wai Brama as they dance around a rice mortar at the central ritual house of the domain in preparation for the *gren mahé* rituals. Watuwolon, October 1980.

Figure 6.7 Asch loads film while Mo'an Koa Tapo looks on. Watuwolon, 1980.

Figure 6.8   Tim and Patsy Asch filming Mo'an Déwa, Mo'an Sina, and Mo'an Koa discussing the exchange of a child between two clans. Munéwolon, 1980.

Figure 6.9   Tim and Patsy Asch filming the discussion of an exchange of a child between two clans. Munéwolon, 1980.

Figure 6.10 Tim Asch writes notes while Mo'an Sina (left) and Mo'an Koa (center, right) chant clan histories. Watuwolon, 1980.

problem occurs, although to a lesser extent, in the translation and subtitling of ordinary speech.

An example will illustrate the point. On the last night of the *gren mahé*, the chanters of the domain divided themselves into two groups. The first, led by Pius Ipir Wai Brama, stood above the ground inside the central ritual hut of the *mahé*. Pius's task was to chant that part of the mythic histories having to do with the origin of the elder of two brothers who founded the Domain of Wai Brama. His father, Sina Ipir Wai Brama, led a group of chanters who stood on the ground facing the hut, whose duty it was to recount the story of the younger of the founding brothers. The full text of a portion of the ritual speech recorded as film sound in this sequence of *A Celebration of Origins* and the subtitles we constructed from it are shown in Table 6.1.

A number of references in the original text would be meaningless to a non-Tana 'Ai audience, even if they were translated fully in subtitles. Mia, Néin, Bapa, and Jago (lines 1–2) and Pipak, Lédu, Kora, and Kilan (lines 17–18) are ancestors of clans in Tana Wai Brama. The import of invoking them in this chant would require more didactic exposition than can reasonably be accommodated in a film. Lines 15–16 are a highly elliptic reference to a key event and the relationship between the peoples of two areas of Tana Wai Brama. The *mahé* of the domain is said to have been located at Waibou at an unspecified time in the history of the domain but,

Table 6.1 Sample text of ritual language with full English translations and subtitles[8]

	Chanter	Original text	English Translation	Subtitles
	Sina:	Da'a Mia nora Néin ko	reach Mia and Néin	∅
2		toma Bapa nora Jago	get to Bapa and Jago	∅
		topo wi'ir wiri wana ko	summon our friends from the left and right	Summon friends from left and right.
4		hawon wi'ir papa ruan	call our companions from both sides	Call companions from both sides.
		ha nulut ha detu	one goes before and the other follows	∅
6		ha wa'at ha depo	one at the head and one behind	∅
		pano tena dolor blon ko	travel in single file	Travel in single file.
8		rema tena lalan lodar	journey one following the other	Journey one behind the other.
		ha lupa ha heron	if one forgets the other will speak	If one forgets the other will speak.
10		ha hulir ha donen	if one leaves out the other will point the way	If one gets lost, the other will point the way.
		oh ...		∅
12	Pius:	Oh, di	Oh, also	∅
		marin molé ganu nué ko	speak also in this way	∅
14		heron molé ganu eté	say this also	
		heron nian ata ué ko	talk of the land who is the older sibling	
16		tat tanat té'é lolon	speak of the earth that rests above	
		da'a Pipak nora Lédu ko	remember Pipak and Lédu	*No subtitles;*
18		da'a Kora nora Kilan	recall Kora and Kilan	*voice-over*
		di mait leku unen ko	who also come to our thoughts within	*translation of Pius's*
20		bawo ola nain	and come up in our inner considerations	*explanation of the*
		baké putik Nian Tana ko	pull out the pointed chisel of the Land and Earth	*chanting;*
22		réan laba Lero Wulan	uproot the broad-faced chisel of the Sun and Moon	*chant on soundtrack in*
		leku leku wali unen ko	from the space for our thoughts within us	*background.*
24		ola ola wali nain	the cavity within which we place our contemplation	
		kirek apak wali mai ko	add to our thoughts within us	∅
26		lagar lagar wali bawo	increase our ideas within us	∅

Table 6.1 Sample text of ritual language with full English translations and subtitles (cont'd)

Chanter	Original text	English Translation	Subtitles
	kirek ganu peru hura ko	make our thoughts like the pattern of the threads	Make our thoughts like the pattern of threads.
28	lagar ganu kélan tola	and color our ideas like the red patola cloth	Color our ideas like the red patola cloth.
	beta beta da'a ha ko	speak to one more true thing	∅
30	pa'en pa'en toma moga	and utter also another metaphor	∅
	apak dira ira napun ko	add the sharpness of the blades of grass of the valley	Add the sharpness of the valley's grasses.
32	apak na dulun wolon ko	add the strength of the hard timber of the mountain	Add the strength of the mountain's timber.

because the people of Waibou were inhospitable to guests attending a gren mahé held there, the mahé was moved to its present location near Watuwolon. Because of its earlier stewardship of the mahé, Waibou is still recognized as the ué (= wué), "elder sibling", of Watuwolon and, by implication, the people of clan Ipir at Waibou are, in the context of the gren mahé, as elder siblings to those at Watuwolon. Thus, Pius continues by invoking the ancestors of clan Ipir at Waibou, Pipak, Lédu, Kora, and Kilan, reminding the gathered ritualists that, even though the people of Watuwolon are now the custodians of the mahé, the links to Waibou as the original site of the mahé are to be remembered and the ancestors of that place are to be summoned to the gren.

Lines 21–22 refer to chisels of the Land and Earth and the Sun and Moon, the four aspects of the deity of the Ata Tana 'Ai. Here, Pius asks the deity to remove the chisels which it has used to open the minds of the ritualists so that memory of the histories may enter them and so that the chanting of the histories of the domain may be complete. These lines invoke conceptions of the person and its relationship to thought that are beyond the capacity of film to explain satisfactorily. Indeed, most of ritual language raises problems of translation which cannot be fully dealt with in a film except by the use of unacceptably intrusive didactic titles or narration.

In subtitling translations of ritual speech for A Celebration of Origins, it proved impossible to provide any sort of a coherent and meaningful (to a western audience) running translation of everything that was being said. The only possible solutions to this problem were to leave ritual speech untitled (in which case the viewer of the film sees only talking heads and is left wondering what is being said) or to focus on one theme of the speech and provide a translation of every other or every fourth couplet pertaining to that theme. This is what we have done (in the sample text, we translated ten of thirty lines of ritual language), even though it does considerable violence to the poetical register of the genre and to the semantic complexity and subtlety of the speech. In other words, what has been required is an intentional abstraction and reduction from the totality captured in film and sound. Our aim has been to convey to the viewer at least a part of that complexity and at the same time to signal that something of considerably greater complexity and interest than what is subtitled is unfolding in the event depicted on the screen.[9]

Film, feedback, and montage

The making of an ethnographic film requires the construction of an edited montage. Editing begins in the choices made by a cinematographer about what to film and what not to film. It continues when the camera is turned on. Only activities within the focused depth of field are recorded clearly and only those within the frame, which can be, within limits, widened or narrowed. Within the limits of cinematographic technology, these are matters of choice on the part of the film-maker who, if the resulting images are to be useful in constructing a meaningful montage, must make his choices in light of a theory[10] of the event being filmed. The theory which informs a dramatic film is encompassed by its screenplay and the shooting script; in ethnographic film-making it lies in the anthropologist/film-maker's understanding of the event before the camera in relation to other events and to persons and their actions as cinematic subjects. It is probably true that the less well developed the theory of the event, the more difficult it is to construct from the camera footage a montage that meaningfully represents the event.[11]

In shooting footage of the *gren mahé*, the Aschs and I had little idea (no reliable theory) of the structure of the event in time, i.e. the sequence of its constituent elements, and very little idea of what the Ata Tana 'Ai themselves considered to be significant about it. In place of an understanding of the temporal order of the specific event we were to film, we drew upon my general knowledge of ritual in the community and decided to follow closely a limited number of persons (among them, Sina, Koa, Déwa, and Pius) who we had good reason to believe would be, as ritual specialists and leaders, central actors in the *gren*. Over several weeks of preparation for the *gren* and during the rituals themselves, Tim filmed much else besides these four men, but he always came back to them because we assumed (i.e. relied on the theory) that, whenever something of central importance in the *gren* occurred, one or more of these people would be present.[12] We hoped that this strategy would allow us to construct a film around the theme of ritual leadership.

This we were able to do, but in editing the film it became apparent that several questions which would likely preoccupy an audience would have to be addressed. First of all, why the focus on these particular men among the hundreds of people who participated in the rites? Why, indeed, the focus on the activities of men and not the women who are visibly present in the footage? Why not focus on some other ritualists or take the viewpoint of a clan headwoman or a young participant? In order for the film to address these questions we resorted to didactic narration, through which we explain the system of ceremonial and mythic precedence which informs ritual action in Tana 'Ai, and in terms of which (1) the actions of the men upon whom we focused can be understood and (2) our choices of subjects can be justified.[13] Much of the material on which the narration is based resulted from extensive interviews with a variety of Ata Tana 'Ai with whom I viewed videotape transfers of the film in 1982 and 1983. We then incorporated the comments of Pius Ipir Wai Brama, who we brought to Canberra in 1984 and with whom I worked extensively to record his exegesis of the events of 1980. This feedback sharpened both our understanding of the event and its place in the social life of Tana Wai Brama, but also enabled us to document the different views of the gren held by different members of the community (see Lewis 1989). Voice-over translations of Pius's remarks on the film and on the gren are a third and very important narrative line in A Celebration of Origins.

The strategy of following the activities of a few selected ritual leaders provided us with the theory we needed for filming. However, it has resulted in a film which raises a second question of importance in relation to the ethnography of Tana Wai Brama. The gren mahé is first and foremost a religious festival. In it, the Ata Tana 'Ai invoke and address directly their deity, Nian Tana Lero Wulan ("the Land and Earth, the Sun and Moon"). The ritual action in which the ritualists engage is aimed at this end or at the invocation of spirits of the land or the ancestral spirits of the clans of the domain. Gods and spirits are, however, notoriously difficult to film, even more difficult, perhaps, than filming the reason for the relative inactivity of women in the mahé forest. It is not sufficient to show the image of a man invoking his clan ancestors and, over that, running a narration to the effect that "Here is so and so addressing his ancestors". Such narration is redundant; worse, it makes for bad film and poor ethnography because, by raising unanswered questions, it confuses rather than clarifies. In any case, the events and individual actions we depict in A Celebration of Origins are hardly marked by a reverent attitude toward the divine or by a submissive demeanor in the presence of ancestors. It would thus be not only ludicrous, but also a gross distortion of the facts, for a disembodied voice to intone, over images of men bashing each other with clubs, words such as "Here are the Ata Tana 'Ai worshipping their deity and honoring their ancestors". The images of the gren are most definitely not the stuff of Millennium (Biniman Productions 1992), in which wizened tribal elders graciously explain to a European-American seeker fundamental, closer-to-nature-than-you-are truths from which all men would benefit. As one of my post-Millennium undergraduate students put it after viewing A Celebration of Origins, "I guess the Ata Tana 'Ai aren't very spiritual, are they?" The answer to this question is simply that, while all peoples demarcate the sacred, attitudes toward it and behavior in its presence are greatly variable, and one thing for certain is that if one comes across a quietly composed Ata Tana 'Ai with his eyes closed, he may be asleep, but he is most certainly not expressing a reverent attitude toward his deity and ancestors.

The *gren mahé* is nonetheless the most profoundly religious event in the ritual repertoire of the Ata Tana 'Ai. The problem is that little of this profundity can be communicated directly in film, for it subsists in ideas and not in action. We can translate the chanting of men "seeking the sources" of creation and Tana Wai Brama's clans, and we can depict the sacrifice of goats, whose severed heads are, for the deity, rubbed roughly on a distinctly paganistic forked tree trunk and monoliths. But how can we communicate in film the profoundly beautiful system of thought which orders what, visually, an audience can mistake to be simply drunken revelry?

Film and ethnography

The answer to the last question is that, as Tim Asch long argued, ethnographic films must be accompanied by written ethnography – preferably, written ethnography which addresses material presented in and addressed by film. This can, of course, mean written materials, such as film study guides or ethnographic film monographs, such as *Jero Tapakan: Balinese Healer* (Connor et al. 1986). But formal ethnographies which do not directly address a related film (such as Lewis 1988) can also fulfil this need.

While Asch's advocacy of written ethnography to complement ethnographic films is of obvious merit, there is another relationship which film can have to ethnographic writing. Film is a research tool which can cast a powerful light upon matters of considerable anthropological interest; indeed, it can reveal unsuspected facets of an ethnographer's subject or focus attention upon previously unrealized aspects of a subject already investigated. I will offer an example to illustrate what I mean.

At two points during the *gren mahé*, Sina Ipir Wai Brama danced to the drums and gongs which were played almost continuously during the rituals.[14] Tim filmed both of these dances, neither of which impressed me as particularly significant; indeed, at the time, Sina's dance did not strike me as especially worthy of filming. During interviews with Ata Tana 'Ai in 1982, in which I used videotape transfers of the *gren* footage to elicit informants' exegeses of the filmed events, a number of informants remarked on Sina's dancing and two or three made extensive comments on it. I had not known before then that ritual leaders were not meant to dance during the *gren* in the free style of the young men and visitors, but were supposed to participate only in the circle dances around the *mahé* altar and for the purpose of leading chants. The unexpected attention which my informants devoted to this incident when reviewing the footage led me to think about the ways in which ritual leaders, through their individual ambitions and intentions, can bring about change in the form and content of a ritual performance. This line of thought led me to consider that, rather than a form of performance or expression which is resistant to change (or conceived by participants to be unchanging), ritual in Tana 'Ai (and especially large-scale rituals) can serve to introduce change in the community or to confirm changes which have already occurred as in accord with *hadat* (Sara Sikka: "custom", "law", "propriety").[15]

Figure 6.11 Asch watches the video of a burial with residents of Watuwolon, 1980. Experimentation with the use of video for elicitation of information from informants
about filmed events was a major aim of the Tana 'Ai film project.

In producing A *Celebration of Origins*, we devoted considerable attention to the
ways in which we had made texts of the events of the *gren mahé*. First, we linked
the visual montage as closely as possible to translated subtitles of speakers on film.
While much information is lost through the linguistic reductions required for
subtitling, the gain is a narrative progression in which the participants in the
filmed events themselves establish the film's principal ethnographic motifs.
Second, we employed a translated voice-over commentary on the events and
people in the film, drawn from the recorded remarks made by Pius Ipir Wai Brama,
a Tana 'Ai ritual leader, as an explanatory narration of some of the events depicted
in the montage. Third, we added where necessary for the film's continuity a voice-
over narration by the anthropologist. We restricted the last narration as much as
possible to avoid its intrusion into the film's thematic development. This narration
serves to provide:

1   running and free translations of myths recounted in ritual language by Tana
     'Ai chanters (shots 7–10);
2   extrapolations from and synopses of the mythic histories of the domain which
     provide contextual information on the filmed events (shots 10–24);
3   introductions to some of the principal characters in the film as they make their
     appearances (shots 18 [Sina], 19–24 [Pius], 34–5 [Rudun, the headwoman],
     39 [Koa], 44–5, 64 [Déwa], and 75 [Om Lawé, the government official]);

4   a bridge between major divisions of the film and to signal intervals of time omitted from montage (shots 28, 30, 36–8, 64, 75, 93).

In addition, shots 143–4 contain a translated quotation of Koa, one of the principals of the *gren mahé* on the subjects of sacrifice and the deity, spoken by the anthropologist, and the film's epilogue has the anthropologist posing a final question about the *gren* to Pius, the commentator. These three narrative lines provide for the accretion of texts, the one descriptive and the others in varying degrees reflexive, which allow the film to move from iconic representation to ethnographic redescription and explanation. However, the film itself played an important role in the research upon which the ethnographic movement from the iconic to the explanatory occurred.

Photo-elicitation: experiments in informant feedback in Tana 'Ai

The advent of portable tape recorders provided anthropologists and linguists with a powerful tool for recording ethnographic data. With the development of small, power-efficient, inexpensive, and dependable audiocassette recorders in the 1970s, a substantial change in the way anthropologists recorded interviews and social events came about. The history of the effects of these technological developments on ethnography has yet to be written, but they have undoubtedly been substantial. So, too, has the advent of portable videocassette recorders, which allow the addition of visual images to recorded sound. Whereas sound recorders allowed anthropologists to record speech and verbal interaction efficiently, the possibilities for studying non-verbal behavior coupled with verbal behavior brought about by video technology are still being explored. Tim Asch was among the anthropologists who first realized the potential for using video recordings for immediate feedback with informants.

An important aim of the Tana 'Ai project was to experiment with methods of using videotape recordings with informants to elicit immediate informant feedback about events recorded with videotape. For this purpose we took to the field a portable videotape recorder and camera with a low intensity vidicon tube and a small, battery-powered video monitor.

On the night of 18 August 1980, Mo'an Ria, the brother of the woman in whose garden we were living, died in his garden some distance from Watuwolon. Ria's body was brought to the house of Du'a Sano Liwu Pigang Bitak, his oldest sister, for burial. Two mornings later, as people gathered at the house for Ria's burial rites, Tim and I consulted with Mo'an Koa about videotaping the burial.[16] Koa agreed to our proposal and Tim made a videotape recording of the event.

On two occasions, four days and nine days after Mo'an Ria's burial, I went through the videotape of the ceremony which Tim had made with Mo'an Sina, the leading ritualist of the community. Sina, who had presided over the burial, commented on many points of the proceedings which I would have undoubtedly overlooked had I relied on observation alone as a means of recording the burial.[17] I was especially interested in a complex sequence of actions carried out at the foot of the grave after the corpse was buried and Tim had taped the whole of this sequence.[18] Sina's comments revealed an order of named actions in the rite which would have been difficult to establish without the videotape as evidence.

An Ata Tana 'Ai is buried at the boundary between the cleared house yard of his mother's *lepo* and the bush which surrounds it. To mark the place of the head of the grave a length of sturdy bamboo, of the species which the Ata Tana 'Ai call *aur*, is driven into the earth precisely at the border between the house yard and the bush. After the grave is dug, the ritualists strike this bamboo in an action called *heput aur*, "to strike the *aur*". This bamboo demarcates the main axis of the ritual of burial, and Sina said that striking it calls the assembled mourners to order. The word *heput* also means (1) "to measure" and (2) "to touch quickly or fleetingly". After the corpse has been buried, a small flat stone is driven upright into the earth at the head of the grave and, before it, another small flat stone, called *blepen*, is laid on the earth as an altar for offerings of tobacco, areca nut, betel leaf and fruit, and lime. The lateral boundaries of the grave are demarcated with lengths of a thin, vine-like bamboo. These markers along the side of the grave are called *leban*. A long length of this thin bamboo is stuck into the ground a meter or so from the foot of the grave. This bamboo is the *sou*, which figures into the ceremonial cooking of rice for the dead after the burial is completed. *Leban* is also the place on the shoulder where one carries a bamboo-carrying pole. These bamboos are for the use of the deceased for transporting the offerings made to him. In addition, *saket*, "stakes", are driven into the earth at each of the four corners of the grave. These are some of the matters concerning the burial which Mo'an Sina explained to me as he and I reviewed the videotape recording of the event.

When I asked about the *leban*, Mo'an Sina responded with a citation of ritual language:

Lepo huler unen,
Woga klakat wutun.

Huler is the first woody plant to re-establish itself in an abandoned garden as the field reverts to forest; *klakat* is the pattern in which the roots of a plant spread out in the earth. These two lines can thus be translated:

The house (is like) the strong wood inside of *huler*,
The visitors' pavilion is rooted strongly in the earth.

Sina thus likened the grave to a construction with the permanence of the *lepo* and one which is intimately associated with it. Furthermore, this phrase reveals a metaphorical association between the recently dead who are entering a new kind of existence as ancestors, and the regeneration of a recently "dead garden" in the form of new forest.

In commenting on the videotape Sina also explicated fully the rite of cooking rice for the dead at the foot of the grave, which I had witnessed before in Tana 'Ai but about which I had previously elicited little detailed information.[19] In this rite, all actions are done in the reverse of normal cooking, which expresses the relationship between the living and dead as one of inversion. With the video recording of the rite before us, Sina explained fully the elements of the sequence and the way in which one led to the next. All of his information revealed much of value about conceptions of death and the relations of the living to the dead.

One of the benefits of the use of videotape recordings of events such as the burial is that it enables the anthropologist to separate the exigent from the contingent in action, especially in the performance of ritual. The striking of the *aur*, for example, is not the contingent action that it might seem; rather, it is something done meaningfully and intentionally. The first clue to this is that it is a named action (*heput aur*); the second is that, upon reviewing the videotape, informants called attention to it and commented on it. In this instance, the use of videotape allowed me to elicit much more finely-grained information about the event than would have been possible by using the technique of recording observations in a notebook. The result was an ethnographic analysis of the event with much greater resolution than would have otherwise been possible.

A video or film recording of an event is not just a text of the event, but an iconic text in which, within the video signal, there is a direct correspondence between the components of the field of observation (the photographic field) and the recorded text (the emulsion or video frame). The employment of iconic recording techniques does not eliminate the need to make decisions about what to record, but it does improve the mnemonic value of the recording over, for example, the memory of the anthropologist or the written field note. Because the camera records more than just the recordist's intended object, the photographic text frequently contains not only information about that object but also further latent and discoverable information.

A good illustration of what I mean occurred during the *gren mahé*. I had witnessed animals being sacrificed in ritual in Tana 'Ai many times. However, close examination of the film we shot of the 1980 *gren mahé* revealed that, before the sacrifice of some of the animals in the *gren*, a ritualist circled the *mahé* altar four times, sprinkling rice on the stones and wood of the altar as he went. In one sequence of the film,[20] he then walked to the nearby place above the altar where other men prepared the animals for sacrifice. With rice left over from his offerings at the altar, the ritualist quickly and almost furtively sprinkled rice onto the neck of the sacrificial animal just before the blade fell on the animal's neck. This was an element in the sacrifice which I had not noticed at the time of the event; nor had I observed it previously in other sacrifices in Tana 'Ai. In reviewing the film with informants in 1982, it became clear from their answers to my questions that the sprinkling of rice on the animal's neck was a consecratory element of some importance in the sacrifice and one which related directly to the main purposes of the sacrifice. The study of visual recordings of events, especially when carried out in

collaboration with informants, can establish many such ethnographically significant relationships between elements of an event which might or might not be
noticed by the keenest observer.

However video and film might improve the corpus of data from which the
anthropologist works, they do not in themselves record the structures of meaning
and patterns of behavior of interest to anthropologists. And however much they
provide improved means for recording data, they do not in themselves improve the
standard of ethnographic analysis for which they provide the empirical ground.
Indeed, rather than making the anthropologist's task easier, in some respects high-
quality iconic records can make it more difficult, first, because of the increased
amount of data which becomes available and second, because the analyst must be
more acute in developing an analysis of these data.

There is also the problem of too much data. As linguists have long known, the
time required properly to analyze a sound recording is an order of magnitude
greater than the length of the recording. The same holds true for videotape and film
as media of recording. For this reason, iconic records must be made selectively and
with particular aims in mind. The most profitable situation in which to use film or
video is thus to record events about which the anthropologist already possesses
some knowledge from previous fieldwork. It is counterproductive, and very
expensive in terms of material and effort, to attempt to record everything that
occurs in a given period of time. In working with Tim Asch, I discovered that
video and film are most valuable as tools for the refinement of knowledge about
subjects of which I already knew something. Visual recordings are thus of particular utility at one stage in the evolution of the heuristic of fieldwork. The case of
Ria's burial is instructive in this regard. Had I not already understood the main
social relationships which a death invokes (as, for example, those between givers
and receivers of husbands) and the patterns of symbolic action which commonly
animate ritual, then no amount of videotape or film would have enabled me to
work out the meanings specific to the burial of Mo'an Ria and the ways in which
they illuminate more general ritual processes in Tana 'Ai. As Tim Asch has
always insisted, the audiovisual iconic recording always points to elements of the
epistemological situation of fieldwork beyond the text itself and the film or video
can thus never stand alone.

The value of a film or video record of an event is never wholly in the images
themselves. Rather, the film image can form an important link in a chain of textual
redescriptions of the event. A concrete example of one such process will help illustrate the point. After filming the *gren mahé* in 1980, the Aschs and I returned to
Tana Wai Brama in 1982 with video transfers of our 16 mm footage and portable
video equipment. I worked with informants to elicit their comments and exegeses
of the events which we filmed. The data thus generated, the informants' exegeses of
the filmed events, have played a crucial role as secondary data in the ethnographic
reconstruction of the *gren mahé* rituals. However, a further stage of analysis has
been made possible. I have also used the texts of informants' exegeses as objects of
further study in collaboration with informants. The results of this work are tertiary

texts which shed light primarily upon the language of interpretation and the participants' exegesis itself. It is at this level of analysis that important discoveries can be made about the logic with which informants approach not the original event, but the representation of that event in language. Each subsequent text not only provides additional data but also a meta-text or theory of the previous text. The chain of textual redescription can be represented in the following diagram.

EVENT →	TEXT$_1$→	TEXT$_2$→	TEXT$_3$→	TEXT$_4$→	TEXT$_n$
	Iconic recording	Informants' exegesis of iconic recording	Informants' exegesis of informants' exegesis	Anthropologists' analysis (film and/or written ethnography)	

In the past, anthropologists largely proceeded directly from field notes and memory of events, behavior, conversations, and the like to an analysis of those events. With film and video, as with, to a lesser extent, sound recordings and photographs, anthropologists can easily interpose informants' redescriptions of the events under study into the chain of redescriptive texts which culminate in a formal ethnographic analysis.[21] The participants' understandings of the event become available to the anthropologist as secondary data through their comments on and exegeses of the cinematic record. The true value of film and video as a research tool is, as Tim Asch long realized, in its quality as an iconic recording of the original event. As a text, the cinematic record is no less selective in its origins than are an ethnographer's field notes, but it removes by one step the need for interpretation and analysis, thereby providing the opportunity for informants themselves to participate directly in the ethnographic interpretation of events. It is, after all, their understandings of events and the meanings which adhere to them that anthropology seeks to comprehend and toward which Tim Asch strove in his career as an anthropological film-maker.

Notes

1 Sorenson and Jablonko themselves come close to the view I develop here. In the work cited above, they further remark:

> When a photographer is filming opportunistically, he flows with the events of the day and cues into them at some personal level, suddenly noticing that "something" is about to happen and following such events intuitively, without a worked-out plan. He takes it as it comes. Thus, the visual data sample achieved reflects the personality of the filmer: it takes its form and content from his interests, inclinations, and style. But *linking the camera to the pattern-recognizing capability of the human mind, the visual data sample reflects prearticulated stages of discovery.* Such footage may not always be directly relevant to a predetermined scientific study, but it can be a powerful resource in the quest for knowledge.
> (Sorenson and Jablonko 1975: 153, emphasis added)

2 Shots 157–70 in *A Celebration of Origins* (Asch, Lewis and Asch 1993).
3 Asch, Lewis and Asch (1993: shots 162–5).
4 Asch, Lewis and Asch (1993: shot 170).
5 Examples of occasions on which the oratorical content of an event, rather than its ostensible content,

prompted filming include meetings of ritual leaders prior to the *gren mahé* in which they discussed plans for the rituals, the discussion of the pig for sacrifice at the *blikon* boundary (Asch, Lewis and Asch 1993: shots 39–43, 46–51), and the chanting of the histories of the domain (depicted briefly in Asch, Lewis and Asch 1993: shots 6–9, 56, and 88–92). The last instance is of interest because the significance of the event is found both in its oratory and its ostension. Generally, film of people speaking in an alien tongue is not of great interest to an audience of non-specialists, however pregnant with ethnographic information the cinematic record of such events may be. We had intended to include uncut the footage of these events in the research film on the *gren mahé* which we planned to make.

6 At one stage in editing *A Celebration of Origins* Patsy Asch and I considered making a series of white-on-black titles with more complete translations of the dialogue of several speakers and interposing these in one such complex speech event. We decided, however, that the continuity of the visual image would be seriously undermined and did not proceed with this plan.

7 One man who chanted during the *gren mahé* sustained his recitation at an average rate of 246.5 words per minute, not an unusual rate of speaking in ritual language among the chanters of Tana Wai Brama.

8 From Asch, Lewis and Asch (1993: shots 88–92).

9 For many years, Tim Asch strongly advocated supplementing ethnographic films with written ethnography. In a written account of an event such as the *gren mahé*, the anthropologist has an opportunity to provide fuller written texts of speech such as the chanted myths of the Ata Tana 'Ai. Thus, film and writing together can provide vastly more ethnographic detail than can either medium alone (see Asch 1992:199).

10 A word which shares its etymology with theater, from the Greek *theoria*, "a looking, a seeing, an observing or a contemplation, hence a speculation" (Partridge 1966).

11 Two faces of the multifaceted problem of meaning arise here. First, let us suppose that, as editors, we wish to construct a sensible montage from a corpus of film resulting entirely from seized opportunities such as those advocated by Sorenson and Jablonko (*supra*). Even though no prior theory informed the shooting of the film, one would be required if the montage is not to be a chaotic jumble of images. That is, as a minimal requirement, the montage must express or reflect some intention on the part of the editor. Second, if the montage is to be sensible not only to one audience, but both to those people whose actions are recorded on the film and to an alien audience, as is commonly the case with ethnographic films, then the montage must not grossly deform the actors' theory of the event. At the same time, it must provide a translation (a second theory) of those actions which is a reasonable transform of the first theory.

12 Or, to turn the proposition around, in the weeks before the *gren*, wherever one of these men happened to be, something of pertinence to the *gren mahé* might occur.

13 The theory which guided our choices on this matter came out of the research I conducted in Tana Wai Brama in 1978 and 1979. It is worth noting that men are enfranchised to perform ritual through their relations to their mothers and sisters, through whom clan and house affiliations are determined. Men thus perform ritual on behalf of the women who are *pu'an*, "source" or "central" (i.e. "trunk") in the major social groups of the community. General points, such as the conception of the Ata Tana 'Ai of women as "source" or "trunk" and men as "peripheral" or "issue", are difficult to establish visually with film because they are elements of a noumenal ideology rather than manifest (and, therefore, filmable) action (see Lewis 1988, especially Chapter XIV, for an analysis of Tana 'Ai gender classifications). One can, of course, overlay image with didactic narration, but this option too easily clutters a film.

14 Asch, Lewis and Asch (1993: shots 101–3 and 113–14).

15 An argument for this thesis, which, I believe, bears on a general theory of social change, has appeared in Lewis (1989). *A Celebration of Origins* grew out of the ethnographic research reported in *People of the Source* (Lewis 1988); other writings on the Ata Tana 'Ai are by-products of the filming which produced *A Celebration of Origins*. The Tana 'Ai film project thus accords with Loizos's thesis that "films do not need to be thought of as 'stand-alone' texts" (Loizos 1992: 50).

16 We decided not to film the burial because we feared that the equipment for filming might be an inconvenience for Ria's family.

17 I have described the burial rituals of Tana Wai Brama in Lewis 1988, Chapters VI and XIII.

18 I had witnessed this ritual sequence once before, at the burial of the old Source of the Domain in 1979, shortly before the conclusion of my first fieldwork in Tana 'Ai. I had not then learned much about it.

19 This rite is described in Lewis (1988: 278–80).

20 Shot number 119 in *A Celebration of Origins*.

21 For a more detailed example of the utility of informants' redescriptions of events for ethnography, see Lewis (1989).

References

Asch, Timothy (1992), "The Ethics of Ethnographic Film-Making". In Peter Ian Crawford and David Turton (eds.), *Film as Ethnography*. Manchester: Manchester University Press, pp. 196–204.

Connor, Linda, Patsy Asch and Timothy Asch (1986), *Jero Tapakan: Balinese Healer. An Ethnographic Film Monograph*. Cambridge: Cambridge University Press.

Crawford, Peter Ian (1992), "Film as Discourse: The Invention of Anthropological Realities". In Peter Ian Crawford and David Turton (eds.), *Film as Ethnography*. Manchester: Manchester University Press, pp. 66–82.

Lewis, E. Douglas (1988), *People of the Source. The Social and Ceremonial Order of Tana Wai Brama on Flores*. Verhandelingen van het Instituut voor Taal-, Land- en Volkenkunde No. 135. Dordrecht, Holland and Providence, Rhode Island, USA: Foris Publications.

—— (1989), "Why Did Sina Dance? Stochasm, Choice and Intentionality in the Ritual Life of the Ata Tana 'Ai of Eastern Flores". In Paul Alexander (ed.), *Creating Indonesian Cultures*. Sydney: Oceania Publications, pp. 175–98.

Loizos, Peter (1992), "Admissible Evidence? Film in Anthropology". In Peter Ian Crawford and David Turton (eds.), *Film as Ethnography*. Manchester: Manchester University Press, pp. 50–65.

Partridge, Eric (1966), *Origins: A Short Etymological Dictionary of Modern English*. Fourth Edition. London: Routledge & Kegan Paul.

Sorenson, E. Richard and Allison Jablonko (1975), "Research Filming of Naturally Occurring Phenomena: Basic Strategies". In Paul Hockings (ed.), *Principles of Visual Anthropology*. The Hague: Mouton Publishers, pp. 151–63.

Films

Asch, Timothy, E. D. Lewis and Patsy Asch (1993), *A Celebration of Origins*. Watertown, Massachusetts: Documentary Educational Resources, Inc. 47 minutes, 16 mm film, sound synch, color.

Biniman Productions (1992), *Millennium*. London: Biniman Productions Ltd, Adrian Malone Productions Ltd, KCET Los Angeles, and BBC-TV in association with The Global Television Network. Video.

Chapter 7

The consequences of conation

Pedagogy and the inductive films of an ethical film-maker[1]

Greg Acciaioli

That's what's exciting about teaching some students: they're willing to suspend preconceived ideas about the world and themselves and concentrate on what it is you're trying to lead them towards ... and they're putting that into their mind, that good mind, with the other things that are there, and they will make some individual mix out of all of this. And out of that will develop something unique of their own, but I'll have had a part in the educational process they're going through ... not shaping their mind but in providing a resource for their own potential to work on, and that's valuable. And film helps a lot, it inspires me to teach the subject in a more exciting way ...

(Tim Asch quoted in Martínez 1995: 56)

Introduction: characterizing Tim Asch's work – from modernist realism to the modernist/post-modernist tension

In his magisterial survey of developments in ethnographic film from the mid-1950s to the mid-1980s, Peter Loizos (1993: 23–9, 39–42) restricts his consideration of Tim Asch's contribution to ethnographic film largely to the project of documentation, the production of films of record. Loizos notes the innovations of "sequence filming", single-event films, and intensive collaboration with anthropologists, but refers to the products of the two seasons of filming with the Yanomamö merely as "documentation films" similar to the "direct cinema" of Leacock and others.[2] Even in presenting Tim Asch's subsequent work, in collaboration with sound recordist and film editor Patsy Asch and anthropologist Linda Connor, and, most importantly, the Balinese medium Jero Tapakan, Loizos (1993: 39) still highlighted the aspect of "documentation filming", treating even the film *Jero on Jero* as a "meta-document ... 'documenting' a process of exogenously-produced change" (Loizos 1993: 41). Loizos assiduously catalogues a number of changes in emphasis that the Jero Tapakan films effected relative to the Yanomamö *oeuvre*, in part echoing aims, such as the depiction of conversation, displaying reactions of the subjects to their own filmic depictions, and the provision of accompanying written materials (such as Connor *et al.* 1986, 1996) that Asch (1996: 34 ff.) himself enunciated. Yet, Loizos's reiteration of the documentation aim emphasizes the continuities of this project with the Yanomamö films – "the goals which Asch took from Venezuela to Bali " (Loizos 1993: 41) – rather than the Bali project's innovations. Even his noting some of the tensions between Patsy Asch's disclaimers of any direct filmic mirroring of reality and the devotion to ethnographic detail in the films associates the films themselves with the naïveté of a past filmic epistemology rather than with the sophisticated self-consciousness and explicit concern with textuality of the films Loizos treats later in his book.

Such an evaluation tends to situate Asch's contribution within the "age of innocence" whose passing Loizos insightfully documents (Acciaioli 1997a: 215). Indeed, some warrant for this characterization can be found in Asch's own writings. In the early manifesto of the principles of ethnographic film co-authored with John Marshall and Peter Spier, Asch emphasized the value of the camera "to do and record what the human eye cannot" (Asch et al. 1973: 179), its function is one of preservation. But the claims made in that article, claims that Asch problematized in his later films and writings, are complex. The article highlights a concern with the structure of events, not only "as interpreted by participants", but also "in the mind of the viewer" (Asch et al. 1973: 179). Although seeming initially to assert a naïve iconism – simple reproduction and preservation – between those two loci of structuring, the authors go on to qualify this position by emphasizing the situated nature of the camera as recording instrument, the delimitation of the event by the agency of the camera operator, the selectivity introduced by editing, and the active participation of the viewers in constructing diverse interpretations. The admission of three levels of restructuring which necessarily occur through the acts of filming, editing, and viewing undercuts the simple assertion of iconicity. Adherence to "the indigenous structure" does not occur automatically; even considered as an ideal to be aimed at, the very phases of making a film doom such an endeavor to failure. Preservation of the " indigenous structure of an event" is in tension with the structuring processes necessary to construct reportage films, the category upon which Asch and his co-authors maintain their focus. Indeed, it is perhaps because Loizos collapses "films of record" with "reportage films"[3] that he underestimates the extent to which Asch's filmic ideals and practice depart from the epistemological innocence of earlier ethnographic film.

In this early piece Asch and his co-writers, perhaps idealistically, envisage the possibility of approaching the mimetic ideal of capturing not only the discrete "units of life" called events, but the larger patterns of culture that give structure to these events (Asch et al. 1973: 182–3). But once again, even in their examples of best practice in achieving this ideal, they tend to emphasize how films fall short, and thus must rely on narration and other devices to fill in the structure of events. The best attempts at reportage are revealed as partial, often succeeding as "films of record" and films that capture "particular behavioral process", but failing to capture "indigenous structure" (Asch et al. 1973: 180). In this early position paper we see the contradiction between an overt text proclaiming the possibility of iconic representation of cultural events, and a subtext declaring the inherent impossibility of this project, due not just to the technical limitations of film-making, but also to the continual perceptual and conceptual restructurings introduced by each step of the process. It is this tension that defines the essential problematique of Asch's life work. His great contribution lies not in resolving this tension – it is indeed irresolvable – but in the honesty and transparency with which he sought to address the problem by a variety of filmic and pedagogical strategies. Asch steadfastly refused to sever this conceptual Gordian knot. He neither reverted to the exhibitionistic auteurism that denies representation of a subject by exalting the artiste's vision through filmic evocation, nor retreated naïvely into the filmic faith of objective recording. By various means, differently emphasized at different points in his career, Asch foregrounded this tension and revealed that it was ultimately not simply a filmic conundrum, but a defining paradox of the anthropological endeavor itself.

Defining Asch's project in these terms situates his endeavors as straddling the modernist/post-modernist divide. Various authors have emphasized one or the other tendency in Asch's work. For example, both Cohen (1979: 62) and Nichols (1981: 269, 272–4), in their emphasis on modes of explanation in *The Ax Fight* (1975), whether conventionally anthropological or narratively encoded, ultimately foreground the realist[4] and hence modernist presuppositions of *The Ax Fight*, aspects which Moore (1995) presumes in his use of the film to demonstrate its utility for the analysis of activity sequences. In contrast, Ruby (1995: 25 ff.), drawing on Asch's own comments, tends to highlight the film's post-modernist innovations (see also Ginsberg, this volume). None of these authors neglects the complementary aspects of the film, but by differential highlighting they obscure the point that, by mobilizing conventions associated with both approaches, Asch's work commits itself to neither perspective exclusively. In effect, the decision as to how to interpret the film then rests more fully with the viewer, the reader of the filmic texts.

Pedagogy and the conative function in Tim Asch's ethnographic film-making

In her introduction to the special module of the *Visual Anthropology Review* devoted to Timothy Asch's work, Lutkehaus (1995: 3), echoing the views of such contributors as Ruby (1995) and Martínez (1995), notes how Asch's project for visual anthropology prioritized the teaching function he envisaged for ethnographic films. Perhaps some of the implications of this concentration can be more clearly drawn by analogy to Roman Jakobson's paradigm of the functions of language. In this paradigm Jakobson (1960: 353–7) isolated six constitutive factors of any speech event: addresser, addressee, message, context (or referent), code, and contact (or channel). A predominant (though not exclusive) focus on any of these six factors can be assessed as a speech function. So a predominant orientation to the context of a message defines the referential or denotative function, while emphasis upon the form of the message itself foregrounds the poetic function of the speech event. Similarly, orientation to the channel or contact specifies the phatic function, and to the code as a whole the metalingual (or metalinguistic) function. Finally, primary emphasis upon the addresser defines the expressive or emotive function of a speech event, while orientation to the addressee defines what Jakobson specifies as the conative function. Transposed to the analysis of filmic modes of communication, a primary concern with the expressive function – "a direct expression of the speaker's attitude toward what he is speaking about" – would be characteristic of the work of an *auteur* (much as Jakobson identifies this function with the lyric genre of poetry), a film-maker stamping her or his signature on every film as an expression of a unique vision of the world. Prioritization of this function in films often considered ethnographic is evident, for example, in the work of those sometimes labelled film poets or painters, including Robert Flaherty (Stoney n.d.) and Robert Gardner (Loizos 1993: 139–167; 1995). A predominant emphasis on the context or referent, the referential or denotative function, would characterize the primary aim of practitioners of "direct cinema", including Leacock and the Maysles.

Whereas the influence on Asch's work of the referential orientation in documentary film, as evident in direct cinema and related approaches, has often been remarked upon – indeed, the notion of "films of record" by definition highlights this function – I would hazard the opinion that the predominant function in filmic communication emphasized by Asch was, rather, the conative. Asch's filmic practice can best be understood by exploring how his methodology attempted above all (although not exclusively) to concentrate on the problem of reception by viewers and on the pedagogical intent of his films. That is not to say that this was the only communicative function to which Asch turned his attention; certainly, the referential and poetic functions were not neglected and indeed were emphasized to various degrees in different films. Yet his primary goal was always to "think of new and more effective ways to integrate film into anthropological instruction" (Asch 1996: 34). Asch ultimately regarded his films as "teaching resources", a view highlighted in the introduction to the catalogue *Films from DER* for the non-profit organization Asch co-founded to further the pedagogical distribution of his own and others' ethnographic films: "Underlying the diversity of DER's film collection is the conviction that ethnographic film is a valuable teaching medium" (Volkman 1982: i). In that emphasis Asch shares with post-modernist writers the problematizing of the relationship with the reader. It is in light of this function that we can re-examine some of the major aspects of Asch's methodology.

Although the conative function is often associated with exhortations and imperatives, it can also be viewed as the primary function of many interrogatives as well. Asch considered that ethnographic films should not provide definitive declarations of what a culture is; indeed, he thought the hour-long thematic film accompanied by an omniscient narration was a mode of film-making largely to be avoided, precisely because it failed to engage the viewer in a process of active thinking and learning:

> The audience, like the participants, needs to work through the event to make sense of it. In a general film about a culture the audience need not work through anything; images are presented to them with a packaged presentation.
>
> (Asch 1996: 33–4)

Instead, ethnographic films should pose questions for their audience and encourage them to reconsider their stereotypes and prejudices in relation to other cultures. The ideal type of film to perform this function was:

> event films, films concerned with a sequence of interactions that occurred spontaneously, in which the edited version maintained the order of the actions recorded and was not intercut with other sequences.
>
> (Asch 1979: 6)

On the one hand, this mode of presentation derives from what some would see as a naïve realist assumption of representation, the simple iconism of the depicted event with the pro-filmic interaction (Nichols 1981). Although Asch's continuing concern with such qualities as "accuracy" and "preservation of indigenous structure" throughout his writings confirms his perseverance in such realist assumptions, in other passages Asch acknowledges that each stage of preparation of the film constitutes a layer of interpretation. Indeed, as noted above, even as early as his 1973 co-authored article, the central diagram representing types of film (Asch *et al.* 1973: 181) clearly emphasizes the three mediations removing the filmic product from the pro-filmic action: "structuring of action by film-maker", "structuring for the screen through editing", and "structure as seen by the audience". What is important is that any interpretations arising through the encoding of the filmic product have no pretension to definitiveness: they must be open rather than closed. Such a characteristic is precisely why such films should be regarded as interrogations rather than declarations. As Asch remarked in relation to the early Ju/'hoansi event films upon which he worked as an editor with John Marshall:

> I had found these films particularly valuable in generating ideas, discussion and insight among students, because they were interrogative or open ended portrayals rather than statements.
>
> (Asch 1979: 6)

However, the conative function of interrogation entails certain responsibilities. Asch believed that simply presenting students with a set of questions by means of a film whose event structure is in need of interpretation without any further guides to potential answers would be, to use Margery Wolf's (1992) term, an "abnegation of ethnographic responsibility". Such a procedure would tend more to elicit and crystallize stereotypes that students already held rather than to lead to any further ethnographic insight, a consequence documented in the work of Martínez (1995 and this volume) on film reception. What Asch required in terms of contextualization of ethnographic film for pedagogical purposes follows from this demand to provide resources that would allow students to answer the questions posed by ethnographic films that challenge their sensibilities.

Filmic ethnography requires that a whole series of films be produced and screened for students, providing an opportunity for examining the range of values informing the diverse behaviors constituting a series of events in that culture. This requirement must be distinguished from Asch's stipulation that all footage taken should be deposited as a research film or data film, including all associated sound recordings, complete transcriptions, and other supporting materials, in an appropriate repository, such as the Human Studies Film Archives of the Smithsonian Institution (Asch et al. 1973: 180; 1979: 7; see also Homiak, this volume). Such film he considered to be of primary importance for other scholars who could use it to conduct research on the documented footage. In other words, it would constitute a publicly accessible corpus of research materials for re-examination.

However, such film would itself not yet constitute teaching materials for students. Such materials are best presented in short films, each dealing with a single event, which should never be used singly but always in association with related films. Which films should be used together for any class would depend upon the topic or theoretical point to be explored. Indeed, the theoretical impetus to Asch's films should not be underestimated. From his own accounts, what sustained Asch in his decision to participate in the first Yanomamö filming season was the allure of making films presenting events that might be interpreted in terms of the theory of gift exchange, alliance, and reciprocity central to Marcel Mauss's (1969 [1925]) The Gift (Asch 1979: 6; 1972: 7; Ruby 1995: 23; Moore 1995: 47–8). Asch also eventually realized that single films such as The Feast (1970) could not be used on their own to illustrate such concepts, for displaying only one type of occasion resulted in portraying only partial aspects of the repertoire of behavior patterns and emotional orientations, not to mention cultural conceptions, of a people, hence reinforcing "negative stereotypes ... [and] Western prejudices" (Asch 1996: 34). So, as Martínez's (1995 and this volume) account of Asch's filmic intentions and in-class pedagogy illustrates, he was determined to use a range of Yanomamö films, those emphasizing both public occasions of fierce display and "gentler domestic interactions" (Martínez 1995: 59), in his teaching sessions in order to portray both the fierce and peaceable sides of the Yanomamö. Since the constituent interactions that were the focus of his event films tended to be dominated by an interactional tone of one sort or the other, averting closure in the process of students coming to conclusions and the reinforcing of stereotypes, that is, maintaining the interrogative rather than declarative intent of the films, required the preparation and presentation of a number of event films selected to raise questions about the concepts represented. In fact, Asch lamented the degree to which other users of the Yanomamö films for instructional purposes failed to follow suit in their use of the films, too often screening only one film (and, in the Yanomamö case, inevitably a film emphasizing their "fierceness") (Martínez 1995: 60). No single text could cover the richness of cultural patterns and emotional expression of a people. Inspiring students to realize this richness and to think about how it all fits together requires an intertextuality fabricated through an ensemble of films.[5]

Collaboration and conation in Tim Asch's film-making

Producing this ensemble and equipping students with the resources to interpret cultural patterns require the assistance of collaborators who can provide an anthropological context for films to be used in teaching. Thus, another entailment of the dominance of the conative function in Asch's vision of the pedagogical use of film was the need to collaborate with an anthropologist. Indeed, Asch stressed that the necessity for such collaboration stemmed from his desire to make "inductive films" (Asch 1979: 7). The idea of "inductive films" implies not the act of inducing, bringing about, or causing a certain message to be received; rather, it refers to the stimulation of interpretation among the viewers. This process results in viewers reaching conclusions that are based on the films, but do not follow necessarily from the films taken as sufficient premises. In other words, the process is an open one, with the films functioning to stimulate diverse reactions, not to convey foregone conclusions. However, such reactions must be guided so that viewers do not fall back into channels that reinforce stereotypes, but move outside of them to widened fields of realization of cultural relativism and other aspects of an anthropological sensibility.

In his own extensive reflections on collaboration, a topic that informs every publication to which he contributed (but see especially Asch [1988]), Asch stressed how this relationship must extend across all stages of the production of ethnographic films, from conceptualization to editing and post-production. This necessity stemmed from his vision of such works as, above all, a form of "ethnographic investigation" (Asch 1988: 4). The process of filming in the field required an anthropologist who could not only fulfill such tasks as taking sound, but who could function even as a sort of director, pointing out the most culturally significant aspects of events, such as rituals, to be filmed and anticipating subsequent actions of key participants. In this capacity, the collaboration of an anthropologist familiar with the people to be filmed was a prerequisite for "sequence filming", since it was her or his long familiarity with the activity sequences (Moore 1995) of a culture that directed the film-maker to the continuity of focus at the heart of Asch's methodology.[6] After filming in the field was completed, the anthropologist was also necessary for transcription of recorded dialogue, the preparation of appropriately nuanced subtitles and intertitles (Asch 1988: 12 ff.), and for advice on editing and other post-production matters. Asch saw such aspects of ethnographic film as the use of subtitles as superseding the "Voice of God" narration of earlier styles of film-making precisely because of the open-ended quality, the plurality of interpretations they allowed viewers, especially students, to make.

> As I see it, if a film has little or no narration it offers greater potential for teaching by obliging students to interpret what they are seeing in relation to their own experiences, reading and lectures, and in discussion with one another.
>
> (Asch 1988: 14)

Central to the students' processes of interpretation was material written by the collaborating anthropologist, which "provides the background necessary for students to explore their interpretations and to answer some of their questions" (Asch 1988: 15).

> Generating interesting questions without providing access to information that might help students to find some of the answer is not fair. Such information is best provided by written materials (although there are times when an additional film, such as *Jero on Jero*, is valuable).
>
> (Asch 1996: 35)

Although the books and articles written by the collaborating anthropologist for diverse purposes and published in various venues could be considered part of the required written contextualization, the ideal was material written with viewers of the films in mind and that specifically addressed the films. Such purpose-written materials range from the early study guides prepared for the event films on which Asch worked, based on both Marshall's sequence filming among the Ju/'hoansi and his own filming among the Yanomamö (e.g. Asch and Seaman 1993), to the full-blown ethnographic film monograph, authored by all those involved in the film-making process, best exemplified by *Jero Tapakan: Balinese Healer. An Ethnographic Film Monograph* (Connor et al. 1986, 1996), a monument in visual anthropology that stands proudly beside Bateson and Mead's (1942) *Balinese Character: A Photographic Analysis*.[7]

Collaboration, however, was a process that Asch envisaged as extending beyond the specific relationship with an anthropologist as co-worker. He increasingly realized that collaboration was the mode of relationship that also had to be promoted and sustained not only with the subjects of ethnographic films, but also with the audiences of the films. These sorts of collaboration were the foundation of his methodology of "feedback" (Asch 1996: 38). One of the main reservations Asch expressed about the Yanomamö films was his inability to take the films back to their subjects for their commentary, in part due to their likely presumption that the souls of participants who had died subsequent to being filmed had been stolen (through their images having been taken) by the film-makers (Asch 1996: 35). In order to redress this shortcoming in the Yanomamö work – " ... Napoleon Chagnon and I had complete control over the filming process and we didn't share it with our subjects. It never even occurred to me that I might share with the Yanomami" (Asch 1993: 5) – taking films back to the community in video format to witness their reactions and obtain their consent became an integral part of his subsequent methodology and a central tenet of his ethics as an ethnographic film-maker (Asch 1992: 200–1).

However, with a view to the ultimately conative function and projected pedagogical context of the use of such films, Asch took this procedure one step further by documenting this process and including it within the films to be released. How this feedback from subjects was incorporated differed in each project. In the Jero Tapakan series, this procedure was the focus of the second film of the tetralogy, *Jero on Jero: a Balinese Trance Seance Observed* (1980), while in *A Celebration of Origins*

(1993) such feedback was used to structure one of the threads of voice-over narration in the film itself:

> Four years after we had filmed in Wai Brama, we invited Pius to come to Australia. We showed him video tape of our footage of the Celebration of Origins. We have used some of Pius's reflections as commentary in the film.
>
> (Lewis 1994: 4 [from the voice-over narration])

In fact, the voice of Pius as narrator is accorded the proverbial "last word" in the voice-over narration, thereby justifying the title accorded the film, as well as the extended focus on the performances of the chanter Sina, as Pius responds to his viewing of the film:

> (PIUS): I was acting as Source of the Domain … As Source of the Domain, I cannot do everything. I just stand and speak. It was the same with Sina, my father. His duty was to seek the origins and source of things. …
>
> (E. D[OUGLAS] L[EWIS]): It has been four years since the Celebration. How have things been?
>
> (PIUS): There have been no problems; our harvests have been good; our animals have been well; yes, and we have watched over our children and all are healthy. There have been deaths, but only one. If a person who is old dies it means the deity has called him, and not that we made errors in the *mahé* and so he died. This means we did the ritual correctly, as our ancestors did them.
>
> (Lewis 1994: 24, 26)

The credit towards the end of the film acknowledging that "[t]he collaboration of the people of the domain of Wai Brama was crucial in recording and in shaping this film" is also accompanied by a "pan over a still shot of people gathered to watch video tape taken in Tana Wai Brama" (Lewis 1994: 24). Thus, in Asch's ethnographic filmic methodology, feedback as part of a collaborative process with the film's subjects becomes not only necessary to contextualization, but also an integral part of the textualization process and the final filmic text itself.

However, feedback also extends to a process of collaboration with the audiences themselves. Asch proclaimed this step as an imperative in the ethics of ethnographic film-making – "Get feedback from sample audiences" (Asch 1992: 200–1). Asch's unpublished 1988 interview with Martínez confirms the centrality of this step as a fundamental aspect of his methodology of ethnographic film-making:

> I'm making it for my students, I show it to my students, they're supposed to understand twenty different ideas in that film, they understand two. "Why don't you understand the other eighteen?" I've got to find out why … I go back with Patsy to the editing room and we look at the film with all this in mind and we change the film; I bring it out three days later and I show it to another group of

students, and I get a little further each time. What have I done when I'm finished with this? I have a film that I've made in collaboration with students ...

(Martínez 1995: 55–56)

Collaboration is a process that embraces not just the anthropologist working with the film-maker, but also the filmic subjects and the intended audiences as well. Ultimately, all this collaboration is in the service of facilitating the understanding of the audience, insuring that "the film is communicating with the audience as you intended" and providing "a context for interpreting what they see" (Asch 1992: 201).[8] This ultimate emphasis upon the communicative success of an ethnographic film, maximizing its potential to elicit reflective interpretation among audience members, highlights most clearly the primary conative function of Tim Asch's ethnographic films.

Tim Asch's ethnographic film-making as both modernist and post-modernist

Martínez (1995: 56) has noted the presence in Tim Asch's pedagogical use of film of "echoes of Edwin Abbott's *Flatland*, the progressive educational philosophy of John Dewey, and Gregory Bateson's ecology of the mind". Certainly, paralleling the Square's attempt to educate his fellow Flatlanders into the third dimension, there is in Asch's work the same sense of a humble author initiating his students into dimensions of culture that are beyond their individual perceptions and everyday interactions (Abbott 1950: ii).[9] Asch regarded ethnographic film as a medium for leading students into ways of learning through reflecting on experience, albeit the filmed experience of other subjects, in ways of which the progressive philosopher of education John Dewey would have approved (cf. Dewey 1938). We should also not forget that Gregory Bateson's contributions to anthropology, psychiatry, evolution, epistemology, and so many other fields (Bateson 1972) stemmed not just from his writings, but also from his own innovations as a pioneer ethnographic photographer and film-maker in his cooperative research with Margaret Mead on Bali (Bateson and Mead 1942). In many respects Asch was carrying forward the program of conducting anthropological research articulated by Bateson and Mead – sometimes jointly, sometimes divergently ([Bateson and Mead] 1977) – in their "experimental innovation" (Bateson and Mead 1942: xi) of taking and using stills and films in Bali to explore a culturally standardized ethos, as well as its ontogenetic origins, in socialization practices. Dissatisfied with the shortcomings of presenting translations of Balinese verbal concepts and descriptions of observed behavior in only written form, Bateson and Mead pioneered the presentation of ethnography through contextualized photography:

By the use of photographs, the wholeness of each piece of behavior can be preserved, while the special cross-referencing desired can be obtained by placing the series of photographs on the same page. It is possible to avoid the artificial construction of a scene at which a man, watching a dance, also looks up at an aeroplane and has a dream; it is also possible to avoid diagramming the single element in these scenes which we wish to stress – the importance of levels in Balinese inter-personal relationships – in such a way that the reality of the scenes themselves is destroyed.

(Bateson and Mead 1942: xii)

Asch's concern with the delimitation of events can be seen as a continuation, in part, of the concern expressed by Mead and Bateson with the "wholeness of each piece of behavior", as can his interest in maintaining the "reality of cultural scenes".[10] Bateson's declaration of his methodology for obtaining a record of Balinese behavior through the use of both still and moving-picture cameras provides one clear source for aspects of Asch's own film work:

We tried to shoot what happened normally and spontaneously, rather than to decide upon the norms and then get Balinese to go through these behaviors in suitable lighting. We treated the cameras in the field as recording instruments, not as devices for illustrating our theses.

(Bateson and Mead 1942: 49)

Bateson and Mead also emphasized how the need for verbal contextualization of photographic records required collaboration between photographer and note-taker, with the latter (i.e. Mead) also "able to do some very necessary directing of the photography" (Bateson and Mead 1942: 50). Asch was later to characterize his work with such collaborators as Chagnon and Connor in similar terms. Mead and Bateson also believed in the combined use of still photography and moving images, as they "assumed that the still photography and the motion-picture film *together* would constitute our record of behavior" (Bateson and Mead 1942: 50). Asch's later incorporation of slides and stills in his event films (see Lewis, Chapter 14) continued this joint usage of the two media in exposition.

After the production of the volume *Balinese Character*, the interests and activities of Bateson and Mead diverged. In fact, Mead worked largely without Bateson's input on the later production of such films from the "Character Formation in Different Cultures Series" as *A Balinese Family* (ca 1951) and *Trance and Dance in Bali* (ca 1952), as well as *Childhood Rivalry in Bali and New Guinea* (ca 1952). Increasingly, their views on the proper manner and interpretation of filming diverged, with Mead touting the virtues of cameras as objective recording instruments and Bateson arguing that films needed also to be art forms in order to convey cultures, given the inherent selectivity of the camera ([Bateson and Mead] 1977). Moore has noted how

Asch has fulfilled the promise that Margaret Mead long ago exacted from ethnographic film; that it would allow us to analyze again, long after the fact of filmic observation, with enhanced or better tools for analysis.

(Moore 1995: 49)

Despite Asch's acknowledgment of the debt he owed to Margaret Mead in the formation of his own anthropological career (Ruby 1995: 20), in many ways his own views on the methodology and interpretation of ethnographic film sided with neither Mead nor Bateson exclusively, instead recognizing the productive tension of these outlooks. On the one hand, in agreement with Mead, Asch emphasized the need to subordinate artistic endeavor to accurate recording of integral events:

> The nature of ethnographic filming itself is a second source of problems [i.e. besides technical problems]. I try to sustain filming of social interaction up to some naturally occurring conclusion, which is often hard to predict and does not fit the length of film rolls ... I try not to let my filming interfere with naturally occurring events ... The primary consideration is the integrity of the event and the people filmed; the urge to construct a creative work of art is in many respects an obstacle. It would be naïve to imagine that I was not influenced by the craft – by every film I have seen, by the technical strengths and limitations of my equipment, by the conventions of my day – but my goal is to make films in which my own artistic drives are eclipsed by the subjects in the film.
>
> (Asch 1996: 42–3)

On the other hand, in accord with Bateson, he acknowledged the need for artistry in his ethnographic films. However, as Martínez (1995: 55) so nicely puts it, "his artistry was profoundly carved in his teaching craft":

> I must say, I have to be honest with you, I'm doing this work probably as an artist as much as an anthropologist, because all the seventy-some odd films that I've made have been made out of a teaching experience ... Most artists work in a little room, and they make their film and they show it to the public and that's it. Not me, I'm making it for my students ... I'm an artist and that's my audience, I have a living audience. Every time I show my work, as a creative thing as much as an anthropological thing, it is a creative experience.
>
> (Asch quoted in Martínez 1995: 55–6)

The criterion for resolving such tension between artistic and recording aims was thus given for Asch in the ultimately conative function of ethnographic film, its relationship to its viewers in the pedagogical context.

However, viewing Tim Asch's work only in terms of its relationship to such forebears as Bateson and Mead would be a disservice. Such an orientation tends to situate his work in terms of past paradigms dominated by notions of "cultural translation", "objective realism" and "transparency" (Martínez 1995: 57) – notions which are indeed central to any evaluation of Asch's work – as well as the epistemological innocence with which Loizos (1993) largely associates Asch's "films of record". However, he was also responding to currents of his time and also setting new trends himself, as David MacDougall (1995: 83) has noted in relation to subtitling and Hildred Geertz, in her review of the Jero Tapakan tetralogy, has articulated more generally:

> With these four films and the monograph accompanying them, film ethnography has been taken another step forward, parallel with the ongoing maturation of written ethnography, away from the old genre conventions of "ethnographic realism" in which a false impression of the truth and wholeness of the portrayal is created through various literary and filmic techniques ... There have now appeared a number of attempts to write ethnography based on the conception of social knowledge as a product of collaborative interpretations. The same attempt to find new forms that embody new assumptions about the nature of the anthropologist's knowledge can be seen in these films.
>
> (Geertz 1984: 811)

Geertz's evaluation remains the exception. All too often the situating of Asch's work with regard to other documentary trends has been largely limited to noting the influence of direct cinema and *cinema vérité* in the 1960s. The influence of modernist forms of documentary on Asch's work is undeniable, but he was also aware of and receptive to subsequent trends in film theory and practice and theoretical anthropology.

In his aptly titled overview of Asch's work, "Out of Sync", Jay Ruby quotes Asch musing upon the significance of how he structured *The Ax Fight* (1975):

> You know the joy of *The Ax Fight* ... is that because Chagnon was so stuck in simple theories that, right away, the film became a real joke. It is funny with its simplistic, straightjacketed, one-sided explanation ... One of the things I liked about it was that it's a pretty funny film. And it's a very dated film if you are going to take it as a piece of serious work. It belongs in another era. But I think also that the film is [a] harbinger of postmodernism long before we get postmodernism ... and I was feeling, you know, halfway into making the film, this great suspicion of the whole field beginning to fall apart before my eyes as I was putting *The Ax Fight* together. I had a powerful piece of material and it was suddenly looking kind of foolish. But it was kind of fun. Actually I wanted to do something like that for a long time. And I realized that when I saw the Oxberry animation stand that I could do it. But now I would love to put on an introduction to it that says, "About Realism".
>
> (Asch quoted in Ruby 1995: 28)

While some of the phrasing of this typically exuberant description of his work on this film may be the result of *ex post facto* rumination upon this film's place in the subsequent development of anthropological theory, the general characterization of the film's significance is remarkably apt. Lewis (Chapter 14, this volume) has remarked upon the considerable humor in Asch's films. Asch himself emphasizes this s dimension in this passage quoted by Ruby, but the funniness of this film lies not in the profilmic scenes depicted, but in the mismatch between the intensity and over-determined character of the scenes and the impoverished anthropological paradigms, especially in the middle sections of the film, invoked in explanation. Whereas such a stance is indeed reminiscent once more of Bateson's (1936) self-conscious expression of dissatisfaction in *Naven* with functional modes of explanation for Iatmul ritual, it also may be seen as in the ironic mode that Marcus and Fischer (1986: 13ff.) have noted as a facet of the crisis of representation in 1980s American anthropology and the post-modern condition generally (Marcus and Fischer 1986: 45).

Of course, it is nothing new for problematizations and innovations in ethnographic film to precede those in written anthropology, as the case of Rouch (Stoller 1992) well illustrates. But few critics have viewed Asch's contribution in similar pioneering terms. For example, as noted above, both Cohen's (1979) and Nichols's (1981: 272–4) evaluations of *The Ax Fight* misconstrue the evident distortions that Asch intentionally incorporates into the final edited section and thus falsely accuse Asch of the fallacious realism and epistemologically naïve representationalism that he is actually attempting to undermine:

> … this last fourth edited version, which I would – if I could have gotten Leni Riefenstahl to edit – I would have. I wanted somebody who was a real expert to edit that final section and, you know, distort it as much as possible but have it look smooth and slick – the way any good ethnographic film looks. Because what we usually see is that last section.
>
> (Asch quoted in Ruby 1995: 27)

In situating Asch's work as part of the "experimental moment in the human sciences" that Marcus and Fischer (1986) have delineated, I am most reminded of the work of Kevin Dwyer (1987) as a written analogue. Marcus and Fischer (1986: 69–70) characterize Dwyer's *Moroccan Dialogues* as a critique of ethnographic inquiry that exposes what conventional textualization techniques conceal concerning the immediate experience of cultural otherness in the local interactional setting. The work is also said to reveal the imperfectness and vulnerability of the cumulative, yet recursive and contingent understanding anthropologists actually attain through their dialogues with their informants, despite the ethnographic authority with which they write. As they conclude,

> Dwyer accomplishes the task of revealing the dialogic roots of ethnographic knowledge, but in so doing, he also disturbingly questions the value of continuing with the project of representation in any of its conventional senses.
>
> (Marcus and Fischer 1986: 70)

Such a conclusion hauntingly echoes Asch's suspicion of "good ethnographic film" and indeed of the anthropological endeavor generally – "the whole field beginning to fall apart before my eyes" – in his recounting of his work on *The Ax Fight*.[11]

Even in smaller details the understandings and ambivalence of Dwyer and Asch converge. Like Asch, Dwyer (1987: 21) is concerned to preserve the "spontaneity and normal behavior of people", thus eschewing a delineated research project that would structure his encounters. His primary aim is to give "full voice" to the Other, especially Faqir Muhammad bin l-'Ayashi Sherardi, his primary interlocutor, attempting to find forms of written presentation that "do not abstract it [the Other's voice] from its context, and that allow it to be heard in a critical address to the Self" (Dwyer 1987: 285). So too, Asch, reflecting upon what he came to regard as the primary deficiencies of his Yanomamö films, sought in his Balinese films to give primary importance to dialogue – "subjects who speak about the central concerns of their lives and participate in spontaneous conversations" (Asch 1996: 32) – deciding that "dialogue as well as the beauty of images, should dictate the filming and editing of a scene" (Asch 1996:32).[12] Like Dwyer, in his dialogic format in these films Asch highlighted one individual, Jero Tapakan, a move not only in keeping with the resurgence of life-history accounts in the experimental moment of the 1980s, but also dialogically and reflexively constituting

> meditations on the relationships of anthropologists with their informants [e.g. Linda Connor with Jero Tapakan], and invok[ing] a model of dialogue revealing how a life history is elicited and jointly constructed.
>
> (Marcus and Fischer 1986: 57)

Asch's own formulation of his filmic goal echoes quite precisely Dwyer's textual goal in regard to the Faqir: "The challenge for us was to enable Jero, in talking about the central concerns of her work and life, to speak for herself" (Asch 1996: 43).

Besides such issues as the emphasis upon dialogue and the rendering of subjects' voices, perhaps the most salient convergence of Asch's and Dwyer's concerns is the problematization of the notion of event. Beginning with what he thought was an unambiguous "'event + dialogue' motif" to structure his account (Dwyer 1987: xvii ff.) – outside happenings providing topics of conversation and lines of inquiry with the Faqir – Dwyer comes increasingly in the course of the text to question the very nature of an outside event as a stimulus to foster dialogue with the Faqir independent of his own interests:

> … I now began to suspect that the sequence "event + dialogue" was not as straightforward as I had imagined. First of all, the encounter with Saleh … had few of the trappings and little of the clear definition of a "traditional" anthropological happening … I could no longer claim, even had I been so inclined before, that our dialogues were essentially an inquiry into external, "objective" events.
>
> (Dwyer 1987: 70)

But my deeper feeling of unease at the notion of the "event" would not go away.

Perhaps I was fundamentally misconceiving the "event" and, in so doing, turning away from what might be very salient elements in our mutual experience.

(Dwyer 1987: 112)

The absence of Faqir Hmed from the Faqir's household appeared, at first glance, to be an event of a new kind, for here my interest had been provoked by something that was *not* happening. This is evidently a superficial observation, but it led me to question my notion of the "event" in new ways ... my seeing this absence as an event had rather more to do with my distinctive experience and perspective. ... The solidity and "objective" character of the event – its existence as something fixed, once and for all, and identical for all those who look at it – was disintegrating.

(Dwyer 1987: 137)

... The "objectivity" of the event, the neutrality of the inquiry, and the information contained in the discussion were all called squarely into question.

(Dwyer 1987: 213–14; cf. Lewis 1989)

The cumulative problematization of the notion of event throughout the course of *Moroccan Dialogues* in certain ways recapitulates the trajectory of Asch's own musings about the event as the basis of his methodology of filming and production of films. In his early writings, the notion of event is rather unproblematic; it is assumed as the profilmic object of ethnographic film: "The aim of ethnographic film is to preserve, in the mind of the viewer, the structure of the events it is recording as interpreted by the participants" (Asch *et al.* 1973: 179). The whole concept of reportage film rests, initially, upon its function in preserving the "indigenous structure of an event":

The subject matter of reportage is always an event or a complete segment of life ... As he [the anthropologist] becomes familiar with his people he can see patterns in their lives, and he can find units of life, with definite beginning and ends, with which the people will agree. It is the filming of these discrete units which constitutes reportage ... Reportage film, that is film shot using the sequence method, presents whole single units of behavior, the units trained anthropologists study.

(Asch *et al.* 1973: 182–4)

However, although Asch seemed relatively more sure of the discreteness of these events when dealing with John Marshall's Ju/'hoansi sequence films, as he became more and more involved with filming himself, the notion of clear boundaries to these units of behavior becomes ever more problematic. This problematization is evident in the conversations among the soundman Craig Johnson, anthropologist Napoleon Chagnon and film-maker Asch that were retained at the end of the first section of *The Ax Fight* as the image on screen went black:

JOHNSON: Sound Reel 14; February 28, 1971; finish of wife-beating sequence.
ASCH: Did you get synch on that?
CHAGNON: Wife-beating sequence, my foot.
JOHNSON: Okay, what is it?
CHAGNON: It was a club fight.
JOHNSON: What was first?

...

JOHNSON: About 3.30 in the afternoon.
CHAGNON: No, about 3.00 it started.

...

ASCH: So this is just the beginning of lots more.

(Ruby 1995: 25)

Ruby's "created" quotations from interviews with Asch concerning *The Ax Fight* reveal that not only did Asch have little idea of what he was shooting at the time – "And then after those first shots of the women crying and what not, Chagnon said, say, come on over and get your camera it's going to start ... meaning it's over there ... whatever it was ... But, whatever was happening was happening down there" – but that he also came to question the delimitation of the event given by the alliance used as the basis of his explanations in the middle sections of the film.

The middle sections of the final film seek to bring closure not only to the explanation of the event, but also to the temporal boundaries of the event itself, as encoded in the final title of the film before the credits: "Several days after the fight, some of the visitors began leaving. Tensions were temporarily relieved" (Biella *et al.* 1997: Frame sequence 1038400). But this closure is undermined by Asch in his inclusion of the slick, distorted section at the end – "The Final Edited Version" – which reveals all too clearly that no one explanation accounts fully for what happens profilmically, and any explanation will fail to contain the excess of the life before the camera (Nichols 1981). Although Nichols does not fully appreciate the ironic mode of this final section (see above), he nicely highlights how the narrative structure of the end version does not reinforce, but provides a counterpoint to, the expository emphasis of the middle sections, "demonstrat[ing] the lack of any one-to-one correlation between what we see, the visible, and what we understand, the conceptual and between observation and explanation" (Nichols, this volume). As Asch himself puts it:

> Show them the second piece, which is our explanation, but let them know that there are other explanations. I mean in this film we are really locked into a very tight simplistic structural–functional explanation here. ... We are dealing with models now, I'm building a model the way anthropologists build models only I am doing it with film. I think one of the biggest contributions to anthropology is to show how film can be manipulated to be an effective model ... I might have still believed wholeheartedly in the structural-functional explanation during the first three to five showings. But after the tenth or twenty-fifth,

I was pretty much jaded. So what I am trying to say is that I went into this fairly naïvely with my anthropology training, thinking that I was making a fascinating truthful translation or representation of culture. But a third of the way through it … because I had to see it so often, I began to get jaded about the whole thing. I mean it almost became a joke. I wasn't aware of any postmodern critiques of representation. I hadn't really picked it up on my own until about five months later … and this whole notion of truth and making an accurate representation blew up in my face.

(Asch quoted in Ruby 1995: 27–8)

Further, as is evident in the description presented for the separate film *Tapir Distribution* (1975) in the Documentary Educational Resources catalogue (Volkman 1982: 29), it is questionable whether the distribution of tapir meat to his brothers-in-law by the Mishimishimaböwei-teri headman Moäwä can be considered an event separate from the dispute shown in *The Ax Fight* that disrupted these alliance relationships. The contextualization of this film undermines the closure brought to the event depicted in *The Ax Fight* by Chagnon's narration and the final title.

Thus, *The Ax Fight* reveals how even events themselves are constructions of the observers and, indeed, of the participants themselves. Asch's apparent loss of faith in direct representation thus parallels the similar realization of Dwyer regarding the anchoring of his dialogues with the Faqir in external events:

As I listened to the various parties to an event offer interpretations of it, I did not see a clear, objective story emerge, but rather a number of convincing, internally coherent yet often indubitably opposed versions. … To what extent, then, was an event the same for the different parties to it? Was the anthropologist's vision of it not simply one among many, seen from a unique standpoint against the background of his own particular and societal interests and concerns, and not from a standpoint that had any claim to be more "objective", more true than the others?

(Dwyer 1987: 214)

Such questioning is further developed in the Jero Tapakan films. Whereas the first film, *A Balinese Trance Seance*, appears in its very title to be a representation of a discrete event in Balinese culture, the nature of this event is then further problematized in the subsequent films of the series rather than within a single film itself, as in the case of *The Ax Fight*. *Jero on Jero: A Balinese Trance Seance Observed* reveals the very different aspects of the first film focused upon by the anthropologist Linda Connor and the subject Jero, while *The Medium Is the Masseuse: A Balinese Massage* moves away from emphasis on a single massage as focal event to include interactions with other patients and an extended interview with one patient, Ida Bagus, and his wife Daya Putu. Finally, *Jero Tapakan: Stories from the Life of a Balinese Healer* problematizes the whole notion of events in a life history: it is unclear to what extent Jero's recounted experiences correspond to any events in the world and to what extent they are visions structured both by her personal afflictions and by the traditional "chronicles" (*babad*), recounting "the adventures of founding ancestors of descent groups, including periods of isolation, privation, and wandering preceding divine inspiration about a course of action" (Connor *et al.* 1996: 204), with which Jero was familiar. As in Dwyer's text, there is a theoretical movement across these four films that increasingly problematizes the objectivity of discrete events and cumulatively prioritizes the subjectivity of dialogically engaged participants.

Ruby (1995: 30) has argued, and I would agree, that Asch never fully relinquished many of the traditional aims of filmic construction and all the shooting and editing techniques these entail. I would argue further that Asch did not completely call into question the project of representation *per se*. In his own words, written long after the making of *The Ax Fight*, "it is important for all of us to learn how to make better and better representations" (Asch 1993: 8). In part, this position flows from Asch's continuing concern with documentation as an ethical imperative: "If these representations don't exist, did those cultures ever exist?" (Asch 1993: 8) As others have noted as well, to deny the project of representation would be to demean the productions, written and filmic, now made by local peoples in the contemporary context, to deny them their voice. Thus, Asch's embracing of aspects of the postmodern project still retains some aspects of modernism; it would not extend to the replacement of representation by evocation, as advocated by Tyler (1987), among others. The variety of post-modernism espoused by Tyler would sit more comfortably with the "science fiction" methodology and surrealist tone of Rouch (DeBouzek 1989; Stoller 1992), to take but one example of an ethnographic filmmaker with a methodology quite different from Asch's.

Asch's position is still, however, consistent with that of a post-modernist like Dwyer, even in a text the latter regards as subverting conventional anthropological canons of representation. In fact, despite overtly calling the representational project into question, Dwyer achieves a position in which he feels it even more important to present unedited dialogues to the reader as accurately as possible without rearranging the temporal sequence in which utterances were made in the interests of a textual organization motivated by the topical and theoretical imperatives of anthropology as a field of inquiry:

> I began to feel very strongly that any effort to appreciate my experience in Morocco and the experience others had of me, and to understand my relationship with the Faqir, would have to respect timing even if one could not hope to reproduce it exactly. At the very least, I suspected that such an appreciation would be irremediably deficient if happening and conversations were reordered and their sequence destroyed, if long segments were eliminated, if the passage of time was ignored, neglecting with this the growing ease and familiarity so essential to the meaning of what was said.
>
> (Dwyer 1987: 156)

Such "respect" for the preservation of dialogical sequence is tantamount to a preservation of many aspects of the representational enterprise. With very little change of wording, such utterances can be applied directly to the continuing aspects of Asch's methodology of sequence filming. Even in the Jero Tapakan films with their increased reflexivity, the need for accuracy never disappears. Such an emphasis is evident not only in the contextualization presented in the accompanying monograph (Connor et al. 1986, 1996), which includes transcriptions of the soundtrack of footage that was excluded from the final films, but even in the films themselves, which display as intertitles precise times and dates of filmed encounters.[13] In both these texts by Dwyer and Asch, written and filmic respectively, there is a recognition that modernist conventions of accuracy and accountability (and a host of others) in documentation, representation and translation remain necessary in pursuing post-modern aims of exploring situated relationships and subjectivity involving both Self and Other. I suspect Dwyer would feel as uncomfortable producing a novel from his dialogues with the Faqir, with all the distortion of temporal sequencing this would allow, as Asch would producing scripted films (Asch et al. 1973: 182; Asch et al. 1991: 103), even with his collaborators in the manner of Rouch (i.e. his methodology of "science fiction" [DeBouzek 1989: 304]).

Conclusion: the ethical film-maker as catalytic pedagogue

Both the retention of modernist standards and the movement from modernist to post-modernist concerns are evident in Asch's later filmic work and his writings about it. Asch's final position with regard to both is expressed perhaps most clearly in his co-authored article of 1991, detailing his role as a "catalyst" (Asch et al. 1991: 104) in a project to teach the Yanomamö to make films of themselves (see also Asch 1993: 6–8). From one view, this project realizes Asch's confrontation with the post-modernist crisis of representation: "who should represent what to whom" (Asch et al. 1991: 102)? Yet, in other ways this project involves not so much a reversal of previous stances as a rebalancing of roles (Asch 1993: 7) in the collaboration which Asch had advocated from the beginning as integral to the methodology of an "ethical film-maker" (Asch 1988, 1992). Asch notes, in terms that once more echo the reflections of Dwyer (1987) and other post-modernists concerning traditions in written anthropological texts, how the transition from the use of "native" to the invocation of the "Other" implies an extension of subjectivity and agency through the right of that "Other" to become an interlocutor who assumes the status of "Self" in the project of representation:

> This name change ought to signify a shift of perspective. The "native" was an object, the object of our studies, the object of our colonization. The "other" is a subject or agent with whom we engaged in a communicative encounter; the "other" implies the expectation of a more balanced interaction. We think now about who has the right to represent whom, to speak for whom. We do it not

simply because we have divined a greater truth, but because we have had to. The people we used to call "natives" have shown us, in many cases, that it is not, and was not, our place to take the power of representation from them.

(Asch 1993: 6)

This position is also a re-specification of the role of addressee for Asch's pedagogical communication as a teacher not only of ethnographic film but also of anthropology. This move is thus ultimately in keeping with Asch's view of the primary function of his films. The problematization of the discreteness of events, the prioritization of voice and dialogue, the transition to exploration of multiple subjectivities (the anthropologists' and film-makers' as well as the local interlocutors'), and the re-specification of the roles of collaborators do not just exemplify the post-modern trends sweeping the textuality of written anthropology since the late 1970s; they also contribute to the open-endedness of Asch's films – their function as interrogations rather than declarations.

Ultimately, these transitions, with their elements of both continuity and discontinuity, can be seen once more within the context of the conative function of Asch's ethnographic film-making project: its concentration upon reception by the addressee. All the facets of his filmic and anthropological endeavors – the necessity for making and showing multiple films to convey cultural patterns, the elaboration of written contextualization, the collaboration that this necessitates, and the movement toward a post-modern sensibility problematizing his earlier assumptions – can be considered in terms of their enhancement of anthropological pedagogy. All these imperatives constitute both a methodology and an ethics focused upon the stimulation of a questioning attitude among students and, as increasingly emphasized in his final musings upon the responsibilities of representation, other audiences as well, a filmic invitation to all these addressees to make sense of others' values and to reconsider their own – "providing a resource for their own potential to work on" (Asch quoted in Martínez 1995: 56). Near the end of his film *How the Myth was Made* (1978), dealing with Robert Flaherty's previous filming of *Man of Aran* (1934), the film-maker George C. Stoney in his voice-over narration refers to Flaherty as "our [documentary film-makers'] greatest film poet". By analogy, I would refer to Tim Asch as visual anthropology's greatest film pedagogue.

Notes

I would like to thank Douglas Lewis, not only for his patience, but also for his helping to bring into my awareness just what I was trying to say. Jim Fox also deserves my gratitude for never losing faith and suggesting back in 1987 that I offer a unit on ethnographic film in my first full year of university teaching.

1 I am not using the term "conation" in this title in its strict sense in psychology as "that portion of mental life having to do with striving, embracing desire and volition" (Delbridge *et al.* 1981: 391). Rather, I am using conation here as the nominal form of the adjective "conative" in the term "conative function", as coined by Roman Jakobson in his typology of communicative functions, which is briefly summarized in the text below. However, I still hope that the use of this term retains the connotations of Tim Asch's sense of moral fervor in the vocation (in the Weberian sense of "calling") of being an ethnographic film-maker.

2 Loizos (1993: 25) does note that the Yanomamö films differed from the "observational films" of Leacock,

Wiseman, and the Maysles in the use of "exegetic assistance in the form of commentary, captions, subtitles and the use of stills". Asch also insisted on study guides and extensive contextualization through background lectures and discussion to accompany the presentation of these films in class.

3 In all fairness to Loizos, I must remark that Asch himself fails to adhere consistently across the range of his writings to the distinction between "film of record" and "reportage film" that he established with his co-authors John Marshall and Peter Spier in their 1973 manifesto. For example, see the title of his early 1979 article "Making a Film Record of the Yanomamö Indians of Southern Venezuela", and Asch's remarks as late as 1992 concerning his earlier "sense of urgent purpose: to depict as accurately and objectively as possible the native cultures which were radically changing, for the ultimate purpose of having a record of what was, so that we could use that record in our scientific purpose" (Asch [with Crane] 1993: 4).

4 Nichols (1991: 70) reiterates the realist sensibility underlying The Ax Fight in his book, Representing Reality: Issues and Concepts in Documentary. More recently, Nichols (this volume) has modified his view to a more favorable evaluation of what the film is attempting, admitting Asch's addition of an "hermeneutic gesture" to complement the "empirical scrutiny" of earlier sections of the film. Although his retention of the views from Ideology and the Image in Part I of his paper bespeaks a continuing characterization of The Ax Fight in the realist tradition, his conclusion of Part II, asserting that this film "both belongs squarely within the tradition of ethnographic film and puts into question many of that tradition's assumptions" converges with my own attempt (see below) to situate Asch's filmic anthropology on the cusp of both modernist and post-modernist paradigms.

5 This phrasing obviously reinforces Lewis's (Chapter 14, this volume) point that Tim Asch's contribution, in its unrelenting insistence upon comparison through multiple filmic texts, constitutes an ethnology based upon filmic and complementary written ethnography.

6 One must acknowledge that Asch also felt the imperative to film aspects of a society other than those fitting the project of a collaborating anthropologist, as his determination to document the gentler side of Yanomamö interactions (Martínez 1995: 59) in counterpoint to Chagnon's emphasis on "fierce" public display indicates. Collaboration did not extend to being dictated to by the anthropologist or any other collaborator.

7 In many ways, the production of a CD-ROM version of a film, with all the documentation and options for open-ended investigation by students it makes available in hypertext format, represents a further step in this process of collaboration among not only anthropologists and film-makers, but also such other contributors as computer programmers and other media specialists. Sadly, Yanomamö Interactive (Biella et al. 1997), as a magnificently contextualized version of The Ax Fight that carries further Asch's project of providing a resource for open-ended interrogation of a culture through visual ethnography, was completed only after his untimely death.

8 Having myself viewed, while finishing my Ph.D. thesis at The Australian National University in the 1980s, a number of rough cuts of A Celebration of Origins, I can personally vouch for the rigor with which Tim and Patsy Asch carried out this imperative of seeking audience feedback.

9 Seen from the perspective of the last pages of Abbott's classic describing the trial and incarceration of "A Square" "for the seditious heresy of the Third Dimension" (Abbott 1950: 96), it is remarkable that, as I revise this piece, there are the first stirrings of an academic interrogation and perhaps trial of some researchers, most notably Napoleon Chagnon and James Neel, involved in the study and representation of the Yanomamö, including focally the filmic representations in which Asch had a primary role (Tierney 2000). What is perhaps most ironic about these first accusations is that while the journalist Tierney castigates the image of Yanomamö fierceness that such films as The Feast (1970) convey, he relies centrally on Asch's own accounts (e.g. Asch 1972) to undermine this image and to contextualize the making of such films. He also neglects the numerous other films produced by Asch to counter this image through a focus on gentle domestic interactions among the Yanomamö, e.g. A Father Washes His Children (1974), A Man and His Wife Weave a Hammock (1975), and Weeding the Garden (1974). It is perhaps one of the fantastic ironies of this incipient controversy that Tierney's view of Yanomamö ethos can be seen as simply continuing a line of critique that Asch himself, ever concerned with the ethics of ethnographic film-making (e.g. Asch 1988, 1992, 1996), has promulgated in his own writings on his collaborative ethnographic film work among the Yanomamö with Chagnon.

10 In fact, besides acknowledging the general inspiration of Margaret Mead in directing him to anthropology, Asch has also noted her direct influence in conceptualizing his focus to include coverage of women's and children's activities for the second filming expedition to the Yanomamö. As she said to him, "'If Yanomamö are so fierce, it is important to know how individuals get to be that way'" (Asch 1988: 9).

11 I argue below, however, that neither Asch nor Dwyer completely abandons the project of representation.

12 I have noted elsewhere (Acciaioli 1997b) the curious change in the phrasing of this passage from "Dialogue rather than the beauty of the images ..." in the first edition of Jero Tapakan: Balinese Healer (1986) to

"Dialogue as well as the beauty of the images …" in the second edition (1996). Whether this difference in phrasing indicates an actual change in Asch's views concerning the relative importance of dialogue and image and hence of scientific (i.e. research) and aesthetic considerations, or is simply an editorial intrusion by some other voice in the preparation of the second edition, remains an interesting subject for speculation.

13 For example, "24 July 1978, 8am–11am" at the end of A Balinese Trance Seance. And again, four titles at the beginning of The Medium Is the Masseuse:

> This is one of four films about Jero Tapakan;
> a spirit medium and masseuse in central Bali;
> 9 am, 19 November 1980, Jero's house yard;
> An hour later after Jero has treated the first two patients.

References

Abbott, Edwin A. (1950), Flatland: A Romance of Many Dimensions. Second revised edition. Oxford: Basil Blackwell.

Acciaioli, Greg (1997a), "Innocence Lost: Evaluating an Experimental Era in Ethnographic Film". TAJA [The Australian Journal of Anthropology] 8 (2): 210–26.

—— (1997b), "Review of Linda Connor, Patsy Asch, and Timothy Ash, Jero Tapakan: Balinese Healer". RIMA [Review of Indonesian and Malaysian Affairs] 31 (1): 270–5.

Asch, Timothy (1972), "Ethnographic Filming and the Yanomamo Indians". Sight Lines 5 (3): 7–12, 17.

—— (1979), "Making a Film Record of the Yanomamo Indians of Southern Venezuela". Perspectives on Film 2: 5–9, 44–7.

—— (1988), "Collaboration in Ethnographic Film Making: A Personal View". In Jack R. Rollwagen (ed.), Anthropological Film-making: Anthropological Perspectives on the Production of Film and Video for General Public Audiences. Chur: Harwood Academic Publishers, pp. 1–30. [Originally published in Canberra Anthropology 5 (1) [1982]: 8–36]

—— (1992), "The Ethics of Ethnographic Film-Making". In Peter Ian Crawford and Ian Turton (eds.), Film as Ethnography. Manchester: Manchester University Press, pp. 196–204.

(1996), "Making the films". In Linda Connor, Patsy Asch, and Timothy Asch, Jero Tapakan: Balinese Healer. An Ethnographic Film Monograph. Second edition, Los Angeles: Ethnographics Press, pp. 32–43.

Asch, Timothy (with Amanda Crane) (1993), "Future prospects for the visualization of culture: Does the native still exist?" In Robert M. Boonzajer Flaes and Douglas Harper (eds.), Eyes across the Water II: Essay on Visual Anthropology and Sociology. Amsterdam: Het Spinhuis, pp. 1–9.

Asch, Timothy, Jesus Ignacio Cardozo, Hortensia Cabellero and Jose Bortoli (1991), "'The Story We Now Want to Hear Is Not Ours to Tell': Relinquishing Control over Representation: Toward Sharing Visual Communication Skills with The Yanomami". Visual Anthropology Review 7 (2): 102–106.

Asch, Timothy, John Marshall, and Peter Spier (1973), "Ethnographic Film: Structure and Function". Annual Review of Anthropology 7: 179–87.

Asch, Timothy and Gary Seaman (eds.) (1993), Yanomamö Film Study Guide. Center for Visual Anthropology, University of Southern California. Los Angeles: Ethnographics Press.

Bateson, Gregory (1936), Naven: A Survey of the Problems Suggested by a Composite Picture of the Culture of a New Guinea Tribe Drawn from Three Points of View. Stanford, California: Stanford University Press.

—— (1972), Steps to an Ecology of Mind: Collected Essays in Anthropology, Psychiatry, Evolution and Epistemology. San Francisco: Chandler Publishing Company.

Bateson, Gregory and Margaret Mead (1942), *Balinese Character: A Photographic Analysis* (Special Publications of the New York Academy of Sciences, Vol. II). New York: The New York Academy of Sciences.

[Bateson, Gregory and Margaret Mead] (1977), "Margaret Mead and Gregory Bateson on the Use of the Camera in Anthropology". *Studies in the Anthropology of Visual Communication* 4 (2): 78–80.

Biella, Peter, Napoleon A. Chagnon and Gary Seaman (1997), *Yanomamö Interactive: The Ax Fight*. CD-ROM. Fort Worth: Harcourt Brace College Publishers.

Cohen Hart (1979), "The Ax Fight: Mapping Anthropology on Film". *Ciné-Tracts* 2 (2): 62–73.

Connor, Linda, Patsy Asch, and Timothy Asch (1986), *Jero Tapakan: Balinese Healer. An Ethnographic Film Monograph*. Cambridge: Cambridge University Press.

—— (1996), *Jero Tapakan: Balinese Healer. An Ethnographic Film Monograph*. Revised edition. Los Angeles: Ethnographics Press.

DeBouzek, Jeanette (1989), "The 'Ethnographic Surrealism' of Jean Rouch". *Visual Anthropology* 2: 301–15.

Delbridge, A. *et al.* (eds.) (1981), *The Macquarie Dictionary*. New South Wales: Macquarie University.

Dewey, John (1938), *Experience and Education*. New York: The Macmillan Company.

Dwyer, Kevin (1987), *Moroccan Dialogues: Anthropology in Question*. Prospect Heights: Waveland Press.

Geertz, Hildred (1984), "Review of the Jero Tapakan film series". *American Anthropologist* 86: 809–11.

Jakobson, Roman (1960), "Concluding Statement: Linguistics and Poetics". In Thomas A. Sebeok (ed.), *Style in Language*. Cambridge, Massachusetts and New York: The Technology Press of the Massachusetts Institute of Technology and John Wiley & Sons, Inc., pp. 350–77.

Lewis, E. Douglas (1989), "Why Did Sina Dance? Stochasm, Choice and Intentionality in the Ritual Life of the Ata Tana 'Ai of Eastern Flores". In Paul Alexander (ed.), *Creating Indonesian Culture*. Sydney: Oceania Publications.

—— (1994), *Shot List (Visuals, Titles, Voice-Over Narration, and Sub-Titles) to* A Celebration of Origins, *A Film by Timothy Asch, E. Douglas Lewis, and Patsy Asch*. Unpublished ms.

Loizos, Peter (1993), *Innovation in Ethnographic Film: From Innocence to Self-consciousness, 1955–1985*. Manchester: Manchester University Press.

—— (1995), "Robert Gardner's *Rivers of Sand*: Toward a Reappraisal". In Leslie Devereaux and Roger Hillman (eds.), *Fields of Vision: Essays in Film Studies, Visual Anthropology and Photography*. Berkeley: University of California Press, pp. 311–28.

Lutkehaus, Nancy (1995), "'Ashes and Tears': To Tim Asch". *Visual Anthropology Review* 11 (1): 2–3.

MacDougall, David (1995), "Subtitling Ethnographic Films: Archetypes into Individualities". *Visual Anthropology Review* 11 (1): 83–90.

Marcus, George E. and Michael M. J. Fischer (1986), *Anthropology as Cultural Critique: An Experimental Moment in the Human Sciences*. Chicago: University of Chicago Press.

Martínez, Wilton (1995), "The Challenges of a Pioneer: Tim Asch, Otherness, and Film Reception". *Visual Anthropology Review* 11 (1): 53–82.

Mauss, Marcel (1969), *The Gift: Forms and Functions of Exchange in Archaic Societies*. Trans. Ian Cunnison. London: Routledge & Kegan Paul.

Mead, Margaret (1962), "Retrospects and Prospects". In *Anthropology and Human Behavior*. Washington DC: Anthropological Society of Washington, pp. 115–49.

—— (1975), "Introduction: Visual Anthropology in a Discipline of Words". In Paul Hockings (ed.), *Principles of Visual Anthropology*. The Hague: Mouton.

Moore, Alexander (1995), "Understanding Event Analysis: Using the Films of Tim Asch". *Visual Anthropology Review* 11 (1): 38–52.

Nichols, Bill (1981), *Ideology and the Image: Social Representation in the Cinema and Other Media*. Bloomington: Indiana University Press.

—— (1991), *Representing Reality: Issues and Concepts in Documentary*. Bloomington: Indiana University Press.

Ruby, Jay (1995), "Out of Sync: The Cinema of Tim Asch". *Visual Anthropology Review* 11 (1): 19–37.

Stoller, Paul (1992), *The Cinematic Griot: The Ethnography of Jean Rouch*. Chicago: University of Chicago Press.

Stoney, George C. (n.d.), "Must a Film-maker Leave His Mark? Some Notes on the Making of a Film about a Film". Unpublished typescript.

Tierney, Patrick (2000), "The Fierce Anthropologist (A Reporter at Large)". *The New Yorker*, 9 October 2000: 50–61.

Tyler, Stephen A. (1987), *The Unspeakable: Discourse, Dialogue and Rhetoric in the Postmodern World*. Madison: University of Wisconsin Press.

Volkman, Toby Alice (1982), *Films from DER*. Watertown, Massachusetts: Documentary Educational Resources.

Wolf, Margery (1992), *A Thrice-Told Tale: Feminism, Postmodernism and Ethnographic Responsibility*. Stanford: Stanford University Press.

Films

Asch, Timothy and Napoleon Chagnon (1970), *The Feast*. Watertown, Massachusetts: Documentary Educational Resources.

—— (1974), *A Father Washes His Children*. Watertown, Massachusetts: Documentary Educational Resources.

—— (1975), *A Man and His Wife Weave a Hammock*. Watertown, Massachusetts: Documentary Educational Resources.

—— (1974), *Weeding the Garden*. Watertown, Massachusetts: Documentary Educational Resources.

—— (1975), *The Ax Fight*. Watertown, Massachusetts: Documentary Educational Resources.

—— (1975), *Tapir Distribution*. Watertown, Massachusetts: Documentary Educational Resources.

Asch, Timothy, Linda Connor and Patsy Asch (1979), *A Balinese Trance Seance*. Watertown, Massachusetts: Documentary Educational Resources.

—— (1981), *Jero on Jero: A Balinese Trance Seance Observed*. Watertown, Massachusetts: Documentary Educational Resources.

—— (1983), *Jero Tapakan: Stories from the Life of a Balinese Healer*. Watertown, Massachusetts: Documentary Educational Resources.

—— (1983), *The Medium Is the Masseuse: A Balinese Massage*. Watertown, Massachusetts: Documentary Educational Resources.

Asch, Timothy, E. Douglas Lewis, and Patsy Asch (1993), *A Celebration of Origins*. Watertown, Massachusetts: Documentary Educational Resources.

Flaherty, Robert (1934), *Man of Aran*. Berkeley: University of California Extension Media

Center.

Mead, Margaret and Gregory Bateson (ca. 1951), *A Balinese Family*. (Character Formation in Different Cultures Series.) University Park, Pennsylvania: Audio Visual Services, Pennsylvania State University.

—— (ca. 1952), *Trance and Dance in Bali*. (Character Formation in Different Cultures Series.) University Park, Pennsylvania: Audio Visual Services, Pennsylvania State University.

—— (ca. 1952), *Childhood Rivalry in Bali and New Guinea*. (Character Formation in Different Cultures Series.) University Park, Pennsylvania: Audio Visual Services, Pennsylvania State University.

Stoney, George C. and James B. Brown (1978), *How the Myth was Made: A Study of Robert Flaherty's* Man of Aran. Chicago: Films, Inc.

Chapter 8

Producing culture

Shifting representations of social theory in the films of Tim Asch[1]

Faye Ginsburg

Introduction

This chapter considers the films Tim Asch produced over a period of twenty-five years in collaboration with various anthropologists and with his partner Patsy Asch. I argue that one can see in both their form and substance the changing epistemological perspectives regarding the production of knowledge taking place over the same period in anthropology more generally. In his essay "Out of Sync: The Cinema of Tim Asch", Jay Ruby argued what might seem to be a paradoxical position, that Asch's

> consistent lack of interest in pursuing current fashion, as well as his lack of synchronicity with the received wisdom of the film world and anthropology, ... allowed him to make significant contributions to both.
>
> (Ruby 1995: 20)

Yet, ironically and sometimes unwittingly, Asch's iconoclastic approach to film-making made him a significant contributor to both anthropology and social theory. While I would agree with Ruby that Asch was certainly never concerned about suiting current fashion, I think his films were, intentionally or not, often in synch with emergent and changing currents in anthropology, a fact that in no way undermines the originality of his ideas and their translation into film.

If one tracks Asch's films from the early Yanomamö series made in collaboration with Napoleon Chagnon from 1968–76, to the series on Jero Tapakan made in Bali with Patsy Asch and Linda Connor from 1978–83 (followed by the publication in 1986 of *Jero Tapakan: A Balinese Healer*), to the films on the island of Roti in eastern Indonesia made with James J. Fox in the 1980s, to the 1993 film *A Celebration of Origins*, made with Patsy Asch and Douglas Lewis in east central Flores in eastern Indonesia, to the workshops he conducted in collaboration with Venezuelan colleagues in which he trained Yanomami in video production in the 1990s, one can see a clear trajectory in the theoretical undergirdings of his films and in his written work that parallels shifts in the theoretical as well as ethical and political constructs that evolved more generally in anthropology in the same period.[2] At the same time, Asch's work cannot be reduced simply to these structuring frameworks (or limits, if you will). This is due, in part, to the quality of "excess", a useful term usually applied to genres such as melodrama, that Bill Nichols (1991) invokes in his discussion of documentary to characterize the impossibility of containing the sensory and narrative aspects of the cinematic material along a single diegetic track,[3] not to mention the complex and unpredictable ways in which audiences respond to images of people of other cultures.

Let me briefly summarize my argument. Asch has explicitly linked the initial work on the Yanomamö material to the inspiration of Marcel Mauss's book *The Gift*, but a number of other influences can be identified. The films are organized around themes in exchange theory and alliance theory but in a structural– functionalist framework, embedded in the untroubled positivism that prevailed in the 1960s and 1970s, along with a more general cultural preoccupation with questions of human aggression (Asch 1993: 1; Martínez 1995: 60). In his development of short sequence films as part of the Yanomamö project, one can see the influence of the Manchester School's focus on event analysis and social dramas as analytic constructs. The next major project, in collaboration with Patsy Asch and Australian anthropologist Linda Connor in Bali, focused on the healer and masseuse Jero Tapakan. The five films in this series are built on a theoretical orientation quite different from the structural–functionalism of the Yanomamö project. Instead, in the Balinese work, the narratives are structured around themes which anthropology explored in the 1970s and 1980s: the social organization of ritual, questions of human agency, personhood, female subjectivity, gendered aspects of social knowledge, and reflexivity. *A Celebration of Origins*, filmed in 1980 and completed in 1993, reflects an increasing concern with what Ortner has called the praxis-oriented approach in social anthropology – influenced by a variety of sources – in which attention is focused on the activities of everyday life as the experience or practice by which cultural sensibilities and structures are constituted. Finally, during that same period, the early 1990s, Asch's efforts to train Yanomami themselves in video production for whatever purposes they saw fit are in keeping with a growing concern for the politics of representation and dialogical approaches to the production of ethnography, issues with which American anthropology has been preoccupied since the late 1980s.

Intentional fallacies and plain speech

Before discussing Asch's films, I want briefly to consider the question of intention: did the shifting theoretical constructs in anthropology that are now apparent to me and others enter self-consciously into Asch's films during their production and editing? Jay Ruby has argued that, in the end, it does not matter what his initial intentions were; the impact of a film like *The Ax Fight*, he suggests, "is to create doubt about the conventions of representation in ethnographic film and about the nature of anthropological explanation" (1995: 30). Asch is not generally known as a theorist. As he put it in a 1993 interview about the recognition of *The Ax Fight* as a "prematurely post-modern" work:

These insights didn't take place through my reading at the time. I did it the way I have always done things in my life, in a practical way through my hands.

(quoted in Ruby 1995: 28)

He tended to speak of his work in concrete and pragmatic terms – discussing problems that arose ethically, institutionally, interpersonally, and pedagogically in the course of making, editing, showing, and teaching with films. Yet he also wanted to make films that represented core theoretical concepts in anthropology (Moore 1995: 47). In addition to his concerns with the film texts themselves, many of the issues Asch raised concerned conditions of production, distribution, and pedagogy. These are crucial to points which are now being argued in more theoretically driven writing on the issues raised in representing cultural difference. But because, in his writing, he used a language of common sense rather than academic jargon and protocol and referred primarily to the concrete experiences of his film-making, Asch's work has an ambiguous status in terms of theory, despite the fact that he was often raising important concerns. His discussion and refinement of the ethics of copyright and royalties arrangements when working with communities are enormously important in their implications for anthropology more generally. However, he did not frame these ideas in terms of more abstract and fashionable concepts about power and knowledge, but kept them tied explicitly to the practical consequences of making a film. For example, books such as *Writing Culture* (Clifford and Marcus 1986) and *Anthropology As Cultural Critique* (Marcus and Fischer 1986), which insisted on more dialogical approaches in the creation of written ethnographic texts, ignored not only ethnographic film's already long-standing experimentation in dialogical approaches to cinematic representation, but also the more concrete but equally (if not more) crucial issues regarding control over copyright, royalties, and distribution that Tim (and others) constantly discussed, and to which he found solutions which he put into practice from the 1970s on. His 1992 article "The Ethics of Ethnographic Film-making" includes a section entitled "Make a royalty arrangement with the people filmed and see that they receive money" in which he wrote,

The notion of sharing royalties was unusual ... [in the 1970s], but once it came up [in the work of Sarah Elder and Leonard Kamerling with Yupik communities], it seemed like a practice that should have been in place long before. ... We gave Jero Tapakan, the Balinese trance healer, a percentage of the royalties for films we made of her and will give a percentage to the Balinese village we worked with on a film of a village cremation ritual. [With] ... our film about the purification ritual in eastern Flores, a percentage of the royalties, as requested by the community elders, will go into an educational fund.

(Asch 1992: 202, 203)

Intellectual property rights are a critical concern that was not included in the more abstract discussions of the quandaries of ethnographic writing that predominated in the 1980s; they are only now becoming hot academic topics, often in relation to more sensational kinds of phenomena such as patenting of human genes. Clearly, Asch addressed many of the issues that preoccupied others at the time, but in ways that were specific to the practice of making ethnographic film and in terms of his constant querying of the ethics and politics of creating and circulating images of the lives of people in other cultures.

The Yanomamö work: from Marcel Mauss to premature post-modernism

The story of the complex relationship that emerged around Tim Asch's and Napoleon Chagnon's collaboration on the Yanomamö project is now almost apocryphal. Chagnon had invited Tim to come and film with him and, after some preliminary reading about the Yanomami, Tim had decided not to go. Then, as Tim recollected,

> When Chagnon phoned ... he kept talking to me ... he said that Marcel Mauss had written a script for a film that he wanted to make. This was quite a shock, it was such an amazing idea to me as a student of anthropology that you could make a film about central concepts. ... to film a central concept in anthropology ... like alliance and reciprocity, and exchange and the gift, and so forth, was really the way I wanted to go. So I found myself saying yes.
>
> (from Freiburg, quoted in Moore 1995: 47–8)

And indeed, as Jay Ruby and others have noted, the resulting film, *The Feast*, shot in 1968 and released in 1970, "is one of the few films produced to illustrate an anthropological idea – Mauss's concept of reciprocity" (Ruby 1995: 23).

In 1971, Asch went back to the Orinoco basin of Venezuela with Chagnon. With funding from a National Science Foundation grant they shot a range of short sequence films, an idea that Asch had developed while working with John Marshall on his Kalahari footage. The resulting short sequence films shot about the Yanomami, works such as *A Man and His Wife Make A Hammock* and *Children's Magical Death* (1974), make up the majority of the Yanomamö *oeuvre* and were conceived primarily as vehicles for teaching anthropology. Shot in an observational style and edited without narration, they were short enough for classroom use, revolved around a single event, and allowed audiences, especially students, to witness and interpret the everyday social life of people of another culture (Ruby 1995: 21). Recent essays on Asch's work have suggested that the idea for this kind of film had a number of sources. Generally, it was a period in American anthropology that was dominated by structural–functionalism as well as a strong post-war interest in the species-wide bases of human aggression; questions about the identities of people and their subjectivity – which became central to the field in the 1980s – were not of great interest. Rather, the activities of daily life, especially in small-scale societies, were studied in order to understand their underlying rationality. For example, the carrying capacity of the land might underlie settlement patterns, kinship structures, war and alliance, all of which were key factors in keeping communities to a certain size that could be sustained in the Amazonian environment. Certainly he was also influenced by his training at Columbia University with Margaret Mead (Moore 1995: 39). Based on the work she and Bateson had done using still and moving images in their *Balinese Character* study in the 1930s, Mead strssed the importance of following natural activity sequences in order to find how cultural patterns were writ small in basic socialization processes of everyday life.

Perhaps the most direct impact on Asch's work was John Marshall's footage and the development of short pieces which captured activity sequences in loving detail uninhibited by the price of film stock (Marshall 1995 personal communication). Even more than Marshall, Asch was concerned with the effectiveness of his work for teaching anthropology (Moore 1995) and constantly tried out his works-in-progress in classrooms to see if they were effective in helping students come to some comprehension of another culture. The short film format was ideal for American undergraduate courses, which meet twice a week for an hour; one can set the context for a ten- or twenty-minute film and still have adequate time for discussion. Indeed, that format was used by the *Man, A Course of Study* (MACOS) experimental curriculum project developed in the Boston area in the 1960s and with which Asch was involved in 1966 (Dow 1991; see Lutkehaus, this volume). Like Asch and Marshall, the creators of MACOS used short films of "fixed action sequences" of animal and human behavior which students would watch and analyze as a vehicle for teaching inductive reasoning to junior high school students.

One cannot ignore the broader film culture that influenced Asch and other key development of ethnographic film in the 1960s and 1970s, such as David and Judith MacDougall. They have mentioned the impact of subtitled foreign films – especially Italian neo-realism – as an inspiration to subtitle their ethnographic films in order to "open a new pathway" to the thoughts and feelings of people from another culture (MacDougall 1995: 83). The Boston area was also a rich center for the development of documentary in the late 1960s and 1970s, in particular through the American direct cinema movement, in which people such as Fred Wiseman and Ricky Leacock were developing observational strategies similar to those used by Marshall and Asch in their work (Ruby 1995); indeed, John Marshall worked on Fred Wiseman's direct cinema masterpiece *Titicut Follies*, and all of these filmmakers, along with Jean Rouch, participated in the Flaherty Film Seminars in the 1970s (Barnouw 1993).

Yet another intellectual source was Asch's studies at Harvard University with Tom Beidelman, who became a lifelong friend and influence. In his teaching, Beidelman used the work of the Manchester school (1995, personal communication), an approach that is especially pertinent to the development of the sequence films. For example, Max Gluckman's famous articulation of extended case studies and situational analysis, as important methodological foci in the analysis of issues of key cultural and social significance, became the building blocks of ethnographic analysis which was sensitive to temporality in understanding the organization of social life. These ideas were later developed by Victor Turner, Gluckman's student, in his work on ritual processes and the concept of the social drama as an analytic tool for understanding the social structure of conflict (Turner 1974).

Whether intentional or not, *The Ax Fight* is exemplary of the use of film to document and demonstrate social drama in specific events, as others have pointed out (cf. Moore 1995: 43 ff.). On his second day in Mishimishimaböwei-teri in 1971, Asch shot eleven minutes of a fight that broke out in the village, footage which became the material for what is arguably the best known of his films. *The Ax Fight* has acquired the status of the *Rashomon* of ethnographic films because it provides several cinematic interpretations of the same material. First, it takes the viewer through unedited sound and visuals; second, it provides a didactic version in slow motion, with a pedagogical narration which explains the fight in terms of alliance theory and by using kinship charts to identify the relationships of the main actors. Finally, the event is recapitulated in a slickly edited version. In 1992, Asch reflected on how he and Chagnon decided to structure the film in this way:

> ... it wasn't really but a few minutes after having discovered how people were related that we could easily make at least a structural–functional analysis of what happened in the ax fight. ...
>
> In 1971 it was perfectly okay. And alliance theory worked out perfectly well with what else we knew about the culture.
>
> (quoted in Ruby 1995: 27)

> ... And it's a very dated film if you are going to take it as a piece of serious work. It belongs in another era. But I think also that the film is [a] harbinger of postmodernism long before we get postmodernism ... and I was feeling, you know, halfway into making the film, this great suspicion of the whole field beginning to fall apart before my eyes as I was putting *The Ax Fight* together. ... But now I would love to put an introduction to it that says "About Realism".
>
> ... I went into this fairly naively with my anthropology training, thinking that I was making a fascinating truthful translation or representation of culture ... I wasn't aware of any postmodern critiques of representation ... this whole notion of truth and making an accurate representation blew up in my face. ... That was when my whole life and commitment to anthropology got really shattered ...
>
> (quoted in Ruby 1995: 28)

The Bali Project: recuperating the subject

It was shortly after that crisis that Asch began his work in Indonesia, first with James Fox in 1977 on the island of Roti in eastern Indonesia. In 1978, while waiting in Bali for Fox to join him on a second trip to Roti, he decided to do some shooting with anthropologist Linda Connor, whom he had met the year before, in order to test his recently repaired camera (Connor *et al.* 1986: 44–5). According to Connor and Patsy Asch:

The first phase of this project began serendipitously in 1978, late in Connor's two-year stay in Central Bali. Connor was undertaking doctoral research and was deeply involved in relationships with Jero Tapakan, the healer who is the subject of four of the films, and other residents of Jero's village. The film-making took place intensively over the six-week period that Tim Asch was in Bali, most of it spent in Jero's village. The second filming and fieldwork trip in 1980 was planned to let us share our footage with the participants, both to offer them something in return for their cooperation and to incorporate their responses into our film corpus to expand the record of their different perspectives on the footage.

(Connor and Asch, this volume)

This change in approach from the Yanomamö project was shaped by a number of circumstances, not the least of which was the shift to research by and about a woman, as well as the kinds of concerns Balinese subjects had about how they were to be represented in film. In an article addressing those issues, Linda Connor and Patsy Asch commented:

In the fieldworld ... the researcher comes to terms with the particular under-standings which constitute the hosts' experience of the world. These indige-nous objectifications of experience challenge and change the categories the anthropologist has brought to "the field", a powerful objectification in itself.

(Connor and Asch, this volume)

Connor and Asch further elaborate this point:

Our narrative motifs, constructed around anthropological theory, emphasized the importance of informal social interactions and ceremonial preparations, as they reveal important elements of village sociality. For our hosts, the peak events, and not the preparations, were the substantial achievements that should be celebrated on film ... the content of the footage reveals a conver-gence of the interests of all of the participants' perspectives, our hosts and ours.

(Connor and Asch, this volume; cf. MacDougall 1995)

In addition, Asch was self-consciously trying to avoid what he had come to regard as the problems of the Yanomamö project. As he recounted in the 1986 monograph *Jero Tapakan*

By the time I began to film with Linda Connor in Bali, I had four main reserva-tions about the Yanomamo films.
1   Unnarrated films of people who look exotic can be, and frequently are, used to reinforce Western prejudices about "primitive" people ...
2   I had intended that the films be integrated with written materials that would provide the needed context to help counter such prejudice and to

make the films more valuable for instruction. …

3   I regretted not filming more Yanomamo conversations, which would have allowed individual Yanomamo to reveal their thoughts and opinions more directly. It is disappointing that so few individual characters emerge in ethnographic films.

4   I was sorry that we dared not take our film back to show to participants. Were Yanomamo to see images of dead relatives they would probably try to kill us, assuming that because we had stolen the dead people's souls (by taking their images) we were responsible for their deaths.

(Connor *et al.* 1986: 43–4)

The representations of Jero Tapakan, then, were intentionally unlike most of the Yanomamö films, in which people are depicted as Durkheimian objects of social fact, typical of the cultural determinism of American anthropology of the 1960s and early 1970s. As Asch came to recognize, people of other "exotic" cultures were portrayed as unproblematically inhabiting a timeless and unchanging ethnographic present; their behavior was of interest insofar as it helped to answer broader general questions about human behavior. There was little opportunity to hear what they thought or engage them in filmic "conversation" (as David and Judith MacDougall did in their work in Africa in the 1970s). While this is the broader paradigm in which much of the Yanomamö work was created, it is also important to note the ways in which Tim Asch also broke that framework, for example by making a film such as *New Tribes Mission* (1975, 12 min.) about the missionaries in the area, and by simple but crucial constructions such as the insistence on placing the date of the film on the film frame.

The Balinese films addressed the perceived shortcomings in the Yanomamö films very directly. First of all, they were developed around the central character of Jero Tapakan, who is a vibrant, lively, and voluble presence in all the films, beginning with the 1978–79 work, *Jero Tapakan: Stories from the Life of a Balinese Healer* (1983), in which Jero talks about her personal history: from her poverty as a peasant farmer to her years wandering as a peddler, to her initiation through mystical visions to the calling of spirit medium. In the film, she is presented as a self-conscious subject, able to represent and interpret her own life in a narrative form comprehensible to a western audience. Jero is very much an intending social actor, an agent whose personhood and subjectivity are richly represented. These concerns are of a piece with the preoccupations of American anthropology in the late 1970s and 1980s, a period which stressed the creativity of individuals as actors in social settings as well as the need for reflexive accounts of the ethnographic encounter, positions that were brilliantly articulated in the ethnographies and films of Barbara Myerhoff (Myerhoff 1974, 1978).[4]

In *A Balinese Trance Seance* (1979), we see Jero in her household shrine where she receives clients seeking to learn the cause of their young son's premature death. While in trance, ancestors speak through Jero, and then the spirit of the young boy, again speaking through Jero, reveals his desire for cremation. According to Tim

Asch, when he showed the film to a class at Flinders University in South Australia, three of the students

> were incensed at the seemingly "imperialistic" and "voyeuristic" quality of the film, ... I suddenly realized that a film of Jero's reactions to seeing herself in the séance film would reveal her attitude toward the project. Furthermore, Jero's reactions might be the best way to answer some of the many difficult questions raised among Western audiences ... particularly the question of whether Jero is a charlatan. Such a film also would demonstrate the value of showing participants a film of themselves as a way of eliciting additional information and interpretations of past events.
>
> (Connor *et al.* 1986: 46)

The resulting film, *Jero on Jero* (1981), is an innovative experiment in reflexivity in film-making, in which the film-makers and anthropologist took *A Balinese Trance Seance* back to Bali and showed it to Jero to ask her for her commentary on the film, on her trance state, the spirits who speak through her, and on her relationship with her clients. I should add, from my experience of teaching the film, that it serves to legitimate the film-makers' and anthropologist's role in filming, as it becomes apparent that she is comfortable with images of herself in trance, which otherwise raised ethical questions for the audience about whether one can get "informed consent" from a person in this state.

In *The Medium Is the Masseuse: A Balinese Massage* (1983), we witness Jero treating a married couple who suffer from infertility, including her use of therapeutic massage which takes place in the midst of a courtyard setting; Jero then talks with the couple and the anthropologists about the husband's illness. Later, the client discusses his treatment. These four films clearly addressed the concerns Tim had of objectifying his subjects. By creating a character whose sense of her subjectivity is very strong, who seems very much in control of the narrative, and whose commentary on her own actions provides a dialogical sense of the production of ethnographic knowledge, the films are in keeping with the issues that emerged more generally in American anthropology of that period. Finally, the ethnographic film monograph *Jero Tapakan: A Balinese Healer* provided the kind of publication – both ethnographically authoritative and filled with detail on the film production itself – that Asch felt was crucial to his pedagogical goals.

The Yanomamö Training Project: reverse shots

In 1990, Asch attended a conference on Yanomamö land rights, where he screened several of the films that he had made about them two decades earlier. Writing about the event in 1991, he reflected:

> They looked at the films attentively and said that while they thought that the films were quite accurate, it would be the "kiss of death" for people to think

that the Yanomami still live today the way they appear to be in the films. They suggested that I make a film about the way they live today .... I am no longer as interested in making films about them as I am in seeing the kinds of films that they might make about themselves. Moreover, I now question my role as an outsider representing their life and concerns to an outside world.

(Asch *et al.* 1991: 102)

I am indebted to the Yanomami for letting me view their lives and film their culture. ... Now, I want to help them communicate their story told in their way to the wider world, if they so choose, and to enable them to use visual media to communicate amongst themselves. Communication may be the most important survival tool in a changing world.

(ibid.: 106)

Asch's practical response was to secure funding from la Fundación Venezolana para la Investigación Antropológica (FUNVENA) and the Rock Foundation to develop training workshops in video production and, along with his Venezuelan colleagues Jesus Cardozo and Hortensia Caballero, run some training programs for interested Yanomami at Mavaca in the spring of 1991. This kind of activity is very much in keeping with a broader trend in visual anthropology to develop indigenous media production. This work began with Sol Worth's Navajo Eyes project in the 1960s (Worth and Adair 1997) and continued with the research of his student, Eric Michaels, with Aboriginal Australians in Central Australia in the 1980s (Michaels 1994), and more recently Terence Turner's (1991) and Vincent Carelli's work with the Kayapo, Waiapi, and other societies in the Amazon. These projects and Asch's work with the Yanomami were a response both to the problematic questions raised by traditional ethnographic film practice and to the increasing self-consciousness and interest in representation of those people who have, in the past, been the ethnographic object.[5]

Conclusion

The trajectory of Asch's career I have sketched, from the early Yanomamö project which employed objective (and objectifying) cinematic techniques to record social behavior, to the reflexive and person-centered approach of the Bali work, to the interest in teaching the Yanomami to film themselves, is one that Asch himself laid out as he reflected on his quarter-century of work as an ethnographic film-maker:

In 1991 the question of who should represent what to whom seems more complicated to me than it did in 1968 when I set out to make my own records of Yanomamo culture. It has always been my conviction that it is important for us (not just in the United States, but the global us) to know about other cultures, to have an appreciation for what is unique about them. Not only might we profit from that knowledge, but we might also care more about the

concerns of members of other cultures. In a world that is becoming increasingly homogenized and, in places, increasingly hostile to cultural diversity it
seems important to increase our knowledge of each other. That conviction has
been and continues to be the foundation of my work. I also remain convinced
that visual media are a powerful means of communication, in many instances,
and particularly in instances of cross-cultural communication, more powerful
than the written or the spoken word. The question which has become
perplexing is: how are these sorts of messages about cultures best conveyed?

(Asch et al. 1991: 102)

In my view, it is this last question that Asch constantly asked himself – how to best
communicate anthropology's concept of culture and his well-known commitment
to pedagogy – that suggests why his work followed such a distinctive path. It is a
question that I think Tim tried to reconsider anew with each project, leading him
to engage in certain kinds of practices that distinguished him from other ethnographic film-makers of his generation.[6]

I would argue that several characteristics made Tim Asch unusually capable of
addressing new perspectives in each project. First, as anyone who met him would
attest, Asch was astonishingly receptive to new ideas and people; perhaps because he
was not tied to any particular "lineage" in anthropology, he did not become
entrenched in a single theoretical position, but kept himself receptive to new possibilities that were compatible with his concerns as a film-maker. Related to that
quality was his insistence on working as a collaborator with different anthropologists,
so that he continued to try out different frameworks for his film projects; his interest
in enabling *their* perspective to come through in the film was a remarkably open and
modest quality for someone working in a field (documentary film-making) more
generally characterized by enormous egos and single-minded *auteurs*. Indeed, he
repeatedly said that he was not an *auteur* with a particular cinematic vision in mind,
but simply one of those anthropologists who continually "seek better ways to record
and translate the beliefs and traditions of human cultures … in unfamiliar, often
distant, and isolated places" (Asch 1992: 196). In the end, Asch's approach to his
work revolved around an overwhelming interest in film-making as a tool for effective
pedagogy about other cultures. That concern is reflected in the unique process he
established of editing and refining his films in relation to feedback from classes and in
his philosophical commitment to the project of ethnographic film in the service of
the much larger ideals he held as a self-avowed evangelist for liberal humanism.

Initially, Asch was somewhat naïve in his presumption that mere exposure to
images and information about people from other societies would provide a tool
against racism. Asch tried continually to be aware of that and other presuppositions, and the shortcomings of prior work, insisting that films should always be
shown in a context in which someone could guide the viewers to a broader understanding of the world indexed by the film. He was perhaps unique in his generation
for his concern with his work's impact, not so much in cinematic but in social
terms, i.e. the actual effects of these images as they circulate in the real world. This

is clear in his response to the research of one his students at USC, Wilton Martínez, who studied the effect of Asch's and other people's ethnographic films on undergraduate attitudes. The project demonstrated that, rather than becoming more relativistic in their views, the students were often confirmed in their racist convictions after watching representations of people from other cultures (see Martínez, this volume). It is hard to imagine another film-maker who would respond in the way that Tim Asch did to these research results.

> ... perhaps the [Yanomamö] films should be removed from circulation. The curriculum was designed to force the USC students out of their set ways, to see the way other cultures see the world. ... The purpose was not to threaten the students' values but to interest them in values we might all share. But if the students' values that they live and grow by are so well-established and [intransigent] or entrenched then what students see on film may only strengthen their values. If that is the case, for the sake of these students and the Yanomami these thirty-nine films should be removed to an archive and not used for teaching.
>
> (quoted in Ruby 1995: 32)

Asch's openness to criticism and new ideas, flexibility, collaboration, and commitment to anthropology as a field made his work remarkably responsive to changing theoretical paradigms. In this sense, his films are as successful as a record of changes in our theories of culture and concerns about representing them, as they are documents of people in diverse societies. In his films, Asch found a medium other than the logocentric language of academic writing, a performative medium through which to present people from other cultures and analyses of them. These works, which will endure as a wonderful legacy to his commitment to cross-cultural understanding, were built out of the cinematic fragments of other people's lives, theoretical understandings of the moment they were made, and the social relations constituted by the circulation of ethnographic imagery from the field to the classroom and back.

Notes

1 My thanks to Barbara Abrash, Douglas Lewis, Meg McLagan, and Fred Myers for their helpful comments on this essay. I want to acknowledge those authors – Patsy Asch, Linda Connor, Nancy Lutkehaus, David MacDougall, Wilton Martínez, Alexander Moore, and Jay Ruby – who contributed to the Spring 1995 issue of *Visual Anthropology Review*, entitled "Out of Sync" and devoted to the cinema of Tim Asch. I recommend that volume to anyone interested in Asch's work. Their articles include a number of retrospective interviews that were done with Tim in the early 1990s and provide some insight into his intentions at the time of making different films and changes in his understandings of those projects many years later. I started drafting this paper in 1993 and then put it aside because of other commitments. In the interim, my colleagues wrote these thoughtful essays which I found both frustrating and enormously helpful when I returned to work on this paper, as a number of ideas I had sketched out in 1993 are now well developed in a number of the pieces.
2 In his 1995 article, "The Challenges of a Pioneer: Tim Asch, Otherness, and Film Reception", a revised version of which is included in this volume, Wilton Martínez made a similar point:

Asch's film-making in collaboration with various anthropologists during the last 30 years – ranging from the disembodied, objectivist representation of the Yanomamö in the sixties to the more personal "reflexive" imaging of Balinese healer Jero Tapakan in the seventies, to his more recent effort in promoting indigenous video production among the Yanomamö – reflects as much about his professional evolution ... as the discipline's different political engagements with the other.

(Martínez 1995: 57)

3 Diegesis refers to the narrative constituted by the filmic reality created by the action enacted within the frame of the screen representation (see Hayward 1996: 67).

4 Myerhoff was instrumental in recruiting Tim Asch to the visual anthropology program at the University of Southern California in the early 1980s.

5 For a further elaboration of this argument see Ginsburg (1994).

6 Other film-makers from Asch's cohort, such as Robert Gardner, have held to an *auteur* kind of vision; or find, as the MacDougalls have written recently, that their work is very much shaped by "complicities of style" required by the diverse performative styles of the people with whom they have worked, such as the Turkana in East Africa or Aboriginal Australians.

References

Asch, Timothy (1992),"The Ethics of Ethnographic Film-making". In Peter Ian Crawford and David Turton (eds.), *Film As Ethnography*. Manchester: Manchester University Press.

—— (1993), "Bias in Ethnographic Reporting and Using the Yanomamo Films in Teaching". In Timothy Asch and Gary Seaman (eds.), *Yanomamo Film Study Guide*. Los Angeles: Ethnographics Press.

Asch, Tim, Jesus Ignacio Cardozo, Hortensia Caballero, and Jose Bortoli (1991), "The Story We Now Want to Hear is Not Ours to Tell: Relinquishing Control Over Representation: Toward Sharing Visual Communication Skills with Yanomami". *Visual Anthropology Review* 7 (2): 102–6.

Barnouw, Erik (1993), *Documentary: A History of the Non-Fiction Film*. New York: Oxford University Press.

Clifford, James and George Marcus, eds. (1986), *Writing Culture: The Poetics and Politics of Ethnography*. Berkeley: University of California Press.

Connor, Linda and Patsy Asch (1995), "Subjects, Images, Voices: Representing Gender in Ethnographic Film". *Visual Anthropology Review* 11 (1): 5–18.

Connor, Linda, Patsy Asch, and Timothy Asch (1986), *Jero Tapakan: A Balinese Healer. An Ethnographic Film Monograph*. Cambridge: Cambridge University Press.

Dow, Peter (1991), *Schoolhouse Politics: Lessons from the Sputnik Era*. Cambridge: Harvard University Press.

Ginsburg, Faye (1994), "Culture/media: A (Mild) Polemic". *Anthropology Today*, vol. 10, no. 2 (April).

Hayward, Susan (1996), *Key Concepts in Cinema Studies*. New York: Routledge.

Lutkehaus, Nancy (1994), "Ashes and Tears: To Timothy Asch". *Visual Anthropology Review* 11 (1): 2–4.

MacDougall, David (1995), "Subtitling Ethnographic Films: Archetypes into Individualities". *Visual Anthropology Review* 11 (1): 83–91.

Marcus, George and Michael Fischer (1986), *Anthropology As Cultural Critique*. Chicago: University of Chicago Press.

Martínez, Wilton (1995), "The Challenges of a Pioneer: Tim Asch, Otherness, and Film Reception". *Visual Anthropology Review* 11 (1): 53–82.

Michaels, Eric (1994), *Bad Aboriginal Art: Tradition, Media, and Technological Horizons*. Minneapolis: University of Minnesota Press.

Moore, Alexander (1995), "Understanding Event Analysis: Using the Films of Tim Asch". *Visual Anthropology Review* 11 (1): 38.

Myerhoff, Barbara (1974), *The Peyote Hunt: The Sacred Journey of the Huichol Indians*. Ithaca, New York: Cornell University Press.

—— (1978), *Number Our Days*. New York: Dutton.

Nichols, Bill (1991), *Representing Reality: Issues and Concepts in Documentary*. Bloomington: Indiana University Press.

Ruby, Jay (1995), "Out of Sync: The Cinema of Tim Asch". *Visual Anthropology Review* 11 (1): 19–37.

Turner, Terence (1991), "Representing, Resisting, Rethinking: Historical Transformations of Kayapo Culture and Anthropological Consciousness". In George W. Stocking (ed.), *Colonial Situations: Essays on the Contextualization of Ethnographic Knowledge*. Madison: University of Wisconsin Press, pp. 285–313.

Turner, Victor (1974), *Dramas, Fields, Metaphors: Symbolic Action in Human Society*. New York: Cornell University Press.

Worth, Sol and John Adair (1997), *Through Navajo Eyes: An Exploration in Film Communication and Anthropology*. Second edition. Albuquerque: University of New Mexico Press.

Chapter 9

Subjects, images, voices

Representations of gender in the films of Timothy Asch[1]

Linda H. Connor and Patsy Asch

Introduction

Early in 1994, many of Tim Asch's friends and colleagues gathered at the University of Southern California to view a retrospective of his films. The films had been selected and shown over three evenings at the Margaret Mead Film Festival in New York the previous October. At an informal gathering, when this book was proposed, we were asked to write about "the introduction of gender" in Tim's films when he began working with Linda Connor in Bali. The request seemed to imply that gender and women are conflated categories and that gender is most appropriately written about by women. We begin from our understanding that all ethnographic film representations are inflected by the gender of their makers. The way in which a film is conceptualized, shot, and edited is inseparable from the interactions of our gendered selves with those of the people we film and with anthropological discourses of the time. As a film-maker, Tim Asch began to address questions of gender in ethnographic film-making when he began collaborating with Linda Connor on films about Jero Tapakan, a Balinese woman.

Because films by and about women are no more or less "gendered" than those by and about men, we will not restrict our discussion to the Bali films, in which we were both closely involved, but will examine a number of films made by Tim Asch in cooperation with other people.[2] Our questions concern ways of understanding ethnographic films as gendered representations, in relation to the process of their making. We explore possible ways of understanding the film-makers' involvement in ethnographic filming, and how this is connected to the representations produced. Questions of gender are necessarily part of our reflections, not least because we are aware that much of the movement toward reflexive interpretation in anthropology, insofar as it has embraced ethnographic film, has neglected gender.[3]

Just as we have found it useful to apply Bakhtin's notion of dialogic communication (Bakhtin 1981) to examine cross-cultural conversations in our films (Asch and Connor, 1994), we have found it productive to apply a dialogic model to gender insofar as it is expressed and experienced differentially in varying situations, rather than to conceive of gender as fixed or immutable. The most useful conceptualization of gender for our purposes comes from Teresa de Lauretis's contention that:

> Like sexuality ... gender is not a property of bodies or something originally existent in human beings, but "the set of effects produced in bodies, behavior, and social relations," in Foucault's words, by the deployment of "a complex political technology."
>
> (1987: 3)

These effects are systems of representations which are culturally constructed. Taking issue with Foucault, who neglected gender, as well as alternative discourses, in his "technologies of sex" de Lauretis argues that gendered identities are constructed through technologies of representation as well as through discursive practices which are differently available to men and women, and between and across this sexual duality. This does not preclude the possibility of reconstructions of gender which resist dominant discourses, and which exist "in the margins of hegemonic discourses" (1987: 18).

We find it productive to think about ethnographic film as a "technology of gender" in anthropology which both produces gendered representations, and is produced by them.[4] Such a frame of reference leads us to investigate the process of ethnographic film-making as a gendered practice, and its potential for reproducing dominant gender representations, as well as for generating different discourses. Anthropology's proclaimed engagement across cultural boundaries and the supposedly inductive methodology of fieldwork provide an opportunity to examine critically processes of representing gender and their effects in specific situations.

Initiating relationships

Like the choices which are made by all ethnographers, the choices we made about where to do fieldwork and filming, and with whom, were circumscribed by personal factors such as age, sex, class, and family situation. In this chapter we discuss four different film and fieldwork projects and sets of relationships, each with different inflections of gender. In Bali, we found our field identities evolved out of the objectifications of our hosts interacting with our self-definitions at the time. Aspects of our personal biographies became implicated in the relationships of the "field-world" (Hastrup 1992: 120). Kirsten Hastrup has discussed at some length the repositioning of the anthropologist as subject in the field through the relations she has with her hosts. The particular circumstances of fieldwork delimit the identification of research problems and the knowledge that is produced from the experience (Hastrup 1992).

We have recounted in greater detail elsewhere a history of the collaborative project involving ourselves, Tim Asch, Jero Tapakan, and other residents of a central Balinese village (Connor et al. 1986). The first phase of this project began serendipitously in 1978, late in Connor's two-year stay in Central Bali.[5] Connor was undertaking doctoral research and was deeply involved in relationships with Jero Tapakan, the healer who is the subject of four of the films, and other residents of Jero's village. The film-making took place intensively over the six-week period that Tim Asch was in Bali, most of it spent in Jero's village. The second filming and fieldwork trip in 1980 was planned to let us share our footage with the participants, both to offer them something in return for their cooperation and to incorporate their responses into our film corpus to expand the record of their different perspec-tives on the footage. Patsy Asch was not present during the first filming, but she participated in the second field trip.

Despite Connor's ambiguous status as a foreign student, villagers commonly referred to Connor as *bujang*, a "young single woman".[6] Rural Balinese women so ascribed are not considered fully adult (only through marriage and child-bearing do they achieve this). They are under the authority and protection of senior male kin and brothers, and independent activity is quite limited. This label created opportu-nities in some contexts of field research and difficulties in others. In terms of the choice of subject for the films, the decision to work with Jero Tapakan grew out of Connor's close relationship with this kind and motherly older woman. Although there were many male healers with practices similar to Jero Tapakan's, it was easier for Connor to take on the various roles of pupil, child, and companion to an older woman than it would have been to negotiate these roles in relation to a male healer.

Choices such as with whom to work closely are heavily influenced by the social constraints of the field-world, particularly with respect to age and gender. One consequence of Connor's choices in the field is that the finished films focus on a woman, not a man, tell the audience about her experiences, and show her work as a healer. In the light of these films, it becomes more difficult to accept a male subject as standing for the "generic person" in Bali.

In retrospect it is apparent that Connor's multiple identities (as foreign woman, student, companion and pupil of Jero, and *bujang*) contributed to the way her anthropological knowledge was shaped through her fieldwork experience.

> LC: As a lone single woman in a Balinese village, a stranger from afar, I might not have had much greater respect or social mobility than a Balinese woman in the same situation. The enhancement of my position by official research permission from the Indonesian government and my high level of education facilitated my access to a broad field of social relations. Thus I was protected in my research by political authoritarianism and the ideological heritage of colo-nialism. This did not prevent me from having to negotiate with specific groups and individuals in order to carry out research on a daily basis. Nevertheless, institutional politics and historical conditions provided the framework in which these negotiations occurred. The legitimacy bestowed by a patriarchal and authoritarian state compensated for some of the difficulties of being a woman researcher in Bali. During my initial period of fieldwork I never confronted the way my presence reproduced colonial relationships, political oppression, and gender inequality, perhaps because I developed research

topics that did not radically challenge my hosts' tolerance of my potentially contradictory identities and categorical ambiguity. It might have been different had I attempted to work in male-dominated domains.

When Tim Asch arrived in the village, the people of the village identified him as Connor's teacher. His age (almost twenty years her senior), sex, and greater wealth (as was apparent in the large amount of sophisticated equipment he brought), made this an unproblematic categorization for villagers. Moreover, Connor was obviously under his tutelage as she struggled to grasp the principles of film-making and learned to operate the Nagra tape recorder. Her assistance as interpreter and cultural guide was readily interpreted by villagers as a subordinate role appropriate to the "pupil" designation. Tim Asch shared the advantages enjoyed by Connor and did not have to resolve the multiple and contradictory roles engendered by the fieldwork.

The differences in experiencing relationships in the field outlined above suggest that discussions of the "privileged" position of women in fieldwork in terms of access to people of both genders tend to leave out of the account the tenacity and emotional resilience required to navigate these complexities on a daily basis (cf. Reisman 1964: xvi; Nader cited in Callaway 1992: 35). Local people are always likely to contest privileges deriving from ambiguities of status or from multiple statuses. These privileges require ongoing assertion throughout the field experience. Prior to the rise of feminist scholarship, during fieldwork many women found that they denied or attempted to obscure the significance of having been raised female. In doing so, they denied one of the most powerful aspects of their sense of self, thereby heightening the sense of alienation from their pre-field-world selves that ethnographers often experience. Patsy Asch reflects on this process as it unfolded during filming in Afghanistan.

> **PA**: My first experiences as a film-maker were in Afghanistan in 1975. Tim and I accompanied Asen Balikci to film a pastoral migration of Pashtoon to their summer pastures. We worked closely with one family, headed by a powerful patriarch, Haji Omar, who seemed to like both the prestige of having a film crew focus on his family, and the money we paid for supplies, food, and rental of pack animals. We began filming in the winter pastures, where we had relatively equal access to men and women. The first ten days we were accompanied by an American woman, Pam Hunte, who spoke Persian fluently and was able to speak with some of the older women. When Tim was struck with a severe bout of dysentery, I taught Pam to record sound. She and I filmed intimate footage of the relationship between a woman and her mother-in-law, exchanges that would have been difficult for Tim to film. We had sought a subject to film that interested us and that we felt comfortable recording. The remainder of the trip Tim filmed and I recorded sound.
>
> With rare exceptions, our footage focused on the activities of men and, when women were involved, they provided a background for the men. Indeed,

Figure 9.1 Tim Asch (seated, background) filming and Patsy Asch (standing, center) recording film sound with Asen Balikci (foreground, left). Afghanistan.

Figure 9.2 Patsy Asch recording film sound. Afghanistan.

Figure 9.3 Tim Asch with Asen Balikci (right, standing) filming in Afghanistan.

in the towns we visited, including one where we filmed for a week, there were no other women visible. Not only did I cover my face and body with Afghan clothing, I felt I should not look directly at people, something difficult to avoid when recording sound. When people outside Haji Omar's family objected to our filming, perhaps because we were strangers in an Islamic country, I was the target of their attacks; I was the person stoned. I engaged in a kind of self-eradication, as well as a denial of my moral and social responsibilities. I felt that I could only argue against filming on the grounds of what would be best for the film rather than for the people we were filming.

I don't believe Tim had a similar experience precisely because of the continuity in his gendered identity that this particular cultural setting permitted. Like the men I traveled with, I accepted male behavior as the norm. If I wanted access to power, in this case the power to represent the lives of others, I should behave like a man, something I was not skilled at doing. At the time, male anthropologists could ignore gender and present their views as though they stood for the generic person but women were caught in a conflict between their sense of themselves as women, and the academic and popular discourses available that assumed a universalist male perspective.

Relations between men and women are expressed very differently in Afghanistan and Bali and my experiences in Bali were completely different from those in Afghanistan. Balinese perceptions of who I was were shaped by Linda's field identities and by assumptions about our relationship, often thought of as younger sister–older sister. My sense of my own competence had grown as I became a more experienced film-maker. I had greater fluency in the Indonesian language than in Persian or Pashtoon. And I felt more comfortable because I wasn't the only woman, of either culture, present much of the time.

A brief consideration of the relationships between the film-makers, Asch and Chagnon, and the Yanomamö, illustrates how gender relations are embedded in the representations produced, while remaining invisible in the conceptualization of the research questions. Whereas the Bali films were made among people that Connor knew well and had worked with for two years, Tim Asch and Chagnon filmed in villages where they had more transient relationships.[7]

In *Studying the Yanomamö* (1974), Chagnon describes how he came to work in Mishimishimaböwei-teri, the village where most of the films were shot. He implies that he took up aspects of the role of fierce headman because he believed that was the safest way to get access to distant villages in order to make a thorough demographic study of the Yanomami: "I had to establish my position in some sort of pecking order of ferocity at each and every village" (Chagnon 1968: 9). Chagnon frequently refers to occasions on which he countered the challenges of the Yanomamö by responding bravely and fiercely. "Whenever I took such action and defended my rights, I got along much better with the Yanomamö" (1968: 10). His book focused almost exclusively on male behavior, not only, it seems, because he was a man but also because, in his view, "Yanomamö society is decidedly masculine, male chauvinistic if you will" (1992: 122).

Asch reports playing a very different role from Chagnon's:

> ... the hosts took us to their shelter, but because they were so annoyed with us,[8] they didn't have a hammock prepared. ... I tried very hard to string mine properly but I had never tied hammock-rope on a smooth pole before. ... I tied both ends of the hammock, went and sat in the middle and slipped to the ground as the hammock-rope slid down the smooth pole. My knees were up to my chin. Although absolutely exhausted, I tied it all once again. Then I sat down very carefully, thinking, "If it should fail this time, I'm just going to have to sit on the ground". It did fail; I sat there with my knees up against my chin.
>
> (Asch 1979: 44)

On the second day while walking in the jungle, I tripped. "He's so harmless he couldn't hit a tapir with a bow and arrow at 20 feet," a headman told Chagnon shortly thereafter. Needless to say, my role was soon one of comic relief compared to Chagnon's macho male. Of course, Chagnon might be justified in arguing that I could afford to play this role because I was under his protection. But frequently, I have found it beneficial to put myself under the protection of others – anthropologists or local people – and to admit my cultural incompetence when I am new to a community.

(Asch 1993: 3)

Gender was not the major theoretical preoccupation of any of the anthropologists involved in the film collaborations we discuss here. This fact is less important than an acknowledgment of the process of "gendered knowing" which informs all ethnographic research, and which works together with other dimensions of difference that are usually identified by universal categories such as age, race and class (Callaway 1992: 35) but which may include more significant indigenous categorizations of difference (including those native to the fieldworker herself). These dimensions of difference constitute discursive arenas which work upon our field-work selves, whether as ethnographer or film-maker, throughout the period of our research and beyond. Fieldwork is potentially destabilizing – and thus usually reconstitutive – of selves. Any conclusions we achieve are conditional and determined more by the professional necessity to produce expert, published knowledge than by existential realities.

Creating subjects

"Subject" is an ambiguous term in social science discourse, because it can be used in the sense of "object" as well as "subject". A person who is an anthropological subject is necessarily an object, not in the context of the person's lived experience as an agent in his or her own life, but by being located in anthropological discourse as an object of knowledge. While it was Asch's goal to record long sequences of social interaction that would allow viewers to see the objects of his filming as subjects in their own lives, the Yanomamö or Balinese or Rotinese remain the object of research and film-making. In the field-world, by contrast, the researcher comes to terms with the particular understandings which constitute the hosts' experience of the world. These indigenous objectifications of experience challenge and change the categories the anthropologist has brought to "the field", a powerful objectification in itself. As Mark Hobart has suggested, if the interpretive frameworks of the hosts can become part of anthropological theory, rather than merely part of the data which anthropological theory addresses, then it may be possible to avoid the "epistemological domination" that occurs when the researcher adopts "academically fashionable criteria for selecting relevant contexts in preference to those used by the participants themselves" (Hobart 1986: 8).

This leads to the question of "which participants' framework?" and to recognition of certain indigenous representations as privileged over others and of the role of gender in this process. In formulating a research problem, the anthropologist, usually armed with at least a research proposal, comes up against hosts' ideas of what is appropriate knowledge for the anthropologist to know, even before beginning to come to terms with the categories of experience through which that knowledge is constituted. Thus, "entering the field" involves the researcher in charting the contours of cultural values pertaining to knowledge, which inevitably modifies the way the research project is realized.

LC: In my case, this trajectory involved resisting definitions of valued knowledge that were current in dominant groups. The process unfolded in the geographical space traversed in "entering the field" (national capital, provincial capital, district town, village).

No doubt all researchers intent on working in a village in Indonesia experience a pull as each nodal point entices the researcher with its lien on culturally valued knowledge. After all, the researcher's presence validates such knowledge. My successive moves through these nodes of power and knowledge rendered me progressively beyond the reach of a higher authority's protection. Just as important, my status dropped with each move to a more distant, poorer location. I moved back and forth between the village and the local town. For my hosts in town, each return was approved and each departure was an occasion for concern. Because I am a woman, these were more pressing concerns than they would be for a man, as men in Bali enjoy much greater social and geographical mobility than women. I sometimes found the weight of my hosts' concern very difficult to endure and yet my attempts to break away from these constraints inevitably compromised my attempts at culturally appropriate behavior on which my successful participation depended.

My intended research did not match well with my hosts' conceptions of what was significant about their community. From the point of view of the elites, it should be about the literate court culture, religion, and the performing arts (the source of Bali's identity in the nation and the world). My interest in village life, not connected with any overt development agenda, was acceptable and supported by academic anthropologists in Bali, but puzzling to others including the town elite who felt that, if I did not have an instrumental

Figure 9.4 Tim Asch and Linda Connor with Jero filming *The Medium Is the Masseuse: A Balinese Massage.*

goal connected with "development" which justified my village location, then their "higher" culture was more worthy of study. In the village, too, I was frequently asked why I wanted to work with "farmers" (*petani*) and "commoners" (*anak jaba*) who "didn't know anything": didn't know anything, that is, about subjects construed as the proper focus of formal study.

By the time the film-making project began toward the end of the second year of fieldwork, these problems had been surmounted as my village hosts became involved in the process of improving my competence in various areas of social life and, perhaps through my curiosity and ignorance, began to appreciate the value of their own knowledge. This process unfolded most clearly with Jero Tapakan, as my ignorance forced her to objectify ever-widening realms of her own taken-for-granted knowledge, in terms that I could understand.

In many ethnographic film projects, a further consideration is the question of access. Often, access to certain domains of social life is restricted for men, or women, or outsiders, or persons in other situationally-defined categories. Patsy Asch's account of her Afghanistan experience illustrates this point. While she felt uncomfortable in male-only settings, Tim Asch felt there were many situations in which he could not film women because of Islamic restrictions on foreign men looking at women. Patsy Asch also encountered restrictions on her movements when filming ceremonies on Flores with Douglas Lewis.[9] In developing the subjects of the Bali films, such restrictions were few. In the village where Connor worked, there is relatively little formal segregation of the sexes, but men and women had separate spheres of activity in most areas of village life. Ceremonies, such as the cremation we filmed in Jero's village (Asch *et al.* 1991), are "work" (*karya*), albeit of an elevated kind. Village women made offerings and cooked food for guests and workers; men assisted with butchering, roasted-meat cooking, and construction jobs in wood and bamboo. Everyone participated in the peak events. Both men and women had major coordinating roles for the ceremonial work.

During the Bali filming, we were welcomed into most of the situations we wanted to film, largely because of Connor's prior development of relationships critical to her research. We were able to move in men's and women's areas of activity, and to converse with anyone who was not too busy. Our filming was not restricted, apart from the need to take care near consecrated areas such as Jero Tapakan's shrine house (where the filmed séance took place) and the offering tables and other important objects used in the cremation. Tim Asch learned to curb his movements if they threatened to impinge on these delimited areas, and bystanders called it to his attention if he did not.

There was no disagreement over selection of subject matter between Tim Asch and Connor because he was committed to filming subjects that Connor was working on as part of her doctoral research. However, the film-making project revived the issues of proper subject matter with Jero and other residents of the village. It was difficult for them to connect their observations of us making

Figure 9.5 Tim Asch and Linda Connor filming a village cremation in Bali, 1978.

representations of them with the visual media representations with which they were most familiar: formal still portraiture, national television (whose content was mainly government propaganda), televised foreign drama, and television studio versions of indigenous performing arts from around the archipelago. Jero decried her ignorance, and told us that literate healers would have more to say. She initially "choreographed" her massage practice for us by making an entrance to the massage area like a traditional masked dancer. Participants in the cremation told us that the ceremonies of the gentry families were bigger and better performed. These and similar protestations had in common a valorization of formal, public culture over everyday events, and elite rather than village representations.

Our narrative motifs, constructed around anthropological theory, emphasized the importance of informal social interactions and ceremonial preparations, as they reveal important elements of village sociality. For our hosts, the peak events, and not the preparations, were the substantial achievements that should be celebrated on film, as testament to their harmonious solidarity and status in the local area. The stages of the ceremony swept us along and we were frequently under the direction of persons on whom we depended to inform us about the course of events. Although Tim Asch largely determined the way the cremation footage was shot, the content of the footage reveals a convergence of the interests of all of the participants' perspectives, our hosts' and ours (see MacDougall 1991).

Connor and Tim Asch have often reflected on the changing temper of their attention to the cremation ceremonies, as a response to their growing involvement with the activities on their hosts' terms.

LC: We began with the decision to make an inexpensive slide tape on prepara-tions for the cremation. We made short visits to the pavilion (visually a very exciting place) where Tim photographed people at work, and I tape recorded conversations with them. As more and more of the group became intensely involved in the preparations and preliminary ceremonies, we found ourselves spending longer periods of time at the work place, and talking to others about the ceremonies. Every day our hosts told us about something new and inter-esting to see – a new offering, a pig-slaughter, the tower that was being crafted by many people. Repeatedly, they asked us if we could use the moving camera to record the main events. Finally, some days before the main ceremonies, we decided to switch to a movie camera, even though our film supplies at that time were uncertain. Tim arranged to have more film sent from Australia, and some days before the main ceremonies we threw ourselves into filming, almost on a 24-hour schedule, such was the level of activity by that time. Caught up, as we were, by the enthusiasm of the participants, we strayed from our original intention to focus on how a poor community could organize such a costly and complex event. We found that most of our resulting footage was about the performance of the ceremonies.

The knowledge produced in ethnographic projects "is doubly mediated by our own presence, and the informant's response to that" (Hastrup 1992: 123). Infor-mants produce not cultural truths, but novel objectifications for the ethnographer who imposes upon them the requirement of self-reflection. Likewise, our film-making imposed a new framework for people to evaluate what they were doing. Their response was not to succumb to our definition of the situation, but to insert their own agendas, which inevitably modified ours (see Connor, Asch and Asch 1986; Asch and Connor 1994).

The manner in which the content of a film evolves also rests upon dialogic inter-actions between people with different expectations about what is appropriate or interesting. Ethnographic film-makers bring not only the theories of anthropology but also the narrative motifs and stylistic conventions of visual media to the task of realizing a film. Does a collaboration between film-maker and subject occur in this realization? What elements of coercion are embedded in it? In David MacDougall's words: "Whose story is it?" (1991). Is the evolution of film content explicitly built into the planning of the project or does an awareness of it emerge, perhaps after the filming is finished? What values about social life and the representation of social life as stories are involved? How are gender relations implicated?

The themes of anthropological research grow not just out of theoretical frame-works of understanding stemming from the discipline of anthropology, but also from the connection of anthropology with social issues of the time in the researcher's own society. These concerns then become projected onto the host group, to whom the anthropologist turns for solutions to problems conceptualized within an alien frame of reference. These connections can be demonstrated in films as well as writing. For example, the films made on Bali by Gregory Bateson resonate with broader concerns about socialization, national character, and psychoanalysis that were current in America in the 1930s. With regard to Tim Asch's films, this point can best be developed through a discussion of the Yanomamö project. We quote from a paper given by Tim Asch at the Royal Anthropological Institute Film Festival in Manchester in 1992:

Chagnon began his research among the Yanomamö in 1964. This was the same year that Robert Gardner completed his film, *Dead Birds*, which focused on warfare among the Dani of Irian Jaya. … By 1966, when Chagnon submitted his Ph.D. dissertation, the United States was increasingly divided over the Vietnam war – ghetto dwellers would soon burn cities and young men burn draft cards. The entire country was preoccupied with the subject of violence. And as is so often the case, anthropological interests were influenced by the concerns of the wider society, particularly the campus community.

In the social and biological sciences there was a swing toward the exploration of the biological roots of behavior epitomized in the 1966 publication of *On Aggression* by Konrad Lorenz and *The Territorial Imperative* by Robert Ardry. Anthropologists, such as Sherwood Washburn and Irven DeVore, were studying primate social behavior in order to see both how aggression was handled within different species and whether we could learn something about human social organization by looking for analogies in the social organization of our closest biological cousins.

Thus, when Chagnon "discovered" the Yanomamö, an isolated society that still engaged in frequent raiding and acts of hostility, his work quickly came to the attention of other social scientists, winning him considerable recognition. Chagnon first published *The Fierce People* in 1968.

(Asch 1993: 1–2)

Although Chagnon (1968) examines relations of power within and among villages that "exchange women", his focus on men coupled with his typification of Yanomamö as "the fierce people" who live in a "decidedly masculine" society, sets up the generic Yanomamö "person" as male. For women, at least, this raises questions about the relationship between fierceness and relations between men and women, as well as the ways in which fierceness is or is not expressed in the behavior of Yanomamö women. In the first edition of *Yanomamö: The Fierce People* Chagnon wrote:

… the Yanomamö are still actively conducting warfare. It is in the nature of man to fight, according to one of their myths, because the blood of "moon" spilled on this layer of the cosmos, causing men to become fierce. I describe the Yanomamö as "The Fierce People" because that is the most accurate single phrase that describes them all. That is how they conceive themselves to be, and that is how they would like others to think of them.

(1968: 1)

"All" Yanomamö men and boys? All Yanomamö women and girls? The almost exclusive focus on men's activities reflects both the impact of Western social science theory of the time (in particular the invisibility of women as social agents) and the masculine dispositions of the film-makers as these bore upon the anthropological interpretation of Yanomamö social life. Film-making, involving as it does the technical characteristics of the recording equipment, the conventional genres of representation, the perspectives audiences bring to viewing, as well as the intentions of the film-makers, produces films that contain a surplus of meaning. Gender may become salient even where it is ignored in the explicit message of the film, as in *The Ax Fight*.

Representations of gender in *The Ax Fight*

In *The Ax Fight* we first hear Chagnon's voice when he tells Asch and Johnson just after the fight that " ... two women were in the garden and one of them was seduced by her 'son'. It was an incestuous relationship and others found out about it and that's what started the fight". Although Chagnon was mistaken, his initial assumption dealt with incest – certainly, among the Yanomamö, a gender issue.

The informal discussion between the film-makers about the fight is followed by a formal analysis of the fight and the genealogical relationships between the participants. *The Feast* and *The Ax Fight* were inspired by Marcel Mauss's theory of alliance and reciprocity (Asch 1988: 8–9) and were influenced by structuralist models of kinship that identified men as social actors and women as objects of exchange. *The Ax Fight* is concerned with the relationship between male visitors and male hosts. This point is made particularly clear in a section that explicates the fight in terms of a kinship diagram.

The narration focuses entirely on the ax fight and how the male participants were related. There is an oblique reference to affines linked by unnamed women. Sinabimi is the only woman named on the diagram and she is never mentioned in Chagnon's narration, which explains the fight in kinship terms. Chagnon concludes: "Members of lineage two were now being forced to divide their loyalties

Simplified structure of the conflict in terms of marriage and descent

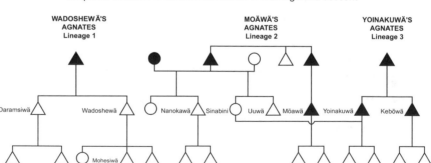

between two groups of affines which emphasized an internal cleavage that already existed." From prior discussion of who is who, we are probably justified in assuming that Chagnon is referring to male members of the lineage. Scant attention is given to the fact that the conflict begins because of Sinabimi's decision not to give food from her garden to a male visitor (at least as far as we know from the film). No mention is made of her kinship relation to the man she refused to feed or to his close relatives. No further reference is made to her, except that we see her crying and her sister comforting her and we are told how her male relatives responded. Many women are involved in the fracas – carrying weapons, comforting wounded men, screaming abuse, adding their voices to those who want to continue and escalate the fight – but the film reveals little about their roles in the event which is its main subject.

The film is concerned with power: a woman refuses to share food, asserting her right or desire to control the distribution of her labor. The reasons are not explored: perhaps to spite the man's wife or daughter or some other women, perhaps because "the visitors refused to work in the garden, yet demanded to be fed", perhaps because her husband told her to. A man beats her, thereby asserting his greater strength or anger or status. When her close relatives learn of the beating, her husband and brother challenge the man, thereby supporting her right to resist. The men fight but their female relatives support them physically and verbally and fight one another with words. The fight is a struggle that concerns the social relations of men and women.

A careful examination of *The Ax Fight* reveals a contrast between the male focus of the analysis and visual evidence that women were active participants who provoked and sustained the fight. As women viewers, who admire the film for its innovative structure and the attention it brings to the process of its construction, we are nonetheless painfully aware when we see the film that women are ignored as social agents. In contrast, there are a number of less well-known Yanomamö films that deal with issues largely overlooked by anthropologists until feminists insisted that domestic relations were a worthy focus of research. These films grew out of Tim Asch's own interest in aspects of social life that were in marked contrast to Chagnon's. Asch wrote:

> On our second trip we continued to focus on events of interest to Chagnon but I thought it important to get additional coverage, particularly women's and children's activities. I was influenced by remarks such as Margaret Mead's: "If the Yanomamö are so fierce, it is important to know how individuals get to be that way." We had lots of footage of Yanomamö displaying fierce behavior, but I thought we should also show gentler domestic interactions. I have found that film images often lead to generalizations. If people only see film of violent behavior then many assume that violence is the only behavior typical of Yanomamö.
>
> (Asch 1988: 9)

Figure 9.6 Yanomamö.

Tim Asch took up this topic again in the paper he gave at Manchester in 1992:

The ten minute film, *A Man and His Wife Weave a Hammock*, shows a loving relationship between a woman and her husband, an unusual focus for an ethnographic film. The film begins with the woman lying in her hammock nursing her child, while she talks with her husband, who is weaving near-by. Their intimacy is conveyed through conversation and through subtle gesture, such as her reaching out to touch his leg. At the end, she joins him, and they work together. When we made *A Man Called "Bee"*, we borrowed a clip from the hammock film to introduce Möawä as one of Chagnon's chief informants. Over shots of Möawä peacefully weaving, Napoleon's narration says that Möawä is one of "the fiercest people he has ever met". Yet the image conveys a very different impression. … I'm not trying to suggest that Möawä is never fierce, but to say that fierce behavior among Yanomamö must be understood in context. Moreover, even men like Möawä, whose behavior is more violent than that of many other Yanomamö men, are not "fierce" most of the time. To label him fierce, while he is engaged in a demonstrably peaceful activity, is to negate the importance of an analysis of when fierce behavior is regarded by Yanomamö as appropriate. I aim this criticism at myself, because I did not challenge this juxtaposition before we produced the film.

(Asch 1992)

Asch goes on to note that, although there are many Yanomamö films like this one that deal with peaceful moments of interaction between men and women,[10] the majority of teachers who use the films use the more dramatic films that focus on violence. Perhaps this is because the content of these films is congruent with the images of Yanomamö presented in literature, not to mention Western stereotypes of violent tribal peoples.

Representations of gender in Asch's Bali and Flores films

When working with people about whom reams of scholarly and popular writings already exist, such as the Balinese, ethnographic film-makers must come to terms with these representations. Many of the representations of Bali that have been popular in the past half-century or so portray a society of calm and gentle people with highly developed artistic skills. Relations between men and women are reputed to be relatively egalitarian (see, for example, Covarrubias 1973 [1936]: 155ff). These judgments are only meaningful in relation to other potent Western representations, such as those of archetypical non-Western groups such as the Yanomamö, or self-representations of the Euro-American bourgeoisie as the yardstick of otherness in anthropology. The Bali films may reinforce commonly held (but erroneous in our view) stereotypes about gender egalitarianism. For example, *A Balinese Trance Seance* shows a spirit medium, who happens to be a woman, conducting a séance. Viewers who do not have access to the accompanying written material (Connor *et al.* 1986) may conclude that all spirit mediums in Bali are women. In *The Medium Is the Masseuse*, the same woman, Jero Tapakan, gives a therapeutic massage to a male client while engaging in conversations and banter with mixed-sex groups of relatives, neighbors, and waiting patients. In *Releasing the Spirits: A Village Cremation in Bali*, we see men and women carrying out preparatory work for the cremation, some in gender-differentiated groups, but in close proximity to one another. The same arrangements hold for most of the ceremonial activity in the film. With minor exceptions, such as the iconography of effigies, corpses of men and women are treated in the same way.

Even when Western audiences see a connection between certain behaviors seen in the films and their own conceptions about gender relations, some of these behaviors may challenge their previously taken-for-granted assumptions. Other parts of the film may contradict Western stereotypes about Balinese gender relations. In *A Balinese Trance Seance*, the revelation that the fatal sorcerer is a woman suggests a cultural ideology of blame that accrues to women who marry outside their patrilineal descent group in a society in which the normatively preferred marriage is endogamous. At other moments, the films' contents may affirm viewers' expectations about gender relations based on their own social experience. The films may also affirm audiences' own values about gender relations, and on this basis emotional involvement may develop. For example, in *Jero on Jero* audiences empathize with the "sisterly" relationship between the anthropologist and the healer. In *Jero Tapakan: Stories from the Life of a Balinese Healer*, they are often moved by Jero Tapakan's weeping as she recounts the difficult circumstances of her earlier life, including her separation from her young children (left in her husband's care) when she becomes an itinerant trader. In other words, the "reading" of gender relations in the films is not objectively present but depends very much on the orientation of different viewers.

Balinese audiences presumably decipher quite different gender codes which are not constructed from Euro-American values regarding appropriate behavior for men and women. One Balinese woman friend told Connor that she was bothered while watching a long segment of the biography film because Connor "was sitting like a man, not like a woman" (i.e. with her legs crossed, but not to the side and tucked under her). Just because gender as an anthropologically defined problematic is not prominent in the manifest subject matter of the films does not mean that gendered representations are absent. Furthermore, the films also suggest that gendered duality is not the only frame of reference guiding the way people act or understand certain situations. Gender as an anthropological category of analysis tells us little about indigenous discourses of difference which, as Hobart has pointed out for Bali, may not rest upon a "substantialized duality" between the two sexes, but may instead be variously divisible and qualifiable depending on situational contexts (Hobart 1995).

Neglect of indigenous discourses of difference is illustrated by the Yanomamö material. Yanomamö men are represented as fierce. Should we conclude that because women rarely appear in Chagnon's writings or in the analysis of *The Ax Fight* that they are not fierce and consequently not important? And is this the view of Yanomamö men, or of the anthropologist and film-maker, or both? Are not there other ways in which gendered selves are discursively constructed among Yanomamö?

Patsy Asch recounts another example in which women are seen only as part of men's stories, this one from *A Celebration of Origins*, a film she and Tim Asch made with the anthropologist Douglas Lewis.

> **PA**: Douglas Lewis asked us to film a major ceremony on the eastern Indonesian island of Flores. Men were the primary social actors visible during the ceremony. Douglas insisted on the importance of women in the public life of this society, but in the film their importance remained largely metaphorical. I cite two of the main comments about women:
> Voice-over narration (E. D. Lewis), shots 34 and 35:
>> Rudun is the Source Mother of clan Ipir because she is the eldest surviving female descent of the founding ancestor.
>>
>> In Wai Brama, rituals are the responsibility of men, but women are said to be the "source" of things.
>>
>> As the Source Mother, Rudun must be present in the *mahé* grove.
> Voice-over Narration, Pius Ipir,[11] shots 48 and 49:
>> When we offer the pig for the *mahé* boundary, women must be present because they have rights over cooking. It is women who are the root of the clan.
>>
>> When we work for a woman in a garden that yields, we only have the right to use the produce; ownership belongs to women. We men travel with empty hands. However, we eat first and the women afterwards (Lewis, Asch and Asch 1994).
> While women are part of these two men's accounts, their lives are not depicted in the film and we do not hear from them directly. Although Rudun is

named, it is not her experiences, her individual life that are significant but her role as "source mother".[12]

One difference between the Bali films and films such as *The Ax Fight*, *The Feast* or *A Celebration of Origins* is that, in the former, women as well as men are present as agents (and in some contexts they are more prominent than men) and, in the latter, they are largely absent. This is not only related to the different way relations between men and women are organized in each society but also to the gendered dispositions of the researchers and film-makers themselves, and to the frameworks of interpretation on which they were drawing at the time. In the Bali films women, as well as men, speak directly to the audience and we learn of their participation in social life through their own words and actions. By contrast, women sometimes appear in the Yanomamö films and in the Flores film but usually in relation to men's lives. We are not arguing against making films that focus on men's activities (or women's activities) but we encourage people to acknowledge that the process of doing so is inflected by aspects of the gender relations of the film-makers and of the people filmed.

Conclusion: ethnographic film as a "technology of gender"

Our quest to understand the gendered nature of ethnographic film projects, in all their stages of development, should not be taken to imply that we are arguing for epistemologies of essential difference between men and women, however these might be constructed. Such an approach, as Patsy Asch found in Afghanistan, defines women in terms of men and maintains the habit of thinking of the masculine as synonymous with universal (de Lauretis 1987: 26).

In her discussion of gender in relation to the question of representation, Teresa de Lauretis proposes that:

> A starting point may be to think of gender along the lines of Michel Foucault's theory of sexuality as a "technology of sex" and to propose that gender, too, both as representation and as self-representation, is the product of various social technologies, such as cinema, and of institutionalized discourses, epistemologies and critical practices, as well as practices of daily life.
>
> (1987: 2)

As a "technology of gender" in anthropology, ethnographic film may perpetuate dominant representations of gender in Western discourses even when purporting to portray other cultures. However, ethnographic film can work as an instrument of alternative practices (feminist or gay–lesbian, for example) and has the potential to explicate different modes of experience and other constructions of gender.

As technologies, the films we make not only reflect gender but also, as de Lauretis argues, shape it in our audiences because films convey ideologies of gender. The representations of the Yanomamö, referred to by Chagnon as "primitive man"

(1968: 3), are cloaked in the scientific, objectivist language of the times. They ignore women, thereby reinforcing in male and female viewers a conception of the relative significance of men and women as social agents and perhaps even suggest to some that this is rooted in our biological past.

In the Bali films, women are prominent as social agents, which may lead Western audiences only to the conclusion that gender differentiation is not highly developed in Balinese social life, and not to the realization that the circumstances of the film-making project gave women a voice.

Although it is always possible to read a text "across the grain" so that it does not preclude the consideration of gender, that is not the way ethnographic films are generally used. If masculine preoccupations go unacknowledged and masculine practices unnoted as such, we will reproduce the dominant ideologies about gender in our society and women will remain, at most, metaphors in men's stories. We have argued that ethnographic films are dialogically constructed through specific practices, by and about specific people, that have the potential to obscure or to challenge prevailing constructions of gender.

Notes

1 Support for the research and film-making on which this paper is based was provided by an Australian Commonwealth Postgraduate Research Award; the Wenner-Gren Foundation for Anthropological Research; the Department of Anthropology, University of Sydney; the Department of Anthropology, Research School of Pacific Studies, The Australian National University; the Center for Visual Anthropology, University of Southern California; the Research Management Committee, University of Newcastle, Australia; and the National Science Foundation. We are grateful for critical comments on earlier drafts from Mark Hobart, Leslie Devereaux, Nancy Lutkehaus, and Faye Ginsburg.

2 In particular, the Yanomamö films made with Napoleon Chagnon, the Afghanistan film made with Asen Balikci and Patsy Asch, and the Flores film made with Douglas Lewis and Patsy Asch.

3 A strong argument about the neglect of gender can be made for written ethnography; see, for example, the debate sparked off by the publication of Writing Culture (1986) edited by Clifford and Marcus, a debate that initially ignored gender and neglected to examine women's earlier experiments in writing ethnography. In contrast, Diane Bell (1993) offers a valuable critique of the neglect of gender in post-modern discourse. She documents many of the ways women have approached ethnographic writing that differ from traditional ethnographies written by men. With the publication of Woman, Native, Other, Trinh T. Minh-ha forced the attention of ethnographic film-makers onto issues related to gender.

4 Of course, one could also look at ethnographic film in relation to other, linked, systems of representation, such as technologies of class or ethnicity or even to less commonly articulated categories.

5 See Connor, Asch and Asch (1986) for a detailed account of the evolution of the Bali project.

6 Belanda, "Dutchman/woman" is a generic term for European. Recently turis, "tourist" has become more popular.

7 Because Chagnon was interested in settlement patterns and in making a demographic study of the Yanomamö, he wanted to visit as many villages as possible.

8 The hosts were angry because Asch and Chagnon arrived very late.

9 For example, she was not permitted to accompany men when they cut down a tree to make a new drum and, unlike Lewis, she was not allowed to stand between the altar and a ceremonial hut to record sound of men's chanting.

10 Among these films are A Father Washes His Children, Weeding the Garden, Sand Play, Bride Service, A Man and His Wife Weave a Hammock and The River Mishimishimaböwei-teri.

11 Pius Ipir Wai Brama was a participant in the rituals depicted in A Celebration of Origins who became the ritual leader of the community after the film was shot. His statements about the rituals are used as commentary throughout the film.

12 I am speaking here about a specific film and not about Lewis's work as an ethnographer. Indeed, he is

currently working on a manuscript entitled *The Paradox of Difference*, in which he looks at gender relations and classifications in relation to dual symbolic classifications generally in Tana 'Ai culture. However, why we might choose to make a film like *A Celebration of Origins* that focuses on the public activities within a ritual grove, and why that results in a film that focuses primarily on men, is not unrelated to the gender of the film-makers, gender roles among the Ata Tana 'Ai, and the theoretical preoccupations of anthropologists at the time, interests influenced by Western academic gender politics.

References

Asch, Timothy (1979), "Making a Film Record of the Yanomamo Indians of Southern Venezuela". *Perspectives on Film* (No. 2). University Park: The Pennsylvania State University.

—— (1988), "Collaboration in Ethnographic Film Making". In Jack Rollwagen (ed.), *Anthropological Filmmaking: Anthropological Perspectives on the Production of Film and Video for General Public Audiences*. Chur, Switzerland: Harwood Academic Publishers.

—— (1992), "Bias in Ethnographic Reporting: A Personal Example From the Yanomamo Ethnography". Paper delivered 14 September at the Royal Anthropological Institute Film Festival, Manchester, UK.

—— (1993), "Bias in Ethnographic Reporting and Using the Yanomamo Films in Teaching". In Timothy Asch and Gary Seaman (eds.), *Yanomamo Film Study Guide*. Los Angeles: Ethnographics Press, Center for Visual Anthropology, University of Southern California.

Asch, Patsy and Linda Connor (1994), "Opportunities for Double-Voicing in Ethnographic Film". *Visual Anthropology Review* 10 (2): 14–28.

Bakhtin, M. M. (1981), *The Dialogic Imagination*. Translated by Caryl Emerson and Michael Holquist. Austin: University of Texas Press.

Bell, Diane (1993), "Introduction 1: The Context". In Diane Bell, Pat Caplan, and Wazir Jahan Karim (eds.), *Gendered fields: Women, Men and Ethnography*. London: Routledge.

Callaway, Helen (1992), "Ethnography and Experience: Gender Implications in Fieldwork and Texts" in Judith Okely and Helen Gallaway (eds.), *Anthropology and Autobiography*. London: Routledge.

Chagnon, Napoleon (1968), *Yanomamö: The Fierce People*. New York: Holt, Rinehart and Winston, Inc.

—— (1974), *Studying the Yanomamö*. New York: Holt, Rinehart and Winston, Inc.

—— (1992), *Yanomamö*. Fourth edition. New York: Holt, Rinehart and Winston, Inc.

Clifford, James and George Marcus (1986), *Writing Culture: The Poetics and Politics of Ethnography*. Berkeley: University of California Press.

Connor, Linda, Patsy Asch, and Timothy Asch (1986), *Jero Tapakan: Balinese Healer. An Ethnographic Film Monograph*. Cambridge: Cambridge University Press.

Covarrubias, Miguel (1973) [1936], *Island of Bali*. New York: Alfred A. Knopf.

Foucault, Michel (1980), *The History of Sexuality, Vol. I*. New York: Vintage Books.

Hastrup, Kirsten (1992), "Writing Ethnography: State of the Art". In Judith Okely and Helen Gallaway (eds.), *Anthropology and Autobiography*. London: Routledge.

Hobart, Mark (1986), "Introduction". In M. Hobart and R. H. Taylor (eds.), *Context, Meaning and Power in Southeast Asia*. Ithaca: Cornell University Press, pp. 7–19.

—— (1995), "Engendering Disquiet: On Kinship and Gender in Bali". In Wazir-Jahan Karim (ed.), *Male and Female in Southeast Asia*. Oxford: Berg Publishers, pp. 121–144.

Lauretis, Teresa de (1987), "The Technology of Gender". In *Technologies of Gender*. Bloomington: Indiana University Press.

MacDougall, David (1991), "Whose Story is it?" *Visual Anthropology Review*. 7 (2): 2–10.
Reisman, D. (1964), "Introduction". In E. S. Bowen, *Return to Laughter*. Garden City: Doubleday & Company, Inc.
Trinh T. Minh-ha (1989), *Woman, Native, Other*. Bloomington: Indiana University Press.

Films

Asch, Timothy and Napoleon Chagnon (1970), *The Feast*. Watertown, Massachusetts: Documentary Educational Resources.
—— (1974), *A Father Washes His Children*. Watertown, Massachusetts: Documentary Educational Resources.
—— (1974), *A Man and His Wife Weave a Hammock*. Watertown, Massachusetts: Documentary Educational Resources.
—— (1974), *Weeding the Garden*. Watertown, Massachusetts: Documentary Educational Resources.
—— (1975), *The Ax Fight*. Watertown, Massachusetts: Documentary Educational Resources.
—— (1975), *Bride Service*. Watertown, Massachusetts: Documentary Educational Resources.
—— (1976), *Children Play in the Rain*. Watertown, Massachusetts: Documentary Educational Resources.
—— (1976), *The River Mishimishimaböwei-teri*. Watertown, Massachusetts: Documentary Educational Resources.
—— (1976), *Sand Play*. Watertown, Massachusetts: Documentary Educational Resources.
Asch, Patsy, Linda Connor, and Timothy Asch (1991), *Releasing the Spirits: A Village Cremation in Bali*. Watertown, Massachusetts: Documentary Educational Resources.
Asch, Timothy, Linda Connor and Patsy Asch (1979), *A Balinese Trance Seance*. Watertown, Massachusetts: Documentary Educational Resources.
—— (1981), *Jero on Jero: A Balinese Trance Seance Observed*. Watertown, Massachusetts: Documentary Educational Resources.
—— (1983), *Jero Tapakan: Stories from the Life of a Balinese Healer*. Watertown, Massachusetts: Documentary Educational Resources.
—— (1983), *The Medium Is the Masseuse: A Balinese Massage*. Watertown, Massachusetts: Documentary Educational Resources.
Asch, Timothy, E. Douglas Lewis, and Patsy Asch (1994), *A Celebration of Origins*. Watertown, Massachusetts: Documentary Educational Resources.
Balikci, Asen, David Newman, Timothy Asch and Patsy Asch (1978), *The Sons of Haji Omar*. Montreal: The National Film Board of Canada.

Chapter 10

Timothy Asch, the rise of visual anthropology, and the Human Studies Film Archives

John P. Homiak

Introduction

One result of anthropology's preoccupation with representation during the 1980s has been a resurgence of interest in ethnographic film both inside and outside of anthropology (see Marcus and Fischer 1986: 45; Nichols 1991). While some anthropologists continue to emphasize films and written texts as complementary media, many more now see films as media of representation in their own right as opposed to seeing ethnographic film-making as merely an adjunct activity to data gathering. At the same time, considerably more attention is now given to the social and political circumstances in which films are produced and to the contexts in which they are distributed, viewed, and interpreted.

Given this turn, it is curious that no one has taken a close look at the institutional factors that led to the formation of visual anthropology as a subdiscipline in American anthropology as it developed from the late 1960s through the 1970s. Reflections on the career of Tim Asch and his association with the Human Studies Film Archives (HSFA) of the Smithsonian Institution provide an opportunity to examine some of these factors. It was there that I first met Tim in 1987.[1] Several times that year, Asch visited the HSFA while he was working on a new and enhanced master print of his film *The Feast*. It is in this facility that the original camera footage from his major film projects is preserved and, in part, catalogued.[2]

The establishment of the HSFA, which was originally called the National Anthropological Film Center, in May of 1975 realized a vision dating back to the early 1960s which Asch shared with a dedicated group of visually oriented anthropologists. This cohort, which included Margaret Mead, Sol Worth, Walter Goldschmidt, John Marshall, and others, articulated methods for visual methodology and communicated their interests widely within the social scientific community.

The origin and initial development of the archives was thus tied closely to the interests of this small group of scholars and their ideas about visual anthropology as a subfield of theory and practice within general anthropology. Between 1965 (when film reviews first began to appear in the *American Anthropologist*) and 1975 (when the National Anthropological Film Center was established at the Smithsonian), the pace of communication in this group accelerated and from that the subdiscipline of visual anthropology emerged. In 1970, this same group of anthropologists and related scholars met at Belmont, the Smithsonian Institution's conference center in Elkridge, Maryland, for a conference sponsored jointly by the National Science Foundation (NSF) and the Smithsonian. There they drafted plans for a national center for research and the preservation of ethnographic film (see Sorenson 1971: 1–2; Asch, Marshall, and Spier 1975: 184–85; Sorenson and Neuberger 1979: 81–98). Revisiting this time in the history of visual anthropology provides an opportunity to appreciate subsequent developments, to review both the achievements and shortcoming of the HSFA, and to understand Tim Asch's contribution to this program and his continuing interest in the concept of research films more generally.

The evolution of a subdiscipline

In the 1960s, an increasing number of American anthropologists became interested in the use of film in their teaching and research. This development paralleled the availability of lightweight cameras with synch-sound recording and a corresponding response by major funding agencies to proposals by independent film-makers, anthropologically oriented and otherwise. In anthropology there had always been an articulate advocacy of visual techniques, but it was pursued largely by individuals on an *ad hoc* basis. Before 1966, when the Program in Ethnographic Film (PIEF) came into existence as a "committee" within the American Anthropological Association (AAA),[3] there was no formal organization through which to communicate about the production and use of film. To promote the use of films in teaching, the PIEF distributed the now well-known catalogue *Films for Anthropological Teaching* under the editorship of Karl Heider and a number of other publications (see Balikci and Brown 1966; Dunlop, 1967; Gajdusek and Sorenson 1968; Worth 1964; and Jablonko 1964). In the spring of 1970 the PIEF began publishing a newsletter five times yearly under the co-editorship of Jay Ruby and Carroll Williams. Asch recalls that he and Jay Ruby discussed the concept of such a newsletter during the 1968 Flaherty Festival held at Wells College outside of Ithaca, New York:

> I can remember that Jay Ruby and I sat on the lawn outside the Flaherty Conference in 1968 when I first showed *The Feast*. And he recognized in the film my interest with developing standards for a methodology of ethnographic film-making in order to promote the use of films in anthropology – which was an interest we both shared. I remember him saying, "Why don't we start by having a publication?" So it was at the next AAA meeting, in 1969 I think, that was when we tried to get together everyone in anthropology who represented or had an interest in ethnographic film. There must have been about thirty of us all in Lita Osmundson's [the Director of the Wenner-Gren Foundation] study. I remember that as when things were beginning to come together.
>
> (taped telephone conversation with Tim Asch, January 7, 1994)

In addition to publishing reviews of films and seminars, the newsletter that developed out of this meeting furthered the group's intention of providing information about the production of films teaching anthropology and provided a forum for debate about visual anthropology and ethnographic film. Until the late 1960s, visual anthropology was thought of as the making of film and photographic records in fieldwork and using these materials to illustrate written accounts of culture or to support aspects of field research. Such visual records reflected anthropology's emphasis on vision, over the other senses, in the acquisition of knowledge and privileged the camera as a means of data collection.[4] Moreover, it reflected the view that knowledge simply exists "out there" in the world waiting to be discovered, rather than being constructed through the questions and methods of researchers.

In the late 1960s Sol Worth began to challenge the idea that film can provide a purely objective record of behavior and events. Worth argued that photographic and film images could not be uncritically accepted as evidence because they always reflected an observer's decisions of when and how to use the camera and that the photographer, through his or her positioning, was thus responsible for constructing the resultant visual product. Worth and Adair's work on the Navajo Film-makers Project sought explicitly to explore this aspect of imaging by assessing how motion picture film conceived, shot, and edited by people such as the Navajo reveals their own cognition and values.

Through this project, Worth and others became interested in film as a phenomenon of culture – as a form of cultural practice – rather than merely as a means of recording evidence about culture (Gross 1980: 8–9). Worth and Ruby introduced this more critical perspective into the Program in Ethnographic Film in the early 1970s when the name of the *PIEF Newsletter* was changed to *Society for the Anthropology of Visual Communication Newsletter* (SAVICOM) in the fall of 1973.[5] This approach in visual anthropology sought to understand the kind of ideological filters associated with film-making, seeing films as a way of constructing knowledge about anthropological subjects. This concern was evident in the journal, *Studies in Visual Communication*, of which Worth was the founding editor.

Discussion of these concerns began to surface more frequently in various national and international ethnographic film conferences held in the late 1960s and early 1970s.[6] The loose collectivity of otherwise disparate visually-oriented anthropologists who participated in these conferences shared the view that their particular interests in visual media would be advanced by a central facility on the national level for research and educational work on anthropological film.

The institutional context of ethnographic film-making from the 1960s

The rise of enthusiasm for the use of film in anthropology from the 1960s can be linked to a political climate in which government spending on science was sufficient to support relatively large-scale film projects for research and education, and to a theoretical orientation which emphasized comparative and generalizing statements in anthropological science. With respect to theory, the emphasis on analyzing social processes, coupled with materialist approaches which foregrounded the relationship between cultural ecology and levels of sociopolitical integration, provided a framework within which film could be used to document and illustrate these factors. At the same time, a humanist concern developed among anthropologists with respect to traditional subjects in the small-scale, "primitive" and tribal societies that had long been the stock-in-trade of fieldworkers and which might soon disappear in a climate of global change. Margaret Mead, in particular, was successful in gaining public support for the idea that anthropologists had an obligation to future generations to record and preserve the traditional life-ways of other cultures before they disappeared altogether or were greatly changed.

Making records of rapidly changing societies as a rationale for anthropological film-making remained strong throughout the 1960s and even into the 1970s, and was in large part a reason for constructing a world ethnographic film sample. Scholars such as Margaret Mead, Alan Lomax and E. Richard Sorenson vigorously promoted this idea. Sorenson, who began his career as an assistant to Carlton Gajdusek at the US National Institutes of Health (NIH), regarded the motion picture camera as a means of "collecting visual data from disappearing cultures for continued study and use" (Sorenson and Jablonko 1975). Both Gajdusek and Sorenson have worked on developing protocols for such films which consisted of raw unedited footage which, after it was shot in the field, would be thoroughly annotated and documented by the film-maker and anthropologists involved in the production. These films, it was reasoned, could be studied and analyzed by future generations of researchers (Sorenson 1967, 1975a, 1975b). Mead, Lomax, and no doubt a few others were enthusiastic supporters of this idea.[7] Sorenson, in fact, would place the study of so-called "cultural isolates" threatened with change at the center of the NAFC's mission over the next several years.

But, as is evident from some of the themes already sketched, there was no single perspective which prevailed with respect to the content and methodology of film studies in anthropology. A number of individuals questioned a primary commitment to the documentation of changing cultures in terms of the larger goals of the discipline. In response to Sorenson's notion about researching "cultural isolates", one of Mead's students, Theodore Schwartz, argued that "Culture does not cease to be worth filming when people put on pants and plastic hats and no longer paint their faces. In the long term business of anthropology, our interest should be just as penetrating without the stimulus of the exotic" (Schwartz 1967: 466).[8]

Nevertheless, a concern with rapidly changing cultures was formalized at the Eighth International Congress of Anthropological and Ethnological Sciences which formed a committee on "urgent anthropology". As a result, many of the film projects carried out during this period were either conceived or promoted in the "spirit of conservators of a passage age" (Gardner and Heider 1968: xii). This was certainly true of the Netsilik series created by Balikci and the made-for-television ethnographic film series *Disappearing Worlds*, which was launched in England by Brian Moser in 1968. The *Faces of Change* series for television, released in 1971 by the American Universities Field Staff (AUFS), was based on the same idea. It is hardly surprising that the proposal which Asch and Chagnon submitted to the NSF in early 1971 for a series of Yanomami films highlighted the importance of filming an isolated culture before it became subject to widespread change. They wrote that

> ... the exposure of a small, fairly homogeneous society such as the Yanomamö to the multiple pressures of acculturation through contact with a large pluralistic and technologically powerful society, frequently results in vast changes in behavior and often disruption or collapse of the social system. Yanomamö isolation affords one of the last opportunities to film an American Indian society before contact with foreign cultures is widespread. The knowledge and insights gained will not only teach us more about the ways in which human groups have been traditionally organized but also afford greater understanding about how the individuals in such societies think and feel and how they may react to change.
>
> (Asch and Chagnon 1971, NSF proposal pp. 7–8)

A preoccupation with documenting presumably isolated cultures on the verge of major change was not the only impetus to anthropological film-making during this period. Ecological–adaptational approaches to culture, which had developed in the 1960s, were seen as a way to organize ideas about the diversity and organizational complexity of cultures. The differences between subsistence patterns found in hunting–gathering, shifting cultivation, pastoralism, and sedentary cultivation could easily be depicted on film and made a favored theme for educational films. At the time, many anthropologists were enthusiastic about the Human Relations Area Files. These members of the profession shared an expectation that comprehensive records of specific cultures could be recorded on film in the field to create a kind of world ethnographic film sample. The resulting film documents, they believed, would be invaluable in the development of educational films focusing on the comparison of cultures and societies. This approach to ethnographic film would be first realized in a film series funded by the NSF and produced by the American Universities Field Staff. The *Faces of Change* series was released in 1971 and was developed around the idea of documenting and comparing societies based on different forms of cultural adaptation. These included adaptations to five basic ecological zones: Bolivian altiplano (Aymara), highland Kenya (the Boran films of James Blue and David MacDougall), the steppes of the Tajik and Afghan Hindu-Kush, Asian lowland wet-rice farming (Taiwan), and South-east Asian insular marine (Cantonese, Soko Islands). Packaged as educational films, each zone was represented by five thematic films. At the time, this comparative dimension was heralded as an important development in educational films for anthropology which would facilitate their flexible use in the classroom.[9] This series, it should be noted, was premiered in Washington DC at the launching of the National Anthropological Film Center before a selected audience of scholars, museum administrators, educators and representatives from the major funding agencies,[10] as well as members of Congress. Showcasing the series in this way was clearly intended to suggest the kind of results which would likely ensue from a coupling of ethnographic film-making and anthropological science at the NAFC. The comparative approach based on ecology and subsistence seems to have been accepted by film-makers who otherwise differed in their styles of cinematic representation. Despite the fact that his own films were consistently poetic and symbolist in form, Robert Gardner would write in 1969 that the idea for making *Dead Birds* (a film on the Dani, sedentary cultivators in Irian Jaya) took shape after working with Marshall on *The Hunters*, a film which purported to illustrate the adaptation of the !Kung San (Ju/'hoansi) as hunters to the harsh environment of the Kalahari. In his reflections on the making of *Dead Birds*, Gardner wrote

> With a film on a primitive hunting society finished, it seemed appropriate to start thinking of one about an agricultural group [the Dani]. Making such a film would mean that two of the three basic ecological adaptations of human society would have been documented. Material I have gathered on three pastoral groups in Ethiopia during 1968 will be released as full-length films in 1971. With their appearance the third pattern, pastoralism, will be represented.
>
> (Gardner 1979: 430)

The Yanomamö proposal submitted by Asch and Chagnon to the NSF in June of 1971 was very much shaped by similar concerns of representation and pedagogy. They proposed to contrast a holistic visual record produced on the Yanomami (which included two half-hour films on political organization and socialization and ten shorter films on specific roles within Yanomami society) with film and ethnography on the hunting-and-gathering !Kung Bushmen of South-west Africa and the pastoral Dodoth of North-west Uganda for the purposes of developing course materials (Asch and Chagnon 1971 NSF proposal, pp. 1, 7–8). They argued that the production of sequence films, to which Asch was already committed, would enable them to represent thematically important social events and to produce films about individuals in different social contexts. This would provide teachers with the flexibility to select among different themes or emphases in developing their own courses of study.[11]

By the late 1960s, the members of that small circle of visually-oriented anthropologists to which Asch belonged were finding ways to increase communication among themselves and to communicate their work more widely within the discipline. In addition, Asch's work was finding its way into this community of film-makers and critics. In 1968, a number of the !Kung sequence films which he had produced with John Marshall were screened at the Colloquium on Ethnographic Film organized by Colin Young and held at the University of California at Los Angeles. Later that year, *The Feast* was screened at the Flaherty Festival. Through this exposure of his work, Asch was coming to be a well-known figure in the emerging field of visual anthropology and to influence the work of other film-makers (see MacDougall 1995: 84).

The Belmont Conference

By the late 1960s a number of funding sources were responding to what they saw as the inchoate status of visual anthropology. Program directors at NSF, who were concerned primarily with the role of anthropological films in curriculum development, sought to close the loop between film-makers and teachers. Leo Baggerly, director of the Undergraduate Science Curriculum Improvement Program at NSF, for example, was interested in the general problem of developing new ways of teaching science at the university level and was consequently interested in anthropological films for the classroom. His interest was further driven by the fact that the number of proposals submitted to the NSF for anthropological films far exceeded their budgetary allocations.

In 1970 Asch approached Baggerly and the NSF to seek funding for a series of films on the Yanomami. This resulted in a formal appeal by the NSF to the nascent community of visual anthropologists within the AAA to determine what methodological and subject priorities should be recognized in the production of anthropological film. This would give the NSF clearer criteria by which to evaluate the increasing number of proposals for film projects. Asch, who had decided to return to the Yanomami after his first visit in 1968, recalled the following conversation with Baggerly and his assistant at the NSF:

> In '69 or thereabouts, I put together a grant to make a series of Yanomami films. When I went to NSF, Baggerly said, "Look, we've already got two grants in here, one from Asen Balikci for half a million, and one from Norman Miller of the American University Field Staff (AUFS) ... and his is for 750 thousand." They told me that they had a lot of pressure on them from Congress ... there were one or two Congressmen involved who were putting pressure on them to fund the AUFS proposal. And I asked them what percentage of their grant funds were pressured in this way – that they had to fund, and they said twenty-five percent. It gives you some insight into where you stand with grants. So I told them right then and there that I could make thirty Yanomami films for 99 thousand. That was a bargain compared to the other two grants.
>
> But it was obvious that they weren't interested in bargains. So they said, "Tim, that's fine. But we don't know what to do about judging or evaluating these grants. You people don't seem to have any professional organization or a list of names that we can go to. You don't seem to represent anything. What you should do is to have a conference and pull all these people together and give some meaning and structure to what seems to be a perfectly legitimate field of inquiry within anthropology."
>
> "Well, fine. Alright, I'll put together a conference – but are you going to fund it?" And they said, "Yes, we'll fund a conference, but what do you know about putting a conference together? Tim, you don't seem to understand. Putting together a conference and making it work requires a tremendous

amount of skill and experience. And no – we're not going to fund something like that if you don't know what you're doing." "Alright, possibly true," I said, "but what about Margaret Mead organizing it?" "You could get Margaret Mead to do that?! Okay, you get Margaret Mead to do it and we will pay for it."
(taped telephone conversation with Tim Asch, January 7, 1994)

According to Asch, he communicated Baggerly's advice to Mead, who supported the idea and who, in her *ad hoc* role as spokesperson for their interests, delegated the responsibility of writing a proposal to fund the conference to Jay Ruby and Gordon Gibson, the latter a curator in African ethnology at the Smithsonian who was interested in film, having made a number of research films among the Himba, Zimba, and Kuvale of Angola.[12]

These efforts resulted in the Belmont Conference on anthropological film. The conference was sponsored jointly by the National Science Foundation and the Smithsonian Institution and met from 30 October to 2 November 1970. Eighteen of the thirty or so participants were either anthropologists or film-makers.[13] The rest represented sponsoring agencies, including the NSF and the Smithsonian. The majority of this core group presented position papers in two main sessions devoted to the "long-range requirements for educational films in anthropology" (session 6) and "guidelines for film funding" (session 7). The other sessions were given over largely to discussing the practical and administrative concerns of establishing a national anthropological film archives and the criteria for materials to be accepted.[14]

Asch gave papers both on the use of films in anthropological teaching and on issues of archiving. He provided the conference with an example of packaging anthropological films with related written materials which reflected his work with John Marshall on the development of sequence films with accompanying study guides. He also spoke on his ideas about research film, which he had adopted from Gajdusek and Sorenson. He outlined a model for a research film which consisted of an uncut image track accompanied by the synch-sound track, a translation of the indigenous speech on the synch-sound track, and an annotation track consisting of ethnographic data and the film's context provided by the anthropologist. The programmatic recommendations that issued from Belmont were very much in line with Asch's research interests and the way he had been working with film up to that point. These included a call for the establishment of an archives which could serve as a national research center and the gathering of a "world ethnographic film sample" to be located at the Smithsonian. The group agreed that cinematic methods employed in films to be included in the archives should be flexible and open to experimentation, but they recommended a style of shooting that would produce footage suitable both for education and research. The Belmont recommendations also supported longitudinal work and the production of written materials, such as study guides to accompany films. Finally, the conference participants agreed that funding decisions should favor proposals for collaboration between film-makers and anthropologists with established research in the field and which allowed for the multiple use of visual materials resulting from the funded projects.

It is difficult to judge the extent to which Asch influenced these recommendations. Certainly, they were consistent with his preoccupations at the time and in the years that followed. This included, in particular, an emphasis on the film-maker–anthropologist collaboration and, following from this, a desire to produce thoroughly documented research films and edited educational films. Along with Sorenson, Gajdusek, and Gibson, Asch was a strong supporter of the need to annotate and archive films and, along with Heider, he emphasized the need for written texts to accompany films.

Belmont had three important administrative results. First, it was agreed that the Smithsonian should be the site for the proposed archive. Second, the participants incorporated themselves as the Anthropological Film Research Institute (AFRI), the purpose of which would be to seek funds for the creation of the archive and to exert influence over its activities as an advisory board.[15] Finally, a search committee composed of Mead, Arensberg, Lomax, Gajdusek and Gibson was formed to review nominations for the directorship of the proposed film archive. Four candidates were nominated, Asch and Sorenson among them. Over the course of the next year the search committee met and communicated on several occasions to select a director. Early on in this process, Asch withdrew his nomination. Thereafter, the committee concentrated on the most frequently named candidate – Richard Sorenson.

For his part, Asch communicated his support for Sorenson to the search committee. He reasoned that Sorenson had already published on research films and had done collaborate work with Gajdusek on such films at NIH since the early 1960s. Moreover, Sorenson and Asch were the strongest supporters for making research films and – at least during this time – Sorenson supported the view held by Asch and others that both research and educational films (as well as the development of a world ethnographic film sample) required the active participation of anthropologists in the field.

From Belmont to the establishment of the National Anthropological Film Center

In 1973, two years before the National Anthropological Film Center formally became a reality, a conference on visual anthropology affiliated with the Ninth International Congress of Anthropological and Ethnological Sciences was held in Chicago. This event lent additional impetus to the resolutions of the Belmont Conference. It brought together a number of important ethnographic film-makers from outside North America, including Jean Rouch, Roger Sandall, and Jorge Preloran. The ICAES conference cast an international light on the proposed national archive and linked it to an international network of scholars interested in ethnographic film. It also reaffirmed the ICAES resolution of 1968 and foregrounded the role of film in the conduct of urgent anthropological research. In this regard, a number of panels were devoted to the role of ethnographic film in salvage ethnography and to archives. Mead, Asch, Sorenson and Lomax figured in all of these sessions.[16] Sorenson would be named the director of the National Anthropological Film Center in late 1974 with the Center officially opening on May 1, 1975.

Alan Horton, Director of the AUFS *Faces of Change* series, and Margaret Mead spoke at the Center's opening. In retrospect, what appears significant about this occasion was that Mead spoke little about the archiving functions of the Center and focused on the Center's role in salvage anthropology. She suggested that the next step would be to begin making films in the field. This was a purpose which the lay public could readily understand and perhaps Mead's words were partly in the service of public relations. But there was uncertainty about whether such film-making would be done by the staff of the newly-launched NAFC or by organizations such as the AUFS. The original design of the NAFC as an archive and research center, however, remained the first priority for the members of AFRI, especially those who had attended the Belmont Conference.

By his own account, Asch played an active role in the first years of the NAFC. In 1974–75 Asch worked at persuading Laurence Marshall (John Marshall's father) to send 25,000 feet of !Kung footage to the NAFC. There, he argued, it could be annotated and would, at the same time, serve as an example which would attract deposits of ethnographic footage by other film-makers. In 1975 Tim and Patsy Asch and Asen Balikci were involved in the Pashtoon Nomad Project in Afghanistan, the first production project at the Center, which was funded jointly by the Canadian Film Board and the NAFC. Modeled after the recommendations of the Belmont Conference which encouraged work between film-makers and anthropologists, this led to one of the first deposits of film in the Center.[17] These materials, along with most of the AUFS *Faces of Change* series, were deposited and readied for translation of sound materials and annotations of image tracks. After shooting 80,000 feet of film, a research film was made according to the protocols set out by Sorenson (i.e. synch-sound matched to the uncut full-film record, a translation track, and an annotation track). For Asch and others close to the Center, this project must have been seen as expressing commitment to research films and to budgeting money to continue their development.

In 1976 Tim and Patsy Asch departed for Australia where Tim accepted a Senior Research Fellowship at The Australian National University, a post which enabled him to continue his film-making working with anthropologists already working in the field. Despite his distance from the Center, Asch continued to work with the expectation of making research films at or for the NAFC and continued to be active as a member of AFRI, which served as the board of directors for the Center. The next six years, however, would be a period of turmoil and contention at the NAFC. Sorenson, with the assistance of Margaret Mead, proved to be an effective fund-raiser and a politically astute strategist in dealing with the Smithsonian bureaucracy. However, almost from the beginning of his tenure as Director, problems developed. From its first year of operation, Sorenson decided to allocate the major part of the NAFC budget into research film-making and to neglect both the archival mission of the Center as well as the expectation that it would support film projects based on collaborations between film-makers and anthropologists with established field research. He quickly established an alternative hand-picked advisory board to the one which had been constituted at the Belmont Conference (i.e. AFRI) and he effectively used Margaret Mead, in her unofficial public role as spokesperson for the discipline, to deflect criticism of this administrative decision. Sorenson's board had only a few anthropologists. Surprisingly, Sorenson mounted a number of research filming projects in Melanesia, Micronesia, India, Nepal, and Mexico with young and inexperienced film-makers who had no anthropological training or field experience and who were not working with anthropologists in the field. He justified these decisions by arguing that the cultures filmed (the Nambas and Mbogate in Vanuatu, Micronesians of the Western Caroline Islands, the Newari of Nepal, and the Huichol of north-west Mexico) constituted "cultural isolates" whose traditional ways of life were threatened and had to be recorded. These projects involved start-up moneys from the NIH and the National Endowment for the Arts that had been allocated even before the formal establishment of the Center in 1975. When various of the Belmont participants, including Jay Ruby and Gordon Gibson, criticized Sorenson for this, Mead defended his decisions, saying that these were just the necessary growing pains of a new organization that had to establish itself. This became a major source of contention between Sorenson and others within the visual anthropological community. Throughout this difficult period, Asch remained optimistic that the Center would ultimately return to its original mission, not only in archiving and annotating research footage, but in providing support for collaborative projects for film-makers like himself working with established anthropologists.

In 1976 the political climate shifted and, under pressure from conservative forces, Congressional funding decisions led to the curriculum development division of the NSF being disbanded (see Balikci 1989: 6–7). Ethnographic film-making in the US became dependent largely on private sources or on the much smaller pool of funds available through the National Endowment for the Humanities, where anthropologists had to compete for funds with large-scale documentary film projects. When Margaret Mead died in 1978, both internal and external criticism of the administration of the NAFC began to mount. In response to strong criticism from the members of AFRI, in 1979 the Smithsonian established an Advisory Committee composed of Karl Heider, Gordon Gibson, Walter Goldschmidt, Adam Kendon, William Fitzhugh, and Caroll Williams to review the workings of the Center and to draft recommendations for changes in its administration. The Committee recommended that the NAFC actively seek applications from scholars with anthropological projects, particularly those in need of "urgent" documentation and that $100,000 of the NAFC budget, be dispersed in the form of "film assistance to ongoing anthropological field projects" in the range of $5,000–10,000 per project based on the submission of competitive proposals. These grants-in-aid would carry an obligation to deposit an annotated work print at the Center for potential research use by others. In this way, the Center would obtain well-documented research footage from ten to twenty professionally qualified anthropologists, thereby fulfilling the mandate of obtaining footage from disappearing or rapidly changing cultures for research. Finally, the Committee argued that the NAFC should actively seek historical footage and attend both to the archiving and indexing of this footage in ways that would make it accessible to scholars. None of these recommendations was ever implemented under Sorenson.[18]

During this time, Asch's position at The Australian National University enabled him to make films in Bali and eastern Indonesia in collaboration with Linda Connor, James Fox, and Douglas Lewis. Among other things, Asch became committed to making a series of films suitable for cross-cultural comparisons and at the same time exploring the use of feedback in the film-making process (see Asch 1979: 6). In 1977 Asch traveled to eastern Indonesia to work with Fox on the island of Roti. The two were well-matched in this project: Asch wanted to work with an anthropologist committed to documenting footage on which they had collaborated, and Fox wanted to annotate and translate the soundtrack of these materials so as to make them an accessible ethnography of Roti.

The collaborative projects Asch carried out in Indonesia with Fox, Connor, and Lewis were squarely within the putative NAFC brief to support fully documented archives of ethnographic film (see Asch 1979). Moreover, Asch's ideas about the production of research films evolved as a result of his work with these colleagues on single-event films which featured dialogue as central to the meaning of the events which were recorded. This included his work with Linda Connor on *A Balinese Trance Seance*, with James Fox on *Spear and Sword: A Ceremonial Payment of Bridewealth*, and with Douglas Lewis on *A Celebration of Origins*. In all of these cases, Asch remained committed to working up research films for deposit at the Center. The films which evolved from his collaborations with anthropologists in Australia were quite clearly intended to be "researchable" by other anthropologists familiar with the culture. Perhaps more importantly, each of Asch's Australian projects was also designed to provide film records of considerable use in the research of the collaborating anthropologists.

As is evident from the films and publications which resulted from their work in Bali (1978–80) with Linda Connor, both Tim and Patsy Asch became responsive to the discipline's growing concern with problems and theories of representation. According to Asch, the evolution of his cinematic style was not simply driven by shifts in anthropological problems and methods; it was also an outgrowth of his experience on the Pashtoon Nomad Project, which originated in the NAFC. Asch has often pointed out that during this filming, Asen Balikci encouraged him to "make him [Balikci] a Fellini". In discussing the film that eventually became *The Sons of Haji Omar*, Asch has said:

> I wanted to use a younger son (of Haji Omar) – the son who didn't get along with his father – as the principal subject of the film. I knew there was a story there and I wanted to make something like a MacDougall film and I started to do it with a vengeance. Well, we had three months there and it didn't take me long to realize that the film I wanted to make would take at least eighteen

months. Even though that film never got made, I learned something from the experience. *The whole experience got me thinking much more about what's going on in peoples' heads as opposed to looking at them as objects and what they do behaviorally.* So the films Patsy and I began to make in Indonesia really came out of the work in Afghanistan.

(taped telephone conversation with Tim Asch, January 7, 1994; italics added)

Most of the Indonesian films, the last which Asch was to make, focused on dialogue and incorporated video feedback to foreground the subjective experiences and understandings of the social actors depicted, something which is absent in the Yanomamö films. Both in the films and in the text which accompanies the Jero series, for example, the Aschs drew attention to the authority of the film-maker and how, as in *A Balinese Trance Seance*, recorded dialogue can influence a film's final form (see Seckinger 1991: 30–31). This concern with dialogue and its complexities also led Asch to feel that shooting styles and the resultant research films must be flexible enough to accommodate a given cultural setting and the interests being pursued by the anthropologist. Asch's Pashtoon experience led him (and Patsy) to pay more attention to the native dialogue and subjects' points of view in his edited films. In retrospect, this concern can probably be traced back as far as his dissatisfaction with *The Ax Fight*, a film which documents but otherwise ignores the role of women in the genesis and persistence of conflict among the Yanomami (see Connor and Asch, this volume). His Indonesian work also made him dissatisfied with how certain kinds of native speech were handled under the research film model followed by Sorenson, a model which focused primarily on observable behavior rather than speech or participants' feelings about their behavior (Sorenson and Jablonko 1975).

The Aschs first voiced these concerns when they evaluated the research film produced at the NAFC in 1977 for the Pashtoon project. It was clear that, in many instances, straightforward running translations in English were not easily accomplished for native speech. From their experience with the Pashtoon project, which was annotated by a native speaker who was not an anthropologist, Tim and Patsy were convinced that this technique posed problems. In some instances it meant collapsing dialogue, it brought the uncertainty of the speaker into focus, and often the English translations were out of synch so that what one heard in English was not the phrase being spoken in Pashtoon. This confused the positionality of speakers in complex and/or coded speaking situations. The Aschs knew that this problem would be magnified for much of their Indonesian materials, which were dense in dialogue centered on ritual. The events he filmed with Fox and Lewis, for example, posed the problems of overlapping and coded speech in which meanings were unstated and implicit and thus extremely difficult to translate sensibly into English and to subtitle succinctly (see Lewis, Chapter 6, this volume).

But Asch was also convinced that in films of single events such as *Spear and Sword* it was important to work with an anthropologist who would commit the time and energy to producing translations and an in-depth analysis, and who would carefully work through the meaning of the nuanced language of such events. With this in mind, he made repeated proposals to the NAFC between 1977 and 1981 requesting approximately $5,000 to produce a research film on Rotinese bridewealth negotiations from the footage he shot with James Fox. These requests were made with the intention of depositing the film at the Center. His plan was to include precise written transcriptions of recorded speech, subtitling of native speech, and an English summary of the dialogue between camera rolls, all of which would require intensive work by the collaborating anthropologist (Asch, NAFC file correspondence 2 June 1980). The project would thus require modifying the basic model of the research film by abridging the purist idea of using only "uncut camera rolls" by minimal discarding of redundant footage. Asch was convinced that this work would result in an important contribution to the concept of the research film. But Asch's extensive correspondence to Sorenson arguing for experimentation on the research film model fell on deaf ears and produced growing frustration. In April 1980, Asch wrote to Sorenson reminding him that he and Patsy

> ... were among the first people to promise a substantial donation of film because we supported the explicit goals of the [National Anthropological Film] Center as first expounded at the 1970 Belmont conference. In the case of our recent Indonesian research film materials, we have been asking you for several years for $5000 to produce a research internegative to "deposit" in your Center's archives. We thought you had budgeted money to continue to develop the concept of research films and that this project would provide a valuable model. At the moment you can count on the fingers of one hand the people who have been able to do extensive research with another person's film from another culture – mainly because most ethnographic film isn't shot and documented well enough to be researchable. [...] I think that one of the N.A.F.C.'s prime activities should be to develop good research films, publicize them, and encourage scholars to do research with them in order to obtain feedback necessary to improve the model. Thus, it seems appropriate to me that your Center experiment with a variety of research film models both to enrich your archives and to encourage film-makers and scholars to be aware of some of the options available in preparing research materials.
>
> (Asch, correspondence, 4 March 1980)

With growing frustration, he followed this with another missive in which he attempted to convince Sorenson of the value of his research film method, saying that

> ... the difference between what we are currently trying and [your] view of a research film is one of focus. We only have limited time from scholars. Our projects – at least those dealing with film of a single event – benefit from in-depth analysis. I feel that if the participating scholar finds the material challenging in his or her own research, then we are likely to generate material that will stimulate others. If he or she wants to reduce material slightly, we don't object since almost all filming is a gross reduction of real three-dimensional

events to begin with. We have insisted that [James] Fox retain anything we feel might convey new ethnographic information. Our hope for the Center's future is that feedback from many scholars using your resource for their own research will teach us how to compile more and more useful documents or packages – film, sound, and written material. To settle for only one model of how this should be done, without reference to either the parameters of a particular project or the skills of those participating, is to close off options before our products have been tested. By our, I mean the whole profession of anthropology. I am convinced that if we are able to produce the research film, *Spear and the Sword*, we will have a model that you will be able to show to other scholars and use to generate ideas about how to proceed.

(Asch, NAFC correspondence file, 2 June 1980).

Asch's request for modest supplementary support to produce a research film was a central point of contention between Sorenson and the NAFC Advisory Committee. In early 1979 the NAFC was under siege both from within the Smithsonian and from its AFRI Advisory Committee members. Not only had Sorenson made his own form of research film-making (choosing not to work with anthropologists) the major component of the NAFC's activities, but he had withdrawn all support for the original group who had chartered the Center at Belmont. Asch, along with Ruby, were the most vocal critics of the direction taken by Sorenson.

Under Sorenson's stewardship, many of the purposes outlined in the Belmont Conference resolutions (e.g. archiving, annotations, and transcriptions) were not pursued. In fact, Sorenson declared that it was impossible to carry out these tasks for lack of funds and that he would not be willing to provide researchers with access to the archived materials until these functions were completed. At the same time, the Center was expending large sums of money on research filming projects conducted by individuals with little or no anthropological training, language competence, or prior field experience. While all of Asch's footage from his filming on Roti is archived at the Smithsonian, sadly none of the research films which he proposed for his Indonesian work was ever made. This foreclosed on the kind of scholarly use and feedback which Asch insisted were necessary for testing and evaluating the usefulness of such films.

Conclusion

Over the course of the NAFC's development from 1975 to 1983, Asch remained the only anthropological film-maker committed to all of the Center's originally proposed functions, including archiving and creating both research and educational films. In 1983, after another internal review, funding for Sorenson's program was discontinued. It is a telling point that during his tenure, none of the major ethnographic film projects which had been produced by the participants at Belmont or by other major ethnographic film-makers (e.g. Asch, Marshall, MacDougall, Sandall) was formally deposited in the NAFC, even though they subsequently found their way into the Archives once its functions had been re-defined. In perhaps a crowning irony, Mead and Bateson's footage shot on Bali in 1936–8 was sent to the Library of Congress rather than to the Film Archives which she helped to create. Now, nearly thirty years down the road from Belmont, the concept of research films and the Archives is a complicated issue to evaluate.

The Human Studies Film Archives, as it is presently called, has grown to a collection of more than eight million feet of original film and video. Unfortunately, in the current era of fiscal restraint and federal cutbacks, it survives with a staff of only two permanent employees and a preservation budget of roughly one-tenth that of the NAFC. Today, the Archives has neither the staff nor the funds to encourage and support the creation of research films of the kind envisioned by Asch. The last significant project of this type completed at the HSFA were the annotations by Colin Turnbull of the 16 mm and 8 mm footage which he shot among the Mbuti Pygmies of Zaire in 1954 and 1974 and of the Ik of Uganda during the 1970s.

The concept of the research film was developed in a time when funding sources were flush and when the Smithsonian was committed to building a national center which would provide support for the development of such films, as well as the staff and facilities to support the broader research endeavor. But the commitment of funds is now increasingly based on the mass appeal of any film being produced. The realization of the concept of the research film very much requires the energy and determined commitment of someone like Tim Asch, who treated filming in the field, subsequent documentation, and ethnographic film-making as part of an overall career commitment.

Perhaps the idea of the research film is now a luxury. But the contemporary HSFA continues to be attuned to Asch's plea for the need to publish and work with archival footage as a way to understand its value (Asch and Asch 1988: 183). In this regard, one of the areas in which work continues to be done involves collections such as dance footage, the contents of which can be repeatedly studied based on style and movement analysis. In recent years this kind of analysis has been done on archival film on dance in the African diaspora. This includes work by scholars such as Lorna McDaniel, Yvonne Daniel, and Maureen Warner-Lewis, using collections of Afro-Cuban, Jamaican, Haitian, and Brazilian footage. The Film Archives has also adopted one of Asch's suggestions for the documentation of ethnographic footage which has already been archived. This involves returning to the field with film records transferred to video in order to elicit feedback from the original subjects or their descendants about visual records which may have been produced decades before (see Asch and Asch 1988: 183). There are at least three projects in which Smithsonian curators or researchers have returned to the field with such film footage transferred to the video medium. These include film records among the King Island Inupiat (Bering Sea), the Tarahumara (north-western Mexico), and among Afro-Jamaicans who are the descendants of post-Emancipation indentured African immigrants.

It is hardly surprising that some people see technology as the solution to facilitating the scholarly use of film archives. Digitizing film on CD-ROMs and making images accessible to researchers on non-linear media clearly have practical advantages over the screening of 16 mm footage in real time. To this end, the HSFA and the Center for Visual Anthropology at the University of Southern California received Smithsonian funds to digitize a major segment of the Yanomami Film Project in 1995–6. But aside from this small project, the Smithsonian is playing catch-up with the rest of the world in the development of electronic databases. But we may ultimately find that it is not technology which makes the critical difference in the use of our holdings. Without the kind of labor-intensive work that Asch supported – the anthropologist's labor which is required to contextualize images – CD-ROM applications will be meaningless novelties. In the end, even with the technology, it may simply be the legacy of Asch's commitment to the film-maker–anthropologist collaboration that will lead us to rethink the value of research films and the role of archival film records in our discipline.

Notes

1 I had recently completed a post-doctoral fellowship in the Smithsonian's Department of Anthropology and, in August 1987, was hired as an ethnographer to catalogue film in the HSFA.
2 The Asch footage archived in the HSFA includes an undetermined amount of footage of the Dodoth shot in Uganda (1961); approximately 100,000 feet of 16 mm film of the Yanomami (1968, 1971); 95,000 feet on the Pashtoon nomads of Afghanistan (1975–76); and over 200,000 feet shot in Bali and eastern Indonesia (1977–81). No single film-maker or anthropologist is associated with more collections in the HSFA.
3 The Program in Ethnographic Film began with a grant from the Wenner-Gren Foundation for Anthropological Research. From 1966 to the spring of 1970 the PIEF was chaired by Asen Balikci at Montreal and Robert Gardner at Harvard.
4 This view can be traced to Boas' early work with the camera and Herskovits. In Mead's view, the turn of researchers to film was a means to "refine and expand the areas of accurate observation" (Mead 1975: 10).
5 See *PIEF Newsletter* 3 (2), Winter 1972.
6 These included the Colloquium on Ethnographic Film organized by Colin Young at the University of California at Los Angeles in 1968; the ethnographic film conference organized by John Middleton, Tim Asch, John Marshall, Jay Ruby, and Karl Heider at NYU in 1969; the annual Conference on Visual Anthropology held throughout the 1970s by Jay Ruby at Temple University; the 1976 conference organized by David and Judith MacDougall at the Institute for Aboriginal Studies in Canberra; and the 1973 sessions at the Ninth International Congress of Anthropological and Ethnological Sciences (ICAES) organized by Paul Hockings. The papers from this symposium were later collected under Hockings' editorship as *Principles of Visual Anthropology* (1975) and published in the same year that the NAFC was formally launched.
7 In her address at the official opening of the National Anthropological Film Center at the Smithsonian's Hirshorn Museum, May 1, 1975, Mead stated that as a graduate student she would wake up every morning saying to herself, "The last man on Raratonga probably died this morning and we have lost something irretrievable." Then she added, "So I'm still saying that the last man on Raratonga died this morning and we haven't made a film of him. Unless we get going [with this new Center] something will be irretrievably lost and we will have failed in our stewardship to future generations." (recorded transcript, 1975, Sorenson files, HSFA). Mead used this justification in her various appearances before Congress to secure operating funds for the NAFC.
8 Schwartz conducted fieldwork and filmed on Manus in the early 1960s. His footage, apparently through the encouragement of Mead, was deposited at NIH with Gajdusek where it remained, along with the footage of John Adair, irretrievable and inaccessible to visual anthropologists until 1997. With Gajdusek's departure from NIH in that year, all of his collected film materials were sent to the Peabody Museum in Salem, Massachusetts.
9 This approach clearly grew out of the prominence which cultural ecology models had gained in American anthropology during the 1960s and the application of this approach to the well-known typology of bands-tribes-chiefdoms-states (see Ortner 1984: 132–8).
10 Including the NSF, the National Endowment for the Arts, the National Endowment for the Humanities, and the Wenner-Gren Foundation for Anthropological Research.

11 These films had a rough parallel in the five AUFS film projects. This series used an observational film-making style and resulted in the production of films with related themes which encouraged viewers to make their own interpretations of the role which ecological factors played in shaping culture.
12 Jay Ruby (personal communication 1994) recalls a less direct role for Mead. According to Ruby, Gordon Gibson and he played a more active role in getting the conference off the ground. In mid-1970, Gibson and Ruby prepared a position paper on plans for an anthropological film archive for the NSF. It appears that a number of individuals who later participated in the Belmont Conference made contact with the NSF prior to the event.
13 Margaret Mead, John Adair, Conrad Arensberg, Walter Goldschmidt, Gordon Gibson, Tim Asch, John Marshall, Robert Gardner, Karl Heider, Asen Balikci, Carlton Gajdusek, John Hitchcock, Alan Lomax, Richard Hawkins, Jay Ruby, Sol Worth, Carroll Williams and E. Richard Sorenson.
14 A collection of the positions papers delivered at Belmont can be found in the Gordon Gibson Papers, Box 27, National Anthropological Archives, Smithsonian Institution.
15 Gordon Gibson was influential in this regard. As an ethnologist who was also an anthropological film-maker, Gibson presented a plan at the Belmont Conference to seek four years of administrative support from the NSF, which would be used by the Smithsonian to run the proposed archive. In his subsequent contacts with Dillon Ripley, the Secretary of the Institution, Gibson argued that the recent creation of the Smithsonian National Anthropological Archives in 1968 made the Smithsonian a logical national center at which to house a national anthropological film archive. During the four years of the anticipated NSF grant, the Smithsonian, for its part, would undertake to obtain support from Congress in the form of a line item in its budget (see Gordon Gibson Papers, Box 27, memo from L. Wardlaw Hamilton to Dillon Ripley, December 9, 1970, National Anthropological Archives).
16 The conference papers would be published under the editorship of Paul Hockings as *Principles of Visual Anthropology* (1975).
17 This project was produced in two stages, a fall and a spring shoot. Tim and Patsy participated in the fall segment while the spring shoot was done by Eugene Boyko of the Film Board of Canada.
18 In 1980 Sorenson changed the name of the center to the National Human Studies Film Center, claiming a broader "humanistic" mandate than was proposed by the participants of Belmont. In 1981, the NAFC's production and archive functions were split administratively. Overseas film-making under Sorenson was officially discontinued in 1983.

References

Asch, Timothy (1972), "Making Ethnographic Film for Teaching and Research". *PIEF Newsletter* 3 (2): 6–10.
—— (1979), "Report from the Australian National University". *SAVICOM Newsletter* 7 (3): 5–8.
Asch, Timothy and Napoleon A. Chagnon (1971), Research Proposal to the National Science Foundation. Unpublished.
Asch, Timothy, John Marshall, and Peter Spier (1975), "Ethnographic Film: Structure and Function". *Annual Review of Anthropology* 2: 179–87.
Asch, Timothy and Patsy Asch (1988), "Film in Anthropological Research". In Paul Hockings and Yasuhiro Omori (eds.), *Cinematographic Theory and New Dimensions in Ethnographic Film*. Senri Ethnological Studies 24. National Museum of Ethnology, Osaka, Japan.
Balikci, Asen (1989), "Anthropology, Film and the Arctic Peoples". *Anthropology Today* 5 (2): 4–10.
Balikci, Asen and Quentin Brown (1966), "Ethnographic Filming and the Netsilik Eskimos". ESI Quarterly Report, Spring–Summer Issue: 19–33. Educational Development Center, Newton, MA.
Dunlop, Ian (1967), *Retrospective Review of Australian Ethnographic Films, 1901–1967.* Australian Commonwealth Film Unit, Lindenfield, N.S.W., Australia.
Gajdusek, D. Carleton and E. Richard Sorenson (1968), "Research Use of Ethnographic

Research Films". A paper presented at the American Anthropological Association Meetings, Seattle.

Gardner, Robert (1979), "A Chronicle of a Human Experience – Dead Birds". In *The Documentary Tradition*, Second edition. Lewis Jacobs (ed.). New York: W. W. Norton.

Gardner, Robert and Karl G. Heider (1968), *Gardens of War: Life and Death in the New Guinea Stone Age*. New York: Random House.

Gross, Larry (1980), "Sol Worth and the Study of Visual Communications". *Studies in Visual Communication* 6 (3): 2–19.

Jablonko, Allison (1964), "Ethnographic Film as Basic Data for Analysis". A paper presented to the VII International Congress of Anthropological and Ethnological Sciences. Moscow.

MacDougall, David (1995), "Subtitling Ethnographic Films: Archetypes into Individualities". *Visual Anthropology Review* 11 (1): 83–91. Spring 1995.

Marcus, George, and Michael Fisher (1986), *Anthropology as Cultural Critique*. Chicago: University of Chicago Press.

Mead, Margaret (1975), "Introduction: Visual Anthropology in a Discipline of Words". In Paul Hockings (ed.), *Principles of Visual Anthropology*. The Hague: Mouton.

Nichols, Bill (1991), "The Ethnographer's Tale". *Visual Anthropology Review* 7 (2): 31–46.

Ortner, Sherry (1984), "Theory in Anthropology since the Sixties". *Comparative Studies in Society and History* 26 (1): 126–66.

Schwartz, Theodore (1967), "Comment" [response to Sorenson]. *Current Anthropology* 8 (5): 462–3.

Seckinger, Beverly (1991), "Filming Culture: Interpretation and Representation in *Trance and Dance in Bali* (1951), *A Balinese Trance Seance* (1980), and *Jero on Jero: A Balinese Trance Seance Observed* (1980)". *CVA Review* Spring, pp. 27–33.

Sorenson, E. Richard (1967), "A Research Film Program in the Study of Changing Man". *Current Anthropology* 8 (5): 443–69.

—— (1971), "Toward a National Anthropological Research Film Center – A Progress Report". *PIEF Newsletter* 3 (1): 1–2.

—— (1975a), "To further Phenomenological Inquiry: The National Anthropological Film Center". *Current Anthropology* 16 (2): 267–9.

—— (1975b), "Visual Records, Human Knowledge and the Future". In *Principles in Visual Anthropology*, Paul Hockings (ed.), The Hague: Mouton.

Sorenson, E. Richard and Allison Jablonko (1975), "Research Filming of Naturally Occurring Phenomena: Basic Strategies". In *Principles in Visual Anthropology*, Paul Hockings (ed.), The Hague: Mouton.

Sorenson, E. Richard and Gay Neuberger (1979), "The National Anthropological Film Center: A Report on its Beginnings and Programs". Washington DC: National Anthropological Film Center, Smithsonian Institution.

Worth, Sol (1964), "Film-making as an Aid to Action Research". A paper presented to the Society for Applied Anthropology, San Juan.

Chapter 11

Tim Asch, otherness, and film reception

Wilton Martínez

Before I took the [anthropology] class I looked at some other cultures like the Yanomamö, I didn't know yet who the Yanomamö were, but, you know, natives hiding in the jungle, as being very bizarre and they just kind of ran around and shot people and ate monkeys and did strange things like that, didn't really have a culture, they were just kind of barbarians.

(male third-year student, 1988)

After reading [Fried, Harris, and Chagnon's] descriptions of the Yanomamö, I felt that to go would be suicide. There seemed no point in dying on my first attempt to test a method for making ethnographic film ... my wife ... wasn't nearly as frightened as I was, but then, she wasn't the one who was going. My friends said that I was out of my mind: two anthropologists said I shouldn't go under any circumstances – I think they really felt for my safety.

(Asch 1979: 8)

Film impact and pedagogical model

In 1973 two Boston University anthropologists, Thomas Hearne and Paul DeVore, conducted the first empirical study of the effects of the Yanomamö books by Napoleon Chagnon and films by Tim Asch on undergraduate students. They were interested in assessing the possibility of change in "student conception of and attitude toward other cultures". Their research involved the screening of twelve of Asch's films[1] and two books: Chagnon's *Yanomamö: The Fierce People* (1968) and Valero's *Yanoama, the Narrative of a White Girl Kidnapped by Amazonian Indians* (1970). The films and books were used in two introductory anthropology courses during seven class sessions. Instead of lecturing, the teachers used student questions as the basis for general discussion in class. The films included some which represent the Yanomamö as "fierce" and others which represent the Yanomamö as "peaceful" and were:

> explicitly organized to offset, or at least minimize, unwarranted and overly facile stereotyping, on the part of the students, of Yanomamö ferocity ... We

were anxious to show that individual Yanomamö have complex and multi-faceted personalities, and they may assume a number of roles and statuses.
(Hearne and DeVore 1973: 2)

In order to determine changes in students' attitudes toward the Yanomamö, Hearne asked students to write essays about their concepts of the "primitive" before and after viewing the films. The study concluded that

> ... it was nevertheless clear in many cases that intensive exposure to Yanomamö films and readings had not appreciably changed ethnocentric attitudes and characterizations. Indeed, the project seemed to reinforce the stereotypes of primitive societies held by some students; in effect, their preconceptions before the project were based on impressions, characterizations, and generally small amounts of data gathered from various media. For these students the Yanomamö material at once reinforced their stereotypes and made them more complex, for now they had a much wider factual base and greater knowledge of a particular society. Thus, while students learned a great deal about the Yanomamö, the overall effect this knowledge had on their preconceptions and stereotypes of other cultures remained questionable.
> (Hearne and DeVore 1973: 5)

Hearne and DeVore tested a systematic and highly context-oriented teaching method. Their critical questioning of audiences' strongly reified stereotypes and of the potentially negative impact of the films carries deep ideological and pedagogical implications for anthropology. Despite some limitations in their presentation of results (e.g. student commentary is not included in the research report), Hearne's study points to the gap that can arise between teaching goals and learning results. Their findings were never published and are not widely known beyond the small ethnographic film circles.

The significance of the negative impact of the Yanomamö films raises complex questions about the effectiveness of using film in teaching anthropology. In particular, such impact posed a pedagogical challenge for Tim Asch, who was involved as a consultant to Hearne's study. Having developed some teaching strategies prior to their research, its conclusions led him to advance further his methodology for teaching with film (Asch 1974, 1975).[2] Asch's teaching method consisted of linking films and written ethnography "to move back and forth between concrete examples of behavior seen within a developing sense of the total social environment in which the behavior occurs, and analysis and application of relevant theory" (Asch 1975: 386). It also combined an inductive problem-solving approach ("making order out of chaos") with a gradual and relatively prolonged familiarization with the "case study" culture, and comparative analyses of the Yanomamö with other cultures and with students' own. Asch also incorporated the use of written study guides to accompany the films and required students to write individual film reports for every film presented in class. A typical case study course is structured around a topical sequencing of films and readings, starting with daily activities and then moving on to belief systems, ritualistic behavior, and ending with the more contemporary missionary films (ibid.). In theory, the course design combines sensitive teaching strategies to avoid stereotyping due to unprocessable culture shock with flexibility for experimentation in its execution.

A major difficulty with the case study approach is that not many teachers are interested in spending a third or more of a semester on the Yanomamö culture, and few are actually interested in screening the "peaceful" films – which are less didactic in structure and less polished than the "fierce" films. Furthermore, as Asch frequently insisted, most anthropology instructors, largely untrained in film theory and practice, commonly show the films but do not work with them that is, they do not seriously analyze their ethnographic and didactic messages and screen films to fill in for lecture time. In consequence, the potential value of the medium and Asch's teaching method are largely limited by the mainstream use of the "violent films" in the context of theme-oriented courses which use a few films on different cultures to illustrate particular anthropological concepts. Indeed, this practice carries greater risks of reinforcing stereotypes. As Asch noted,

> ... there has been a classical pedagogical dilemma: whether to use palatable material that will bypass the prejudices of the viewer but grossly misrepresent the society, or use powerful data that more closely display indigenous behavior but can reinforce prejudice. It has been true in my experience that the more powerful material can help overcome prejudice and become valuable for instruction only in the context of a broad film resource that rests on good written material.
>
> (1975: 400)

In addition to Asch, several anthropologists (for example, Heider [1976], Rollwagen [1988], and Banks [1992]) have also suggested that the main strategy to minimize or avoid viewers' stereotypical misreadings of film consists of providing a detailed and comprehensive ethnographic context. While crucial to providing a more informed and well-rounded anthropological understanding of the people represented in film, this assumption entails a number of problematic questions, central of which is: why is it that only the represented "other" needs contextualization and not the "self" (i.e. the ideological discourses of the text itself, of the film-maker, instructor, and viewers), since the problem starts with the representation and with the academic consumption pattern discussed above? Also, what are the requirements for a proper "contextualization" of the other? How is the ethnographic context bounded by racial, cultural, and national politics of selfhood and otherness? Finally, what are the criteria and measure, if any, of pedagogical success?

These are some of the central questions I have attempted to answer in my research on the production, distribution, and consumption of ethnographic film

(Martínez 1994, 1998). My inquiry into student responses to the Yanomamö films is framed within a larger analysis of viewers' reception of classic, conventional, and more contemporary film and videos. The results of the research suggest that the problem of stereotyping is pervasive, in different degrees, in most anthropological media (Martínez 1990a, 1990b, 1992). Further, my research indicates that this problem is largely the result of instructors' widespread use of film and videos merely as anthropological illustrations of the other, while neglecting critical analysis of the textual politics of representation and its articulation within popular stereotypes of otherness. As I argue below, the Yanomamö films constitute a unique case but they should not be isolated from the larger context of the problem of anthropological representation.

The stereotype as fetish: masking difference

From 1987–92 I conducted research on the production, pedagogical use, and student reception of ethnographic film at the University of Southern California. The study was primarily of an introductory anthropology course entitled "Exploring Culture through Film" taught at USC. Before discussing in detail students' responses to the Yanomamö films, I shall briefly refer to the notion of cultural stereotyping, a critical issue in cross-cultural communication yet one largely unaddressed by visual anthropologists. Stereotyping and stereotypes about "primitive" cultures among student viewers need to be understood, not only because they powerfully influence all pedagogical projects dealing with difference and otherness, but also because the anthropological medium itself is inscribed in the wider Western discourses about the "savage", and may contribute to perpetuating such stereotypes.

In my research I have found that many students come to introductory courses in anthropology with ingrained prefigurations of the other based on popular media stereotypes:

> I thought they [the Yanomamö] were, I didn't really know like the exact people, but I thought people like that were headhunters and, you know, just gross ... I got those impressions from movies, people paint their faces and stuff, people go to the Brazilian forest and stuff, that's my only source, *Tarzan*, *The Mission*, *Indiana Jones*, that's all you see, Indians throwing spears ... you know, stupid.
>
> (No. 1, female second-year student, 1992)

> I didn't have any initial perceptions about them other than they're not too civilized ... I guess National Geographic pictures of them just in war paint and no clothes on [laughs]. I never thought of the Yanomamö actually growing their own bananas and stuff, so that was new to me ... they were what I thought they were, I guess ... they have some intelligence you know, even

though they don't have running water or anything, you know, modern, I guess, it's not as if they cannot learn it, I think.

(No. 2, male second-year student, 1992).

These simplistic perceptions of the "primitive" proved to be common among the majority of University of Southern California students interviewed in my research.

Data on student preconceptions were collected in 32 interviews and from essays students wrote on the topic "primitiveness".[3] Roughly 85 percent of the students surveyed produced the basic media caricature of the "primitive" as essentially prehistorical. While some of them explicitly distanced themselves from this view and satirized it, in most cases they had no knowledge with which to counter the media stereotypes. The popular stereotypes of the "primitive" were also linked to students' ambivalent attitudes toward the romanticized, "good" savage and the vilified barbarian. The former was generally described as simple, naïve, pure, innocent, originary, and as a victim of civilization and thus subject to sympathy and protection. Descriptions of the "bad" savage as uncivilized, violent, lacking morals and values, immature and dangerous were generally more distant and conveyed a sense of general disapproval. Seventeen percent of the students in the sample backed their definitions with references to their experiences as tourists in "primitive societies". About ten percent of the students made explicit their relativistic views by arguing that the notion of primitiveness depends on one's own arbitrary point of view and can only be determined in comparison to relatively more civilized ways of life. A minority of five percent criticized the concept of "primitive". One said:

> "Primitive", to me, has held an open-ended definition. It's like one of those words that has to be defined in accordance to the context it is used in. I think it is a loaded term that allows Westernized individuals to criticize and even condemn those non-modernized, non-industrialized (essentially non-capitalistic) nations while simultaneously adding to an overwhelming sense of ethnocentrism and prejudice.
>
> (No. 3, male third-year student, 1988)

Besides these rare views, the predominantly media-derived stereotypes characteristic of most undergraduate students at USC in the late 1980s were virtually identical to those of the Boston University students analyzed by Hearne in 1973. In their study, they found the same evolutionary narratives:

> Primitive societies were often described as original, not developed or evolved, basic, simple, and people with savage ape-like headhunters, living in prehistoric times, speaking in monosyllabic language, lacking the intellectual sophistication of Western man and, indeed, knowing very little of the world and universe.
>
> (Hearne and DeVore 1973: 4)

The popular conception of the "primitive" seems indeed frozen twenty years later, despite the relative sophistication of media images of otherness and the increasing popularization of anthropological knowledge on television.

Student stereotypes of the "primitive" (see Nos. 1 and 2) reflect contemporary media images of the "Westernized savage" as spectacle, images that are nevertheless rooted in the whole repertoire of stereotypes of the "good", "bad", "childlike", and "noble" savage. Stereotypes are based precisely on repetition, mutual referentiality, and circularity of correlated images. More specifically, stereotypes are ruled by a logic of simplification and a generalization of cultural identities, a logic that denies individuality and which is generally structured in positive or negative terms (i.e. as good or bad), a dualism that condenses the fundamental ambivalence in attitudes and value-judgments toward alterity (White 1978; Todorov 1984; Gilman 1985; Pieterse 1992; Bhabha 1994). As Gilman argues, the dynamic of stereotyping is also characterized by the projection of qualities, fears, and desires onto otherness, projective mechanisms by means of which the "self" is constituted and normalized:

> The Other is invested with all the qualities of the "bad" or the "good". The "bad" self, with its repressed sadistic impulses, becomes the "bad" Other; the "good" self, with its infallible correctness, becomes the antithesis to the flawed image of the self, the self out of control. The "bad" Other becomes the negative stereo-type; the "good" Other becomes the positive stereotype. The former is that which we fear to become; the latter, that which we fear we cannot achieve.
>
> (Gilman 1985: 18)

The mechanism of projection is the key to understanding the dualistic and ambiva-lent stereotyping in the perception of otherness, for this mechanism reflects internal contradictions within the self. As I will argue below, a similar pattern of projection can be found in student responses to the Yanomamö films, a pattern that originates in students' preconceptions of the primitive and that is also motivated by the dual themes of the film series (the Yanomamö as fierce/peaceful). The question that remains is: why are stereotypes so central in self-construction? Where lies the power of stereotypes?

White's (1978) analysis of the noble savage "metaphor" in terms of fetishism, as a kind of belief, devotion and psychological posture, is helpful to understand the psycho-social workings of stereotypes:

> ... the very notion of a Noble Savage was fetishistic, given the very context in which it was elaborated as a putative description of a type of humanity. That is to say, belief in the idea of a Noble Savage was magical, was extravagant and irrational in the kind of devotion it was meant to inspire, and, in the end, displayed the kind of pathological displacement of libidinal interest that we normally associate with the forms of racism that depend on the idea of a "wild humanity" for their justification.
>
> (White 1978: 184)

What needs to be examined is how these pervasive stereotypes are recreated or deconstructed in response to ethnographic film. In the remainder of this chapter I will examine student reception of the Yanomamö films and the dynamics of stereotyping in light of the theoretical perspectives discussed above, and, in particular, by using Bhabha's four-term stereotyping strategy as an analytical model. It will be assumed, firstly, that viewers' (narcissistic) identification with the film subjects may result in positive projections of qualities and desires onto the other by means of "masking" and normalizing it in the form of the "good" stereotype. Secondly, viewers' alienation from or aggressive identification with the Yanomamö may result in negative projections and the concealing of such "lack" with the image of the "bad" savage. Instances in which stereotypes are reflexively recognized and criticized as such, and, moreover, cases in which the representation in itself is contested, will be discussed as instances of relative "pedagogical success" (considering instructors' goals of minimizing or eliminating stereotypical responses). While using psychoanalytical categories, my analysis will focus not on psychic mechanisms in themselves but on the processes by which viewers reconstruct identities of otherness and the articulation of these reconstructions with the filmic representation of the Yanomamö and with the pedagogical strategies employed by instructors.

Fierceness as difference: reception of *The Ax Fight*

We were just watching these people yelling and screaming and pretty soon these guys were running around with axes and it was so brutal and they're actually hitting each other. I just kind of jumped out of my seat when they started doing that, I thought "these people they're psycho, they're crazy … he's not gonna hit him with that ax," you see him running up like this, "no, he's not gonna hit him" … I just thought "this is unreal, these people are barbaric, they're animals, they're bizarre". Nobody really hits someone with an ax … that's all I was thinking about these people, "they're just crazy".

(No. 4, male third-year student, 1988)

In *The Ax Fight* it was quite disturbing to me because I don't like any violence, but it just shows you how the Yanomamö people are, they are the fierce people, there's a lot of corruption, a lot of disturbance in their culture. They are opposing visitors, I mean, they don't like any visitors and that's what *The Ax Fight* was about … And with the quality of the film, I mean, with the three parts to it, I felt that each part was quite repetitive … I just felt in the third part that they really didn't have a need to show that, I mean, because after hearing that lady at the end scream so many times, you know, her shrieking voice, it just really bothered me.

(No. 5, female second-year student, 1988)

These comments dramatically convey the shock of viewing *The Ax Fight* and the view of the Yanomamö as "fierce" that my interviews with several USC undergraduates revealed in 1988.[4] Such responses may not be too surprising if we consider, first, the film's primary focus, a spontaneous conflict that quickly escalates into a fight with clubs, machetes, and axes among a large group of men and women, and, second, if we take into account that these students only viewed two of the most "fierce" Yanomamö films, *The Ax Fight* and *Magical Death*, in the context of a theme-oriented introductory anthropology class.[5] It could be more surprising to some, however, to find that the two viewers who explicitly stated their stereotypical construction of the Yanomamö were students who demonstrated a fair understanding of the dynamics of the fight and the film itself, fulfilled the course requirements, and received average grades for the course. In their written reports on *The Ax Fight* and essay papers, these two students provided an interpretation that closely matched Chagnon's explanation in the film's study guide and had apparently acquired a basic understanding of the role of kinship links in the filmed event, and the dynamics of escalation of violence and conflict resolution.

However, in the more casual context of the interview, the students openly expressed their blatant stereotyping of the film subjects.[6] The male student's (No. 4) interpretation of Yanomamö behavior as animalistic conveys the classic stereotype of a remote but terrifying barbarian further enhanced by the image of the typical "psycho" and the wicked madness of horror movies, a media genre that evokes primal fantasies of castration. The female student's (No. 5) apparent confusion regarding her assumption that the Yanomamö do not like visitors clearly represents an aberrant reconstruction of the film's explanation as well as a facile projection of the fixed notion of the "fierce people" who, hostile by nature, attack *any* people indiscriminately. Both students were anxious about the differences between the Yanomamö and themselves and were emphatic about not identifying with the Yanomamö. The consequent masking of the Yanomamö with the bad savage stereotype served to normalize the viewers' frightening experience of otherness as "lack".

The contrast between these students' learning of ethnographic information and their stereotyping of the Yanomamö was by no means rare in the introductory anthropology class. Considering that most instructors in these courses aimed not only to teach factual information but also to fight ethnocentrism and help students develop relativistic views of foreign cultures, the contrast is indeed problematic. It clearly indicates a failure to achieve teaching goals. Although such difficulties may be inevitable when teaching about radical cultural difference, evidence of negative results in significant proportions which are strongly linked to particular films should make us rethink our pedagogical methods.

This teaching failure was also manifest in my earlier analysis of undergraduates' reactions to *The Ax Fight* (Martínez 1990a, 1990b). In an examination of students' written responses to the film, which was presented as part of their coursework, a very similar pattern of stereotypical readings emerged from a sample of twelve students who took a similar introductory course in 1987 and who saw *The Ax Fight* in the context of a theme-oriented course.[7] My inquiry revealed that the films shocked and appalled the students. In many cases, viewers misconstrued the textual explanation and felt largely alienated from the Yanomamö, but largely construed Yanomamö behavior as "barbaric", "stupid", and "reprehensible".

When compared to Asch's teaching approach, the 1987 and 1988 courses (in which Asch did not teach) did not offer the ethnographic contextualization of *The Ax Fight* that could have potentially reduced the number of stereotypical readings of the Yanomamö. For example, had those students seen the films which depict the Yanomamö as peaceful, their responses might have been more informed and less stereotypical. As I will show below, when students view both the films which depict the Yanomamö as violent and those which present them as peaceful, their responses are more sophisticated, but the responses are still negative and reveal negative impressions of the Yanomamö.

For now, let us return to the 1988 introductory course to analyze the fewer but more elaborated and apparently less stereotypical responses found.

> I think the main value was to make people understand how organization can change something from chaos to something that makes sense to them. Like for example … looking at the film before it was edited and before you knew what was happening, you had a total surprise and negative view about it but then after you figured out what was going on, you understood and therefore with understanding you felt better about it, you know what I mean?
>
> (No. 6, female second-year student, 1988)

> What I thought really helped about seeing *The Ax Fight* was having Timothy Asch in class, he could come to the class and explain what his intentions were before we even saw the film. Also, you kind of pay more attention when you know the film-maker is there watching your reactions. When I first saw it, the first part of it, I was real confused about it, I didn't know what was going on. Then as he broke the film down and started to explain a little bit about the people in the Yanomamö it became really fascinating and instead of becoming just this chaotic scene that I didn't understand, it began to make sense. And when Timothy Asch explained that that's what anthropologists do, what he tried to do as a film-maker, make order out of chaos, it kind of clicked in that that's kind of part of what all of the films that we're watching were trying to do, to kind of somehow bring an event together in a coherent way.
>
> (No. 7, female fourth-year student, 1988)

While demonstrating their understanding of the film's explanation of the event in terms of Yanomamö kinship and politics, these students were often more reserved about their subjective views of the Yanomamö, whether it was because they did not want to be or appear judgmental or because their analytical views precluded easy stereotyping. In any case, their comments show that they identified with Chagnon's narrative voice and with Asch's invitation to make anthropological order out of the apparent chaos of Yanomamö behavior. This identification made them feel better about their initial surprise and confusion while also helping them to learn ethnographic information. These students' film reports were more elaborate in their anthropological details than those of the first two students cited (Nos. 4 and 5) but did not depart much from the explanation provided in the study guide. They neither challenged nor criticized the representation of the Yanomamö in the films. In terms of their construction of the Yanomamö, it remains unclear to what degree these viewers' conceptions of the Yanomamö may have served to deconstruct or simply to erase or suppress their initial negative masking of the films' subjects.

> *The Ax Fight*, I liked it for one specific reason, in that it was almost like "here's how an ethnographic film is made". That was interesting, to start with the raw footage and then explain what we just saw, and then show it all cut together. It wasn't incredibly filmic, it was pretty flat; it doesn't bother me in that instance because he [Asch] wasn't trying to make a beautiful movie, he wasn't trying to be Spielberg junior. He was trying to make a point about the ax fight, and so, that was the focus, and that's what I was drawn towards. It was confusing at first, but then it was all explained, I just found it very fascinating. It's funny because you think of America as such – we talk about violence in America, and the film-maker, Tim Asch, warned us, he goes "now their behavior may seem a little extreme to you," and it didn't! I mean, compared to what we do, it seemed very rational. It seemed like the old ways that we used to fight, in civil war days, or even pre-Revolutionary war where it was very chivalric ... it's kind of like, "I'm going to start off just punching you, and then I'm going to pick up my stick, and then I'm going to get my ax, I'm going to hit you with the blunt end of it, don't let me get to the sharp end". It's like war games almost, it was kind of interesting, it was making statements through the violence without actually – it wasn't like enraged violence, it was like calculated and had meaning to it.
>
> (No. 8, male third-year student, 1988)

This response from a screen-writing major with professional experience in film production seems better to match Asch's teaching goals: the student appreciated the film for its informational value and self-reflexive dimension and also learned the ethnographic information while questioning the stereotype. His response could be seen as an example of pedagogical success. But then again, to what extent does the viewer's reconstruction of the fight as "war games", a mere ritualized "chivalric" gesture, convey an erasure (or re-masking) of the represented violence and thus a suppression of the "bad" savage stereotype? As suggested above, the "repertoire of conflicting positions" that accompanies racial stereotyping entails more than just suppressing radical difference in order to construe a more "normal" image of other-ness. The assimilation of a normalized other into the realm of the self is always prob-lematic: while it offers a basis for students' humanist and relativist appreciation of cultural difference, it domesticates the other without necessarily questioning the self. For example, apart from his reference to American history, to his own cultural past, the student's comparison of Yanomamö violence with "what we do" remains ambig-uous. Other students were more explicit in their reference to this fictive "we".

I think it was upsetting to see this people do something like that, get into an ax fight with deadly weapons, although I was surprised at how they held back actually, they had these axes there and they turned the blunt edges and were hitting each other with those. I mean if it would've been here, they would have used the sharp edges; we're a much more violent society than they are ...

Who is this 'we' you are talking about?

Western, American society ...

Where in Western or American society?

Right around here, yeah, I know it's very violent, you go five blocks away and probably be in more danger than you'd would ever be among the Yanomamö ... I have been harassed on the street and they have been, you know, the same type of people, and now I'm actually scared when running to my apartment.

(No. 9, female third-year student, 1988)

These "we" found "right around here", in the Los Angeles inner-city area surrounding the university, are not quite part of the more intimate student self. They are the mostly black and Latino population living in the common American scene of urban poverty, crime, gang warfare, and violence. In general, students live in constant fear of this mostly unknown, potentially dangerous, and largely stereotyped other. As Bhabha argues, "the stereotype requires, for its successful signification, a continual and repetitive chain of other stereotypes" (1994: 77). This co-referentiality suggests that the assimilation of a normalized "primitive" violence into American violence constituted, for some students, an ideological displacement or re-masking of cultural/racial difference: the fierce other was recast as the ethnic other. The self remained largely untouched.

It's fun, you know, when you think of gangs, of kids here, and that's news; that's the startling thing, we live in a city that has more gang violence than any other city in America, and that's always news. So, all this violence with the Yanomamö is kind of news and interesting and fun, but it's not what their life is all about, most of the time. Most of the time their life is about keeping things together and living a good life the way, you know, just the way we're trying to. I mean, in a different way, it's a different environment altogether ... they love their gardens, their gardens are a model, a beautiful thing to look at. So, it's not all violence; the violence is only a part of it, a small part. But, that's what we're getting, that's what I have to deal with.

(Asch 1988)

As a film-maker, Asch was highly sensitive to the social impact of violence as spectacle in contemporary America and to how *The Ax Fight* may play into the media commodification of endemic violence. Although chivalric to some, the exotic Yanomamö "fierceness" nonetheless provided many viewers with grounds for concluding that the Yanomamö are stereotypical savages and bad. Even if some of the more informed students absorbed Asch's attempt to relativize violence and assimilate the other, such "assimilation" could be indicating in some cases an ideological displacement and, eventually, a restoration of the original fear of difference. Paradoxically, their endorsement of the voice of anthropology led some students to return, more informed and sophisticated, to the hyperbolic view of the "fierce" people.

> I still feel that they're – they have a tendency for violence that is a part of culture that I personally don't like, but that's their culture, that's what they do, that's the way they've been brought up, that they live, and I have to accept that. But I think I'm finding that they're more than just a savage people, that they do have a culture just as I have a culture, they have a way of life that's uniquely theirs.
>
> (No. 10, female fourth-year student, 1988)

The realization that the Yanomamö have a unique culture was probably the central anthropological lesson students learned in the class. The savage was thereby reconfigured into a new image of an organized yet violent *culture*. This anthropological reconstruction of otherness is the basic goal of most introductory courses, yet it raises two related problems. The first has to do with the reification of culture as a totalizing concept, which, by commonly failing to provide a theory of praxis, "commits anthropology forever to imputing (if not outright imposing) motives, beliefs, meanings, and functions to the societies it studies from a perspective outside and above" (Fabian 1983: 156–7). The second problem is tied to the notion of cultural difference, which affirms and normalizes otherness within a discourse of relativity while masking anthropology's privileged role in representing difference.

This critical perspective is useful to question further the extent to which the film's anthropological explanation helped students deconstruct or simply elaborate their stereotypical views of Yanomamö otherness. In the case of the student quoted above (No. 10), the latter seemed to be the case. The comment "but that's their culture" encapsulates Yanomamö society as a unified body, fixated in its difference and normalized in its "equality", more than just "savage" but ultimately essentialized as a *violent culture*. Although differing much in their rhetorical strategies and aims, the popular stereotypical discourse and the anthropologically informed knowledge share a common process of masking radical difference via the fixation of otherness. In other words, an identification of the Yanomamö as a "fierce" culture may produce a similar effect on viewers as does the reductive hegemonic categorization of stereotypical discourse. This problematic conclusion raises serious concerns about the mainstream exclusive screening of the "fierce" films, as was the case with the 1988 introductory course, and it raises problems for particular representational strategies in anthropology and ethnographic film. To explore these issues further, I turn to an analysis of the reception of some of the other Yanomamö films.

Figure 11.1 Tim Asch (right) and Craig Johnson filming *Climbing the Peach Palm*, 1971. Note the Yanomamö immediately below the crown of the palm tree.

Figure 11.2 Tim Asch filming *New Tribes Mission*, 1971.

The good, the bad, and the ugly: reception of the film series

> Having seen approximately fourteen to sixteen films on the Yanomamö, I think that some of them or a lot of them deal with curing ceremonies and trying to kill the *hekura* spirits, and I don't think that we need that many representations on how they cure. I know it's a main point of their culture but I think that we need to learn more about them as people.
>
> (No. 11, female second-year student, 1989)

> I don't know if my intention was always there, 'cause, sometimes like *Weeding the Garden*, I think that's essential to learning about the Yanomamö because that's their life and you've got to film their life and that's what it is, but it's not actually the most exciting thing to watch, you know, so sometimes I kind of get a little restless.
>
> (No. 12, female first-year student, 1992)

> The way that the films paid so much attention to the bizarre behavior of the Yanomamö, the drug snuff coming out of their mouth and picking lice on each other and that sort of thing, was kind of taking advantage of the things about them that are shocking to us and, in another way, it's sort of acceptable because you want your films to hold the attention of your audience, I think. I mean, very few film-makers like to think that they're gonna make a film just for the intellectual elite to sit around and think about.
>
> (No. 13, male second-year student, 1989)

The tension between wanting to see the Yanomamö as "people" and being bored by the "peaceful" films mirrors the larger split between a desire for exciting films and the aggressive denial of boring media and objectifying representations. I have observed a similar pattern of students' film evaluation before (Martínez 1990a): a preference for the more "cooked" TV anthropological documentaries over conventional ethnographic films, which most students found less entertaining and "raw" in style and also more alienating. Students read ethnographic films in aberrant ways more often than other documentaries and linked them to "rawer" stereotypical figurations.[8] As a whole, the Yanomamö film series evoked a similar media consumption pattern: even if some viewers found some of the films somehow exploitative in intention and style, this was considered "acceptable" as a means to hold their attention (No. 13).

In this section I discuss in more detail how particular films captured students' interest and how they influenced viewers' constructions of the Yanomamö by focusing on two groups of students who saw both the films and read published ethnographies of the Yanomamö. In the introductory anthropology classes of 1989 and 1992, students saw thirteen and ten Yanomamö films respectively, in courses using Asch's case study approach.[9] Asch himself taught the course in 1989 while the instructor in the 1992 class followed Asch's teaching methods. Students' responses to the films' styles can help us understand how the films' rhetoric of form is related to viewers' reconstruction of the films' content.

For some reason when we were watching *Moonblood* or *Myth of Naro*, or *The Feast*, or *Tapir Distribution*, or one of those, you didn't feel as close to the Yanomamö. They were talking straight to the camera, which the !Kung did do, but for some reason the camera was so far away and you just didn't, it was very far away, it was almost like some of it was staged, it seemed, not as natural as the !Kung was, very organized, but I mean that is part of their culture, I think the Yanomamö culture is more organized as a culture than the !Kung are, they are more organized and probably more distant.

(No. 14, female third-year student, 1992)

I guess that one reason that I'm not dispelled [*sic.*] that much by the violence in Yanomamö culture is the fact that it was treated so clinically. I felt like I wasn't really ... if I were there I wouldn't be threatened by it, that's something that exists in their realm, is a part of their culture and I wouldn't be subjected to it, if I was there, any more than the anthropologist seemed to be.

(No. 15, male second-year student, 1989)

Here are some classic reception problems with the observational and monologic style of conventional ethnographic film, problems which started in our case with the frightening viewfinder image of the Yanomamö and with the ethnographic film trope of positivist and unreflective realism dominant during the 1970s ("whole bodies, whole people, whole acts"). In the narration, Chagnon dissects, describes, and explains the film subjects, further distancing them from the viewer. The film style then produces the double effect of freezing the other and, to some extent, "numbing" the viewer to the mute Yanomamö (No. 15). It is also interesting to note how student No. 14 collapses both form and content, constructing a homology between the films' objectifying style and the "distance" of the Yanomamö as a culture, a distance linked to their "organization" or lack of naturalness, unlike her image of the "warmer" !Kung people. While numbing some students, however, the anxious order of the films (especially the "fierce" ones) and their anti-romantic, rationalist fixation of difference cannot suppress the *excessive* difference of the Yanomamö.

They just seem like a very vulgar group of people there, even the children have filthy language, the women are almost barbaric in the way they yell back and forth to each other, like in relation to the !Kung ... the Yanomamö seem constantly to either be out of it because they are on drugs or worried about the *hekura* spirits or, they're very sexually involved, at least in the books that I read they were not described as very passive, sensitive people, they were kind of greedy almost. The whole gift-giving process was just very self-involved, you

know, what they're gonna get from this group of visitors, if they don't get it, you know, we'll start a fight, and I don't think that's a way of life that should be led.
(No. 16, female second-year student, 1989)

They are kind of warlike in that they don't conduct themselves in a proper manner, I think that all this taking drugs and stuff kind of gave me an impression, I don't know, I don't really feel anything towards these people. I don't really find that much interest in seeing films about drugs and fighting and things like that.
(No. 17, female first-year student, 1989)

They had a strange legend, I couldn't stand watching them take their drugs, I hated that, it was really gross, and the way they don't talk about their dead ones. I just thought that their religion was very strange, all the Moonblood and all that kind of stuff, it was pretty violent too, kind of a violent religion, about eating the children and blood. I thought it was weird, and all the trance and stuff like that, talking to the *hekura* spirits and everything. I don't understand it, I mean, I can understand what they thought but I don't understand why they want to believe in it, I couldn't relate to it.
(No. 18, male second-year student, 1992)

The main features of Yanomamö culture to which these viewers reacted – violence, use of drugs, religious beliefs, sexuality – conform to an image of a primordial savage, excessive in his behavior and beliefs, and radically other. Confronting these features of Yanomamö life led many students to feel alienated from the Yanomamö. These students engaged in a relation of aggressive non-identification and resorted to masking the threatening difference with the fetish object/image of the barbarian in direct opposition to the (mirror) image of the docile !Kung as the "good" primitive. This ethnocentric and racist masking of difference was then inscribed into a desire to domesticate the subaltern other into passivity and "proper manners" (Nos. 16 and 17).

The ethnographic contextualization of the films through reading published ethnography seems to have had little impact on the way Nos. 16, 17, and 18 (and a significant proportion of the class) stereotypically reconstructed the Yanomamö as lacking culture. Indeed, the addition of written ethnography to the curriculum resulted in more informed stereotypes, in the addition of another body of evidence to the students' fixation of difference. For example, a perception of the Yanomamö as greedy was reinforced by a student's reference to the class readings (No. 16). Exposure to the written ethnography provided the students with the means of further developing a stereotype of the Yanomamö as inhuman and ugly.

In contrast, some students saw another Yanomamö:

I still don't even know about the Yanomamö ... the only thing I know about the Yanomamö is that they act on their raw passions, they are very primitive people. It seems that they don't even think before they act. They are very violent people that just go raiding other villages, they take drugs and they freak out on drugs, and on drugs they've been known to attack people. They can take drugs and that's a good excuse to be violent. They love their own little family but they can't even have a village over fifty people because they start to clash on ideas and become violent ... I don't wanna hang out with them because I'd probably get arrows on my back, that's how I think, that's too bad. I wonder if that's the real deal or not.

(No. 19, male second-year student, 1992)

This rather ironic reading of the Yanomamö-as-stereotype seems to convey a critique of its reductionist character. Apparently feeling unable to confront the ethnographic "facts" about Yanomamö violence *outside* of the representation, e.g. by comparison with other texts or through more direct experience, this student was left with a number of doubts about the "real" Yanomamö. This healthy suspicion of the representation, however, did not necessarily lead to a deconstruction of the stereotype; on the contrary, the difficulty in reconstructing the radical otherness of the Yanomamö in an alternative light seemed to have trapped this viewer into reluctantly "giving in" to the rhetorical power of the filmic and written material: "that's how I think, that's too bad".

Asch was aware of these problems in using the Yanomamö as a case study:

I feel a battle every time I go in the classroom and I use these films ... I'm there at the stage, I've got the students out there in the audience. I've got the readings that some of them have done in their heads and that I've got in my head. And then I've got these visual images that we share together, and in the sharing, it's a fight, it's a struggle ... not to get them to see it my way, but ... to get them to see those two things and deal with them and reckon with them and, what are they really? ... And I'm negotiating that process, and it's very hard. I'm exhausted at the end of every class ... A lot of the films deal with some pretty hard, raw, strong elements that are very new to the students and difficult for them to deal with. I find it difficult to deal with them. I find it difficult to use the Yanomamö to talk about another phase of economic and cultural development in positive ways. And yet, I know them to be a great people, interesting, energetic, full of life, full of the great desire to learn, full of tremendous energy. And yet, the material I have to work with, the written material at the moment, and the film material, it in itself tends to reinforce these basic prejudices, because, you know, The Fierce People: look, hey man, these people are really fierce, and you can see it.

(Asch 1988)

The films which included footage of violent behavior, such as *The Ax Fight* and *Magical Death*, made the strongest impressions on many students and apparently overpowered the impressions left by the "peaceful" films (see the comments of Nos. 11, 13, 17 and 18). These viewers produced their mostly stereotypical impressions regardless of the course input and class discussions in which the films were critiqued by instructors and students. As Asch notes, a major challenge for him in class was trying to undo viewers' negative impressions by critiquing Chagnon's characterization of the Yanomamö and by juxtaposing his own contrasting perspective on them. The results were mixed: while some students gave priority to Chagnon's characterization over Asch's, arguing that it was more "objective", others endorsed Asch's critique, and probably most of them negotiated meanings between the two positions.

> We've already heard the deal of Chagnon, he had this idea that the Yanomamö are fierce and he's gonna make them seem fierce, and, also, a book sells better when it says "the fierce people" on the cover rather than "the nice people" ... If it were not by Asch, I would've bought the whole thing because I don't know better, you know.
>
> (No. 20, male second-year student, 1989)

> I have trouble believing everything Tim Asch says because he and Chagnon don't get along in their opinions, but then again, I don't believe everything Chagnon says either. ... Having heard Asch's, whose opinion I respect, I can see that the Yanomamö are not that fierce, and then reading Chagnon's book I can see where he was, you know, a little afraid of these people and maybe threatened by them.
>
> (No. 21, male third-year student, 1989)

Asch's critical framing of the films in terms of the producers' personal biases indeed provided a valuable counterpoint to the image of the Yanomamö as fierce and offered students the opportunity to analyze the constructedness of the representation. In any case, students supported one view of the Yanomamö or the other and negotiated their interpretations of the films' subjects guided by their own concerns and interpretations.

To what extent did Asch's "peaceful" films facilitate students' identification with the Yanomamö and help subvert the "bad" savage stereotype?

> After seeing the films my impression is that they are no more violent or fierce than any other people. I guess a lot of the films focused on some of the violent nature of the people but I can think of one film in particular, which is *Weeding the Garden*, where Dedeheiwa was weeding his garden and playing with his kids and playing with his wife. That was a very peaceful and happy kind of scene and that really made me realize that the Yanomamö people are just as fun-loving and peace-loving as anybody else.
>
> (No. 22, male first-year student, 1989)

> *Moawa Burns Felled Timber* and *Weeding the Garden* were touching films, to see these giants playing with their kids and weeding the garden. It was really

impressive to see these people that had been made out to be such bad people playing with their kids and letting their kids give 'em a backrub or a massage. … That really hammered it home that these are just not people we're studying, they're humans and they love their kids as all parents do.

(No. 23, male third-year student, 1992)

These "peaceful" films seem to have worked as a counter-balance to the violence in the other films for these students. As I have noted, the observational style of these event films does not vary much from that of the violent ones; there is no narration in the peaceful films, which employ simple editing to emphasize real time, and are thus less polished. Perhaps for this reason, the films in themselves did not seem to capture students' attention as much as their subject matter did (the other as "people") and the way it was framed critically by Asch in class as an exposé of the other side of the Yanomamö. In their film reports and essays, many students referred to *Weeding the Garden* and *Moawa Burns Felled Timber* as evidence that the Yanomamö are not fierce but peaceful and "human". In the interviews, I noticed that male students recalled these films more often than female students, perhaps responding to images of Dedeheiwa and Moäwä as good and fun-loving fathers. In contrast, while some female students shared this positive image of the good male, several of them emphasized their relative indifference or boredom toward these films (see No. 12) and even criticized them:

Some of the films are like really romanticized too, you know, like I think it was the Wasp Nest where they were kind of in the field and, and even the Yanomamö, I think it was in *Weeding the Garden* when it shows like the women just smiling, a big smile on their face, a little bit romanticized I guess … which kind of makes it a little bit less objective than other films.

(No. 24, female second-year student, 1992)

This student raises the issue of romanticism as a form of masking the more "objective" (i.e. "real") behavior. In other words, her critical perception of the free-wheeling and smiling women does not seem to convey the supposedly oppressive reality of "primitive" women. Certainly, the image of the loving male did not touch this viewer much. This indicates that, given the consistent and pervasive silencing of women in the film series as a whole, the potential of the "peaceful" films for subverting the image of the "fierce" Yanomamö needs to be read along gender lines.

Conclusion: the challenges of the representer

I have discussed in this paper how student reception of the Yanomamö films poses serious challenges to ethnographic film-makers and instructors who use ethnographic film in university teaching. These pedagogical and representational challenges are all the more acute in relation to the Yanomamö films. As texts, many of the Yanomamö films focus on male violence. The influence of these features of

Yanomamö behavior on students' perception of the Yanomamö as people is powerful and perhaps results in part from the distancing which results from their observational style, a style which objectifies the people who are their subjects. Labeling the Yanomamö "the fierce people" contributes to students' negative reactions to the Yanomamö. At the exegetical level, we have the pedagogical context (i.e. course design, lectures, books, discussions) in which students see the films, the historical horizon of reception of the films (in our case, the gap between students' reception of the films in the early 1990s and the films' late 1960s' politics of representation) and, more generally, the insertion of anthropological discourse within American and Western political and social discourses and media stereotypes. I have attempted to show how all these textual and extra-textual factors were articulated in contradictory and complementary ways to produce more or less stereotypical interpretations of otherness.

As an author, teacher, and film-maker, Tim Asch responded creatively to both pedagogical and representational challenges. Asch's teaching methods and strategies, which aimed at providing extensive documentation of the Yanomamö through film and written ethnography, have proved to be the most consistent with the goals of minimizing stereotypical readings and countering the communicational "impasse", much more so than the mainstream use of the "fierce" films in theme-oriented courses. The instances of pedagogical success found among students were largely the result of Asch's personal intervention as translator. His experimental strategies for negotiating textual and exegetical meanings with students and his self-critical attitude toward representation resulted in many cases in the more negotiated and reflective and less stereotypical readings of the films. The significant proportion of stereotypical readings, however, indicates that there are limits to the effectiveness of the "case study" method, the detailed ethnographic contextualizations, and to Asch's personal intervention – limitations posed mainly by viewers' subject positionings and by the rhetorical power of the representation itself. An important way to confront these limits is to reassert Asch's proposal that instructors use films more consciously and critically. Furthermore, we need to build on Asch's pedagogical tactics.

In this direction, I have argued that an alternative to the educational impasse with the Yanomamö films, and with ethnographic film in general, is to move from an ethnographic contextualization of the other to a critical contextualizing of the self in class. This will necessarily entail moving from the analysis of film-makers' " biases" to a classroom critique of the representation itself as a cultural and historical construct, to seriously engaging students in a reflexive critique of American and Western racial stereotypes of otherness.

In many important ways, Tim Asch catalyzed and contributed to innovative figurations of alterity in ethnographic film and video, from his early Yanomamö films to his Jero Tapakan film series and his commitment to promoting indigenous media among the Yanomamö, in which he was engaged at the time of his death. Much of his professional development can be seen as original responses to the challenge posed by the academic and student reception of the Yanomamö films.

After making the series of films on Bali, Asch wrote about his main reservations regarding the Yanomamö films (Asch 1986: 43–4). From the perspective of his later work, he saw that some of the Yanomamö films can powerfully reinforce Western prejudices and stereotypes of the "primitive". He argued that films need to be more closely integrated with written materials in university anthropology courses. He concluded that the lack of Yanomamö voices in the films contributed to distancing them from viewers. And he regretted not being able to show the films to the Yanomamö themselves. In his later films on Roti, Bali, and Flores, Asch experimented with ways of overcoming these limitations.

Even during the production of the Yanomamö films, Asch set himself the task of countering the image of the Yanomamö as fierce by offering viewers alternative images of the Yanomamö as peaceful people engaged in ordinary daily activities in which violence had no part. For many students, the humanist message of the peaceful films worked as an antidote to the stereotype of the bad savage and provided a bridge between them and the radical Yanomamö otherness communicated in the violent films. However, the humanistic view of the peaceful Yanomamö led some students to romanticize them as the good and noble savage. While countering Chagnon's perspective, Asch's dualistic framing of Yanomamö otherness in the film series created other difficulties in teaching.

Anthropological representations of otherness are frequently articulated within the dualistic and fetishistic dynamics of racial stereotyping in western spectatorship. The dynamics of students' maskings of the Yanomamö as "bad" or "good" savage are all but metonymic of larger cultural discourses of alterity affecting the reception of all anthropological media. The few students who contested the Yanomamö representation clearly pointed at the complicit relation between the monologic, objectifying discourses of anthropology and the larger media discourses of and about "others". These commentaries make all the more imperative ethnographic film's challenge and need to develop alternative representations, perhaps more evocative, dialogic and reflexive in form, but necessarily more democratic, anti-stereotypical, and decolonizing in their politics. Students' critical responses also address the crucial fact that the agenda and theoretical framework for teaching introductory anthropology need to be rethought if instructors want to avoid converting their central notions of *culture* and *cultural difference* into "illustrated" stereotypes of otherness and assimilating them within hegemonic constructions of sameness.

In our media-saturated times of increasing hybridization and commodification of cultures, the demands for more democratic and dialogical representations of alterity are stronger than ever. From this angle, the Yanomamö film series needs to be seen both as an historical product with its own potentials and limitations and as a cultural legacy with corrective lessons to offer. As Asch argued in his recent writings on the ethics of anthropological filmic representation (Asch 1992), the responsibilities of contemporary film-makers have become much more complex and include engaging in economic, legal, political, and ethical negotiations with the film subjects that were unacknowledged in his early pioneering efforts.

Asch's perspective is fundamental to consider in response to the challenges posed by the reception of the Yanomamö films, for it suggests the need to historicize the processes of representation and reception of otherness. A critical use of visual media in teaching anthropology demands framing the ethical concerns and the politics of representation of a given time; it requires historicizing texts and the contexts in which they are constructed and initially received. Such a perspective can help viewers deal with their re-enactment of fantasies and fears of difference, and contribute to minimizing communicational problems that arise when there is a mismatch between texts and viewers' horizons of expectation.

Notes

The research reported here was funded by the Spencer Foundation, the Fulbright Commission, the Center for Visual Anthropology at USC, the Haynes Foundation, and the Organization of American States. The research is the subject of several research reports and related papers (Martínez 1990a, 1990b, 1992, 1994) and my doctoral dissertation (Martínez 1998).

I wish to thank Susan Reed for her invaluable help in reading and commenting on earlier versions of this chapter.

1 Hearne and DeVore name the following Yanomamö films which they originally planned to use in their study. They do not say specifically which twelve films from this list they used. 1. *Morning Flowers*; 2. *Children in the Rain*; 3. *Moawa Burns the Garden*; 4. *Dedeheiwa Weeds His Garden*; 5. *Myth of Naro as Told by Dedeheiwa*; 6. *Myth of Naro as Told by Kaobawa*; 7. *Woman Spins*; 8. *Moawa Weaves*; 9. *The Ax Fight*; 10. *Mouth Wrestling*; 11. *The Feast*; 12. *Children Roast Meat*; 13. *Magical Death*; 14. *Children's Magical Death*; 15. *Ocamo is My Town*; 16. *New Tribes Mission*.

2 During the 1960s Asch collaborated on the project *Man, A Course of Study* which developed an anthropology curriculum for elementary schools. Later, he used his teaching experiences with the !Kung and Yanomamö films to develop his methods for teaching with the use of film. As part of his evaluation of introductory anthropology courses he taught at Brandeis and Harvard universities, Asch presented a series of student-written comments about the successful use of the Yanomamö films (Asch 1975: 395–8). Students' comments, however, did not focus on the represented Yanomamö as much as on the communicational qualities of visual media, i.e. providing "accurate" and "truthful" representations, enhancing the information provided in books, providing a sense of "immediacy", and "bringing to life" the people represented. Overall, students celebrated the use of visual images as a valuable teaching tool.

3 From 1987–91, I collected 316 essays on "primitiveness" written by students at USC. On the first day of class, students were asked to write a one- to two-page essay containing a definition of the term "primitive" and a description of "primitive society" based on either media-based impressions or direct experience; descriptions included aspects such as peoples' appearance, daily life, beliefs and values, and their views of modern societies.

4 In the spring semester of 1988 I conducted interviews with fifteen students randomly selected from a class of 108. Each student was interviewed at least once during the semester and then again by the end of the course.

5 "Exploring Culture through Film" is one of the most popular general education requirements among undergraduates at USC. Ethnographic films and videos play an important role in the course, in which instructors screen between ten and more than twenty films during a single semester. Although the course structure varies with each instructor, in 1988 the films were organized around specific anthropological topics. In particular, the two Yanomamö films were shown within a thematic unit on violence entitled "Cultural Contrasts: War and Peace in Yanomamö society". The films were also screened to trigger discussion about the issue of stereotyping in film (e.g. in comparison with the film *The Emerald Forest*, which was also shown in class). As guest speaker Asch addressed students before screening *The Ax Fight*, but he was not present during class discussion. Chagnon's *Yanomamö: The Fierce People* (1983) was listed as recommended reading while the film's study guide was required material for class and small discussion groups.

6 The stark contrast between responses given in required assignments (which also asked students about their personal reactions) and in the interviews may be also indexing a pattern of deceptive responses on the part of students. Many students quickly learn what to say to an instructor in order to get better grades. As one student said: "Sometimes in order to get a good grade in lab report you had to get pretty cheesy about your answers, and I wanted to just answer the question, move along but you get a B if you do that; if you want to get an A, you have to give a lot of flowery garbage about how it related to your entire life ... If you made some great statement about how the film changed your life, then, you know, I'd get little comments, like 'great ideas', 'good' ... and so once I figured that out, I started getting As" (male third-year student, 1988).

7 Students in the 1987 class were required to read Chagnon's ethnography (1983) and, while they did not read the film's study guide, they had access to written transcripts of the lectures sold at a local bookstore. Students were also required to write two-page film reports on most of the films they saw in class. Asch participated as a guest speaker in a session previous to the screening of *The Ax Fight*.

8 While different in character, most ethnographic films (e.g. *The Ax Fight, Trance and Dance in Bali, The Feast, The Nuer*) were linked to stereotypical interpretations of the "bad" savage, e.g. violent, superstitious, bizarre, backward, irrational.

9 Yanomamö films screened in spring 1989: *Young Shaman, A Man Called 'Bee': Studying the Yanomamö, Myth of Naro as Told by Kaobawa, Magical Death, Children's Magical Death, Moonblood: A Yanomamö Creation Myth, A Father Washes his Children, Weeding the Garden, The Feast, Tapir Distribution, New Tribes Mission*, and *Ocamo is My Town*. Yanomamö films screened in spring 1992: *Yanomamö: a Multi-Disciplinary Study, Moonblood: A Yanomamö Creation Myth, Yanomamö Myth of Naro as told by Kaobawa, Weeding the Garden, Moawa Burns Felled Timber, The Ax Fight, Tapir Distribution, The Feast, Ocamo is My Town*, and *New Tribes Mission*. The other ethnographic cases included in the course were the !Kung, Balinese, and American societies. Each class devoted three to four weeks to each case study society and used five to thirteen films on each of them. Asch himself taught the 1989 course, assigning Chagnon's *Yanomamö: The Fierce People* (1983) and Lizot's *Tales of the Yanomami* (1985) as reading and study guides for most of the films screened. Students also had to write two-page reports on every film they saw. In the 1992 class, the instructor followed Asch's "case study" methodology; students were assigned the same material (Lizot's book was suggested reading) and also wrote film reports. As guest speaker in this class, Asch presented three films (*The Ax Fight, Tapir Distribution*, and *Weeding the Garden*) and discussed them with the students.

References

Asch, Timothy (1974),"New Methods for Making and Using Ethnographic Film". In George Spindler (ed.), *Education and Cultural Process: Towards an Anthropology of Education*. New York: Holt, Rinehart and Winston.

—— (1975), "Using Film in Teaching Anthropology: One Pedagogical Approach". In Paul Hockings (ed.), *Principles of Visual Anthropology*. Chicago: Mouton Publishers.

—— (1979), "Making a Film Record of the Yanomamö Indians of Southern Venezuela". *Perspectives on Film* 2: 4–9, 44–9.

—— (1986), "How and Why the Films Were Made". In Linda Connor, P. Asch and T. Asch, *Jero Tapakan: A Balinese Healer*. New York: Cambridge University Press.

—— (1988), Unpublished interview with Wilton Martínez. Los Angeles: University of Southern California.

—— (1992), "The Ethics of Ethnographic Film-making". In Peter Crawford and David Turton (eds.), *Film as Ethnography*. Manchester: Manchester University Press.

Banks, Marcus (1992), "Which Films Are the Ethnographic Films?" In Peter Crawford and David Turton (eds.), *Film As Ethnography*. Manchester: Manchester University Press.

Bhabha, Homi (1994),*The Location of Culture*. New York: Routledge.

Chagnon, Napoleon (1968), *Yanomamö: The Fierce People*. First edition. New York: Holt, Rinehart and Winston.

—— (1983), *Yanomamö: The Fierce People*. Third edition. New York: Holt, Rinehart and Winston.

Fabian, Johannes (1983), *Time and the Other: How Anthropology Makes Its Object*. New York:

Columbia University Press.

Gilman, Sander (1985), *Difference and Pathology: Stereotypes of Sexuality, Race, and Madness.* Ithaca: Cornell University Press.

Hearne, Thomas and P. DeVore (1973), "The Yanomamö on Film and Paper". Paper presented at the Anthropological Film Conference, Smithsonian Institution, May 12.

Heider, Karl G. (1976), *Ethnographic Film.* Austin: University of Texas Press.

Lizot, Jacques (1985), *Tales of the Yanomami: Daily Life in the Venezuelan Forest.* Cambridge: Cambridge University Press.

Martínez, Wilton (1988), Interview with Timothy Asch. Los Angeles: University of Southern California. (Unpublished.)

—— (1990a), "The Ethnographic Film Spectator and the Crisis of Representation in Visual Anthropology". M.A. thesis. Los Angeles: University of Southern California.

—— (1990b), "Critical Studies and Visual Anthropology: Aberrant Versus Anticipated Readings of Ethnographic Film". *Commission for Visual Anthropology Review* Spring 1990.

(1992), "Who Constructs Anthropological Knowledge? Toward a Theory of Ethnographic Film Spectatorship". In Peter Crawford and D. Turton (eds.), *Film As Ethnography.* Manchester: University of Manchester Press.

—— (1994), "Deconstructing the 'Viewer': From Ethnography of the Visual to Critique of the Occult". In Peter Crawford and S. Hafsteinsson (eds.), *The Construction of the Viewer: Media Ethnography and the Anthropology of Audiences*, NAFA 3. Højbjerg, Denmark: Intervention Press.

—— (1998), *Imaging Alterity: Discourse, Pedagogy, and the Reception of Ethnographic Film.* Ph.D. dissertation. Los Angeles: University of Southern California.

Pieterse, Jan N. (1992), *White on Black: Images of Africa and Blacks in Popular Culture.* New Haven: Yale University Press.

Rollwagen, Jack R. (ed.) (1988), *Anthropological Filmmaking: Anthropological Perspectives on the Production of Film and Video for General Public Audiences.* Chur: Harwood Academic Publishers.

Todorov, Tzvetan (1984), *The Conquest of America.* Richard Howard (trans.) New York: Harper and Row.

Valero, Helena (1970), *Yanoama, the Narrative of a White Girl Kidnapped by Amazonian Indians, as Told to Ettore Biocca.* New York: E. P. Dutton and Co.

White, Hayden (1978), *Tropics of Discourse: Essays in Cultural Criticism.* Baltimore: The Johns Hopkins University Press.

Chapter 12

What really happened

A reassessment of *The Ax Fight*

Bill Nichols

This chapter is in two parts. The first part presents a slightly revised version of remarks in *Ideology and the Image* (Nichols 1981) in which I responded to *The Ax Fight* by film-maker Tim Asch and anthropologist Napoleon Chagnon, one of the central works in their series of films on the Yanomamö Indians of the Orinoco and Ocamo river basins in southern Venezuela. The second part offers a reconsideration and different angle of vision on the film, examining it less in terms of narrative structure and more in terms of historiographic concerns. The complex relation of narrative to the process of sustaining and representing both a sense of culture and history serves as a central preoccupation.

Part I

Many ethnographic films such as *The Lion Hunters* (Rouch 1970), *Dead Birds* (Gardner 1963), *Les Maîtres Fous* (Rouch 1953), Asen Balikci's and Guy Mary-Rourselière's Netsilik Eskimo series, Asch's and Chagnon's Yanomamö series, and Marshall's Bushman series use a relatively simple narrative structure. These films exhibit a single chain of causally-linked events that move from a beginning to a resolution; they fabricate a coherent expanse of time and space populated by social actors, people around whom actions and enigmas unfold. Some, like *Les Maîtres Fous*, employ the surprise ending common to the structure of short stories, an O. Henry twist that reinterprets what has gone before. But perhaps the most interesting film to discuss in some detail is *The Ax Fight* (1975) from the larger Yanomamö series of films.

The film has five parts. First, we see a fight break out in a Yanomamö village. The fight is shot in long takes with synch sound. As the fight breaks up, the sequence concludes with a woman hurling extremely derogatory epithets at visitors from another village – presumably she and they were antagonists in the conflict. Next, the screen goes black as we hear the voices of Napoleon Chagnon, Tim Asch, and Craig Johnson (the anthropologist, film-maker, and sound recordist respectively) speculate on the cause, apparently at or very near the time when the fight subsides and the first part ends. On the basis of what an informant tells him, Chagnon attributes the fight to an alleged incident of incest although, if the voice-off comments are simultaneous with the event, when this information was conveyed is left unclear. Two white-on-black titles explain that this speculation was incorrect and that the fight arose from an argument between a woman of the village and a visitor.[1] The visiting man had demanded food from the woman and hit her when she refused. Her return to the village, wailing, prompted two of her relatives to begin a fight with the visitor. In the third part, the original footage is replayed with direct-address commentary and superimposed pointers highlighting aspects of the images that correspond to the correct explanation. This part turns to diagrams which illustrate the three lineages involved in the fight and how the various combatants are related. Finally, a white-on-black title announces, "A final edited version of the fight follows" and the film-makers present an edited version of the original footage with synch sound but without commentary. This final part begins and ends with the woman who hurled epithets at the visitors at the conclusion of part one.

Several points can be made about this attempt to demonstrate the relationship between observation and explanation, and the film's use of both exposition and narrative. First, commentary in the third part stresses conflict between lineages and some of the ways in which specific choices of action, such as striking with the blunt side of an ax rather than its edge, serve to moderate violence. Other sources of moderation, such as the hierarchy of authority represented by the village chief, who intercedes at one point, receive only passing mention, possibly because they are not as visually manifest in the footage. In fact, brief mention of the chief poses one of those marginal enigmas that question the adequacy of the explanation adduced: what role does a chief, or a broader network of power, hierarchy, and responsibility, play in moderating lineage conflicts when such factors are less available to observation than the manner of wielding an ax?

The whole issue of how film provides entrée to the conceptual or non-visible remains under-examined. We assume that films offer visible evidence of what took place before a camera but much of what we see depends on framing concepts for its meaning. Two women may grip the palm and fingers of each other's right hand and then join in a coordinated, rocking motion of their hands, but even this form of "self-evident" greeting relies on prior knowledge that allows us to apply the term "handshake" and then go on either simply to note this as a fact or to infer more particularized meanings from the specific manner in which this handshake is conducted. *The Ax Fight* clearly wants to ascribe meaning to the witnessed events, but it does so with what seems to be a preoccupation with the sense of physical threat and mortal danger that the use of axes and machetes interjects. This emphasis is perhaps most obvious in the thud that is dubbed into the soundtrack in synch with the striking of the ax blow when no other blows yield audible sound and none of the words uttered by the chief is made available. (A similar choice of dubbed sound for dramatic emphasis occurs in the Academy Award-winning Holocaust documentary, *The Last Days*, during a clip of silent 16 mm footage that shows a group of Jewish men standing in an open trench. Soldiers on the side of the trench open fire, killing the entire group. The only sound we hear is of the guns firing. This dubbed sound has a chilling effect: it heightens the intensity of a historical event, ironically by shifting the visible evidence from raw footage to realist representation.) The same choice in *The Ax Fight* coincides with the film's stress on explaining *why* something as dramatic as an ax fight took place at all, rather than on exploring *how* a complex set of modulations of violence and negotiation surrounds the acting out of social conflict in this situation.

Part four raises questions about the relation between written and visual ethnography since the most precise anthropological explanation (the lineage diagrams and voice-over commentary) is also at the greatest remove from the indexical representation of the pro-filmic event (the long take, synch footage of events as they unfolded before the camera. What becomes of the visual excess represented by the footage but not addressed by the explanation? Does part three provide a scientific explanation that remains inadequate to the footage? What other explanations are possible? Is it even possible to explain the structure and function of the social codes (of combat, self-control, and lineage relations, for example) an individual internalizes without recourse to explanatory models that remove moving pictures from their full indexicality? Can the emotional, experiential, and affective dimensions of social interaction remain evident in the form of an explanation, or must they inevitably be an excess in need of containment? Few films confront these questions directly, but *The Ax Fight* raises them indirectly. The best ethnographic films identify problems still in need of resolution and no paradigmatic answers are at hand. That these problems recur across much of documentary, if not the cinema as a whole, is part of what makes the need to confront them so urgent.

Finally, part five of *The Ax Fight* offers an explanation of the event independent of the anthropological explanation developed in parts two, three, and four. It is a tacit answer to the question just posed above, since the explanation is based on the original footage itself rather than written comments or kinship diagrams. Part five explains because it is a narrative in which the change between the beginning and the end is accounted for by the middle. Narrative structure itself gives us an explanation of the event: a woman provokes visitors, a fight breaks out, the woman gloats over vanquished visitors; therefore, the provocations of women cause men to fight. The physical altercation satisfies the women's anger and indignation. Narrative structure, then, "contains" the original footage, but at a considerable price. Part five reinforces parts two through four by suggesting that the raw footage is not self-explanatory, and poses implicitly the question of whether a narrative or expository reorganization and use of that footage provides the more adequate explanation.

This narrative explanation, on which the film offers no additional comment, presents at least two major inadequacies. First, relationships between social actors are not identified: we see the same woman at the beginning and end of the fight, but neither her relationships to the combatants nor the combatants' relationships among themselves receive clarification. Lineage conflict (or incest, for that matter) does not appear as an evident explanation, nor even as a possibility in the footage itself. These explanations remain invisible. We can infer them from the commentary in part three but the footage fails to offer evidence of this idea; it works, instead, to advance its own account, based on the editing. Second, the editing of this part leaves us with an (unidentified) image of a woman as provocateur of physical violence between men, a violence moderated only by their obedience to rules of conflict resolution. This flirts with an ethnocentric essentialism – an assumption about the "given" nature of women that is peculiar to our culture, namely the notion of the eternally feminine as "bitch" (reserving whore, mother, goddess for other occasions). The narrative sequence requires no further explanation: that's the way women are (as we all know, it seems to say).

The Ax Fight demonstrates the lack of any one-to-one correlation between what we see, the visible, and what we understand, the conceptual, and between observation and explanation, yet it does not make this demonstration openly. No discussion of these questions occurs; the film seems to assume an unproblematic transparency between part one and parts two through four and a non-contradictory, reinforcing transparency in part five. In this way, the film as a whole repeats the style of tacit argumentation made by narrative form in part five alone. The Ax Fight demonstrates the need to answer the question of how we give adequate representation to people and their behavior. How may we account for an "ensemble of social relations" without lapsing into essentialism at the level of explanation or an "ontology" of the self-evident image?

Part II

One of the persistent challenges of historiography and ethnography is the effort we devote to recounting wie es eigentlich gewesen ("how it actually was", or "what really happened"), as the nineteenth-century German historian, Leopold von Ranke, first termed the impulse toward scrupulous documentation, reliance upon primary sources, and the exclusion of the merely speculative. Documentary film and both written and filmed ethnography carry forward something of von Rank's effort to found historiography in historical method, an objectivity that would distinguish it from Romantic Idealism and fanciful speculation. Film in particular gives us an apparently unassailable answer to such questions as how did things look; how did people, social actors, conduct themselves; what shape did events exhibit; and how did situations unfold in time? We can see for ourselves what had heretofore been available only through written and verbal accounts heir to all of the slippage between word and event that language allows. With film, rigorous description attains a qualitatively distinct level.

And yet this is obviously not the end of the story. Written accounts have continued to prevail. A number of reasons may lie behind this fact, but the one of particular relevance here is that the filmed record of actual events is not quite as firm a guarantee of what really happened as we may have at first thought. The problematic relation of descriptive fact to interpretive frame was already evident in von Ranke's time, before the advent of film. It resulted from the way in which the demand for scrupulous attention to the historical record became coupled with the need for an intuitive grasp of what bound specific facts, incidents, details, and events together. This larger coherence, or pattern, though, must not be the work of the imagination alone, even if, as a method, it holds much in common with artistic practice: for the nineteenth-century historian (or the realist ethnographer), the larger pattern must derive from actual events truly recounted. Pattern, therefore, had to be both in the events from the outset, and actively constructed by the historian by means of narrative form. Narrative interpretation drew out and made more apparent the latent image, or "big picture", that keen investigation discovered. In this way, the same actual events could yield multiple narratives and different constructed interpretations.

Such a process of intuitive inference, even if bound by principles of verification, approached the realm of art. In film, its practice has often been associated with the work of the man usually acclaimed as the father of both documentary and ethnographic film, Robert Flaherty. In the spirit of an Eskimo carver confronted with a piece of stone, Flaherty loved to tease meaning from his footage. In the depths of the stone such an artist discerned the final shape of the carving and his task was more to release than to make. On another level, inferring pattern has often stood as a problematic model for the task of historical or ethnographic representation in general; problematic because of the desire to have it both ways: to posit as already there what must in large measure be brought out by the interpreter, often in the spirit of natural congruence.

This account of the problems of using film as a historiographic or ethnographic instrument is clearly moving in a theoretical direction that is actually at odds with the primary direction I wish to take. But it sets the stage, however cursorily and sparsely. On this stage I would like to reintroduce the protagonist of this tribute, Tim Asch, and his and Napoleon Chagnon's Yanomamö film *The Ax Fight*. Although I continue to agree with most of the passage from *Ideology and the Image* with which this essay begins, I wish to complicate that initial reading in ways that try to take better account of the film's very considerable appeal. I have used it continuously for over fifteen years in teaching classes in documentary film, ethnographic film, and cross-cultural representation. It continues to stimulate lively debate. But I have not given it, or Asch, the full credit that is their due.

As a film-maker, Tim Asch always sought to use film as an instrument of anthropological knowledge. He has abided by the rigors of close scrutiny and careful observation and has contributed, with his cinematic skills, to the discovery of social processes and cultural patterns that remain invisible to the eye. More an ethnographer's ethnographer than a popularizer, Asch has helped us understand the complex ways in which we strive to produce a fit between the coherence we desire and the events we observe, between the patterns we infer and the assumptions we hold. He is, paradoxically, like the other major pioneers of visual anthropology, both a collaborator in the development of a collective discipline and a singular voice, with a distinctive style, within it.

In retrospect, *The Ax Fight* puts on display, without resolving, the paradoxes of description and interpretation, and the challenges of reproducing the external appearance of an event and inferring something of its inner form.

The Ax Fight enjoys some of its very special status precisely because it calls into question the adequacy of accurate observation and faithful representation. Long takes, wide-angle shots, synchronous sound – the basic principles of holistic representation – do not in and of themselves yield an account of what really happened, even though they are the most faithful representation of what happened that can be offered (in terms of temporal duration or spatial configuration). Nor do these techniques yield "facts" as they are normally regarded or encountered, in service to a subsequent interpretation. More than a set of semi- or disconnected facts to be strung together, the opening footage of an ax fight that suddenly erupts in front of the unprepared Chagnon and Asch represents "what actually happened" in a comprehensive but nonetheless inadequate sense. We can see with our own eyes and ears what the camera and tape recorder have provided for us. It is already more than a chronicle or assembly of data – much more. It has the same mix of transparent obviousness (often absent from data) and impenetrability (often abundant in data) that forms of lived encounter also possess. Unlike data or facts, this representation appears already to be a narrative, with a beginning and an end determined by the duration of the shot-sequence rather than the event itself, but a narrative whose meaning remains obscure. It calls for an interpretive supplement that exceeds the original representation, even as this representation exceeds mere description or data collection. It calls for something in excess of empirical scrutiny. It calls for what might go by the name of the hermeneutic gesture.

Tim Asch has given us a vivid representation of a classic ethnographic conundrum. What we see is what there was, but what we see does not account for what there was. What really happened eludes us and what we reveal as we set out to explain what happened is who we are, what we value, and how we go about understanding the world around us (our own assumptions, that is, rather than the latent meanings embedded in the surrounding world). Verification procedures involving the authenticity of evidence via informants and other means allow access to the question of what really happened that differentiates ethnography and its fieldwork from other forms of cross-cultural speculation but, as Douglas Lewis pointed out in a written communication to me,

> ... the people who participated in the event and without whose behavior there would have been no event ... would understand the film well without narration, subtitled translations of speech, animated kinship charts, and redundant projection of the images. ... The problem is: as distances of time, space, language, and culture increase, so too does the need for interpretation of the images and explanation of the behavior which they depict. Hence, the job of the ethnographer.
> (letter to B. Nichols, 20 September 1996)

What von Ranke sought to do with the historical past, ethnographers seek to do with the cultural present. Instead of turning to the archive as the font of knowledge, ethnography turns to the field, but in the same spirit of scrupulous, disciplined inquiry. What Tim Asch has done in *The Ax Fight* is to remind us of how incomplete this inquiry is until yoked to those interpretive strategies and gestures that characterize the specific film-maker or ethnographer, on the one hand, and the general field or discipline of documentary or ethnographic film on the other.

Asch gives evidence of finding considerable comfort in the thick of the initial conundrum he has so skillfully represented. The middle sections of *The Ax Fight* move through a series of explanations that become progressively more complete until we are left to settle on an account of long-standing lineage conflict and the immediate spark of confrontation and violence in a village garden. This is anthropological interpretation in full flower. It clearly exceeds the original representation; in fact, it calls for other, more schematic forms of symbolization such as lineage charts or diagrams. The final segment of the film, however, returns us to the original scene, and both Asch and the interpretive, more than the explanatory conundrum he has given to us, return to center stage.

In the final segment the original footage of the apparently spontaneous outbreak of an ax fight is once again put to use, but now it is in an edited form. What originally constituted beginning and end no longer do. By re-editing the footage, Asch has given us a visual, narrative and non-verbal analogy of (but not an explanation of) lineage conflict. But it is an interpretation more than an explanation, a representation of meaning in an immediate, affective form rather than as abstracted content. Seen in isolation, akin to that sudden, unexpected irruption of the ax fight itself, the final segment reintroduces the vivid sense of both representational fullness and inadequacy. What formal coherence joins this particular array of shots and sounds together? What larger pattern arises, greater than the sum of its parts, as an ordering principle? None is stated, and what can be inferred is what Asch has also inferred: it is the pattern of a narrative, a story, that gives meaning to these events, even if it does not fully explain them. "What really happened" is that a story has been told. It is in this sense that the event has achieved full textual representation even though this representation also retains that sense of mystery which a more positivistic science would wish to dispel.

In this context, the final segment takes on the quality of a visual analogy of the more schematic and verbal anthropological explanation in the middle parts. Once we regard this segment in the framing context of what has come before, its sounds and images take on an exemplary tone rather than a strictly empirical one. The angry woman who hurls a series of cruel epithets with which the segment begins, for example, may not simply represent the eternally feminine as "bitch" (as I previously interpreted her); she may also represent (if not be – her actual historical status as a social actor is not specified) an aggrieved woman insulted and injured during the unfilmed altercation in the village garden. The ensuing shots of the actual ax fight would then represent how a violent confrontation unfolded among villagers. And the concluding shots of the woman again hurling insults would offer a form of narrative closure to this particular incident on which the anthropological explanations can be overlaid without fully exhausting the subjective complexity and affective intensity of the specific event. We behold a story which, through its form, makes sense of what has gone before. Asch's hermeneutic gesture allows us to discover, or construct, meaning within an encounter whose full meaning remains inexhaustible. This is not only good history but good ethnography as well.

In later work, such as *A Celebration of Origins* (1993), Asch and Lewis opt for a different strategy that achieves a similar result by engaging the participants in an event to provide their own interpretation. The event, a ritual enactment of origin myths, lacks the elements of the sudden and unplanned that made the ax fight so enigmatic but, as the commentary offered, after the fact, by one of the event's participants makes clear, the event nonetheless calls for a narrative act of interpretation if it is to be made intelligible to those who were not immediate participants. A somewhat different, more carefully planned hermeneutic gesture is at work but it is one that retains a similar balance between the constructed representation of an ethnographic explanation and of a participant's or observer's experience.

The final segment of *The Ax Fight* arrives with a voice-over introduction that positions it as a revision of the "raw footage" in keeping with the final level of understanding attained. But Asch withholds any further form of explanatory gesture. Words and images, once again, as they did in the beginning, speak for themselves. But do they? That is the conundrum. Asch insists that we have it both ways. We now read the series of words and images in the context of a larger, inferred pattern, but also experience them in the full immediacy with which they arrive. We can "see" a hermeneutic gesture or a scrupulous representation of the actual contours and dimensions of the original event to which an explanatory frame has been fit (via the charts and diagrams).

The Ax Fight, and this is the accomplishment to which I wish to pay special tribute, both belongs squarely within the tradition of ethnographic film and puts into question many of that tradition's assumptions. The question of what really happened becomes both answered and unanswered, or answerable and unanswerable, within the terms used to pose the question in the first place. "What really happened?" receives as response, "What really happens" (i.e. the act of telling stories of the past or of other cultures). The unprecedented descriptive accuracy of a visual record of what actually happened still contains within it both the promise of a certainty and the delivery of a mystery. Tim Asch has given us both at once. In doing so he has challenged us to reassess the ground on which we stand, even if there may not appear to be any other ground available to us. This act of reassessment, I see Asch suggesting, may itself provide the alternative ground we would not otherwise discover.

Note

1   The titles read:

First impressions can be mistaken. When the fight first started, one informant told us that it was about incest. However, subsequent work with other informants revealed that the fight stemmed from quite a different cause.

We learned that several former members of the village were visiting. These visitors were invited back by some of their kinsmen. However, they also had old enemies in the village, so the situation was volatile. The visitors refused to work in the garden, yet demanded to be fed, and thus, tension grew until the fight erupted. One of the visitors – Mohesiwä – demanded plantains from a woman, Sinabimi. She refused him. He beat her and she ran into the village screaming and crying.

Reference

Nichols, Bill (1981), *Ideology and the Image: Social Representation in the Cinema and Other Media*. Bloomington: Indiana University Press.

Films

Asch, Timothy and Napoleon Chagnon, (1975), *The Ax Fight*. 16 mm film. Watertown, Massachusetts: Documentary Educational Resources.

Asch, Timothy, E. Douglas Lewis, and Patsy Asch (1993), *A Celebration of Origins*. 16 mm film. Watertown, Massachusetts: Documentary Educational Resources, Inc.

Gardner, Robert (1963), *Dead Birds*. 16 mm film. Cambridge, Massachusetts: Film Study Center, Harvard University.

Rouch, Jean (1953), *Les Maîtres Fous*. 16 mm film. Paris: Films de la Pleiade.

—— (1970), *The Lion Hunters*. 16 mm film. Paris: Films de la Pleiade.

Chapter 13

The Ax Fight on CD-ROM

Peter Biella

Introduction to *Yanomamö Interactive*

In the last hundred years, the development of audio and film recording technologies created new opportunities both for exposition and analysis in the social sciences (Fewkes 1890; Hilton-Simpson and Haeseler 1925; Gessell 1935; Dyhrenfurth 1952; de Brigard 1975). In the past, these technologies contributed insights into practical and theoretical problems in the social sciences. This chapter describes the uses of a new expository and analytical technology in anthropology, CD-ROM, and one of the first published works using that technology. *Yanomamö Interactive* (Biella, Chagnon and Seaman 1997) offers a variety of educational and research documents about Tim Asch's and Napoleon Chagnon's film masterpiece, *The Ax Fight* (1975). The film and *Yanomamö Interactive* are about conflict resolution and village dynamics among the Yanomamö of Venezuela. The two works also explore the vagaries of ethnographic analysis and explanation.

In *Yanomamö Interactive*, both text and film are stored digitally on CD-ROM. Both can be viewed and reviewed non-linearly, as often as desired, and in any number of juxtapositions. Figure 13.1 is a sample screen from the CD. The screen is divided into four quadrants. In the upper left is a digital version of the half-hour *The Ax Fight* film. The film is the hub around which the user can organize detailed explorations by accessing information in the other three quadrants. The upper right is reserved for enlargeable graphic works, including frames of the film, photographs, maps, and genealogies. The lower left quadrant displays textual descriptions and analyses of the film and essays related to it. Finally, the lower right provides a location where users can request and have displayed biographical information about the individuals identified in the film.

Yanomamö Interactive, like *The Ax Fight*, is concerned both with the social dynamics of the filmed event and its place in the biographies of individuals. Each person identified in the film is assigned a *People* screen chapter in the CD in which his or her activities on screen are isolated and explained.

A series of mouse-driven menu buttons stretches across the top of every screen. Figure 13.2 gives an exploded view of the options. Two of the menus guide users to different screens: the *Contents* menu provides access to various descriptions and

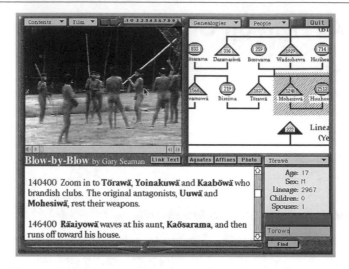

Figure 13.1 A sample screen from *Yanomamö Interactive* with quadrants for different instructional purposes.

analyses of the film and the *People* menu gives access to screens that feature each of the Yanomamö. Two additional menus allow comparative material to be brought forward to the current *Analysis* or *People* screen. *Genealogies* displays three alternate diagrams of village kinship relationships. Selections from the *Film* menu instantly scroll the movie to any of thirty-five pre-selected moments.

Yanomamö Interactive's seven *Analysis* screens and its fifty *People* screens all have the same four-part design, and all have the same capacity to juxtapose an assortment of audiovisual and database materials with printed texts. Its design is similar to that of an earlier work-in-progress CD, *Maasai Interactive* (Biella 1993a). In both, the rigidity of quadrants and the fluidity with which material may be juxtaposed in them reflect two fundamental educational premises. The first concerns control and open-endedness. Users need systematic analytical guidance to the film and the accompanying materials, a predictable screen interface which allows them to keep their bearings, and a design that facilitates unexpected juxtapositions and discoveries (Landow 1991). In keeping with the first part of this premise, *Yanomamö Interactive* includes an introductory tour and *Help* screens that guide users through information stored in the different quadrants. Users can also create unprecedented juxtapositions of text, film, photos, graphics and statistical information.

The second educational premise of *Yanomamö Interactive* relates to C. Wright Mills' insight that the sociological imagination is the recognition of biography in history (1959: 143–164). One of the great boons of all ethnographic film, and of Asch's and Chagnon's *The Ax Fight* in particular, is the capacity to render biographical detail. The film depicts an historical incident which involved dozens of people.

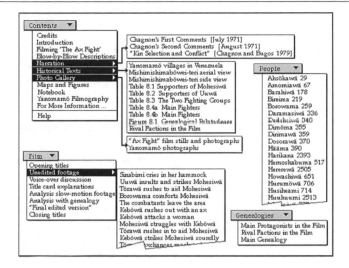

Figure 13.2 Contents of *Yanomamö Interactive*'s menus and options available through the menu buttons.

Through slow-motion footage and narration, the film also emphasizes individual biographies within that complexity.

The CD extends the expositional method employed by Asch and Chagnon in *The Ax Fight*. This is made possible by the major innovation of multimedia technology, the capacity to link time-based audio and video media to any number of different texts. Users of *Yanomamö Interactive* are provided with analytical texts which allow them to study the same few moments of footage several times while concentrating on the perspectives of many different Yanomamö men and women. Non-linear access to the film and unlimited user-initiated viewings render real-time recordings much more amenable to scholarly research than was possible in the past. With guided, repeated viewings, the acts of individuals on film can be distinguished in the welter of events.

Description of screens in *Yanomamö Interactive*

The capacity to link text and film is the basis for *Yanomamö Interactive*'s primary descriptive tool, a chapter of the CD by Gary Seaman called "Blow-by-Blow Descriptions".[1] The descriptions divide the film's ten-and-a-half minutes of unedited footage into some 380 "current moments" which range from a few frames to a few seconds in length. Seaman wrote a paragraph for each of these moments and each paragraph describes the individuals and activities which he and Chagnon judged to be most important for an understanding of the moment currently in view. A mouse-click on a "Blow-by-Blow" paragraph causes the film to scroll forward or backward to the moment that the paragraph describes. A mouse-click on a person's name in these paragraphs causes the mouse to leap up to the movie screen and point out the individual (Figure 13.1).

A linear reading of all "Blow-by-Blow" paragraphs together reveals the dynamics of this Yanomamö dispute settlement in broad outline. Reading any of the CD's *People* chapters, on the other hand, provides the user exclusively with those paragraphs that describe actions of the one person featured in that chapter. *People* chapters offer concise biographical vignettes and help users to develop ideas about the motives of individual Yanomamö men and women. This provides information indirectly about Yanomamö culture as a whole. Each *People* screen contains a photographic portrait of the featured individual, a collection of daily-life photographs in which he or she appears, and vital statistics.

The same descriptive paragraphs about "current moments" in the film are used in the historical "Blow-by-Blows" and the biographical *People* screens. However, the significance of a paragraph and the corresponding moment of the film in the two contexts are very different. As Bateson (1972) argues, not only does the juxtaposition of information in different contexts create a difference that makes a difference, it also helps students of anthropology become accustomed to interrogating the same data from alternative interpretive schema.

Analysis screens in Yanomamö Interactive

The Yanomamö have remained vital to the teaching of anthropology in the United States partly because of the theoretical controversies which surround Chagnon's arguments. My *Introduction* to the CD, excerpted below, proposes ways that students can query *The Ax Fight* as a means to becoming engaged in the controversies of evolutionary biology, cultural materialism and gender roles that discussions of Chagnon's Yanomamö inevitably evoke. In addition, the *Introduction* suggests explorations of the film which will interest students of the film's structure and engage them in basic epistemological questions about the interpretation of ethnographic data.

Four other *Analysis* screens in the CD provide further text-based opportunities to study the film. In 1971 Chagnon tape recorded comments on two occasions when he first saw the film footage. These two texts are transcribed in the CD and linked to the moments in the film that Chagnon describes. Comparison of the two transcriptions reveals how Chagnon developed his ideas, corrected a few errors, and arrived at his conclusions. Reading them provides a rare glimpse into the process by which anthropological analysis proceeds (Figure 13.3).

An essay by Chagnon and Bugos (1979), another of the *Analysis* chapters of the CD, provides an additional perspective on the film and research method. This work uses *The Ax Fight*'s footage as data for an evolutionary argument about Yanomamö kin selection and conflict. As will be described below, the Chagnon and Bugos essay offers opportunities for students to engage in an experience that is like fieldwork in interesting ways. They can use *The Ax Fight* as primary data and can investigate the process by which the authors transformed the behavior streams it depicts

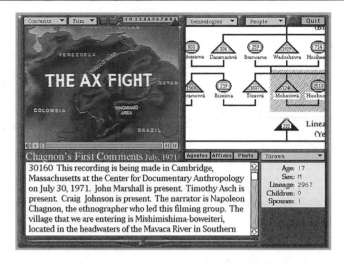

Figure 13.3 Screen showing Chagnon's first comments on footage of the ax fight. In the CD they can be read in synch with the moments of the film that they describe.

into data for statistical analysis. They can also query the footage in terms of alternative deductive hypotheses.

In a fourth *Analysis* screen, Chagnon presents a sometimes dark autobiographical essay which describes the context of making *The Ax Fight*. It emphasizes in particular his difficult relationship with film-maker Tim Asch. Echoes of their tense collaboration can be found in section 2 of the film. Chagnon's autobiographical essay provides another contextual vantage point from which the footage can be understood.[2]

Graphic resources in Yanomamö Interactive

The juxtaposition of descriptive and analytical texts with motion picture film provides a learning context that is unique to multimedia. In *Yanomamö Interactive*, film and text are brought together with a wide array of additional graphic resources. A dozen crucial freeze frames of *The Ax Fight* are available for full-screen viewing. In addition, a roll of still photographs that Chagnon took from a close perspective while the 16 mm film was being shot can be viewed beside it. More than a hundred other photographs by Chagnon are also included. They depict many non-violent aspects of Yanomamö life and provide a useful counterpoint to the film.

Much of the analysis presented in the film's narration is based on a theory of kinship relations and village fissioning. For this reason, the CD includes three genealogical diagrams drawn with different levels of detail. Frequent reference to these guides enables users to keep track of individuals and the claims that the film makes about their obligations to one another (Figure 13.4).

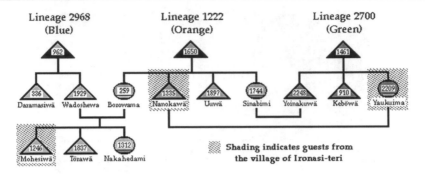

Figure 13.4 Yanomamö genealogy, first level of detail, showing main protagonists in *The Ax Fight*. This genealogy may be viewed from any screen of *Yanomamö Interactive*.

Other contextual graphic information is available in maps of the region and drawings of Mishimishimaböwei-teri, the village where *The Ax Fight* was shot. The drawing locate the living and sleeping areas of all major protagonists in the film and identifies camera positions and the location of the fights.

Lastly, in the CD but independent from its multimedia component, Chagnon has included several large data files. These contain vital statistics, not only of the thirty-eight villagers identified in the film, but of all 268 residents of Mishimishimaböwei-teri at the time of filming. Chagnon has created a number of computer-based research exercises that students may conduct with his primary data.

To understand the goals and organization of *Yanomamö Interactive*, it is first necessary to understand those of *The Ax Fight*. Much of the film's strength stems from the wealth of contextual materials that Chagnon has provided. These materials also enrich the CD. Another principal strength is the reiterative approach that *The Ax Fight* takes to its footage: some shots are shown three times and others are frozen on screen. The film's concern with subjecting footage to repeated analysis is the foundation of *Yanomamö Interactive*'s interactive multimedia approach. The CD-ROM and hypermedia technology make this reiteration possible and convenient for users.

Five ways of looking at *The Ax Fight*

Almost a third of a century has passed since *The Ax Fight* was shot in the Yanomamö village of Mishimishimaböwei-teri. The film has subsequently been recognized as one of the most original in the social sciences. Its most brilliant innovations are based on a simple insight: filmed cultural activities are difficult or impossible to understand when they are viewed once and in real time. Nevertheless, complex behavior and interactions can be understood, questioned, and reformulated when footage is repeatedly considered by a knowledgeable analyst.

For years, the complex structure of the film has fascinated anthropologists and film scholars.[3] Nichols (1981 and this volume) writes that the film has five easily identifiable sections and that much of *The Ax Fight*'s power lies in the way that it redisplays or re-interprets a single event in the five sections.

Section One   Confusion in fieldwork

In the first section of *The Ax Fight*, viewers are shown ten-and-a-half minutes of unedited 16 mm footage, exactly as it came from the camera. The footage documents a sequence of violent encounters that escalated in the plaza and living areas of a Venezuelan Yanomamö village in 1971. Five minutes of the footage in section one were recorded in a single, uninterrupted run of film. This is followed by several shorter takes. All of the footage in section one is unedited. For this reason, it has the air of authenticity. It is also chaotic.

As the unedited footage unfolds, it depicts a quarrel that escalated into fighting in the village. The incident began with shouting and progressed to the use of axes. Violence then de-escalated to shouting as one man recovered from blows he received. At the height of the engagement, more than fifty men and women, in the village of 268 people, rushed about the principal antagonists. Close inspection of the footage reveals a variety of activities: some individuals sought to maintain peace, some criticized the fighters, and others swung their weapons. All but the last of these details are lost on first-time viewers of this section of the film. The fact that a blur of violence is remembered best was anticipated by the editors of the film.

Just before filming, informants had warned Chagnon that a fight was about to erupt. Chagnon quickly alerted cinematographer Tim Asch, who had only a few moments to prepare his equipment. Then, for five minutes, events unfolded in quick succession, permitting no time to turn the camera off and move it nearer to the fight. This and several other factors rendered the footage not only confusing but also representative of the kinds of difficulties that field anthropologists often encounter in such circumstances. The single perspective of the camera and the distance between it and its subject were responsible for crucial details of the fight being hidden by the crowd. Important actions were hidden in shadow. When the camera zoomed out to wide-angle, detail of the fighting was lost. When it zoomed in to telephoto, distances between bodies were distorted by foreshortening. This is corrected in part by many photographs that Chagnon took simultaneously from another vantage point and that are available in the CD (Figure 13.5). In addition, principal actors in the event moved rapidly and wore little clothing that observers could have used to distinguish individuals. Also confusing for viewers, the audio track is little more than unintelligible screams, punctuated with the sounds of ax on flesh. The sounds provoke an emotion that is difficult for the audience to ignore.[4]

Chagnon and Asch included unedited footage as part of *The Ax Fight* because of the emotions it raises and its partial unintelligibility. The film-makers' goal was to recreate for their audience the state of confusion that the fieldworkers experienced.

Figure 13.5 On the left, the extreme telephoto lens of Asch's movie camera causes fore-shortening and makes combatants appear to be inches apart from each other. Chagnon's 35 mm photograph, right, was taken at nearly the same instant but with a wide-angle lens and very near the action. In this case, distances are depicted more clearly.

Just as Asch and Chagnon understood little of the event, viewers of the first section of the film can understand little. The film thus begins with an emphasis on the difficulties of anthropological interpretation and fieldwork. It also gives reason to question anthropological films that make interpretation seem easy.

Section Two   Methodology backstage

With the beginning of section two, *The Ax Fight* cuts to black. In the field, the camera had run out of film, but soundman Craig Johnson continued to record audio. The film audience now monitors something of the film-makers' subjective experience, by hearing their unrehearsed, private conversation. The projection of the anthropologists into the film and this revelation of what was going on "backstage" were as unprecedented as *The Ax Fight*'s use of unedited footage.[5]

Over a black screen, the film-makers are heard attempting to make sense of the fights they had just seen. Chagnon describes an ax blow that was hidden from the camera. He then repeats for Asch and Johnson information that he was given by a Yanomamö informant. According to the informant, before filming began, a woman named Sinabimi had been assaulted by Mohesiwä, a man classified as her "son" in Yanomamö kinship terminology. The fight, Chagnon had been told, broke out because of incest.

The film audience is drawn into the Yanomamö incest story as it would be into a Western soap opera. Listeners feel something of the thrill that Asch expresses when he hears that incest had been committed. "No kidding!" he exclaims over the black screen. Before section two of the film ends, a final plot element is introduced: Möawä, headman of the village, can be heard asking Chagnon for a bar of soap. The anthropologist complains that this is the tenth person that day who has made the request. Asch tries to assuage the situation by offering to give Möawä his own bar of soap when they depart from the village. Chagnon heatedly rejects the idea. The Yanomamö, he says, will "make damn sure we leave in a hurry if we keep promising them everything when we go home".

Years later, Asch criticized Chagnon for his own aggressiveness and his characterization of Yanomamö as "fierce". At this point in the filming, Asch foreshadows his disapproval with deceptive mildness. He says, "*Shoriwä* (brother-in-law), living in your village is going to be tiresome." Memory still fresh with the violence of the ax fight, Chagnon simply replies: "Thought I was shitting you about 'the fierce people', huh?"

Section Three   Interpretation, creativity, and error-correction

In section three, the film shifts from a representation of the phenomenological, subjective experience of the film-makers to interpretation and analysis. A subtitle over a black screen explains that an error has been made. It reads:

> First impressions can be mistaken. When the fight first started, one informant told us that it was about incest. However, subsequent work with other informants revealed that the fight stemmed from quite a different cause.

The mistaken initial interpretation was discovered in the days following the fight. Chagnon conducted several more interviews. He learned that Mohesiwä was a non-contributing visitor from another village who had confronted Sinabimi in her garden and demanded that she feed him. Obeying her husband's admonition against catering to the visitors, Sinabimi refused to do so and Mohesiwä hit her with a club. It was this act that Chagnon's informants understood to have started the fight. While the fight was taking place, however, the informants simply explained to him that Mohesiwä's offense was *yawaremou* (incest).

In subsequent interviews with Yanomamö informants, Chagnon learned that when he had heard the first explanation, he had understood the word *yawaremou* in its most common meaning, "sexual relations with a close kinsperson". In this case, however, a second meaning of the Yanomamö word was intended, "a physical assault on (or any intimate contact with) a woman in a proscribed kinship category".

The admission here that the anthropologist made a mistake may seem trivial, but it deserves considerable respect. Ethnographic film-makers had never before been so honest about the difficulties of fieldwork. With this revelation, section three introduces a problem that confronts all field anthropologists. Even in the best circumstances – with multiple informants, excellent visual documentation, and good language skills – errors occur and interpretations need revision. Thus, *The Ax Fight* offers another insight into the creative process of anthropological interpretation. Contrary to the illusion produced by slickly-edited documentaries, this process is not simple. Interpretation is created in fits and starts. Meaning has a history.

Although the film is now almost half over, a satisfactory explanation for the fight is still missing. Even though the beating of Sinabimi was forbidden by Yanomamö incest restrictions, Chagnon could not believe that, *by itself*, a man hitting his classificatory "mother" would have provoked fifty people to the extremes that are documented in the film. Intrigued but caught up in other demands of filming and fieldwork, Chagnon could not develop his interpretation of the fight until five months later. Only then was he able to examine the evidence of the footage and, with the help of other field data, establish more precisely its ethnographic context.

As will be seen, Chagnon's process of researching the footage was an inspiration for the editing and design of *The Ax Fight*'s third section. Chagnon first viewed the footage in an editing room with film-makers John Marshall, Tim Asch, and Craig Johnson. As he watched, Chagnon tape recorded his reactions and comments. Citing foot-and-frame numbers in the film, watching the footage in slow motion, and pointing out individuals, Chagnon identified as many people as he could and explained what he saw. As described above, the tape recording of Chagnon's first reactions to the footage was transcribed and is available in the CD (Figure 13.3).

For several weeks after viewing the footage, Chagnon went over the identification photographs and field notes he had taken in the village. The photographs ultimately allowed him to connect names to the images of thirty-eight people who were on camera during the fight.[6] Chagnon's field notes allowed him to determine the lineages of people on camera as well as their genealogical relationships with others involved in the fight. Using his ethnographic knowledge of the village, Chagnon was finally prepared to formulate an interpretation of the fight that was more plausible to him than "incest". Now able to describe what he saw with increased precision, Chagnon then returned to the editing room. Again, he tape recorded his analysis, which is included in the CD as "Chagnon's Second Comments".

Chagnon's two comments provide the opportunity for the study of field methodology: when the two sets of comments are compared, they show how the anthropologist corrected errors, formulated ideas, and followed up on early suspicions.

In the remainder of section three – following the subtitle that rejects incest as an explanation – Chagnon's film research process is replicated. The film represents much of the original footage, but this time it uses optical techniques familiar to film editors, including slow motion, freeze-frames, optical enlargements, and arrows identifying individuals. Chagnon presents a formal version of his "First and Second Comments".[7] In the narration, he identifies the principal antagonists and describes their behavior, making constant reference to the empirical evidence of the footage. Moving from empirical description, the narration then gives a preliminary interpretation of the fight, based on Chagnon's understanding of the motives of the individuals.[8]

Chagnon's interpretation in this section of the film is carefully illustrated and it is compelling. In less than nine minutes of screen time, however, he can only describe what he considers to be the most important people, actions, and motives. Only twelve people of more than fifty are identified genealogically or by name. Chagnon does not attempt to provide the detail of his transcribed 1971 comments. Instead, he simplifies them for the voice-over presentation. He also reserves for section four of the film a more theoretical explanation of the fight.

The chaos of fieldwork that is represented in the first section of *The Ax Fight* establishes the problem of anthropological interpretation that the remainder of the film addresses. Section three demonstrates how film footage, appropriately trimmed, slowed down, and enlarged, can provide empirical evidence needed to make a credible interpretation.

Section Four   Genealogies, contradiction, and fission

As the footage fades out, *The Ax Fight* introduces another innovation to anthropological film: genealogical diagrams of the male protagonists. Over these diagrams, Chagnon offers a complex interpretation that assumes the motives described in section three and complements them with more abstract theoretical constructs. The narration explains the occurrence of the ax fight in terms of village loyalties that shifted with the efforts to satisfy two contradictory needs. On one hand, Chagnon explains, villagers in the film had recently sought to rid themselves of problems that resulted when two men competed for the same role as headman. This tension was relieved by a division, or fission, of the entire village. On the other hand, a group of villagers had also sought to renew the alliance between the divided villages.[9]

Despite its effort at precision, this section of the film is unclear to many viewers. The confusion comes in part from the poor visual quality of the genealogical diagrams and a series of clumsy cuts and pans. More than this, the argument itself is difficult: not only is it presented verbally and only once, but it is incomplete and describes a rather subtle contradiction. It also necessarily leaves a large number of questions unanswered. To make matters worse, before viewers can even begin to understand the argument they must first associate different faces in the film with genealogical icons, and comprehend the genealogical relationships between the faces. The latter task by itself is difficult to master.

In retrospect, it is difficult to imagine a way that this section of the film could have overcome the problems inherent in presenting complex and abstract information with the medium of film using voice-over narration. A film necessarily rushes on, regardless of the viewer's comprehension. Complex communications can best be understood when studied at leisure. Non-linear technologies, like printed text, permit leisurely and repeated study. CD versions of films help make up for the fact that they are difficult to understand fully when they are viewed only once. Section four's theory of contradiction and village alliance is transcribed in the "Narration" chapter of the CD (accessible from the *Contents* menu.) There, the transcription is synched with corresponding sound and image. The text and film may be reviewed as often as necessary for comprehension and evaluation.

Section Five   Slick editing, default meaning

The Ax Fight's unprecedented display of unedited footage, unrehearsed conversation, slow-motion analysis, genealogical diagrams, and ethnographic theory exposes by its example the conservatism – or the failure of imagination – in earlier anthropological films. In another unprecedented move, the fifth section of The Ax Fight again confronts the limitations of earlier works. The last section begins with a title card: "The final edited version". It is followed by a new edit of the footage that is unimaginative, polished, and too familiar.

Asch intended the final section of The Ax Fight to be read as ironic (Ruby 1995: 28), a mockery of standard ethnographic film style. It is ironic for viewers – who have just been subjected to an overdose of anthropological explanation – to find that in the final section nothing is explained! The ending is fast-paced and without narration. Concern with complex relationships between villagers, painstakingly introduced in sections three and four, has vanished.

In the absence of these subtleties, however, the "final edited version" of the film is far from meaningless. What remains is a stereotype familiar to every viewer: naked savages swinging weapons at each other. A default meaning, borrowed from a thousand Hollywood movies, fills the void.[10]

In section five, the stereotype of "violent savages" has been offered for viewers' passive assimilation. In light of the previous examinations, assimilation of this stereotype is difficult. Subtleties about the incident that viewers have already learned cannot be erased by a version that ignores them. The simultaneous presence of the details in memory and their absence on screen is disturbing. This dissonance not only undermines the stereotypes but asks the viewers to consider what they would have thought about Yanomamö violence if the film had been made as most anthropological films are made, polished and fast-paced.

On the surface, section five is a parody of stereotypes that link savagery with race.[11] The plausibility of the stereotypes is sustained by the absence of corrective interpretation. It will be argued below that the absence of alternatives is also a feature of weak scholarly argument.

The last section of the film contains one final irony. As Ruby (1995) draws out in his interview with Asch, all sections of the film are self-reflexive, but this section questions the validity of the film's anthropological theory. As described above, on the day that The Ax Fight was shot, Asch was already objecting to Chagnon's interpretations of Yanomamö behavior. His objections there were not limited to the audio track of section two.

The "final edited version" can be read as the film's auto-critique, but its message is ambiguous. At one interpretive extreme, the last section of the film could be read as Asch's acknowledgment of something that might be called the Rashomon effect, a concept based on the Kurosawa film (1951). This is the idea that, because all versions of an event are biased and incomplete, none is more plausible than the others. The conclusion is anathema to most anthropologists, including those who, like Chagnon, understand their work to be in the tradition of positivistic science.

While scientists accept the idea that theories can always be improved and are always incomplete, they do not conclude from these premises that all theories are equally plausible. The practice of science is designed to weed out errors through rigorous tests.

At the other interpretive extreme, it is possible to read the final version as Asch's criticism of Chagnon as a rejection of the narrator's particular emphases and suppressions. It may be that Asch wished to suggest, with the example of artistic manipulation in the "final edited version", a problem analogous to the scientific manipulation earlier in the film.[12]

The Ax Fight re-takes and digital interpretations

The Ax Fight provides a model for scholarship in visual anthropology that has been adopted and extended in *Yanomamö Interactive*. In the CD, users can reconsider *The Ax Fight* in two ways. First, they are provided with the means of studying and making more complete empirical descriptions of the incident than is possible with the film. Second, users can integrate the film with anthropological theory.

Resources in the CD can be used as a means to engage in theoretical controversies, but there is no easy way to decide which of competing interpretations is correct. No single ethnographic observation, piece of film footage, or informant-generated report can settle a theoretical problem. Nevertheless, anthropologists value field data very highly because the empirical clues they provide are essential for justifying a stand within theoretical controversies. Theoretical controversy within scholarly disciplines is equally important: theory becomes more comprehensive, and more useful, when scholarly traditions persist and compete. New perspectives on data are essential for the discovery of theoretical blind spots and misemphases.

For these reasons, *The Ax Fight* film is an extremely valuable document. It is rich ethnographically, it is supported by an array of supplementary ethnographic materials, and it sheds light on important controversies such as that about violence and social control. Studying *The Ax Fight* thus provides students with an experience that is like fieldwork in interesting ways.

Reconsidering controversies with researchable film

Most ethnographic field research includes a portion of work that is based on deductive hypotheses. In other words, working deductively, ethnographers seek evidence that tends to confirm or disconfirm theoretical ideas proposed in advance. Research exercises that use resources in the CD are proposed below. They are based on a number of the hypotheses that have made debates about the Yanomamö so fruitful and heated.[13] Additional exercises, based on new hypotheses, can certainly be devised.

The most famous theoretical debate over Yanomamö ethnography was begun by Marvin Harris (1974, 1984). He and Chagnon disagree about the ultimate cause of Yanomamö violence and warfare. For both, however, the cause lies outside conscious awareness and control. For Harris, it is a combination of nutritional requirements and environmental limiting factors. Yanomamö men promote a male-centered ideology, and engage in population-depleting wars, Harris argues, not because of their conscious dislike of one another (which is often extreme), but because the Amazonian environment in which they live has only enough high-quality animal protein to support a low-density human population. Wars occur before the protein supply is irreversibly depleted.

For Chagnon (e.g. 1988), in contrast, the ultimate cause of violence and warfare is Darwinian. He argues that Yanomamö male violence takes many forms, from displays with clubs and axes to the killing of enemies, because violence is rewarded with reproductive success. According to his statistics, Chagnon says the most violent Yanomamö males have a greater number of offspring who will carry forward their genes. As in Harris's argument, the ultimate cause of violence for Chagnon is not conscious. It is not the enjoyment of sex, parenthood, or being *waiteri* ("fierce"), all of which Yanomamö men do praise. The ultimate goal of Yanomamö, and of all organisms, is reproductive survival.

In 1979, Chagnon and Paul Bugos, Jr., the editor of *The Ax Fight*, wrote an essay entitled "Kin Selection and Conflict", available in the CD. The Chagnon and Bugos essay provides the opportunity for a number of exercises using *Yanomamö Interactive*. *The Ax Fight* plays a crucial role in the essay, and its rich ethnographic material can be explored in relation to the essay. Chagnon and Bugos interpret the behavioral evidence recorded in the film in their effort to make an evolutionary argument. They first distinguish between two groups of Yanomamö villagers. One group is designated the "supporters" of Mohesiwä in the ax fight while the other group is designated "supporters" of his antagonists, Uuwä and Keböwä. The essay then summarizes the data in four Tables which compare the "supporters'" genealogical relatedness to the two combatants. Evidence for the evolutionary argument takes the form of statistics in these Tables which suggest that "supporters" share more genetic material with the man whom they supported than with the man they opposed.[14] Thus, Chagnon and Bugos argue, people take sides consistent with predictions from evolutionary theory: they support close kin over distant kin. The argument is that violent men are rewarded by more offspring who share their genetic material. It also proposes that all activities that promote differential fertility are selected for evolutionarily.[15]

Translating filmed behavior streams into discrete data

A possible exercise in field method with *The Ax Fight* begins with reading "Kin Selection and Conflict". With this background, users can recreate the analytical process of Chagnon and Bugos.[16] For each person who is designated as a "supporter" in the essay's Tables 8.4a and 8.4b, users can confirm or disconfirm the designation. Accessing footage in the *People* screens of the identified people, users can find the "raw" observations, the continuous, multifaceted streams of behavior, that Chagnon and Bugos designate as "support". These designations constitute the essay's "data", the discrete, discontinuous units of information that can be subjected to statistical analysis.

The translation of "behavior streams" into "data" requires discussion. Close inspection of the footage confirms that more than half of the thirty people identified by Chagnon and Bugos to be "supporters" do act supportingly: they bait or physically threaten the opponents of those whom they are said to help. This fact weakly confirms Chagnon's and Bugos's argument.[17] The example of one "supporter" in particular demonstrates further points about the translation of field observation into statistical data. Mohesiwä's classificatory "father", Yoroshianawä, is identified by Chagnon and Bugos to be Mohesiwä's "supporter" (Chagnon and Bugos, Table 8.4a). Observation of Yoroshianawä's activities reveals, however, that on at least three occasions he *prevented* an attack against Mohesiwä's antagonist. Superficially, this seems to constitute a misidentification of "support", although, as will be seen, the identification may ultimately be correct. The first point to be made, however, is the importance of close observation and clearly-defined coding criteria when footage and field observations are translated into data.

A second point about this example was raised by Gary Seaman (personal communication). Although Yoroshianawä prevented attacks on Mohesiwä's antagonist, this de-escalation of violence may have prevented Mohesiwä from being killed by a powerful opponent. Yoroshianawä had good reason to believe that his classificatory "son" was in considerable danger. In addition, Yoroshianawä's action probably had the long-term consequence of promoting the survival of Mohesiwä's lineage. Members of this lineage were vulnerable at the time and extremely dependent on the goodwill of Mohesiwä's antagonists. Ironically, Yoroshianawä's "failure to support" violence in this case would have had Darwinian consequences that affirm the Chagnon and Bugos hypothesis: Mohesiwä's survival in the ax fight may not only have been necessary for the reproduction of his own genes but instrumental for the reproduction of his lineage's gene pool. "Support" – here defined as action that advances the reproductive survival of individuals – is not a simple thing to recognize.

Reductionism: pushing film research to the limits

Another exercise concerns the extent to which field observations and ethnographic film footage can justify a choice among competing theories. *The Ax Fight* and the "Kin Selection" essay were not produced explicitly for the purpose of debating Marvin Harris's ecological theory of violence, but they can be considered in that light. With access to *The Ax Fight*'s footage and Chagnon's meticulously-collected genealogies, users are in a good position to evaluate whether Harris's argument could predict the fact that so many close kinsmen support each other in a fight. Is something more than the need for protein required to explain the actions recorded in the film? Are a need to reproduce one's genes and a need to sustain a supply of protein mutually exclusive?

In the social sciences, theories that search for a single, all-powerful explanation are called reductionistic. All factors that contribute to the existence of a phenomenon are "reduced" to only one. Both Harris (1984: 196) and Chagnon (e.g. 1989) argue that their goals are not reductionistic because they acknowledge many factors that contribute to Yanomamö behavior.[18]

In many cases, however, reductionistic explanations are difficult to avoid because they are not recognized as such. Documentary films, for example, often tempt viewers to interpret reductionistically. Viewers are presented with a brief moment recorded in the stream of history. They are then asked to believe that the recording is "truthful" and the moment is representative of a larger whole.

At best, films that present a single moment in history and a single interpretation of that moment restrict contextual understanding. At worst, they promote a closed-minded analysis by actively inhibiting supplemental or alternative arguments. The Ax Fight offers five versions of a moment in history, and suggests that none is the definitive truth. In that sense, it is a corrective to reductionism. The best antidote to a reductionist interpretation is a non-reductionist alternative. The film's emphasis on ten-and-a-half minutes of violence, however, necessarily ignores many things, notably the many sociable aspects of Yanomamö village life.[19] The range of behavior in the sample is not representative of the current whole.

The same problem of interpretive reductionism also has an historical aspect. If viewers of The Ax Fight had no other evidence, they might easily make interpretations of the Yanomamö that are ahistorical. They would have difficulty recognizing the extent to which recent history has transformed Yanomamö life. The change that is most obvious in the film, once it is pointed out, is the introduction of steel axes into the village. It is intriguing and disturbing to speculate about other changes brought by contact with the West. Albert (1989: 637) hypothesizes that Yanomamö villages which are relatively close to Western settlements have been inclined to unprecedented violence by the introduction of steel tools and the population explosion that resulted from them: the violence in The Ax Fight may be in part a distant consequence of Western expansion. Chagnon disagrees with Albert's hypothesis, but affirms that many external developments have had devastating consequences for the Yanomamö.[20]

Theory, biography, and history

Chagnon argues that Yanomamö women play a relatively passive and minor role in political affairs, compared to the violent and dominant role of men. A few anthropologists have debated his interpretation and qualified it with the suggestion that women display considerable power behind the scenes (Ramos 1979; Lizot 1976). The debate suggests a deductive foundation for research exercises in Yanomamö Interactive. Selections from the People menu allow users access to brief ethnographic records of women's activities. In terms of women's roles, the footage of Nakahedami and Yaukuima, sisters of the principal male antagonists in the fight, shows them to be much more active than many other women. Footage of several men – of Keböwä, Uuwä, Mohesiwä, and Törawä – clearly illustrates the ideal of Yanomamö male behavior, *waiteri,* that Chagnon frequently describes. The footage of Yoroshianawä, on the other hand, like that of Nanokawä and Möawä (discussed in Chagnon's narration), suggests that there are times when Yanomamö men give peace a chance, when alternative male strategies are preferred. A particularly striking case of non-*waiteri* behavior is that of Yoinakuwä, the man who was probably most responsible for escalating the violence in the ax fight.[21] In every piece of action described in the "Blow-by-Blows", Yoinakuwä displays an uncanny ability to promote violence while keeping himself far away from the swinging axes.

The depictions of many individuals in *The Ax Fight* present short but suggestive biographies that can be read in the *People* screens. Sinabimi's young son Räaiyowä, for example, offers users the opportunity to pursue a footage-based exercise in biographical research. On first screening, the ten-year-old boy is nameless and invisible. When his movements are tracked over time, however, he is discovered everywhere. Räaiyowä is concerned about his mother's plight and anxious to study the ways by which Yanomamö men avenge abuse.

Tools to analyze the structure of *The Ax Fight*

Yanomamö Interactive also makes possible explorations that should interest students of film, as distinct from students of anthropology. As described above, sections three and five of *The Ax Fight* are re-edits of the unedited, original footage of section one. A special feature, for users who wish to understand editing decisions in *The Ax Fight*, permits non-linear navigation between precise frames in the edited sections and the equivalent frames in the original. This feature is available in the "Narration" chapter (accessible from the *Contents* menu). There, descriptive paragraphs for sections three and five contain bolded "REF" footnote numbers. A mouse-click on any part of a paragraph that is not in bold will cause the movie to synch with the current moment that is described in the paragraph. A click on the "REF" number itself will jump the movie back to the equivalent picture frame in the unedited footage.[22] Students of film should also be interested in the still photographs that Chagnon took while *The Ax Fight* was being shot (Figure 13.5). The alternative compositions and perspectives that these photographs provide reveal the limits of single-camera film production.

Selective perception in field observation and ethnographic film

The last exercises I suggest with the footage are intended for viewers of ethnographic film in general. They explore the way that narration focuses and unfocuses attention. Here is a case in point, a line of Chagnon's narration near the middle of the fight:

> Alarmed by this new threat, a woman from Keböwä's group seizes his [Törawä's] ax handle, turns the sharp side back down and drags him out of the fight.

The narration thus emphasizes Törawä's failure of purpose, mentions no one except Törawä and a woman, and gives no special emphasis to the fact that it is a woman who blocks a man so effectively. Both the emphasis and de-emphasis have consequences for viewers.

Before I began work on the CD, I had taught with and viewed *The Ax Fight* about ten times. In all of those viewings, I had concentrated on Törawä's failure, following the narration's emphasis. I did not find it particularly interesting that a woman (Keböwä's sister, Yaukuima) had "out-manned" a Yanomamö man. Now, having reconsidered the footage since reading Ramos (1979), I have become intrigued. Inspection of the footage also reveals that, at the moment when Törawä is blocked by the woman, Yaukuima, Törawä's classificatory "father" (in an apparent effort to de-escalate the violence) shoves Törawä off balance. I had never noticed Yoroshianawä shove Törawä, though he does it in plain sight. I now realize that the interpretation of the incident given in Chagnon's narration not only emphasizes the failure of the weak Törawä; it also de-emphasizes the active role of the woman, Yaukuima, and the "non-support" of the classificatory "father", Yoroshianawä.

Earlier in the film, another example of this phenomenon occurs. The narration describes Keböwä's dash across the village plaza in his effort to injure Mohesiwä:

> Keböwä attacks Mohesiwä, but Mohesiwä's kinswomen seize the ax handle and try to prevent him from striking.

Believing this to be the case, Gary Seaman needed dozens of slow-motion viewings before he realized that Keböwä's intended victim was actually someone else. Seaman had been blinded by the narration. Yet the narrator's mistake is logical: since Mohesiwä had attacked Uuwä, Keböwä's ally in the club fight that just ended, it would make sense for Keböwä now to attack Mohesiwä in return. The film evidence of Keböwä's actual victim, however, indicates that a different logic was at work: earlier in the day, Mohesiwä had also attacked Sinabimi, Keböwä's classificatory "wife". Keböwä is here apparently retaliating against a woman in Mohesiwä's group, probably *his* wife! (See Figure 13.6 for a stop-frame rendering of Keböwä's attack, created for the CD by Jeanne Fitzsimmons.)

Ethnographic film narration serves a complex function. On one hand, it provides the crucial role of helping viewers to make sense of visual chaos. *The Ax Fight* demonstrates this point perfectly in the contrast of its first and third sections. Narration must be directive and must interpret footage according to the priorities of the ethnographer. On the other hand, even the best narration is coercive: by directing attention to one perspective, it manifestly desensitizes viewers to other perspectives.[23]

To study this phenomenon, users may employ the film and "Blow-by-Blow Descriptions" in exercises that direct the perceptions and interpretations of others. An exercise that can help hone the skills of field observation and ethnographic argument is to produce a number of different narrations for a single moment in the film. The narrations could emphasize alternative aspects of a single action or present different (perhaps mutually exclusive) theoretical slants on it.[24]

Figure 13.6 Selected still frames from the film reveal that Keböwä's victim is a woman (probably Mohesiwä's wife, Huuhuumi) and not Mohesiwä, as the voice-over narration suggests. The narration is so compelling at this point that viewers do not recognize the error.

Conclusion

The paradox of blinding interpretive light defines *The Ax Fight* and has influenced the design of *Yanomamö Interactive*. It affects all analysis, all people who make films, and all who try to make films out. The best way, I believe, to contend with the essential difficulties of interpretation is to follow the practices of scholarship. Keep close watch on priorities, keep reading alternative perspectives, and keep checking that the data make the case.

Interactive media have the potential to integrate the best resources of scholarship in anthropology (Biella 1993b). Anthropology grows through the competition of theoretical interpretations, but the discipline is also based on a foundation of non-recurrent empirical observations. Ethnographic film, with the essential tool of narration, makes a good beginning at documenting and interpreting these observations. Before the advent of interactive media, however, anthropological images were difficult to unlink from the coercive interpretations of their makers. Because of this resistance to scholarship, ethnographic film has not always seemed serious. Like its precursor, *The Ax Fight*, interactive media offers important correctives. It slows down the footage and allows changing relationships to be considered repeatedly. Non-linear links to texts release interpretation and open ethnographic film more fully to the search for new meaning.

Notes

1 The "Blow-by-Blows" were written by Gary Seaman in 1996 as part of a close reinvestigation of *The Ax Fight* footage. The original identifications and genealogies of the people in the film, which made Seaman's descriptions possible, were supplied by Chagnon, who has extensive knowledge of the Mishimishimaböwei-teri villagers. Seth Reichlin's analysis (1993) of *The Ax Fight* also contributed to the "Blow-by-Blows". Reichlin was an anthropology major at Harvard who was hired to write a study guide by the film's distributor, Documentary Educational Resources. Chagnon read, corrected, and approved all of Seaman's "Blow-by-Blows". I also spent many hours going over them to make sure that what they described can be seen in the film.

2 See http://www.anth.ucsb.edu/projects/axfight/index.html for links to downloadable textual and graphic resources in *Yanomamö Interactive*.

3 Essays that discuss *The Ax Fight* include Asch (1991), Bugos, Carter and Asch (1993), Chagnon and Bugos (1979; available in the CD), Cohen (1979), Klein and Klein (1977), Loizos (1993), Marks (1995), Moore (1995), Nichols (1981 [see also Nichols, this volume]), Reichlin (1993), Ruby (1995), and Weinberger (1994).

4 Several of Asch's students and colleagues have mentioned to me that he spoke openly and with some amusement of recreating for *The Ax Fight's* soundtrack the repeated, clearly-discernable crunches of axes on flesh: Asch reportedly produced the effect in a Boston soundstage by striking a mallet against a watermelon. Anyone who has tried, at a distance, to record subtle sounds in the midst of an acoustic mêlée will understand that Asch's microphone was much too distant from the village fight to register its faint details, significant as they may have been. Asch assumed that he would need to recreate the crunching sounds if he wished his film audience to be aware when blows were struck. Further, as I argue above, Asch promoted this awareness in order to serve two purposes, informational and emotion-generating. I have tested Asch's assumption about the consequences of adding the artificial crunching sounds of the ax on occasions when I have screened the film to students. Usually I leave the sound up, but sometimes I turn it off during the raw-footage sequence. Based on student reactions, the acoustic watermelon punctuation marks create in viewers a sense of awareness and shock that is absent in those who try to understand the film's image without the recreated acoustic guidance. Like Chagnon's pointed narration, the artificial sound of blows tells viewers what to think and feel.

Tierney (2000) has recently claimed that Asch and Chagnon staged Yanomamö fights for the camera. In light of Asch's open admissions that he recreated the sound of ax blows, and in light of his many statements, subsequent to release of the film, in which he repudiates Chagnon for exaggerating Yanomamö violence, I conclude that if Asch had harbored any suspicions that the fights were staged, he would eventually have expressed them (a more detailed argument for this conclusion appears in Biella [2000]).

5 Rouch's and Morin's path-breaking documentary *Chronicle of a Summer* (1960) includes conversations between the film-makers, but the talks were premeditated and took place for inclusion in the film.

6 Identification photographs in *Yanomamö Interactive* can be seen by selecting an individual's name from the *Vital Statistics* menu and clicking the "Photos" button.

7 When *The Ax Fight* was released in 1975, it was not unique stylistically. Its viewers may have recalled the optical enlargements and slow zooms found in such fiction films as Antonioni's *Blow-Up* (1966) and *Zabriski Point* (1969). Nevertheless, in the social sciences, the optical fireworks of section three of *The Ax Fight* were unprecedented and stunning. Apart from the film's optical effects, the repetition of the footage was itself remarkable. Similar techniques had been used less effectively by John Marshall in *An Argument About A Marriage* (1958) and by Asch and Chagnon themselves in their earlier Tanonmamö film *The Feast* (1968). Only Gregory Bateson and Margaret Mead, Asch's mentor, had previously advocated such close attention to the use of 16 mm film as empirical evidence in anthropology (Bateson and Mead 1942). No one before Asch and Chagnon had gone to so much trouble to integrate evidence with theory in an anthropological film.

8 The "Narration" is transcribed and synched with the footage. It is accessible in the *Contents* menu.

9 Chagnon's argument is left somewhat unfinished at this point: the narration offers no motive to explain

why villagers again wanted alliance. Students of Chagnon's case study (1992, 1997), however, would expect these motives to include the need for mutual protection against enemies, men's desire for sister-exchange, and women's desire to live in villages where their brothers also reside.

10 For more on the "savage slot" in anthropology's ideological niches, see Trouillot (1991) and Dumont (1988).

11 Research on film reception has demonstrated that the parody is too subtle for many student viewers to grasp (Martínez 1990 and this volume).

12 Is the implicit conclusion of the "final edited version" that all analysis, everywhere, is illusion? Asch implies something to this effect in his interview with Ruby (1995), but he may have been reading contemporary post-modernism backward into his work of 1975. The claim that all interpretations are equally invalid because they are all born of human illusion is called solipsism. The film's ambiguity on this philosophical question is no doubt intentional but, as far as I am concerned, the ambiguity is a weakness. In any case, if the claim were that all interpretation is illusion, then further investigation of *The Ax Fight*'s footage would be no more than an exercise in interpretive aesthetics. There could be no superior interpretation because there are no real patterns in human action or culture.

The position of solipsism is self-negating. People who claim to know that all knowledge is merely an interpretation or illusion are really claiming to know nothing, since by their argument any knowledge would merely be an interpretation or an illusion.

13 For a recent summary of the theoretical controversies in which Chagnon's work has played a major role, see Monaghan (1994), an essay that is biased toward the views of Chagnon's detractors.

14 Chagnon's and Bugos's four Tables, 8.1, 8.2, 8.3, and 8.4 (*a* and *b*) are available in the CD. The Tables illustrating the Chagnon and Bugos argument can also be accessed from the *Illustrations* menu of the "Kin Selection and Conflict" screen. The mathematical calculations used in the Tables can be verified using data provided in the "Carved and Dyadic" and "Census and Participants" data files that Chagnon gathered in the field. The data are presented elsewhere in the CD but should be weighed in light of the caveat presented in footnote 17.

15 In his written comments on an earlier draft of this essay, Chagnon adds that factors which contribute to reproductive success of Yanomamö men include much more than the capacity for violence. They also include having skill as a shaman, multiple wives, membership in a powerful lineage, exceptionally numerous matrilateral kin, and exceptionally numerous ascending generation kin.

16 *The Ax Fight* footage was the "raw" observational record from which Chagnon and Bugos designated villagers to be "supporters" of one faction or the other. While users' access to this footage and to Chagnon's genealogical data (stored in "People" screens and elsewhere in the CD) does not reproduce for users the original fieldwork experience, it replicates very well the conditions under which the analysis was made.

Like the extraordinarily frank material that Chagnon includes in his *Studying the Yanomamö* (1974), the "raw" footage of *The Ax Fight* and the genealogical material in the CD are the sort of field data that anthropologists ordinarily repress. Honesty facilitates what is likely often to be hostile outside critique. In the past, it has been the absence of such extensive honesty (in conjunction with the absence of imagination in the use of audiovisual and digital technologies, one might add) that has prevented anthropology from providing data which independent observers can verify.

17 Chagnon's and Bugos's (1979) essay claims to use the film footage as the basis for statistical evidence concerning "support" by thirty genealogically-close relatives. However, twelve of the thirty people named in the essay as "supporters" have not to my knowledge been identified in the film. Their names are not mentioned in either Chagnon's or Seaman's descriptions of the footage. It is clear in any case that the film's tiny sample of behavior, whether composed of eighteen or thirty "supporters", would be incapable of affording Chagnon's argument statistical significance.

18 See Chagnon (1997: 91–7) for his comments on "The Great Protein Debate". In written comments on a draft of this essay, Chagnon made the following remarks:

Harris's "theory" about the male-supremacist complex was borrowed directly from one of my own publications – a chapter in a book Harris edited with Morton Fried and Robert Murphy (Chagnon 1968). I characterized it as the "waiteri complex", but it all hinged logically on whether or not it was empirically true that Yanomamö infanticide was female preferential infanticide: that Yanomamö killed more female babies at birth than males. … I could not demonstrate empirically a female sex bias in Yanomamö infanticides, rendering both the logic of my "waiteri complex" hypothesis untenable and the logic of Harris's derivative version equally untenable. Harris's version is now widely identified in his re-wording of his earlier arguments (Divale and Harris 1976). …

While cultural determinists such as Marvin Harris argue that the behavior of tribesmen is almost exclusively determined by material factors – they do things that lead to the economic survival of their cultures – I argue that individuals in all cultures tend to do things that promote their selfish individual reproductive survival: they do not exist to promote the survival of groups, villages, tribes and cultures.

They exist to promote their own reproductive interests. Harris reduces conflict and warfare to material causes – struggles for food, meat, water holes, territory, etc. I expand the repertoire, advised by modern biological theory, and include many other causes of human conflict, including conflicts over reproductive resources – females – that Harris rejects as "too biological". Yet Harris's own theory rests on the same, but unstated, assumption: food is a biological necessity for survival. Ultimately, Harris's theory is as "biologically reductionist" as mine. It would even be possible and logical to claim that Harris is positing a "gene" for maximizing protein intake or material well-being. If this isn't the mechanism that causes people to strive to get more protein (and water holes, territory, etc.), then what does Harris posit as the "cause" for this striving? How different is Harris's basic assumption from my own?

19 Only two days after the fight occurred, for example, Yanomamö elders promoted an impromptu meat distribution feast. Asch and Chagnon (1975) made a film about this event, but the work is rarely screened and its cultural significance – in counterpoint to the famous film about ax violence – is rarely recognized. Moore's (1995) essay on the subject is an important exception.

20 Chagnon considers Albert's hypothesis that capitalist expansion has increased Yanomamö violence to be groundless speculation. He states that Albert promotes wishful thinking about Western myths of the peaceful Noble Savage.

It is true that, beginning in the 1950s, steel axes were introduced to Yanomamö villages as trade goods offered by missionaries and other Westerners. Chagnon has frequently discussed the modification of Yanomamö culture due to the introduction of steel axes. He argues, for example, that axes have been integrated into Yanomamö stages and rituals of violence (Chagnon 1992: 64, Chagnon and Bugos 1979). More recently, the introduction of shotguns has made inter-village disputes more lethal. Chagnon reports incidents in which heavily-armed miners have slaughtered Yanomamö, and, as an investigation of the causes of death listed in *People* screens of the CD will show, great devastation has been brought to Yanomamö by epidemics, often of Western diseases. See Chagnon (1997: 227–60) for additional data on mortality due to Western contact.

21 Yoinakuwä also may be said to have started the fight by instructing his wife, Sinabimi, to stop feeding the visitors.

22 When this occurs, the "Return" button, in the lower right of the screen, is activated and a click on it will re-cue the movie back to the current moment. On a few occasions, original and edited frames linked together with "REF" numbers are not identical; this is the case because some film information was lost when the film was digitized at 15 frames per second.

23 As pointed out above, in the absence of narration, informal guidelines are always available to fill the void. Stereotypes like "primitive, savage violence", though unspoken most of the time, are also blinding and coercive.

24 The "Blow-by-Blow Descriptions" were written with the goal of maintaining a reasonable degree of objectivity. By this is meant, first, that they describe almost exclusively what can be seen on camera at the current moment. Second, they are written, almost exclusively and to the extent possible, in language that minimizes value judgments and psychological or cultural interpretations (exceptions are usually marked off in brackets). The design of the "Blow-by-Blows" is restricted in this way in order to acknowledge uncertainty about indigenous Yanomamö meanings and motives, and to leave unprejudiced, as much as is possible, users' interpretations that will be based on the descriptions. While descriptions of behavior carry their own theoretical baggage, the writing style of the "Blow-by-Blows" is not intended to promote a reductionistic model of human action.

References

Albert, Bruce (1989), "Yanomami 'Violence': Inclusive Fitness or Ethnographer's Representation?" *Current Anthropology* 30 (5): 637–40.

Asch, Timothy (1991), "The Story We Now Want to Hear is Not Ours to Tell – Relinquishing Control Over Representation: Toward Sharing Visual Communication Skills with the Yanomamö". *Visual Anthropology Review* 7 (2): 102–6.

Bateson, Gregory (1972), "Style, Grace and Information in Primitive Art". In *Steps to an Ecology of Mind*, pp. 128–52. New York: Ballantine.

Bateson, Gregory and Margaret Mead (1942), *Balinese Character: A Photographic Analysis.* New York: The New York Academy of Sciences.

Biella, Peter (1993a), "The Design of Ethnographic Hypermedia". In Jack R. Rollwagen (ed.), *Anthropological Filmmaking in the 1990s*. Brockport, New York: The Institute, Inc., pp. 293–341.

—— (1993b), "Beyond Ethnographic Film: Hypermedia and Scholarship". In Jack R. Rollwagen (ed.), *Anthropological Filmmaking in the 1990s*. Brockport, New York: The Institute, Inc., pp. 131–76.

—— (2000), "Of Watermelons and Emperors: Implausibility of Momentous Deception in the Asch–Chagnon Films". Paper presented in the session "Visual Anthropology in the Public Sphere," Annual Meetings of the American Anthropological Association, San Francisco, November.

Brigard, Émilie de (1975), "The History of Ethnographic Film". In Paul Hockings (ed.), *Principles of Visual Anthropology*. The Hague: Mouton, pp. 13–43.

Bugos, Paul, Jr., Stephan Carter, and Timothy Asch (1993), "*The Ax Fight*: Film Notes". In Timothy Asch and Gary Seaman (eds.), *Yanomamö Film Study Guide*. Los Angeles: Ethnographics Press, University of Southern California, pp. 132–44.

Chagnon, Napoleon (1968), "Yanomamö Social Organization and Warfare". In Morton Fried, Marvin Harris and Robert Murphy (eds.), *War: The Anthropology of Armed Conflict and Aggression*. Garden City, New York: Doubleday, pp. 109–59.

—— (1974), *Studying the Yanomamö*. New York: Holt, Rinehart and Winston.

—— (1988), "Life Histories, Blood Revenge, and Warfare in a Tribal Population". *Science* 239: 985–92.

—— (1989), "Reply to Ferguson". *American Ethnologist* 16 (3): 565–9.

—— (1992), *Yanomamö*; Fourth edition. Fort Worth: Harcourt Brace College Publishers.

—— (1997), *Yanomamö*. Fifth edition. Fort Worth: Harcourt Brace College Publishers.

Chagnon, Napoleon and Paul Bugos, Jr. (1979), "Kin Selection and Conflict". In N. A. Chagnon and William Irons (eds.), *Evolutionary Biology and Human Social Behavior: An Anthropological Perspective*. North Scituate, Massachusetts: Duxbury Press. [Also available in the CD.]

Cohen, Hart (1979), "Mapping Anthropology on Film". *Ciné-Tracts* 2 (2): 62–73.

Divale, W. and Marvin Harris (1976), "Population, Warfare and the Male Supremacist Complex". *American Anthropologist* 78: 521–38.

Dumont, Jean-Paul (1988), "The Tasaday, Which and Whose? Toward the Political Economy of an Ethnographic Sign". *Cultural Anthropology* 3 (3): 261–75.

Dyhrenfurth, N. (1952), "Filmmaking for Scientific Film-makers". *American Anthropologist* 80 (4): 1020–2.

Fewkes, J. (1890), "A Contribution to Passamaquoddy Folklore". *Journal of American Folklore* 3: 257–80.

Gessell, A. (1935), "Cinemanalysis: A Method of Behavior Study". *Journal of Genetic Psychology* 47 (1): 3–16.

Harris, Marvin (1974), *Cows, Pigs, Wars and Witches: The Riddles of Culture*. New York: Random House.

—— (1984), "Animal Capture and Yanomamö Warfare: Retrospect and New Evidence". *Journal of Anthropological Research* 40: 183–201.

Hilton-Simpson, M. and J. Haeseler (1925), "Cinema and Ethnology". *Discovery* 6 (69): 325–30.

Klein, Patricia and John F. Klein (1977), "Review: The Ax Fight". *American Anthropologist* 79 (3): 747.

Landow, G. (1991), "The Rhetoric of Hypermedia: Some Rules for Authors". In Paul Delany and George P. Landow (eds.), *Hypermedia and Literary Studies*. Cambridge, Massachusetts: MIT Press, pp. 81–103.

Lizot, Jacques (1976), "Population, Resources and Warfare among the Yanomami". *Man* (n.s.) 12: 497–517.

Loizos, Peter (1993), *Innovation in Ethnographic Film: From Innocence to Self-Consciousness 1955–1985*. Manchester: Manchester University Press.

Marks, Dan (1995), "Ethnography and Ethnographic Film: From Flaherty to Asch and After". *American Anthropologist* 97 (2): 339–47.

Martínez, Wilton (1990), "Critical Studies and Visual Anthropology: Aberrant Versus Anticipated Readings in Ethnographic Film". *Commission for Visual Anthropology Review* Spring 34–74.

Mills, C. Wright (1959), *The Sociological Imagination*. London: Oxford University Press.

Monaghan, Peter (1994), "Bitter Warfare in Anthropology". *Chronicle of Higher Education* 41 (9) [Oct. 26]: A10, A18–19.

Moore, Alexander (1995), "Understanding Event Analysis Using the Films of Tim Asch". *Visual Anthropology Review* 11 (1): 38–52.

Nichols, Bill (1981). *Ideology and the Image: Social Representation in the Cinema and Other Media*. Bloomington: Indiana University Press.

Ramos, Alcida R. (1979), "On Women's Status in Yanoama Societies". *Current Anthropology* 20 (1): 185–7.

Reichlin, Seth (1993), "*The Ax Fight*: A Study Guide". In Timothy Asch and Gary Seaman (eds.), *Yanomamö Film Study Guide*. Los Angeles: Ethnographics Press, University of Southern California, pp. 90–130.

Ruby, Jay (1995), "Out of Sync: The Cinema of Tim Asch". *Visual Anthropology Review* 11 (1): 19–35.

Tierney, Patrick (2000), *Darkness in El Dorado: How Scientists and Journalists Devastated the Amazon*. New York: W. W. Norton.

Trouillot, Michel-Rolph (1991), "Anthropology and the Savage Slot: The Poetics and Politics of Otherness". In Richard G. Fox (ed.), *Recapturing Anthropology: Working in the Present*. Santa Fe, New Mexico: School of American Research Press, pp. 17–44.

Weinberger, Eliot (1994), "The Camera People". In Lucien Taylor (ed.), *Visualizing Theory: Selected Essays From V.A.R. 1990–1994*. New York and London: Routledge, pp. 3–26.

Films

Antonioni, Michelangelo (Director) (1966), *Blow-Up*. Film. Hollywood: Metro-Goldwyn-Mayer.

—— (1969), *Zabriski Point*. Film. Hollywood: Metro-Goldwyn-Mayer.

Asch, Timothy and Napoleon Chagnon (1968), *The Feast*. Film. Watertown, Massachusetts: Documentary Educational Resources.

—— (1975), *The Ax Fight*. Film. Watertown, Massachusetts: Documentary Educational Resources.

Biella, Peter, Napoleon Chagnon, and Gary Seaman (1997), *Yanomamö Interactive: The Ax Fight*. CD-ROM. Fort Worth: Harcourt Brace College Publishers. (For excerpts, see also http://www.anth.ucsb.edu/projects/axfight/index.html.)

Chagnon, Napoleon and Timothy Asch (1975), *Tapir Distribution*. Film. Watertown, Massachusetts: Documentary Educational Resources.

Kurosawa, Akira (1951), *Rashomon*. Film. Tokyo: TAMA.

Marshall, John (1958), *An Argument About A Marriage*. Film. Watertown: Massachusetts: Documentary Educational Resources.

Rouch, Jean and Edgar Morin (1960), *Chronicle of a Summer*. Film. Paris: Argos.

Chapter 14

Person, event, and the location of the cinematic subject in Timothy Asch's films on Indonesia

E. D. Lewis

Tim Asch carried out research and made films in Canada, Africa, Trinidad, Venezuela, Afghanistan, and Indonesia. Of these, the best known and most widely screened are three or four films of the series about the Yanomamö Indians of Venezuela. From 1976 until his return to the United States in 1982, Asch worked in Australia, where he devoted his professional energies to film-making in Indonesia. The films on Indonesia are perhaps less well known than the Yanomamö films but are, in my opinion, his finest work.

Asch's work in Indonesia began shortly after his arrival in Canberra to take up a position in The Australian National University's Research School of Pacific Studies. In December 1976, Asch and James J. Fox submitted an application for research funds to the United States National Science Foundation entitled "The Ceremonies of Savu: The Development of a Methodology for the Analysis of Large-Scale Ritual Performances via the use of Film and Video-Tape". The NSF proposal set out the aims of Asch's work and his collaboration with Fox:

> (1) to study the indigenous rituals of the island of Savu in eastern Indonesia, (2) to focus on social relations and multi-personal interactions within a formal ceremonial setting, and (3) to develop a methodology, via the use of film, for the analysis of large-scale ritual performances. These closely related aims are intended to advance the comparative understanding of ritual systems in Indonesia, to test certain hypotheses about the nature of ritual on Savu, and to demonstrate the research potential of film in the study of specific anthropological problems.
>
> (Asch and Fox 1976)

The project was to be the first stage of a long-term "cross-cultural study of ritual on several islands in Indonesia". Asch and Fox gave their project

> ... a modular design intended to be carried out in sequential fashion. Each individual project could stand on its own but the value of the whole lies in producing a body of comparative materials from diverse groups within a particular area of the world. ... If, as we suspect, our understanding of Savunese

ritual is enhanced greatly, then we will be in an excellent position to extend our explorations to other, contrasting groups. ...

(ibid.)

From its inception, Asch's work in Indonesia aimed at using film for research in comparative ethnology. As Asch and Fox made their case to the NSF:

> Eastern Indonesia is a prime area for this kind of project because of its extraordinary diversity. The ecology of the islands ranges from tropical rainforest to savannah to semi-arid regions. For centuries, Hinduism, Islam, Christianity and a wide range of local religions have existed side-by-side on separate islands. Economically, subsistence patterns include foraging, herding, sailing, slash-and-burn agriculture, palm-tapping and highly developed rice cultivation systems. But despite this diversity at all levels, there are numerous, clearly evident cultural patterns that unite these many different people. The intention of the filming project as a whole would be to maintain a focus on selected cultural similarities in the midst of diversity.

(ibid.)

The five cultures selected for study were those of the Savunese, the Rotinese, the Balinese, the Mambai of Timor, and an Islamic sailing population of southern Sulawesi (Salayar or Buton). Filming on Sava proved impracticable because of difficulties in obtaining research permits from the Indonesia government within the timetable Asch and Fox had in mind, and it was not possible to work among the Mambai in East Timor because of the Indonesian take-over of the Portuguese colony. Filming in Tana 'Ai on Flores replaced the Savu component of the research, while work on Roti and Bali proceeded as Asch and Fox had planned.

The program of research in Indonesia also had a methodological aim, which was to develop techniques for using film and video in the study of behavior in complex social situations. In their NSF proposal, Asch and Fox commented:

> Film is able to capture the full sequencing of an otherwise transitory series of events; it can encompass the simultaneous actions of a number of different participants; it can recall these events to participants to stimulate comment on them, even after a considerable lapse of time; it offers a means of repeated viewing for the purposes of analysis; and, finally, having provided the simplicity and clarity necessary for a frame-by-frame examination, it can represent some measure of the complexity of the original events.

(ibid.)

Asch had perhaps been disappointed that, despite Napoleon Chagnon's intensive sociological analysis of some of the Yanomamö film (such as that of the ax fight), the footage had never been used to elicit the perspectives of Yanomamö themselves on the events that had been filmed. In their NSF proposal, Asch and Fox note that

Chagnon was working on an analysis of the ax fight that would "relate this incident to the previous pattern of alliance and hostility among [the] Yanomamö" depicted in the film. But they went on to say:

> This film has not been shown to Yanomamö participants, which is one of the ways in which analysis is to be carried out among the Savunese. Furthermore, at the time when [*The Ax Fight*] was made, there was no attempt to record the varied interpretations of the incident from among its different participants.
>
> (ibid.)

The involvement of informants in filming and experiments with the use of the film to elicit "informant feedback" on the filmed events would be a principal aim of the Indonesia research.[1]

The corpus of Asch's Indonesia films includes a series of five films made with Dr Linda Connor on the island of Bali, two films made in collaboration with Professor James J. Fox on the island of Roti in eastern Indonesia, and a film about the Ata Tana 'Ai of the eastern Indonesian island of Flores, the first of a planned series of three or four films and the last of Asch's films to be released before his death.[2] The films and their release dates are:

1979 *A Balinese Trance Seance*. Patsy Asch, editor, co-producer; Timothy Asch, ethnographic film-maker, co-producer; Linda Connor, anthropologist, sound-person, narrator, translator.

1981 *Jero on Jero: A Balinese Trance Seance Observed*. A film by Timothy Asch, ethnographic film-maker; Linda Connor, anthropologist; Patsy Asch, editor and co-producer.

1983 *The Water of Words: A Cultural Ecology of an Eastern Indonesian Island*. James J. Fox, anthropologist, sound recordist and translator; Timothy Asch, film-maker and co-producer; Patsy Asch, editor and co-producer.

1983 *The Medium Is the Masseuse: A Balinese Massage*. Timothy Asch, ethnographic film-maker; Linda Connor, anthropologist and sound recordist; Patsy Asch, editor and producer.

1983 *Jero Tapakan: Stories from the Life of a Balinese Healer*. A film by Timothy Asch, Linda Connor and Patsy Asch.

1988 *Spear and Sword: A Ceremonial Payment of Bridewealth. The Island of Roti, Eastern Indonesia*. James J. Fox, anthropologist, sound recordist, translator; Timothy Asch and Patsy Asch, ethnographic film-makers; E. M. Pono, participant and transcriber.

1991 *Releasing the Spirits: A Village Cremation in Bali*. A film collaboration between Patsy Asch, Linda Connor, Timothy Asch, and Balinese participants in a group cremation.

1993 *A Celebration of Origins* (Tana Wai Brama, Flores). E. Douglas Lewis, anthropologist, translator, narrator; Patsy Asch, sound recordist, co-producer, editor; Timothy Asch, cinematographer, co-producer.

Asch's Indonesia films share at least five salient features. First, all of the films were made in collaborations between Asch and anthropologists who were intimately acquainted with the communities in which they were shot. Second, the styles of the films range from the more didactic (*The Water of Words*) to the more reflexive (*Jero on Jero*) while all combine elements of didactic exposition of their subjects with reflexive narration in which the films themselves provide exegeses of the subjects and narrative continuity. As a corpus, the Indonesia films are thus a series of notable experiments in the representation of the essential relationships which sustain ethnographic film: between individual persons as cinematic subjects, between anthropologist and informant, between ethnographic cinematographer and subject, between anthropologist and cinematographer, and between film-makers and their audience. Third, while depicting events, all of the films focus closely upon particular individuals in the societies they address. In each case, the individuals are not simply identified, but their personalities, positions in the communities, and interests in the film are fully set out. Indeed, two of the Bali films (*Jero on Jero* and *Jero Tapakan*) are *about* an individual, Jero Tapakan, a Balinese healer. In all of the films, the words of these individuals are employed as narration or as informed narrative about the events depicted in the films. In some cases, these narratives are complex (as in *A Celebration of Origins* [3]) and involve both the subtitled translation of the person's speech on film and the person's subtitled or translated voice-over comments on and exegeses of the events which are the film's subject.

Fourth, in all but *The Water of Words*, Asch and his collaborators set out to experiment with what Asch referred to as "informant feedback"[4] in both the collection of ethnographic data on the filmed events and in the construction of self-explicating films for distribution. Last, all of the films address, at least to a degree, ritual in the societies in which they were shot and it is ritual, as a kind of event and as a category of social action and anthropological analysis, which all of the films but one (*Jero Tapakan: Stories from the Life of a Balinese Healer*) share as an ethnographic subject. In this regard, all are either films of events (*A Balinese Trance Seance*, *The Medium Is the Masseuse: A Balinese Massage*, *Spear and Sword*, *Releasing the Spirits: A Village Cremation in Bali*, and *A Celebration of Origins*), films in which informants speak about and comment on events (*Jero on Jero* and *Jero Tapakan*), or employ footage of "typical" events in the life of the community as a thematic thread (*The Water of Words*). In this respect, all of the Indonesia films carry on the development of event films[5] for which Asch is justifiably well known in anthropology (see Moore 1995).

Tim Asch is still perhaps best known in the United States for the films on the Yanomamö in the late 1960s and 1970s. Several of the films of the Yanomamö series quickly established themselves among the most frequently screened films in the repertory of ethnographic films used in undergraduate teaching in America. When screened in conjunction with setting Chagnon's *Yanomamö: The Fierce People* (the title of the fourth edition of the volume was changed to *The Yanomamö*) as reading, films such as *The Ax Fight*, *The Feast*, *Tapir Distribution*, and *New Tribes*

Mission appealed to both lecturers and their undergraduate students. The influence of these films remains substantial and their place in the American curriculum in Anthropology remains prominent today: the June 1995 issue of the *American Anthropologist* featured a review article by Daniel Marks, who was one of Asch's students in the graduate program in ethnographic film at USC in the 1980s, largely devoted to an analysis of *The Ax Fight*.

Tim Asch's Indonesia films have yet to establish themselves in the teaching curriculum in anthropology to the degree that the Yanomamö films have done and are perhaps less well known. The reason for this may not be difficult to find. Asch's Indonesia films were also his Australian films. In 1976, Tim Asch left Cambridge, Massachusetts, to join the Department of Anthropology in the Research School of Pacific Studies (now the Research School of Pacific and Asian Studies) in the Institute of Advanced Studies of The Australian National University. He worked in Canberra for six years, to 1982. These six years were perhaps the most productive of Asch's career. During this brief time, he carried out fieldwork and film production among the peoples of three islands in eastern Indonesia (Roti, Bali and Flores) in collaboration with three anthropologists based in Australia (Fox, Connor, and Lewis). Eight films have so far been made from footage shot while Asch was at The ANU, and a further two, possibly three, films on Flores were in post-production at the time of his death.[6]

Three important factors must be taken into consideration in addressing the Indonesia films. First, Asch worked with a different anthropologist in each of his Indonesia projects and the shape and subjects of each set of films directly reflect the research interests of his collaborators.[7] Second, post-production of the Roti, Bali and Flores films overlapped. There were times in the years 1980 (the year in which the footage for *Jero on Jero* and *A Celebration of Origins* was shot) to 1988 (the year in which *Spear and Sword* was released) in which the Aschs worked on two or three of the projects simultaneously (Table 14.1). Perhaps most importantly, the editing of the films made on the three islands overlapped in time. The making of each film thus influenced the making of the others. Third, Patsy Asch was the editor of all of the Indonesia films, a circumstance which is undoubtedly responsible, to a major extent, for the stylistic and anthropological coherence of the Indonesia films as a corpus of work.

Elements of style in Asch's Indonesia films

Asch's interest in building a cinematic anthropology, kindled during his own anthropological studies with Margaret Mead and Morton Fried at Columbia University in the 1950s, began to take form during the period of his work with John Marshall in the early 1960s. It was then that they developed the notion of sequence films devoted to brief activities such as the tug-of-war in the short film of that title.[8] The sequence approach to ethnographic film-making was not only an innovation at the time; it contributed to rounding out the representation of the Ju/'hoansi in such a way as to counteract the archetypes that dominated Marshall's *The Hunters* (1957).[9] Asch's focus on quotidian events as a cinematic and ethnographic subject

Table 14.1 Chronology of filming and post-production for Asch's Indonesia films

Project	Filming	Additional fieldwork	Subject
Roti	1977		Footage for *The Water of Words* (lontar tapping, ritual language); footage of bridewealth payment (*Spear and Sword*).
	1978		Footage of mortuary ceremonies (for film to be called *A Death in a Clan*); footage of a church service and additional footage of everyday life in Roti.
Bali	1978		Trance séance, Jero's practice as a masseuse, Jero's biography, village cremation.
	1980		Feedback for *Jero on Jero*; footage for *The Medium Is the Masseuse*.
		1982	PA and TA returned to Bali to show participants footage of *The Medium Is the Masseuse*.
		1983, 1984	Linda Connor returned to Bali: discussions with Jero about the massage footage.
Flores	1980		Filming ritual in Tana Wai Brama.
		1982, 1983	Informant feedback work on all footage.
		1984–1985	Pius Ipir Wai Brama visited Canberra to assist with informant feedback, transcription and translation, and editing.

saw its full development in the Yanomamö films. For Asch, sequence filming was both a method of filming in the field and a type of film useful for teaching and research (see Fox, this volume). A *Celebration of Origins* was edited largely by condensing our footage of sequences that were part of this event. The importance of filming sequences lay in its usefulness in ethnographic research: sequence filming was the most effective way to get research data because actions are placed in a social context. Asch also showed that sequences were valuable pedagogical tools because they were brief and could be embedded in a lecture or used to stimulate discussion, and because they encouraged students to compare similar sequences from different societies and contexts as a way of making sense of what they were seeing.

Many of us who use Asch's films in teaching have come to realize that these short films which focus on single activities may be more important, both anthropologically and in the history of ethnographic cinema, than the "blockbuster" films such as *The Feast* and *The Ax Fight*. While the idea of sequences grew out of Asch's early experience of working with John Marshall's footage of the Ju/'hoansi, these films may be Asch's most important contribution to the cinematic anthropology he spent half a lifetime building. Tim himself spoke of the Yanomamö sequence films, such as A *Father Washes His Children* (1974), as important for countering the stereotype of the Yanomami as the "fierce people" and as balancing films such as *The Feast* and *The Ax Fight*, which dwelt upon violent elements in Yanomamö life. As Tim well knew, fierceness was a part of the Yanomamö ethos, but it was not the whole story. In the sequence films, Tim contributed to a much more rounded image of the Yanomamö than had Chagnon, his collaborator, in the earliest editions of

Yanomamö: The Fierce People in the Holt, Rinehart and Winston Case Studies in Anthropology series.

Asch was a brilliant event film-maker and all of his Indonesia films focus on performances of particular ritual events or, like *The Water of Words*, include footage of such events. Because of the shared theoretical orientation of the anthropologists who were his collaborators (or perhaps because his collaborators had the Aschs in common), the films address a number of closely related problems in the ethnographic study of ritual, myth, and religion. Asch's Indonesian work thus ranks among the most coherent corpora of ethnographic films on any region in the world.

Asch's method as an anthropologist and film-maker was to combine programmed filming based on his collaborator's theoretical and ethnological interests with opportunistic filming of events which arose in the life of the community in which he worked.[10] There are advantages and disadvantages to this method. Opportunistic filming can produce a valuable record of the serendipitous events which inform social life and the surprising ethnographic results that mark the best of exploratory science. But editing film made in this way can present unusual challenges and problems. While footage of events is, as Asch argued, unquestionably superior to scripted footage as a source of data and information for ethnographic research, how, for example, can a film for general screening, which must tell or narrate a *story* of some kind, be created from essentially unplanned shooting? Shooting in this way can make production a joy but post-production a nightmare. If the evolution of an event is taken to provide a "plot", what can a film editor do when the shots required to establish and contextualize a sequence are not to be found in the corpus of footage? This was certainly a recurring problem for Patsy Asch as she struggled to make editorial sense and maximum use of the Indonesia footage available for cutting. Over the years in which they produced the Indonesia films, she and Tim developed a number of innovative stylistic devices that are common to all of the films in the series to overcome these post-production problems. They include the use of supplementary still photographs in a number of situations to overcome problems generated by shortages of pertinent footage. Many of the films employ still photographs under closing titles and also in the body of the films as well. In *A Balinese Trance Seance*, stills are used under narration, as cutaways, as a bridge over sound for which there is no image, and to establish the film-makers' identity and their location with respect to subjects in the film. A good example of the last device is in the opening sequence of three shots in *Jero on Jero*. The first shot (without title) is a still close-up of Jero, over which appears the main title ("*Jero on Jero: A Balinese Trance Seance Observed*"). The title disappears and the still of Jero resolves into a moving image of Jero speaking animatedly. As she turns and throws up her right hand, the frame freezes as another still. This entire but brief sequence is accompanied by the sound of Jero speaking. The second shot is a still photograph of Jero's house compound taken from a tree outside the compound walls under the title "In 1978 we filmed a trance séance held at the home of a Balinese spirit medium, Jero Tapakan".[11] The third shot is of Tim, Arriflex on his shoulder in his typical pose of triangularly braced arms, filming Jero and Linda Connor as they watch a video monitor. The title over this still reads, "Two years later we brought Jero to a neighboring town to view a videocassette of the completed film, 'A Balinese Trance Seance.'" The accompanying sound is of Patsy Asch who, as sound recordist, whispered into her microphone, "October seventeenth, nineteen eighty, ten twenty a.m". The result is an astonishingly effective and extremely elegant lead-in to the main sequences of the film.

In *A Celebration of Origins*, Patsy labored to introduce the main characters in the *gren mahé* rites in order to establish their positions in the community and relationships to one another. We had good stills and moving images of all the characters except Mo'an Rapa Ipir Wai Brama, the old Source of the Domain and ritual leader of the community who had died the year before we filmed. We wanted to introduce Mo'an Rapa as the initiating force behind the *gren* and as the man whose position in the community was assumed by two other ritual specialists in the events we filmed. When I ransacked my collection of photographs from my 1978–79 fieldwork, I was surprised to find that I had very few photographs of Mo'an Rapa, who had been one of my main friends, supporters, and informants during my first two years of fieldwork in Tana Wai Brama. I did have a good series of photographs of Mo'an Rapa's burial in 1979. Patsy intercut pictures from that series to very good effect in the part of the film devoted to introducing him. Indeed, the photographs of his burial served to establish Rapa as an historical figure while the black-and-white portrait of him which I had used as the frontispiece to my book *People of the Source* established him as a ghostly presence behind the rites we filmed with, to my mind, considerable efficacy.[12]

To my knowledge, no one has commented in print on the humorous and occasional comic elements in Tim Asch's films. There are many, and they sometimes produce a somewhat uncomfortable reaction in his audiences.[13] I have experienced this reaction of students in using his films in teaching. Audiences of ethnographic films, and especially, it seems, students, expect ethnographic film to be rigidly serious. It thus comes as something of a shock (the shock of the funny?) to be confronted with humor in an ethnographic film. Beyond the confounding of expectation lies another, more serious difficulty, and that is a reluctance to laugh while viewing such a film: after all, one should not laugh at people, especially if, as a student, one has been inculcated with the idea of cultural relativism. What is funny to *us* might not be funny to *them* and, in any case, it is not nice to laugh at people. While this is true, Tim Asch occasionally invites his audience to laugh *with* his film subjects and I find it a shame that audiences of the Indonesia films frequently do not take up his invitation. Many film-makers would leave out such incidents as Jero's clients tape recording the séance or humorous moments in *A Celebration of Origins*, such as the confusion over a goat's sex. The goat sacrificed in the *gren mahé* so that the success of the rites can be divined should be a billy goat, but the goat at hand during the divination was a nanny goat. The ever-resourceful ritualists of Tana 'Ai neatly solved this impasse, in the following exchange:

UNIDENTIFIED MAN: Bring the she-goat.
SINA: Two nights ago

Gati and Bago said
that goat would be [a]
black and white [billy goat],
and now I see it
for myself.
If you cut the she-goat
and cut a small pig,
that's the same as a he-goat.

UNIDENTIFIED MAN: This is now a male goat.

SINA: It will remove our sins.

One may think that ritual is serious business, but the expressions of good-humored exasperation visible on the faces of his fellow ritualists as they react to Sina's *ad hoc* pronouncement indicate otherwise. And then there is Pak Mias Kiuk smiling impishly into Asch's camera, the better to instruct his unseen audience about the source of Rotinese superiority: "Even though we only drink lontar juice, our brains are like gold," he declaims. Asch and his collaborators on the Indonesia films have left in moments such as these, and to good cinematic and ethnographic effect. Humor is reflexivity: participants standing back momentarily to reflect on paradoxes and occasionally on minor absurdities of their own actions (and sometimes the actions of the film-makers). Such moments help to de-exoticize the films' subjects, a problem about which Tim Asch worried from the beginning of his career as a film-maker, and to establish the common humanity between the sometimes alien-looking people on screen and the audience.[14]

There are other elements of style that clearly identify the Indonesia films as Asch productions. Tim has written of the annoying but unavoidable "vignetting" in close-up wide-angle shots in the Bali footage caused by the lens he used on the Arriflex camera in shooting all the Indonesia footage. But close-up was for Tim an important element in shooting which he used partly as a means of focusing attention on a subject and partly because of the intimacy with his subjects that close-ups provide the audience. In all cases, this element in Asch's work relates to his consistent inclinations to establish the identities of his films' subjects as fully as possible and to engender rapport between the subjects and the films' audiences.

Frequently, the close-ups Tim filmed were of hands doing things, a technique which other film-makers have also employed. Not all such shots have been incorporated in films for release, but those that have include Mo'an Koa's hands rolling a lontar-leaf cigarette in *Mula Puda*, Jero's hand motions in the séance, and the hands of the musician plucking the strings of the Rotinese *sesandu* in one of the final shots in *The Water of Words*.

The results of informant feedback are incorporated in the Bali and Tana Wai Brama films and, to a lesser extent in *The Water of Words*, in which Mias Kiuk is interviewed on film (not about the footage, but about the film's subject). Feedback involves taking footage back to the community in which it was shot, showing it to participants in the filmed events and others, and recording (sometimes on film) the participants' comments, exegeses, and explanations of what was going on in the film. The method is especially useful for an anthropologist when dealing with ritual. First, it provides fine-grained information about ritual action and the social relations which ritual action manifests, which might otherwise be missed. Second, it helps the ethnographer separate the contingent from the exigent in ritual and thereby better to define what makes an event a ritual. It also helps to identify the extent to which the personalities of the performers give a ritual its character. In all the rituals in the Indonesia films, the intimacy and the personalities of the participants invite a close examination of the phenomenology of spirituality in Indonesia.

Perhaps most importantly, from the viewpoint of making films for release, recording informant feedback provides the film-maker with a means of locating the anthropologist and film-makers themselves in the filmed event. The purpose of this location is not merely to celebrate the anthropologist, nor to authenticate the film. The relationship of the anthropologist and film-maker to their subjects becomes an important scientific datum, one which allows for a check on the subject event itself. The information gained through feedback also serves the important end of indexing the significance and reliability of the information presented in the primary corpus of film by allowing participants themselves to comment on both the film and the events it depicts.

In the opening shots of *Jero on Jero* and in the fight sequence toward the end of *A Celebration of Origins* we see Patsy Asch taking sound. Whereas many film-makers would cut accidental intrusions of the film-makers into the film frame, the Aschs intentionally included a few such intrusions in the Bali and Flores films to establish the film-makers' identity and location with respect to their subjects and the filmed events, but without belaboring the point. In every case, the presence of the film-makers/anthropologists is presented as an element in the situation within which the event being filmed evolves.

A Balinese Trance Seance and *Jero on Jero* are exceptional films in this respect. Not only do the two films reflect upon the séance which is their subject, but they present the relationship between anthropologist and her subject (Connor and Jero) in some detail. More than that, they establish that *trance* is a category of action in Bali and is addressable by an anthropologist in collaboration with her subject. The films thus serve to refute those who nowadays make claims about the impossibility of anthropology ever comprehending the subjectivities of cultural experience. These films, which in my view should always be screened in tandem, are both an instance of reflexivity and a good example of second-order analysis in which the text of the subject becomes the subject of a further text.

If *Jero on Jero* is meta-film-making, at the end of *Jero on Jero* we get a glimpse of meta-meta-film-making: Linda Connor turns to Patsy Asch and expresses her delight at the results of the session with Jero: "That was," she remarks with some animation, "just fantastic. Just incredible!"

A single stylistic, thematic, and anthropological thread connects all of the Indonesia films and links them to Tim Asch's earlier work. Asch has written that:

I prefer not to film with the intention of editing a documentary that paints a broad canvas to show a culture in one hour, as many have done. An hour-long film is unlikely to reveal the complexities of a group's social relationships.

(Asch 1986: 42)

In a sense, Asch thought that "culture" was something that cannot be filmed. It follows that a film which "depicts a culture" cannot be made. What can be filmed are people doing things with each other. The focus is thus necessarily upon interaction and social relationships, which can be filmed. "Culture" is, then, not a thing in the phenomenal world, but a perspective on individuals, their actions, and interactions with others. Culture is, in other words, a *theory of* observable (and filmable) action, interactions, and events. One films individuals; one communicates the identity of those individuals through film editing and montage; and one constructs an explanation (or understanding) of those things as a culture. *Jero on Jero* is not about Balinese culture; it is about Jero, a Balinese *balian* (healer). We learn of Bali through what we learn of Jero as a person; to the extent that we have done so, we are in a position to construct a theory of Bali – i.e. a set of ideas to which we can refer as "Balinese culture". In *Jero on Jero*, we see the anthropologist and her informant, who is also the subject of a previous film, constructing that culture through negotiations revolving around the interpretation of images common (and commonly available in the "public domain") to both the anthropologist and subject. Put simply, we see the anthropologist at work. And we see how it is that ethnography is not simply subjective reportage, something akin to writing novels.

The Indonesia corpus as ethnological films

In 1935, the Dutch ethnologist F. A. E. van Wouden wrote that myth, ritual, and social structure are the main axes around which society turns in that region of Indonesia the Dutch call the *Groote Oost*, the archipelagos of east and south-east Indonesia. The societies of the region, in which we can certainly include Bali, are an identifiable sub-set of the great Austronesian culture complex. The ceremonial systems of the Lesser Sunda Islands and the various rituals which make up the ceremonial systems are similar to a degree sufficient for useful comparisons. Bali is a significant counterpoint to these ceremonial systems. Despite the overlay of religious ideas traceable to India and a social organization which has incorporated elements of Indian society such as caste (albeit with a considerably different force and result), Bali retains social and cultural affinities with the islands of the archipelagos to the east.[15] The Island of Bali is thus a significant ethnological counterpoint to the eastern islands and serves always to remind the anthropologist of the sometimes profound effects of historical events and alien influences on culture and society. In all of these islands, ritual is at once a dramatic and photogenic field of social activity and a problem of considerable ethnological significance.

The main focus in the Indonesia films is on ritual in all three of the societies that the films address. Myth, ritual, cosmology, and religion have been topics of abiding interest among anthropologists since the days of the earliest Dutch interest in the ethnology of eastern Indonesia and the work of van Wouden (1968 [1935]). These topics have been foci of the research of all three of Asch's collaborators in Indonesia.[16] There was a congruence of anthropological interests and concerns among the three of us, and all of us, including Asch, came out of a strongly empirical tradition of ethnography. It is perhaps because of the intellectual links among Asch's collaborators that the differences between the three societies in which he filmed emerge clearly in the films; the differences in the film ethnographies reflect accurately differences among the three societies.

Edmund Leach once remarked that ritual is not a kind of action, but an element, present to a greater or lesser degree, in all human action. This proposition is abundantly established in Tim Asch's Indonesia films. The films address a variety of different rituals in eastern Indonesia and aspects of ritual which are found in a range of activities in the societies treated in the films. In the case of *The Water of Words*, traces and evocations of ritual are explicated in what, for the Rotinese, are the most mundane of subsistence activities.

In eastern Indonesia, ritual addresses a number of different concerns. There are throughout the region life-cycle rituals (including initiation and other rites of passage), garden rituals, and what may be termed rituals of the domain. Not all are found in every society of the region, nor are the details of performance the same from one society to another. Asch's Indonesia cycle includes film of life-cycle rituals (a funeral on Roti, which has yet to be made into a film, the second-stage mortuary rites of the late Source of the Domain of Tana Wai Brama which will be included in a future film of the Tana 'Ai series, and *Spear and Sword*, which is about a Rotinese bridewealth exchange). *A Celebration of Origins* is about the rituals of the domain of Wai Brama.[17] Missing from the corpus is footage of garden rites, which would be an excellent subject of future filming in eastern Indonesia. The Balinese films treat a trance séance, in which the spirits of ancestors and deities are addressed (a theme also present in the rituals of Tana Wai Brama), a massage (an example of curing rites, which are also found in eastern Indonesia), and a cremation (a step in a protracted complex of mortuary rites, also a feature of some eastern Indonesian death cycles, such as in Tana Wai Brama).

Among the three societies which are the subjects of the Indonesia films, those of Roti and Tana Wai Brama bear the closest similarities, on linguistic, historical, and social-structural grounds. These two societies are "mutually interpretable" (P. E. de Josselin de Jong 1980) and, taken together, form a point of comparison with Bali. Nevertheless, differences between Roti and Tana Wai Brama are abundantly illustrated in the films. As Fox has described them and as the films depict them, the Rotinese are indifferent ritualists among whom oratory is of paramount importance on ceremonial occasions, on which participants frequently call upon knowledgeable elders to recite ritual language, the special poetical register of language in which myths are narrated. In Tana Wai Brama, ritual is important in itself and ritual language is an inherent part of ritual performance. In this society, formal oratory is less common than in Rotinese ceremonial situations; when it occurs, it punctuates proceedings when ritualists must negotiate the next step in a ceremony, a feature of ritual illustrated in A *Celebration of Origins*.

Ethnology, the systematic comparison of ethnographic data from different societies, operates at two levels. First, it seeks to identify and to explain the commonalities, continuities, and similarities of social structure, the forms of ritual, and the themes of myth which are found between societies in what J. P. B. de Josselin de Jong (1935) called an *ethnologisch studieveld*, a "field of ethnological study". Second, it seeks to identify, analyze, and explain the manifest differences between societies. In other words, ethnology studies both the unique and contingent in specific societies and those features of society and culture which societies share and about which generalizations can be made, which hold for all the societies within a defined culture complex.

In terms of these twin concerns of ethnology, each series of Asch's Indonesia films are *ethnographic* films which explore the details of life in particular communities while, taken as a corpus of work, they can be said to be *ethnological* films which invite formal comparison. Such corpora of mutually interpretive films are exceedingly rare in anthropology. Indeed, the Indonesia films may be the only case in the history of anthropological film-making of an ethnographic cinematographer working with three anthropologists in three societies of a single-culture complex. The result has been the creation of a body of ethnological work which may well be unique in anthropology and is certainly of extraordinary value.

Tim Asch has written:

> In order to make ethnographic film that is both tied to research and technically adequate to produce instructional films for others, collaboration between an ethnographically trained film-maker and an anthropologist is probably the best strategy. ... For example, Jero does not know the nature of her clients' problem in A *Balinese Trance Seance*, but they have come to contact the spirit of their dead son and the audience can see how their purpose slowly emerges and how, in the process, they are drawn into new concerns. In *Jero on Jero* it becomes clear that Linda has specific topics she wants to cover but that Jero is interested in quite different issues. The audience, like the participants, needs to work through the event to make sense of it. In a general film about a culture the audience need not work through anything; images are presented to them with a packaged presentation.
>
> (Asch 1986: 42)

The Water of Words is the closest Asch came in his Indonesian work to the "broad canvas" to show the whole of a culture. Even so, the film has a determined focus on myth, mythic narration, and ecology. It is not a "culture in an hour"; it is, rather, in the spirit of Marcel Mauss, the depiction of a total social fact. The film treats a paradox: Rotinese on film say they live on the lontar palm, but the images of Roti and its people in the film clearly show rice cultivation (wet rice in the opening shot), vegetable gardening, and women fishing with small nets in tidal pools at the beach; elsewhere, an abundance of pigs and chickens in evidence.

The film begins with a voice-over introduction of two Rotinese men:

> Two Rotinese narrate this film. The one a poet and story teller, the other a clan headman and local leader. Each presents a view of life on the island and speaks of the importance of the lontar palm. The clan headman, Mias Kiuk, is a practical man, full of wit and humor. His speech is direct, but he enjoys exaggerating to emphasize his views. The poet, Petrus Malesi, is a ritual specialist. He draws on a diverse oral tradition, sometimes speaking in the paired language of poetry, sometimes in ordinary dialect.
>
> (J. Fox, voice-over narration, beginning of *The Water of Words*)

Thus, even in the most didactic of the Indonesia films, the narrative focus is upon individuals, the two men whose words in translation will narrate the film.

The film treats a single theme: Rotinese representations of the peculiar ecology of the island as expressed in ritual language and in commentaries by Rotinese on film. The film addresses an event, albeit not as a continuous flow of images: the tapping of lontar palms, the processing of the collected lontar juice, and the uses to which the Rotinese put the harvest of this unusual palm.

Fox has described Tim Asch's reaction to arriving on the island of Roti in 1977:

> Compared to the lush greens of Bali or Java, Roti was stark and bare. Worse still, there was nothing that resembled the ceremonies of the Kraton of Solo or the temple pageantry of Bali. Indeed, as I had warned Tim, the Rotinese are, for the most part, notable non-ritualists. ... Language is everything; performance counts for little. The challenge we faced was therefore to make a film about ritual where ritual is primarily verbal performance, not visual performance.
>
> (Fox, this volume)

The Water of Words is thus as much about language, specifically Rotinese ritual language, as it is about action. The results of Asch's willingness to film people speaking and Patsy Asch's experimentation with cutting film to speech rather than to action can clearly be seen in all of the Indonesia films, but most especially in *A Balinese Trance Seance* and *A Celebration of Origins*. And *Jero on Jero* is, of course, essentially a film about conversation.

On 6 August 1977, Asch and Fox shot footage of a bridewealth payment and its negotiation that would become the film *Spear and Sword*, which is also about ritual. In Fox's words:

> The bridewealth payment ceremony was an easily circumscribed event and certainly showed the way Rotinese talk themselves through ceremonies. ...

The film itself follows closely what we recorded and we had only to fill in the gaps that occurred when the camera was not running but the tape recorder remained on. The film conveys the seriousness of such ritual negotiations as well as their humor. It also makes evident the ordinary reality behind high-sounding "ritual frames", such as "Spear and Sword". Clearly, the participants were enlivened by the presence of the camera and tape recorder but negotiations retained their usual character. By the time drinking began, the self-consciousness of the performance diminished.

(Fox, this volume)

Unlike Savu or Tana Wai Brama, ritual events are relatively rare on Roti, a society which places a higher value on oratory than on ostension (Fox 1979). It was perhaps for this reason that *The Water of Words* is unique among the Indonesia films in that it is not about a single event (ritual or otherwise), but is a synthetic depiction of two interrelated themes in Rotinese life: myth (which is communicated in speech), and the ecology of the island and the peculiar economy of its people (see Fox, this volume).

I have heard Tim express dissatisfaction with *The Water of Words*. But to my mind, it is a superb film, both aesthetically and for teaching. The sharp, direct, unshadowed, and overwhelming light, which Fox reports Asch remarked upon when he arrived on Timor, and the starkness and barrenness of the Rotinese landscape filmed beautifully. If the light quality on Roti was a shock to Asch, it is visually unexpected for an audience who, knowing Roti is in Indonesia, might come to the film expecting landscapes reminiscent of the verdant central islands. The opening sequence of a lone horseman riding across a broken, almost desert-like savanna with a sapphire sea in the background (see Figure 5.2) makes an indelible visual impression and alerts audiences to an Indonesia beyond Java and Bali. Perhaps it is the starkness of the landscape and the harshness of the light that make the richness of Rotinese social life and thought stand out in high relief from the landscape in which they take place and which they address.[18]

While *The Water of Words* is not constructed as one of the vacuous "culture in an hour" films which Asch himself derided, it nevertheless provides its audience with sufficient information about Rotinese society and culture to contextualize meaningfully the specific events the film depicts, a contextualization that Asch argued can be fully provided only through written ethnography. In this respect, the film is excellent for teaching, not only because Fox's voluminous writings on the Rotinese are available for collateral study, but also as a general introduction to the dry tropics of Indonesia. Its focus on language, myth, and indigenous representations of life make it eminently useful for comparison with other peoples of eastern Indonesia. I must confess, *The Water of Words* is perhaps my favorite among Asch's Indonesia films.[19]

One of the most salutary things the Indonesia films teaches us about eastern Indonesia, a lesson that has profound implications for the anthropological study of ritual, is that ritual is by no means habitual action, the outcomes of which are certain to the extent that ritual form is followed. *Spear and Sword: A Ceremonial Payment of Bridewealth* is a film largely about talking. More than that, it is about speech, the formal and ritualized speech of negotiations between two Rotinese clans as it is employed in the negotiation of a payment of bridewealth. Here, the defining feature of a ceremonial occasion is the uncertainty of its outcome and the contingent actions of its participants in constructing the outcome. The "spear and sword" of the film's title and "the rope of the spear and sword" ("The rope consists of money and small animals" [film narration]) are two of a series of payments over a span of time which make up a complete bridewealth transaction. As in Sikka on the island of Flores, the larger payment (bridewealth) consists of smaller gifts negotiated and given over as a sequence of *prestations*. Elements of each gift are interchangeable (" … we have added money instead of seven goats," says one of the negotiators in *Spear and Sword*) and the monetary value of each animal must be negotiated and agreed. Then, because there are more billy goats than nanny goats making up the six to be given in lieu of cash, a fine must be paid. The fine is the subject of further negotiation and agreement between the two sides. Then, from a man speaking for the husband's people, comes one of the clearest possible statements of Rotinese ideas about gender and the complementarity of symbolic classifications:

MALESI: What if, what if the goats are mostly male?
[MAN FROM WOMAN'S SIDE]: *Then you must pay a fine, even though males give good fortune.*
[MAN FROM HUSBAND'S SIDE]: Increase comes from males.
[MAN FROM WOMAN'S SIDE]: *Everything comes from males.*
If there were no males the earth would be empty.
Without males the earth would not conceive.
What we're doing here [the bridewealth negotiation] *would never happen.*
If there were only women:
Who would take whom? Who would know whom?
From females and males comes everything good.
Put the two together.
[MAN FROM HUSBAND'S SIDE]: Like chewing betel and areca.[20]

Conceptions of *adat* (Bahasa Indonesia: "custom, tradition, propriety") in relation to Christianity are a point of reference in the negotiations. As in *A Celebration of Origins*, the conceptual separation of *adat* and Christianity arises in the course of the ritual. While the two sides share a meal to mark their agreement, conversation continues and the following exchange between the husband's representatives (non-italics) and the wife's representatives (italics) occurs:

We have to pray.
We can't!
And it's adat not to pray.
Adat stands between darkness and light so there is no praying.
But now we follow Christian adat.

Whether Christian or not, this is Rotinese adat.[21]

Clearly, however, what is *adat* is apparently itself the subject of negotiation. This film raises a very interesting question: if the ritual consists, as it does in this Rotinese bridewealth ceremony, of the negotiated construction of the event, then what is ritual? The same problem arises out of the footage of A *Celebration of Origins* in which the performance of a series of rites is punctuated by meetings of ritual specialists in which they negotiate (and sometimes quarrel about) the next steps in the ritual.

Conclusion

Anthropologists face a difficult problem. Open any introductory textbook on anthropology and somewhere on the first page you will be told (as are thousands of university students every year) that anthropology is the study of culture or society – or something semantically equivalent. But this is not, strictly speaking, what anthropologists study at all. Anthropologists study what they record of life in a community, and life anywhere consists of people doing things. The records themselves commonly consist of written field notes, photographs, sound recordings, film, and video.

The difficulty with the textbooks' claim is that culture and society exist as noumena rather than as phenomena. Their ontology does not mean they cannot be known, but it does mean that they cannot be filmed.

Tim Asch's Indonesia films are good examples of films which focus on people doing things of significance in their own societies and cultures. It might be said that all anthropological films are of people doing things, but in Indonesia Tim focused on events, i.e. people doing things in situations they themselves define as happenings of a named and recurring type. Tim Asch is not the only film-maker to have focused on individuals and events, but he helped form what has come to be widely recognized in the discipline of anthropology as a most useful way of making ethnographic films. In the case of the Indonesia films, five events in three societies are taken as the subjects of five of the eight films. All are rituals: the *gren mahé* of Tana Wai Brama (A *Celebration of Origins*), a trance séance in Bali (A *Balinese Trance Seance*), a curing ritual in Bali (*The Medium is the Masseuse*), a ceremonial nogotiation of bridewealth on Roti (*Spear and Sword*), and a village cremation in Bali (*Releasing the Spirits*). Two of the remaining three films are about Jero Tapakan, one of Linda Connor's main informants in Bali and a principal subject in all the Bali films. *The Water of Words* does not deal with a single event or person, as do the other films, but looks didactically and synthetically at events of a number of different kinds (mainly lontar-palm tapping and gardening). The film is held together through the words of two men, Mias Kiuk and Petrus Malesi, who, like Jero and the ritualists of Tana Wai Brama, are both subjects and narrators of the film.

How are these subjects located, if not in culture? As much as possible through the translation of their own words. But this is never entirely sufficient because words must be fully contextualized to be understood. Rather than setting the events he filmed into possibly spurious cultures, Asch contextualized the action on film by making clear the interactions of subjects and their interactions with the anthropologist and film-maker. In this way, Asch avoids the logical circularity of many ethnographic films in which culture is assumed as animating peoples' actions, which are explained by their "culture". The *culture* in such films is often provided by a scripted "Voice of God" voice-over narration. Instead of attempting to film *culture*, Tim Asch's films on Indonesia identify *persons* who are seen on screen acting meaningfully in various events according to their individual intentions. In the interplay of person and event we do not see culture, but are instead provided with sufficient information to construct a culture as a theory of the persons, actions, and events we see and hear on film.

Thus, social persons, who are identified as agents in evolving events captured on film, are Asch's main cinematic subjects.

Notes

1 Asch and his collaborators not only employed the feedback technique successfully in the field. In the 1980s Fox and I brought two of our main informants (E. M. Pono from Roti and Pius Ipir Wai Brama from Flores) to Canberra to assist with the post-production analysis of the Roti and Tana 'Ai footage.

2 There is additional footage from the Roti filming expeditions which has not yet been edited for release. It is possible that two additional films on Roti can be made, one on a church service and one to be called *A Death in a Clan* (Fox, this volume). Two additional films about Tana 'Ai ritual were in post-production at the time of Asch's death. These were tentatively titled *Mula Puda. A Tana 'Ai Child Exchange* and *To Retire the Flesh and Cool the Blood. The Likon Rites of the Ata Tana 'Ai*. Patsy Asch and I also planned a fourth film to treat the theme of boundaries in the thought and culture of the Ata Tana 'Ai.

3 See Chapter 6, this volume.

4 See Chapter 6, this volume.

5 There is a danger of confounding concepts here: early in his career Asch became interested in filming natural sequences of human activity (Moore 1995: 39) and he often spoke of the need to film complete sequences for research. Many of the Yanomamö films are of sequences: *A Father Washes His Children*, *Climbing the Peach Palm*, *Firewood*, *Weeding the Garden* and *Tug of War* are good examples. An event (see Lewis 1989) is an activity or occurrence that is named (i.e. it is a category in a culturally constituted classification of activities and occurrences) and is recognized as such by participants themselves. Events consist of activity sequences, but not all activity sequences are events. While Asch filmed activity sequences in the Indonesian societies in which he worked, most of these sequences occurred in the context of the events on which he focused, such as Jero's trance séance in *A Balinese Trance Seance*, the massage in *The Medium Is the Masseuse*, the bridewealth payment in *Spear and Sword*, and the rites of the *gren mahé* in *A Celebration of Origins*.

6 Much of the post-production work on many of these films was done at USC after Tim relocated to Los Angeles.

7 It is perhaps worth noting that Connor and I were still Ph.D. students when Asch shot the footage for the Bali and Tana 'Ai films. In both cases, Asch set out with the specific intention of filming events of central pertinence to our thesis research. The initial intention of Asch's collaboration with Professor James Fox was to film large-scale ceremonial contests on the island of Savu. When this project proved not to be feasible, they shifted their filming to Roti.

8 Asch later produced a short film on a Yanomami tug-of-war which contrasts interestingly with the Ju/ 'hoansi film of the same activity and there is footage from Roti of children playing tug-of-war.

9 *The Hunters*, which is about a giraffe hunt by four men, was made from footage of several hunts filmed in 1952–53. As Marshall has written, the film "celebrates hunting despite the fact that 80 percent of the people's food was derived from gathering bush foods" by both men and women (Marshall in Ruby [ed.] 1993: 233).

10 I have suggested (Chapter 6, this volume) that a better term than "opportunistic filming" for Tim's method would be "heuristic filming".

11 Tim Asch's penchant for climbing trees for location shots was a source of nervously humorous stories when his collaborators had occasion to meet after working with him. He laboriously cut foot notches into quite a tall tree in Tana Wai Brama, from which, perched in the high crotch of the tree, he filmed wonderful location shots of Watuwolon, the hamlet of ritual houses where we lived during production of the Tana 'Ai films (see Figures 6.3 and 6.4). I recall Napoleon Chagnon in 1986, years after the fact, complaining to me of the risks Tim took in climbing trees in Yanomamö country. With evident disappointment, Asch reported to me on one occasion that the Rotinese would not let him climb a lontar palm when he was in Termanu.

12 Tim Asch trained as a still photographer in his youth and, throughout his career as a film-maker and teacher, urged his students and colleagues to experiment with slide tapes as an inexpensive but highly effective replacement for film. He had no difficulty whatsoever in combining moving images with still frames, often with considerable impact.

13 Jay Ruby has perspicuously pointed out the subversive nature of The Ax Fight, citing the soundtrack which includes the following dialogue between Chagnon and Asch at the end of the first presentation of the footage of the fight:

ASCH: Did you figure out how many there were in the village?

CHAGNON: No. I haven't counted them yet – there are over 200 there. [He turns to talk to Moäwä in Yanomamö.] Aaah, that's about the tenth person today that's asked me for my soap.

ASCH: Tell him I'll give him my soap …

CHAGNON: No you won't give him your soap!

ASCH: … when I go home.

CHAGNON: They're going to make damn sure we leave in a hurry if we keep promising them everything when we go home.

ASCH: Shoriwä (brother-in-law), living in your village is going to be tiresome.

CHAGNON: Thought I was shitting you about the fierce people, huh?

Ruby notes that in this film and, in particular, its opening moments, "the conventions of documentary/ethnographic realism and the 'scientific' certainty of anthropological explanations are called into question" (Ruby 1995: 25). With this judgment I agree, but, as an ethnographer, I also think this is simply one of the funniest moments ever in ethnographic film.

To be sure, this incident is one which involves the anthropologists as much as the subjects of the film. Others involve the filmed subjects alone. For example, A Celebration of Origins includes a sequence in which an official from the local District Office, who is Sikkanese and not from Tana 'Ai, lectures the ritual specialists on how to proceed with the gren mahé rites. Florenese and other Indonesians who have seen the film think this sequence is quite hilarious. And so it is to Western viewers when they know that such officials, almost all of whom are Catholic, regularly lecture the mountain people on the wastefulness and general backwardness of their religious practices – with little effect.

14 The concern with humor and the difference between laughing at someone and laughing with someone is explicitly addressed in the as-yet-uncompleted second film about Tana 'Ai, Mula Puda, or, the Woman You Never See, in which the difficulties the Aschs and I encountered in keeping up with the events of a ceremonial child-exchange between two clans are exploited as a theme in the film and to explain gaps in our footage of the event.

15 Without underestimating the uniqueness of Balinese culture and social life, at a formal level Bali is perhaps more similar to the other Austronesian societies to the east than is commonly recognized. Bali has long been the subject of specialized anthropological investigation and "Baliologists" (as they are sometimes jokingly called), caught up in the intricacies of Balinese culture and pointing to the unique religious heritage of the island, tend to forget that the island's cultures and societies bear unmistakable affinities to other Indonesian societies. The work of at least one recent ethnographer, Dr Thomas Reuter of The University of Melbourne, will go a long way toward situating Bali in the larger field of comparative Austronesian ethnology (see Reuter 1998, 2002a, and 2002b).

16 I was a student of James J. Fox. Linda Connor's Ph.D. research and her thesis, In Darkness and Light: A Study of Peasant Intellectuals in Bali (University of Sydney, 1982), were supervised by Dr Douglas Miles.

17 Dr Michael P. Vischer, a Visiting Fellow of the Department of Anthropology, Research School of Pacific and Asian Studies, The Australian National University, is currently producing films on the rituals of the domain of Ko'a on Palu'é, an island off the north coast of Flores (Vischer 1996). The Palu'é footage will be an extremely useful complement to the gren mahé footage from Tana Wai Brama.

18 Two other scenes make this point. In the first, a man occupied by making a lontar-leaf basket converses with women cooking lontar syrup in the meager shade of a thinly-leafed acacia tree. The background is a washed-out and over-exposed whiteness. In the next scene, a man making a lontar-basket and a woman preparing areca nut squat in the narrow umbra of a tree trunk. The surrounding earth is in a cataract of

white light in which no details at all are visible and the man and women seem to be working on an island in the midst of a blinding sea of light.

19 Another element in the film's stylistic and aesthetic appeal is the superb English voice-over of translated Rotinese ritual language. The reader is Professor Wang Gung-Wu, who was, at the time of the film's production, Director of the Research School of Pacific Studies (now the Research School of Pacific and Asian Studies in The Australian National University and who later became Vice-Chancellor of the University of Hong Kong. Gung-Wu's voice and reading style are models for the narration of ethnographic films.

20 *Spear and Sword*, film subtitles.

21 *Spear and Sword*, film subtitles.

References

Asch, Timothy, 1986, "How and Why the Films Were Made". In Linda Connor, Patsy Asch, and Timothy Asch, *Jero Tapakan: Balinese Healer. An Ethnographic Film Monograph.* Cambridge: Cambridge University Press.

Asch, Timothy and James J. Fox, 1976, The Ceremonies of Savu: The Development of a Methodology for the Analysis of Large-Scale Ritual Performances via the use of Film and Video-Tape. Research proposal to the U. S. National Science Foundation (unpublished).

Connor, Linda, Patsy Asch and Timothy Asch, 1986, *Jero Tapakan, Balinese Healer: An Ethnographic Film Monograph.* Cambridge: Cambridge University Press.

Fox, James J., 1979, "The Ceremonial system of Savu". In A. Becker and A. A. Yengoyan (eds.), *The Imagination of Reality: Essays on Southeast Asian Coherence Systems*, pp. 145–73. Norwood, N.J.: Ablex Publishing Corporation.

Josselin de Jong, J. P. B. de, 1935, *De Maleische Archipel als Ethnologisch Studieveld.* Leiden: Universiteitsboekhandel en Antiquariaat J. Ginsberg.

Josselin de Jong, P. E. de, 1980, "The Concept of the Field of Ethnological Study". In J. J. Fox. Cambridge, Mass.: Harvard University Press.

Lewis, E. D., 1989, "Why Did Sina Dance? Stochasm, Choice, and Intentionality in the Ritual Life of the Ata Tana 'Ai of Eastern Flores". In Paul Alexander (ed.), *Creating Indonesian Cultures.* Oceania Ethnographies 3. Sydney: Oceania Publication.

Marks, Dan, 1995, "Ethnography and Ethnographic Film: From Flaherty to Asch and After". *American Anthropologist* 97 (2): 339–347.

Moore, Alexander, 1995, "Understanding Event Analysis: Using the Films of Timothy Asch". *Visual Anthropology Review* 11(1): 38–52.

Reuter, Thomas A., 1998, "The Banua of Pura Pucak and Penulisan: A Ritual Domain in the Highlands of Bali". *Review of Indonesian and Malaysian Affairs* 32 (1): 55–109.

— (2002a) *Custodians of the Sacred Mountains: Culture and Society in the Highlands of Bali.* Honolulu: University of Hawaii Press.

— (2002b) *The House of our Ancestors: Precedence and Dualism in Highland Balinese Society.* Verhandelingen Series. Leiden: KITLV Press.

Ruby, Jay, 1995, "Out of Sync: The Cinema of Tim Asch". *Visual Anthropology Review* 11 (1): 19–35.

Ruby, Jay (ed.), 1993, *The Cinema of John Marshall.* Chur: Harwood Academic Publishers.

Vischer, Michael P., 1996, *Contestations. Dynamics and Precedence in an Eastern Indonesian Domain.* Canberra: The Ethnographic Film Unit, Department of Anthropology Research School of Pacific and Asian Studies, The Australian National University. Video (55 minutes).

Wouden, F. A. E. van, 1968 [1935], *Types of Social Structure in Eastern Indonesia.* Rodney Needham (translator). The Hague: Martinus Nijhoff.

Appendix
Writings and films of Timothy Asch

E. D. Lewis

Published work and unpublished manuscripts

Asch, Timothy (1965), "A Proposal for Making Ethnographic Film". Paper presented at the American Anthropological Association annual meeting, New York.
—— (1967), "Comment" [in response to Sorenson], *Current Anthropology* 8 (5): 462–3.
—— (1968), "New Methods for Making and Using Ethnographic Film". Paper presented at the American Academy of Sciences, Washington DC.
—— (1971), "Ethnographic Film Production". *Film Comment* 7 (1): 40–2.
—— (1971), "Report from the Field: Filming the Yanomamo in Southern Venezuela". *Program in Ethnographic Film Newsletter* 3 (1): 3–5.
—— (1972), "Ethnographic Filming and the Yanomamo Indians". *Sightlines* 5 (3): 7–17.
—— (1972), "New Methods for Making and Using Ethnographic Film". Paper presented to the Research Film Committee, African Studies Association, Philadelphia. (Revision of Asch 1968.)
—— (1972), "Making Ethnographic Film for Teaching and Research". *Program in Ethnographic Film Newsletter* 3 (2): 6–10.
—— (1974), "Audiovisual Materials in the Teaching of Anthropology From the Elementary School Through College". In George D. Spindler (ed.), *Education and Cultural Process: Toward an Anthropology of Education*. New York: Holt, Rinehart and Winston, pp. 463–90.
—— (1974), "New Methods for Making and Using Ethnographic Film". In George D. Spindler (ed.), *Education and Cultural Process: Toward an Anthropology of Education*. New York: Holt, Rinehart and Winston, pp. 463–90.
—— (1975), "Using Film in Teaching Anthropology: One Pedagogical Approach". In Paul Hockings (ed.), *Principles of Visual Anthropology*. The Hague: Mouton, pp. 385–420.
—— (1979), "Making a Film Record of the Yanomamo Indians of Southern Venezuela". *Perspectives on Film* 2 (August): 4–9, 44–9. University Park: The Pennsylvania State University.
—— (1979), "Report from The Australian National University on First Stage of Comparative Ethnographic Filming in Indonesia". *SAVICOM Newsletter* 7 (3): 5–8.
—— (1982), "Collaboration in Ethnographic Film Making: A Personal View". *Canberra Anthropology* 5 (1): 8–36.
—— (1982), "Ethnographic Film: Its Theory and Application". Anthropology News (Proceedings of the Anthropological Society of Western Australia) 19 (4): 53–6.
—— (1983), Review of *To Find the Baruya Story*, *American Anthropologist* 85 (3): 751–2.

—— (1983), Review of *Her Name Came on Arrows*, *American Anthropologist* 85 (3): 752–3.

—— (1985), "Introduction". In Jacques Lizot, *Tales of the Yanomami: Daily Life in the Vene-zuelan Forest*. Cambridge: Cambridge University Press.

(1986), "Report from Beijing: The Commission for Visual Anthropology and the University of Southern California's Collaboration with China's Central Institute of Nationalities". *SVA Newsletter* 2 (1): 2–3.

—— (1986), "How and Why the Films Were Made". In Linda Connor, Patsy Asch and Timothy Asch, *Jero Tapakan: Balinese Healer. An Ethnographic Film Monograph.* Cambridge and New York: Cambridge University Press, pp. 39–53. (Reissued in Connor, Asch, and Asch [1996].)

—— (1987), "Film Biography and the Translation of Culture". *Arts and Artisans: A Celebration of the Margaret Mead Festival.* A monograph to accompany a film exposition and exhibit traveling throughout the United States in 1987, 1988, and 1989.

—— (1988), "Film in Anthropological Research". In Paul Hockings and Yasuhiro Omori (eds.), *Cinematographic Theory and New Dimensions in Ethnographic Film*. Senri Ethnological Studies No. 24. Osaka: National Museum of Ethnology, pp. 165–89.

—— (1988), "Collaboration in Ethnographic Filmmaking: A Personal View". In Jack R. Rollwagen (ed.), *Anthropological Filmmaking: Anthropological Perspectives on the Production of Film and Video for General Public Audiences.* Chur: Harwood Academic Publishers, pp. 1–29. (Revision of *Canberra Anthropology* 1982 paper.)

—— (1989), "L'uso del film nella didattica dell'antropologia". *Il Nuovo Spettatore* 12: 99–115.

—— (1989), "Cuyagua (Devil Dancers and The Saint with Two Faces)". *Visual Anthropology* 2 (3 & 4): 210–12.

—— (1991), "Sequence Filming and the Representation of Culture". Unpublished manuscript (version dated 2 February 1991).

—— (1991), "Das Filmen in Sequenzen und die Darstellung von Kultur (Sequence Filming and the Representation of Culture)". In Reinhard Kapfer, Werner Petermann, and Ralph Thoms (eds.), *Jäger und Gejagte: John Marshall und seine Filme*. München: Trickster Verlag, pp. 123–34.

—— (1991), "The Defense of Yanomami Society and Culture: Its Importance and Significance". *La Iglesia Amazonas*, XII No. 53: 35–8.

—— (1992), "The Ethics of Ethnographic Film-making". In Peter Ian Crawford and David Turton (eds.), *Film as Ethnography*. Manchester: Manchester University Press, pp. 196–204.

—— (1992), "Bias in Ethnographic Reporting: A Personal Example from the Yanomamo Ethnography". Paper delivered 14 September at the Royal Anthropological Institute Film Festival, Manchester, UK.

—— (1992), "J'enseigne L'anthropologie". In *"Cinem-Actions – Demain, le Cinéma Ethnographique?"* Paris: Corlet-Telerama, pp. 122–7.

—— (1992), "La Formacion de Antropologos Visuales". *Fundamentos de Anthropologia.* Grenada: Centro de Investigaciones Etnologicas, pp. 114–21.

—— (1993), "Films on the Yanomamo Indians of Southern Venezuela by Napoleon Chagnon and Timothy Asch". Ms.

—— (1993), Bias in Ethnographic Reporting and Using the Yanomamo Films in Teaching". In Timothy Asch and Gary Seaman (eds.), *Yanomamo Film Study Guide*. Los Angeles: Ethnographics Press, University of Southern California, pp. 1–12.

At the time of his death Tim Asch and Patsy Asch had begun work on a collection of his essays, which were to be revised and published as a book. The collection carried the working title *Film and Anthropology* and included the following chapters:

Asch, Timothy and Patsy Asch
"Introduction".
Asch, Timothy
"Development of a Methodology for Ethnographic Filming".
"Ethics". (Expanded version of Asch, "The Ethics of Ethnographic Film-making", 1992 and Asch *et al.* "'The Story We Now Want to Hear Is Not Ours to Tell' – Relinquishing Control over Representation. Toward Sharing Visual Communication Skills with the Yanomami," 1991.)
"Collaboration". (Article first published as "Collaboration in Ethnographic Film Making: A Personal View" in *Canberra Anthropology* 5 [1982], with revisions.)
"Film in Anthropological Research". (Based on "Film in Anthropological Research". In Paul Hockings and Yasuhiro Omori [eds], *Cinematic Theory and New Dimensions in Ethnographic Film.* Senri Ethnological Studies No. 24. Osaka: National Museum of Ethnology, pp. 165–89. 1988.)
"Bias: A Personal Example from the Yanomamo Ethnography". (First drafted in 1982 or 1983 and subsequently published in different forms in 1992 and 1993.)
"Teaching".

Co-authored writings

Asch, Timothy and Patsy Asch (1987), "Images That Represent Ideas: The Use of Films on the !Kung to Teach Anthropology". In Megan Biesele, Robert Gordon, and Richard B. Lee (eds.), *The Past and Future of !Kung Ethnography: Critical Reflections and Symbolic Perspectives.* Hamburg: Helmut Buske Verlag, pp. 327–58.
—— (1988), "Film in Anthropological Research". In Paul Hockings and Yasuhiro Omori (eds.), *Cinematographic Theory and New Dimensions in Ethnographic Film.* Senri Ethnological Studies No. 24. Osaka: National Museum of Ethnology, pp. 165–89.
—— (1995), "Film in Ethnographic Research". In Paul Hockings (ed.), *Principles of Visual Anthropology.* Second edition. Berlin: Mouton de Gruyter, pp. 335–60.
Asch, Timothy, Patsy Asch, and Linda Connor (1980), "*A Balinese Trance Seance.* Ethnography for the Film". Watertown, Massachusetts: Documentary Educational Resources.
—— (1981), "*Jero on Jero: A Balinese Trance Seance* Observed (Jero Tapakan Series)". Watertown, Massachusetts: Documentary Educational Resources.
Asch, Timothy, Jesus Ignacio Cardozo, Hortensia Caballero, and Jose Bortoli (1991),"The Story We Now Want to Hear Is Not Ours to Tell – Relinquishing Control over Representation. Toward Sharing Visual Communication Skills with the Yanomami". *Visual Anthropology Review* 7 (2): 102–6.
Asch, Timothy, John Marshall, and Peter Spier (1975), "Ethnographic Film: Structure and Function". *Annual Review of Anthropology* 2: 179–87.
Asch, Timothy, Jay Ruby and Carroll Williams (1970), "Notes on Anthropological Film".

Rural Africana 12: 29–36.

Asch, Timothy and Gary Seaman (1993), "Acknowledgments". In Timothy Asch and Gary Seaman (eds.), *Yanomamo Film Study Guide*. Los Angeles: Ethnographics Press, University of Southern California, p. v.

Asch, Timothy and Gary Seaman (eds.) (1993), *Yanomamo Film Study Guide*. Los Angeles: Ethnographics Press, University of Southern California.

Asch, Timothy and Lucien Taylor (1991), "Contributo all'antropologia. Jean Rouch cineaste etnografico (Jean Rouch's Contribution to Anthropology as an Ethnographic Filmmaker)". In *Jean Rouch le renard pâle*. Torino: Centre Cultural Français de Turin and Museo Nazionale del Cinema di Torino, pp. 157–64.

Atkins, David and Timothy Asch (1975), "Yanomamo: A Multidisciplinary Study. A Film by James V. Neel, Timothy Asch and Napoleon Chagnon. Film Notes". Somerville, Massachusetts: Documentary Educational Resources.

—— (1993), "Yanomamo: A Multidisciplinary Study in Human Genetics". In Timothy Asch and Gary Seaman (eds.), *Yanomamo Film Study Guide*. Los Angeles: Ethnographics Press, University of Southern California, pp. 14–40.

Bashor, Christen R., Paul Bugos, Jr., and Timothy Asch (1975), "*Magical Death. A Film by Napoleon Chagnon*. Film Notes". Somerville, Massachusetts: Documentary Educational Resources.

—— (1993), "Magical Death: A Study Guide". In Timothy Asch and Gary Seaman (eds.), *Yanomamo Film Study Guide*. Los Angeles: Ethnographics Press, University of Southern California, pp. 58–68.

Bugos, Paul, Jr. and Timothy Asch (1975), "*Tapir Distribution. A Film by Napoleon Chagnon and Timothy Asch*. Film Notes". Somerville, Massachusetts: Documentary Educational Resources.

—— (1993), "Tapir Distribution". In Timothy Asch and Gary Seaman (eds.), *Yanomamo Film Study Guide*. Los Angeles: Ethnographics Press, University of Southern California, pp. 146–57.

Bugos, Paul Jr., Stephan Carter, and Timothy Asch (1975), "*The Ax Fight. A Film by Timothy Asch and Napoleon Chagnon*. Film Notes". Somerville, Massachusetts: Documentary Educational Resources.

—— (1993), "The Ax Fight: Film Notes". In Timothy Asch and Gary Seaman (eds.), *Yanomamo Film Study Guide*. Los Angeles: Ethnographics Press, University of Southern California, pp. 132–44.

Connor, Linda, Patsy Asch and Timothy Asch (1986), *Jero Tapakan: Balinese Healer. An Ethnographic Film Monograph*. Cambridge and New York: Cambridge University Press.

—— (1996), *Jero Tapakan: Balinese Healer. An Ethnographic Film Monograph*. Revised edition. Los Angeles: Ethnographics Press.

Ennis, Scott and Timothy Asch (1993), "The Feast: A Study Guide". In Timothy Asch and Gary Seaman (eds.), *Yanomamo Film Study Guide*. Los Angeles: Ethnographics Press, University of Southern California, pp. 74–88.

Films

Asch, Timothy
1963   *Dodoth Morning*, 16 mm, color, 15 mins. Distributed by Documentary Educational Resources, Inc., Watertown, Massachusetts.

1965   *An Instructional Interview*, with Margaret Donaldson. Distributed by Education Development Center, Cambridge, Massachusetts.

1978   *The Sons of Haji Omar*, with Asen Balikci, David Newman, and Patsy Asch. Distributed by Audio Visual Service, Pennsylvania State University, University Park, Pennsylvania.

1979   *A Balinese Trance Seance*, with Linda Connor and Patsy Asch. Distributed by Documentary Educational Resources, Inc., Watertown, Massachusetts.

1981   *Jero on Jero: A Balinese Trance Seance Observed*, with Linda Connor and Patsy Asch. Distributed by Documentary Educational Resources, Inc., Watertown, Massachusetts.

1983   *Jero Tapakan: Stories from the Life of a Balinese Healer*, with Linda Connor and Patsy Asch. Distributed by Documentary Educational Resources, Inc., Watertown, Massachusetts.

1983   *The Medium Is the Masseuse: A Balinese Massage*, with Linda Connor and Patsy Asch. Distributed by Documentary Educational Resources, Inc., Watertown, Massachusetts.

1983   *The Water of Words: A Cultural Ecology of an Eastern Indonesian Island*, with James J. Fox and Patsy Asch. 30 mins. Distributed by Documentary Educational Resources, Inc., Watertown, Massachusetts.

1985   *Air Kata Kata*, Indonesian version of the 16 mm film *The Water of Words*. Distributed by Department of Anthropology, Research School of Pacific and Asian Studies, The Australian National University, Canberra, A.C.T., Australia.

1989   *Spear and Sword: A Ceremonial Payment of Bridewealth*, with James J. Fox and Patsy Asch. 30 mins. Distributed by Documentary Educational Resources, Inc., Watertown, Massachusetts.

1991   *Releasing the Spirits: A Village Cremation in Bali*, with Linda Connor and Patsy Asch. 45 mins. Distributed by Documentary Educational Resources, Inc., Watertown, Massachusetts.

1993   *A Celebration of Origins*, with E. Douglas Lewis and Patsy Asch. 47 mins. Distributed by Documentary Educational Resources, Inc., Watertown, Massachusetts.

The Yanomamö Series, with Napoleon Chagnon

Some of Asch's Yanomamö films were still in various stages of post-production at the time of his death. As a result, different titles are to be found cited in the literature and in various lists of the Yanomamö films. For example, many of the titles in one of Asch's own lists of his films (Asch 1975: 410–14) differ from later lists, such as that which appears on page 144 of *Visual Anthropology Review* 11 (1) (Spring 1995). Alternative titles of the films in the following list appear in square brackets. Seaman (1993) has published a very useful list of the films with a short description of each. In compiling this list, I have taken as definitive the titles, dates of release, and timings published by Documentary Educational Resources, Inc. (2001) on their web site. However, not all of the films listed below appear on the DER list. Those films listed as "slopticals" (Asch's term for his unfinished films with optical rather than magnetic soundtracks) and those which are otherwise not in their finished form are taken from the Yanomamö Series as listed in Heider and Hermer (1995: 285–8). Inquiries about Asch's films can be directed to DER, which distributes all of the films of the Yanomamö series:

Documentary Educational Resources
101 Morse St., Watertown, MA 02472 USA
Phone: 617–926–0491; Fax: 617–926–9519
URL: www.der.org
Email: docued@der.org

Arrows [*Arrow Game*]. 1974. 10 mins. DER.
The Ax Fight. 1975. 30 mins. DER.
Bride Service. 1975. 10 mins. DER.
Children at Reahumou Play. 6 mins. Sloptical. DER.
Children Grooming for Lice in Front of Dedeheiwa's House [*Grooming Before Dedeheiwa's House*]. 7 mins. Sloptical. DER.
Children of the Hammock [*Children Making a Toy Hammock; Children Making a Hammock*]. 7 mins. Sloptical. DER.
Children Playing in the Rain [*Children Play in the Rain; Children in the Rain*]. 10 mins. Sloptical. DER.
Children's Evening Play at Patanowa-teri. 8 mins. Sloptical. DER.
Children's Magical Death. 1974. 7 mins. DER.
Climbing the Peach Palm [*Collecting Rasha Fruit*]. 1974. 9 mins. DER.
Death of a Prominent Man. 15 mins. Sloptical. DER.
Dedeheiwa Rests in His Garden. 6 mins. Sloptical. DER.
Dedeheiwa's Sons Gardening. 20 mins. Sloptical. DER.
A Father Washes His Children [*Dedeheiwa Washes His Children*]. 1974. 15 mins. DER.
The Feast. 1970. 29 mins. DER.
The Fierce People. 1972. BBC Special "Horizons of Science," 60 mins.
Firewood [*Chopping Wood*]. 1974. 10 mins. DER.
Hunting Crickets. 10 mins. Sloptical. DER.
Jaguar: A Yanomamo Twin-Cycle Myth as Told by Daramasiwa [*The Twin Cycle Myths; Jaguar: A Yanomamo Twin Cycle Myth as Told By Daramasiwa, Part I*]. 1976. 22 mins. DER.
Kaobawa Trades with the Reyabobowei-teri. 8 mins. Sloptical. DER.
Magical Death. 1973. 29 mins. DER.
A Man and His Wife Weave a Hammock [*Moawa Making a Hammock; A Man and His Wife Make a Hammock*]. 1975. 12 mins. DER
A Man Called 'Bee': Studying the Yanomamo [*Doing Anthropological Fieldwork in Mishimishi-mabowei-teri*]. 1974. 40 mins. DER.
Moawa Burns Felled Timber. 9 mins. Sloptical. DER.
Moonblood: A Yanomamo Creation Myth as told by Dedeheiwa. 1976. 14 mins. DER.
Morning Flowers. 20 mins. Sloptical. DER.
Mouth Wrestling. 5 mins. Sloptical. DER.
Myth of Naro as Told by Dedeheiwa [*The Yanomamo Myth of Naro as Told by Dedeheiwa*].

1975. 22 mins. DER.

Myth of Naro as Told by Kaobawa [*The Yanomamo Myth of Naro as Told by Kaobawa*]. 1975. 22 mins. DER.

New Tribes Mission [*New Tribes*]. 1975. 12 mins. DER.

Ocamo Is My Town. 1974. 23 mins. DER.

The River Mishimishimabowei-teri. 20 mins. Sloptical. DER.

Sand Play. 19 mins. Sloptical. DER.

Tapir Distribution [*Reahumou*]. 1975. 15 mins. DER.

Tug of War. 1975. 9 mins. DER.

Weeding the Garden [*Dedeheiwa Weeds His Garden*]. 1974. 14 mins. DER.

Woman Spins Cotton, A [*Woman Spins*]. 8 mins. Sloptical. DER.

Yanomamo Hekura Spirits. 14 mins. Sloptical. DER.

Yanomamo of the Orinoco. 1987. 29 mins. DER.

The Yanomamo Tribe in War and Peace. Produced in collaboration with Nippon A-V Production.

Yanomamo: A Multidisciplinary Study. 1968. 44 mins.

Young Shaman. 10 mins. Sloptical. DER.

References

Asch, Timothy (1975), "Using Film in Teaching Anthropology: One Pedagogical Approach". In Paul Hockings (ed.), *Principles of Visual Anthropology*. The Hague: Mouton Publishers.

Documentary Educational Resources, Inc. (2001), http://www.der.org

Heider, Karl G. and Carol Hermer (1995), *Films for Anthropological Teaching*. Eighth edition. Special Publication of the American Anthropological Association Number 29. Arlington, Virginia: American Anthropological Association.

Seaman, Gary (1993), "The Yanomamo Indians of Southern Venezuela and Northern Brazil: Filmography". In Timothy Asch and Gary Seaman (eds.), *Yanomamo Film Study Guide*. Los Angeles: Ethnographics Press, University of Southern California, pp. 160–77.

Index

bold type indicates an illustration

AAA *see* American Anthropological Association

activity sequences 10, 16n5, 125, 129, 153, 280n5; *see also* sequence films

Adair 158, 185, 187, 201n8

Adams, Ansel 2, 17, 18, 24, 25, 26, 29, 55, 56n6, 60, 63, 76

aesthetics 2

Afghanistan 1, 4, 17, 81, 166–8, 172, 181, 194, 197, 263

AFRI *see* Anthropological Film Research Institute

Air Kata-Kata (Indonesian language version of *The Water of Words*) 95

alliance 59, 67, 128, 139, 140, 150, 152, 153, 154, 176, 249, 265

Altars of Fire 80

American Anthropological Association xxii, 57, 64, 186

American Anthropologist 16, 83, 185, 267

American Universities Field Staff 189

Anderson, Lindsay 77

Annenberg School of Communications 79

Anthropological Film Research Institute 193

anthropological theory 135, 155, 170, 173, 250, 251

Arensberg, Conrad 43, 44, 193

Argument About A Marriage, An 258n7

Asahi Shinbun 2

Asch, Patsy xx–xxi, xxiii, 2, 4, 6, 7, 10, **12**, 14, 16, 60, 64, 78, 81, 95, 97, 100, **107**, **108**, 121n6, 123, 124, 149, 150, 154, 155, 160, 163, 165, 166, **167**, 172, 180–2, 194, 196, 265, 267, 269, 270, 272, 276

Afghanistan project 166–8

Bali project 168

Asch, Timothy xix, xxi–xxii, xxiv, 1, 4, **5**, 7–9, **11**, **12**, 13, 15, 16n4, 17–55, 57, 60, 66, 68, 70, 75, **77**, 82, 83, 88–90, 95, 97, 98, 100, **103**, **104**, **105**, **107**, **108**, **109**, 114, **115**, 116, 119, 120, 123, 125, 129, 132, 134, 143, 149, 152, 155, 156, 159–61, 163–6, **167**, **168–9**, 171–3, 175, 178, 180, 185, 186, 192, 197, 200–2, 205, 206, 213, 214, **217**, 222, 224, 229, 233, 234, 236, 239, 243, 245, 248, 263, 265, 266, 267, 270–2, 274–6, 279–81, 283, 285

Afghanistan project 166–9

in Africa 45–50

aims of research and filming 10, 11, 97, 99, 104, 112, 115, 116, 134, 137, 138, 263–5

on anthropology 42–3

apprenticeship with Minor White 25–9

and audience feedback 9–10, 130, 131, 144n8

in Australia 1976–82, 4, 84–6, 194, 196

awards 14

Bali project 5–6, 86–7, 154–7, 166

and Beidelman, Thomas 50–1, 153

in Cambridge, Massachusetts 33, 76–82, 83–4

Cape Breton project 19, 29–34

collaboration 129–32

  with Patsy Asch 166–8

  with Napoleon A. Chagnon 3, 130, 133, 135, 149, 152, 169, 177, 189–90, 266

  with Linda Connor 5–6, 7, 80, 86–7,

133, 150, 154–7, 164–6, 171, 173, 196, 265, 267
  with James Fox 84–95
  with E. Douglas Lewis 6–13, 80, 196
Dodoth (Uganda) photography 2, 45–50, 79, 190, 201n2
early life 1–4, 20–5
editing John Marshall's films 2, 18, 43, 59, 75, 76, 80–1, 268
as event film-maker 92, 127, 130, 196, 197, 266, 269
as film review editor *American Anthropologist* 83
Harvard course on ethnographic film 83–4
humor in Asch's films 91, 135, 270–1, 281n14
Indonesia films 197–8, 263–80
influence of Margaret Mead 59
in Japan 34–42
and Ju/'hoansi films 75, 76
and Peter Loizos at Harvard 75–6, 78
and Man, A Course of Study 2, 3, 60, 71n3, 80
and Margaret Mead 2, 42, 43, 44, 54, 59, 76, 133–4, 153, 267
  filming Margaret Mead in Bali 5, 86–7
National Science Foundation grant application with James J. Fox 95, 263
representations of gender in films of 163–82
Roti project 5, 87–93
social theory in films of 149–60
still photography 18, 19, 53–5
Tana 'Ai project 6–13, 98–120
as teacher 1, 3, 4, 7, 15, 82, 224, 281
teaching with film 57–9, 128
teaching Yanomamö to make videos 157–8
at the University of Southern California 14
in the U.S. 1982–94 14–15
use of films and written ethnography 1, 7, 8, 114, 121n9, 144n5, 206, 220, 224, 277
on visual anthropology 43–5
Yanomamö training project 157–8
Ata Tana 'Ai *see* Tana 'Ai
audience 10, 58, 84, 109, 111, 112, 114, 121, 126, 127, 132, 134, 156, 157, 165, 181, 189, 218, 221, 245, 246, 266, 270, 271, 273, 275, 277

AUFS *see* American Universities Field Staff
Australia xxiv, 4, 6, 13, 14, 17, 53, 55, 57, 68, 84, 92, 131, 157, 158, 174, 194, 196, 263, 267
Australian National University 4, 5, 53, 57, 84, 95, 194, 196, 263, 267, 281, 282
auteur, film-maker as 126, 159, 161n6
auteurism 125
Ax Fight, The xxiii, 3, 4, 58, 70, 71n9, 84, 92, 94, 125, 135, 136, 138–41, 144n4, 150, 154, 176–8, 180–1, 197, 211–15, 221, 229–36, 239–58, 259n16, 265–8, 281
  blow-by-blow description 241–2, 258n1, 259n24
  confusion in fieldwork 245–6
  error correction in 247–9
  kinship analysis in 176–7, 243–4
  reductionism in 253–4
  as researchable film 4
  reception by students 211–16
  representation of gender in 176–8, 181, 197
  structure of 58, 255

Bakhtin, M. 163
Bali 4, 5, 6, 7, 43, 44, 85, 86, 87, 88, 93, 98, 124, 132, 133, 145, 149, 150, 154, 155, 157, 158, 163–5, 168, 169, 171–4, 179–82, 196, 199, 200, 225, 227, 264–8, 271–4, 276, 277, 279
Bali films 6, 179, 181, 279, 281n15
Balikci, Asen xxi, 3, 4, 9, 60, 64, 66, 68, 80, 166, **167**, **168**, 185, 186, 188, 191, 194, 195, 196, 229
Balinese *see* Bali
Balinese Family, A 133
Balinese Trance Seance, A 6, 9, 92, 130, 140, 145, 156, 157, 179, 196, 197, 265, 266, 269, 270, 272, 275, 276, 279
Bard College 2, 29
Bateson, Gregory 59, 70, 130, 132, 133, 134, 136, 153, 174, 200, 242
BBC 81
Beidelman, Thomas 2, 50, **51**, 153
Belmont Conference 186, 191–3, 194, 195, 198, 199, 200, 202n15
  Margaret Mead's role in 192
Bhabha, H. 210, 211, 215
Biella, Peter xix, xxiii, 4, 139, 239, 240, 257
Blitz, Daniel 16

Blow Up 258n7
Bogdanovich, Mitch 77
Boston Marathon 79
Boston University 2, 49, 56n12, 205, 209
Brandeis University 3, 4, 17, 57
Brattle, The 77
Breathless 77
bridewealth 90, 91, 198, 268, 274, 276, 278, 279
Brown, Penelope 85
Brown, Quentin 66
Bruner, Jerome 2, 52, 60, 61, 62, 63, 64, 65, 66, 67, 68, 71n3, 80
budgets for film-making 68, 85, 102, 194, 195, 200
burial rites 115, 116, 117, 118, 119, 121, 270
Bushman Woman 52

California xxii–xxiii, 2, 4, 8, 14, 15, 17, 18, 19, 24, 25, 26, 27, 28, 56n5, 57, 68, 163, 190, 208, 209
California School of Fine Arts 25, 26, 56n5
Canada 1, 2, 31, 50, 263
Canadian Film Board 194
Cape Breton Island 2, **30**
Celebration of Origins 7, 10, 14, 92, 97, 109, 111, 113, 115, 120, 121, 130, 131, 144n8, 149, 150, 180–3, 196, 236, 265–8, 270, 272, 274–6, 278–81
     editing 10, 102, 112, 121, 268, 269
     fight sequence 100–2, 272
     representation of gender in 180–1, 182, 183n12
Center for Visual Anthropology xxi, 4, 15, 57, 161n4,
Chagnon, Napoleon A. xx, xxi, 3, 9, 17, 59, 70, 80, 130, 133, 135, 138, 139, 140, 149, 152, 154, 169, 175, 176, 177, 178, 180, 181, 189, 190, 205, 212, 213, 219, 222, 225, 229, 233, 234, 239–56, 260, 264, 265, 266, 268, 281, 287
Childhood Rivalry in Bali and New Guinea 133
Chronicle of a Summer 258n5
Climbing the Peach Palm **217**
collaboration 3, 4, 5, 6, 7, 8–11, 49, 57, 61, 80, 81, 83, 84, 86, 87, 91, 93, 98, 119, 123, 129–32, 133, 142–3, 149, 150, 152, 160, 174, 192, 193, 196, 243, 263, 265, 266, 267, 272, 275
Collier, John 19, 29, 31, 32, 33
colonialism 165

Columbia University 2, 18, 59, 64, 76, 153, 267
commentary 69, 115, 130, 131, 157, 206, 230, 231, 236
Comparative Eastern Indonesia Project 85
conative 126, 127, 129, 130, 132, 134, 143n1
conative function 125–30, 132, 134, 143
Conlan, John B. 68, 69
Connor, Linda xix, xxi, xxiii, 5, 6, 7, 9, 80, 86, 87, 95n3, 98, 114, 123, 130, 133, 137, 140, 141, 142, 149, 150, 154, 155, 156, 157, 160, 163, 164, 165, 166, 169, **171**, 172, **173**, 174, 179, 180, 196, 197, 265, 267, 268, 270, 272, 279
Cornell University 19
Crystal, Eric 84
cultural stereotyping 208
Cyprus 81

dance 49, 87, 101, 105, **107**, 114, 133, 200
Dead Birds 52, 76, 84, 175, 190, 229
DER *see* Documentary Educational Resources, Inc.
DeVore, Irven 60, 66
DeVore, Paul 70
Dewey, John 59, 132
dialogic communication 163
diegesis 150, 161n3
direct cinema 123, 126, 135, 153
Disappearing Worlds 188
Documentary Educational Research, Inc. 3, 126, 288
documentation films 123
Dodoth 1, 2, 48, 49, 79, 190, 201n2
Dodoth Morning 1, 2, **48**, **49**, 56n11
Dwyer, Kevin 136, 137, 138, 140, 141, 142

editing xix, xxii, 8, 10, 15, 18, 19, 20, 33, 34, 59, 66, 75, 76, 78, 102, 112, 121, 124, 127, 129, 131, 137, 141, 150, 151, 159, 223, 231, 248, 250, 255, 267, 268, 269, 273, 275
ethics 14–15, 81, 130, 131, 142–3, 144n9, 151–2, 157, 225–6
ethnographers, relationship to subjects 164–70
ethnographic film
     institutional context of production 187–90
     subjects in 170–6
     in teaching 58–9, 206–26
Evans-Pritchard, E. E. 50

event films 92, 123, 127, 128, 130, 196, 197, 223, 269
excess cinematic, 71, 139, 150, 231
exchange theory 150

Faces of Change 188, 189, 194
Farrebique 77
Father Washes his Children, A 144n9, 227
Feast, The 3, 84, 92, 128, 152, 176, 181, 185, 186, 190, 212, 213, 219, 266, 268
feedback
    informant 9, 10, 19, 112, 116, 265, 266, 268, 271, 272
    audience 9, 10, 131, 144n8
Feldmesser, Robert 62
field notes 120, 248, 279
field of ethnological study 275
fieldwork 3, 4, 6, 7, 11, 31, 35, 67, 98, 99, 104, 119, 121, 155, 164, 165, 166, 170, 172, 187, 242, 245, 246, 247, 248, 249, 251, 267, 270
film reception xxiii, 4, 70–1, 126, 143, 205–27
    study by Hearne and DeVore 205–6
    of The Ax Fight 211–16, 221–2
    of Yanomamö films 218–23
Fishing at the Stone Weir 66
Flaherty, Robert 14, 126, 143, 153, 186, 190, 233
Flores 4, 5, 7, 8, 10, 85, 97, 98, 149, 151, 172, 179–82, 199, 225, 264, 265, 267, 268, 272, 278
Ford Foundation 64
Fox, James J. xx, xxi, xxiii, 4, 5, 6, 7, 9, 80, 83, 84, 85, 91, 92, 95, 98, 143, 149, 154, 196, 197, 198, 199, 263, 264, 265, 267, 268, 274, 276, 277
Freeman, Derek 4, 84, 85
Fried, Morton 42, 43, 44, 205, 267
funeral 91, 274

Gajdusek, Carlton 52, 185, 186, 188, 192, 193
Gardner, Robert 1, 2, 33, 34, 43, 44, 45, 48, 55, 75, 76, 77, 78, 79, 80, 81, 82n2, 126, 175, 185, 188, 190, 193, 229
Geertz, Hildred 135
gender xxiii, 121, 163–82, 183, 223, 242, 278
    in The Ax Fight 176–8
    in Bali films 179–80, 181
    in A Celebration of Origins 180–1
    technology of 181–2

Gibson, Gordon 185, 192, 193, 195, 202n15
Gluckman, Max 50, 153, 154
Goldschmidt, Walter 185, 195
Grass 84
gren mahé see Tana 'Ai, celebration of origins
Group of Women, A 76
Gung-Wu, Wang 282

Happy Mother's Day 84
Harper, Douglas xix, xxiii, 2, 17, 25
Harris, Marvin 205, 251, 252, 253, 254, 260
Harvard University xix, xxiii, 2, 3, 4, 75, 153
Harvest of the Palm 7, 92, 93
Hastrup, Kirsten 164, 174
Haviland, John 85
Hearne, Thomas 70, 205, 206, 209
Heider, Karl 185, 186, 188, 193, 195, 207, 288
heuristic filming 97–100, 280
Hobart, Mark 170, 180
Horton, Allan 194
Human Ethology and Ethnographic Film Laboratory 4, 84, 85
Human Relations Area Files 189
Human Studies Film Archives xxiii, 128, 185–201
Hunters, The 44, 75, 77, 79, 81, 84, 190, 229, 267, 280
hypertext 4, 144n7

iconic text 118
ideology 121, 179, 252
indigenous structure 124, 127, 138
Indonesia xxii, xxiii, 1, 4, 10, 17, 81, 83, 84, 85, 86, 88, 95, 97, 98, 99, 149, 154, 171, 196, 197, 263, 264, 265, 266, 267, 268, 269, 270, 271, 272, 273, 274, 275, 276, 277, 278, 279, 280
Indonesia films 4, 197, 265–7, 269–72, 274–7, 279
    elements of style in 267–73
    as ethnological films 273–9
    features of 266
    subjects in 279–80
inductive films 123, 129
informant feedback 9, 10, 116, 265, 266, 268, 271, 272
International Congress of Anthropological and Ethnological Sciences 188, 193

Ipir Wai Brama, Pius 10, 101, 109, 110, 111, 112, 113, 115, 116, 131, 180, 182n11, 268, 280
Ipir Wai Brama, Rapa 104, 270
Ipir Wai Brama, Sina 101, 108–10, 112, 114–18, 131, 270, 271

Jaguar 84
Jakobson, Roman 125, 126, 143n1
Japan **36, 37, 38, 39, 40**
Jero on Jero 9, 10, 123, 130, 140, 157, 179, 265, 266, 267, 268, 269, 272, 273, 275, 276
Jigging for Lake Trout 66
Johnson, Craig **217**, 230
Joking Relationship, A 76
Josselin de Jong, P. E. de 274, 275
Ju/'hoansi 2, 3, 16, 18, 59, 66, 67, 71n8, 75, 127, 130, 138, 267, 268, 280

Kendon, Adam 4, 84, 195
kinship 59, 153, 154, 176, 177, 212, 213, 231, 234, 240, 243, 246, 247
Kiuk, Mias 89, 271, 276, 279
Kozol, Jonathan 18, 19,

Laboratory for the Iconic Recording of Human Behaviour 85
Last Days, The 230
Last of the Cuivas 84
Lauretis, Teresa de 164, 181
Leach, Edmund 274
Leacock, Richard 77, 123, 126, 143, 153
Lembaga Ilmu Pengetahuan Indonesia 85
Les Maîtres Fous 84, 229
Levinson, Stephen 85
Lewis, E. Douglas xx, xxiii, 1, 6, 16, 80, 97, 113, 114, 120, 121, 131, 133, 135, 138, 143, 149, 160, 172, 180, 182–3n12, 196, 197, 200, 234, 236, 263, 265, 267, 280, 283
Leyton, Alexander 30
life history 137, 140
Lion Hunters, The 230
Loizos, Peter xx, xxiii, 2, 3, 60, 64, 75, 102, 121, 123, 124, 126, 134, 143
Lomax, Alan 188, 193, 194
lontar palm 7, 89, 90, 92, 268, 271, 275, 276, 279

MacDougall, David and Judith 1, 48, 135, 153, 155, 156, 160, 173, 174, 189, 190, 196, 199

Magical Death 152, 212, 221
Mainichi Shinbun 2
Malesi, Petrus 90, 91, 92, 276, 278, 279
Man and His Wife Weave a Hammock, A 144n9, 178
Man, A Course of Study 2, 52, 58–73
congressional debate about 68–70
Manchester school 153
Margaret Mead Ethnographic Film and Video Festival 14, 18, 19, 163
Marks, Daniel 14, 59, 267
Marshall, John 1, 2, 3, 33, 43, 47, 48, 59, 60, 75, 76, 79, 80, 81, 85, 124, 127, 138, 152, 153, 185, 190, 192, 194, 248, 267, 268
Marshall, Laurence 16, 44, 194
Martínez, Wilton 4, 8, 123, 125, 127, 128, 131, 132, 134, 143, 150, 160, 205, 208, 212, 218
Mauss, Marcel 67, 128, 150, 152, 176, 275
Maysles brothers 77
Mead, Margaret xxii, 2, 5, 14, 18, 19, **40**, 42, 43, 44, 47, 54, 55, 57, 59, 66, 69, 70, 71n1, 76, 86, 87, 95n4, 130, 132, 133, 134, 144n10, 153, 163, 174, 177, 185, 188, 192, 193, 194, 195, 200, 201n7, 267
and the Anthropological Film Research Institute 193
and the Belmont Conference 192
and the National Anthropological Film Center 194, 201n7
meaning 121n11
Medium is the Masseuse, The 145, 157, 179, 268, 279
Millennium 113
Mills, C. Wright 240
Moawa Burns Felled Timber 222, 223, 227
modernism and postmodernism 123–5, 132–42
montage 100, 102, 112, 115, 116, 121, 273
Moser, Brian 188
Myerhoff, Barbara 156, 161n4

Nagra tape recorder 77, 87, 166
Nanook of the North 84
narrative 10, 19, 31, 33, 44, 46, 53, 84, 93, 94, 113, 115, 116, 139, 150, 155, 156, 157, 173, 174, 213, 229, 230, 231, 232, 233, 234, 235, 236, 266, 276
National Anthropological Film Center 57, 185, 189, 193–9, 201n7
National Defense Education Act 61

National Endowment for the Arts 195
National Endowment for the Humanities 195
National Science Foundation, U.S. 4, 60, 61, 68, 85, 152, 186, 192, 263
Netsilik 3, 60, 64, 65, 66, 67, 188, 229
New Tribes Mission 156, **217**, 266–7
New York University 3, 57
Nichols, Bill xxiii, 3, 58, 80, 125, 127, 136, 139, 144n4, 150, 185, 229, 234, 245,
Nippon Times 2
North Country School 1, 21, **22**, **23**, 55n1, 59
NSF *see* National Science Foundation

objective record 187
objectivity 138, 141, 232, 260
observational documentary 77, 79
observational style 152, 223, 202n11, 224
Old Amish Order, The 84
One Day of Many 33
opportunistic filming 98–9, 120n1, 269, 280
oratory and ostension 120–1n5
Osmundson, Lita 186

Palu'é Island, Indonesia 281n17
Peabody Museum 2, 33, 44, 48, 55, 75
photo-elicitation *see* feedback
postmodernism 123–5, 135, 141, 154, 150–1
Preloran, Jorge 193
Primary 77, 79
primitive, student stereotyping of 67, 69, 155, 181, 188, 190, 206, 208, 209, 210, 215, 220, 223, 225, 260
Putney School xix, 1, 18, 19, 23, 24, 32, 55n1, 59

Quandt, Bill 29

Ranke, Leopold von 232, 234
realism 82, 134, 135, 136, 153, 219
reception of ethnographic film *see* film reception
reciprocity 67, 128, 152, 176
reflexivity 142, 150, 157, 271, 272
Releasing the Spirits 10, 179, 265, 266, 279
research film 52, 57, 121, 128, 192, 194, 197–200, 251–2
Research School of Pacific and Asian Studies 4, 5, 6, 84, 263, 267
Reuter, Thomas A. 281n15

Reynolds, Peter 4
ritual xxiii, 5, 7, **9**, 10, 12, 45, 47, 50, 79, 84, 85, 86, 88, 90–4, 97–9, 100, 102, 104–7, 109, 111–15, 117, 118, 119, 121, 131, 136, 150, 151, 154, 183, 197, 236, 263, 264, 266, 268, 269, 270, 271, 272, 273, 274, 275, 276, 277, 278, 279, 280
ritual language 92, 104, 106, 110–11, 112, 115, 117, 121, 268, 274, 275, 276, 282
Roti xxiii, 4, 5, 6, 7, 83, 85, 86, 87, 88, 89, 90, 91, 92, 93, 95, 98, 149, 154, 196, 199, 225, 264, 265, 267, 268, 274, 275, 276, 277, 279
Rouch, Jean 1, 136, 141, 142, 153, 193, 229, 258n5
royalties for ethnographic films 151
Ruby, Jay xix, xxiii, 59, 125, 128, 134, 135, 136, 139, 140, 141, 149, 150, 151, 152, 153, 154, 160, 185, 186, 187, 192, 195, 199, 250

salvage ethnography 194
Sandall, Roger 193, 199
Sapir, David 2, 21, **23**, 25, 50
Savu 5, 85, 86, 90, 92, 93, 95, 102, 263, 264, 277, 280
Schwartz, Theodore 188, 201n8
Seaman, Gary xix, xxi, 241, 253, 256
sequence film 3, 8, 44, 47, 50, 52, 59, 60, 65–7, 71n1, 76, 79, 92, 93, 123, 129, 130, 138, 142, 150, 152, 453, 190, 192, 267, 268, 280n5
slide tape 18, 71n7, 174
Smith, Eugene W. 2, 25, 55n1
Smithsonian Institution xx, xxiii, 4, 57, 128, 185, 186, 192
social organization 7, 63, 67, 99, 106, 150, 175, 273
social structure 154, 273, 275
Society for the Anthropology of Visual Communication Newsletter 187
Society for Visual Anthropology Newsletter xix, 14
solipsism 259n12
Sons of Haji Omar 4, 196
Sorenson, Richard 52, 98, 120, 121, 185, 186, 188, 192, 193, 194, 195, 196, 197, 198, 199
sound recording 92, 104, 119, 186
Source of the Domain, Tana 'Ai 7, 97, 104, 121, 131, 270, 274
Spear and Sword 5, 91, 92, 94, 95, 196, 197, 265–8, 274, 276–80, 282

Staal, Franz 80
Stars and Stripes 2, 18, 76
stereotyping of film subjects by audiences 205, 207, 208–14, 225
Stieglitz, Alfred 24
Stryker, Roy 19, 32, 56n8
Studies in Visual Communication 187
study guides 57, 91, 93 5, 114, 130, 192, 206, 212, 214
subjectivity 141, 142, 150, 152, 156, 157
subjects in ethnographic film 170–3
subtitles 10, 104–12, 115, 129, 153, 197, 247, 248, 282
Sulawesi 84, 95, 264
Suwandi, Raharjo 95
synch sound 16, 77, 79, 82, 149, 186, 192, 194, 197, 229, 230, 231, 243, 255

Tana 'Ai xxiii, 6, 9, 11, 12, 13, 15, 85, 97, 98–120, 121, 183, 264, 270, 274
    celebration of origins 7, 10, 92, 97–102, 105, **107**, 109, 111–16, 118, 119, 121, 270, 279
    fight sequence 100–2
Tana Wai Brama *see* Tana 'Ai
Tapir Distribution 140
Tapo, Koa **107**
Taylor, Lucien 14
television 52, 58, 62, 173, 188, 210
textualization 102, 119–20, 131, 136
Thomas, Elizabeth Marshall xxi, 2, 18, 19, 45–50, 51, 70, 79, 205
Three Domestics 84
Tierney, Patrick 144n9, 258n4
Time for Learning, A 71n7
Timor 85, 88, 102, 264, 277
Titicut Follies 76, 153
Toraja 84
Town, The 84
translation in ethnographic film 95, 104, 106, 109, 110, 111, 121, 134, 140, 142, 149, 154, 192, 194, 253, 266, 268, 276, 279
Trinidad 18, 263
Turner, Victor 154, 158

Uganda 2, 48, 49, 190, 200, 201n2
USC (University of Southern California) xxii, 14, 15, 18, 160, 208, 209, 211, 267, 280

Venezuela 1, 3, 10, 15, 17, 81, 124, 229, 239, 263, 266
Vischer, Michael P. 281n17
visual anthropology 1, 2, 3, 14, 16, 17, 57, 95, 125, 130, 143, 158, 185, 186, 187, 190, 191, 193, 233, 251
Visual Anthropology Review xix, xxii, 14, 125, 160, 287
Visual Sociology 2
voice-over narration 8, 115, 131, 143, 248, 249, 257, 276, 280

Water of Words, The 5, 7, 83, 84, 89, 90, 92, 93, 94, 95, 265, 266, 268, 269, 271, 274, 275, 276, 277, 279
Wedding of Paolo, The 84
Weeding the Garden 144n9, 218, 222, 223, 227, 280
Wenner-Gren Foundation for Anthropological Research 186
Weston, Edward 2, 17, 18, 24, 25, 29, 53, 55, 76
What Makes Man Human 71n1
White, Minor xx, 2, 16, 17, 18, 24, 25, 26, **27**, **28**, 29, 53, 55, 56n6, 76, 205, 210
wie es eigentlich gewesen ("what really happened") 232
Williams, Carroll 185, 186, 195
Wiseman, Frederick 76, 153
Wolf, Margery 127
Woods Hole 61, 62, 68
Worth, Sol 79, 158, 185, 186, 187
Wouden, F. A. E. 273, 274
Wylie, Laurence 43

Yang, John xix, xx, 2, 23, **24**, 50
Yanomamö 1, 3, 16, 17, 59, 67, 70, 81, 83, 84, 123, 124, 128, 130, 137, 142–3, 149, 150, 152, 155–158, 160, 169, 170, 175–82, 189, 190, 197, 205–208, 210–27, 229, 233, 239–248, 250–2, 254–60, 263–9
Yanomamö films 3, 128, 205–26, 263, 287; *see also The Ax Fight*
    reception of 218–23
    representation of otherness in 225
Yanomamö Interactive (CD-ROM) 239–60
    screens in 241–244
Yanomamö training project 15, 157–8
Young, Colin 190, 227

Zabriski Point 258n7